VICKERS

VISCOUNT AND VANGUARD

Other titles in the Crowood Aviation Series

Aichi D3A1/2 Val	Peter C. Smith
Airco – The Aircraft Manufacturing Company	Mick Davis
Avro Lancaster	Ken Delve
Avro Shackleton	Barry Jones
BAC One-Eleven	Malcolm L. Hill
Boeing 737	Malcolm L. Hill
Boeing 747	Martin W. Bowman
Boeing B-17 Flying Fortress	Martin W. Bowman
Boeing B-29 Superfortress	Steve Pace
Bristol Beaufighter	Jerry Scutts
Bristol Britannia	Charles Woodley
British Experimental Turbojet Aircraft	Barry Jones
Concorde	Kev Darling
Consolidated B-24 Liberator	Martin W. Bowman
Curtiss SB2C Helldiver	Peter C. Smith
Douglas A-26 and B-26 Invader	Scott Thompson
Douglas Havoc and Boston	Scott Thompson
English Electric Canberra	Barry Jones
English Electric Lightning	Martin W. Bowman
Fairchild Republic A-10 Thunderbolt II	Peter C. Smith
Fairey Swordfish and Albacore	Bill Harrison
Hawker Hunter	Barry Jones
Hawker Typhoon, Tempest and Sea Fury	Kev Darling
Heinkel He 111	Ron Mackay
Ilyushin Il-2 and Il-10 Shturmovik	Yefim Gordon and Sergey Kommissarov
Lockheed F-104 Starfighter	Martin W. Bowman
McDonnell Douglas A-4 Skyhawk	Brad Elward
Messerschmitt Bf 110	Ron Mackay
Messerschmitt Me 262	David Baker
Nieuport Aircraft of World War One	Ray Sanger
North American B-25 Mitchell	Jerry Scutts
North American F-86 Sabre	Duncan Curtis
North American F-100 Super Sabre	Peter E. Davies
North American T-6	Peter C. Smith
Panavia Tornado	Andy Evans
Petlyakov Pe-2 *Peshka*	Peter C. Smith
V-Bombers	Barry Jones
Vickers VC10	Lance Cole
Vought F4U Corsair	Martin W. Bowman

VICKERS VISCOUNT AND VANGUARD

Malcolm L. Hill

The Crowood Press

First published in 2004 by
The Crowood Press Ltd
Ramsbury, Marlborough
Wiltshire SN8 2HR

www.crowood.com

British Library Cataloguing-in-Publication Data
A catalogue record for this book is available from the British Library.

ISBN 1 86126 669 3

Acknowledgements
Grateful thanks are extended to all the following individuals and organizations whose invaluable funds of information; material, co-operation and time have made this book possible:

Aer Lingus, Afavia, Air Canada, Air France, Air New Zealand, Rafael Arteaga, Aviation Hobby Shop, Will Blunt, David Castle, Thom Cliffe, Cyprus Airways, Stephen Ford, Global Air Image, Patrice Gousenbouger, Jenny Gradidge, Barbara Hanson, Cameron Hill, Luxair, Bill Mellberg, Military Aircraft Photographs, Joseph P. Noto, Jon Proctor, Steve Richards, Bill Sheridan, THY Turkish Airlines, Bob Turner, United Airlines Archive, Tony Ward, Steve Williams.

Whilst every effort has been made to identify the source of illustrations used in this publication, this has not been possible in all cases, due to the passage of time and dispersal of the material. All persons claiming accreditation should contact the author via the publisher and any omission or error will be corrected in subsequent editions.

Typefaces used: Goudy (*text*), Cheltenham (*headings*).

Typeset and designed by
D & N Publishing
Lowesden Business Park, Hungerford, Berkshire.

Printed and bound in Great Britain by CPI Group, Bath.

Contents

CHAPTER ONE

The First One

The Reason Why

When the Vickers-Armstrongs Type 630 Viscount prototype took to the air for the first time, on 16 July 1948, it only did so for a mere twenty minutes. Nonetheless, those twenty minutes marked the beginning of one of the most prestigious and profitable periods in British airliner production. Even after production ceased, the descendants of that single aircraft were set to enjoy decades of reliable, profitable service for their numerous operators. The Viscounts by the hundred, and the much fewer, bigger-brother Vanguards by the dozens, which followed the sole Type 630 Viscount into the air, were to earn the Vickers turboprop airliner designs a very special place in aviation history.

At the time of that first brief flight, though, there was little sign of the success story that would eventually follow. Whether or not any more aircraft would be built after the prototype was still in serious doubt, and the Viscount could easily have been one of the many post-Second World War 'experimental' types that failed to attain production. The airline for which it had mainly been designed in the first place seemed to be losing interest. Doubts were even being expressed in high places as to the very practicality of its groundbreaking new form of propulsion, the propeller-turbine. It was taking a great affirmation of faith in the future prospects of their design for the Vickers management team to press on with the project.

The commercial airways of the time were solely the domain of the piston engine, as they had been since airlines had carried their first fare-paying passengers thirty years before. Even the brand-new airliner types, finally beginning to replace the few pre-war survivors and hundreds of converted wartime transports which then made up the majority of the world's air fleets, were piston powered. The piston engines were certainly getting more powerful, enabling aircraft to carry heavier loads over greater distances. They were also flying higher, most newly designed aircraft having pressurized

ABOVE: Whirling propellers, viewed through panoramic windows during a smooth ride, become the hallmarks of travel by Vickers turboprop airliner from the 1950s right through to the next century. Joseph P. Noto

BELOW: Starting up the Viscount prototype's Rolls-Royce Dart engines before its first flight was the high-pitched prelude to over fifty years of air transport history. Author's collection

The world's post-war airlines were still relying heavily on the Douglas DC-3, basically a pre-war design, for their short- and medium-haul operations. Sabena via author

fuselages and taking their passengers to smoother levels, way above the rougher air encountered at lower altitudes. The war had at least yielded a spurt of technical development that produced many improvements in engine and airframe design. However, all the extra power required meant that the engines were also getting much more complex, noisier, and creating increasingly uncomfortable vibration for the passengers and crews.

Proposed by Committee

The first of the many projects that were destined to form the core of Britain's post-war civil airliner production owed their existence to the formation of the Brabazon Committee. As early as 1942, when the war could barely be seen to be starting to go the Allies' way, thoughts were turning to future civil aviation production. Lord Brabazon of Tara, the first Briton to hold a pilot's licence in the early years of powered flight, chaired the committee, which soon became labelled with his name.

The Brabazon Committee was charged with examining post-war civil air transport requirements. Their aim was to inspire and encourage Britain's beleaguered aircraft industry to begin looking ahead, beyond purely military production. The committee's prompting soon led to the manufacturers' studying a number of possible projects. Although the manufacturers were all heavily pre-occupied with producing military aircraft, a co-ordinated post-war plan was seen to be needed to give the British industry a chance of competing in the new era. It was already clear that the US aircraft industry, its factories already well geared-up for mass production and having operated beyond the range of hostile bombing, would be in a very favourable position to dominate both the civil and military aircraft markets once peace returned.

The major achievement of the Brabazon Committee's studies was the outlining of various categories of airliner designs that it surmised would be needed post-war. These categories varied from large trans-oceanic aircraft for mass travel to smaller feederliners. Among the eventual resulting production aircraft would be the Bristol Britannia turboprop transport and the de Havilland Comet jet airliner.

Pure Jet or Prop Power?

The gas turbine (jet) engine had first appeared, at least in an experimental form, before world war had broken out. The military pressures to develop this new and faster form of propulsion to a practical stage for combat use led to the first jet-powered fighters entering service on both sides of the conflict in the last months of the hostilities. With the advent of peace, thoughts could be turned to civil applications for the new engines. As well as the pure jet engine, another option, in which the jet thrust was used to drive a propeller, also attracted serious consideration for civil use in addition to military applications.

The first experiments in this direction were made using a Gloster Meteor jet fighter in 1945. Its Rolls-Royce Derwent jet engines were modified with added reduction gearing and extended compressor shafts which allowed propellers to be driven by the jet engines, proving the feasibility of the theory. The turboprop promised to offer speeds close or even equivalent to those of the pure jet, but with much lower fuel consumption and, consequently, much lower costs. The turboprop was expected to offer high reliability, much quieter running with low vibration and a higher power-to-weight ratio than the piston engines of the day. It also offered much more flexibility over a variety of stage lengths than the early pure-jet designs.

Rolls-Royce's aero-engine division was a pioneer in both pure-jet and propjet technology, and worked closely with the aircraft manufacturers. It produced early propjet designs such as the Trent and the Clyde, as well as the Derwent, Nene and Avon jet engines. Other British aero-engine companies such as Armstrong Siddeley, Bristol and Napier were developing rival designs, often with a view to powering the emerging products from their own associated aircraft manufacturing companies.

Vickers' Proposals

One important Brabazon category was for an economic airliner for European routes, and it was this that attracted most of the attention of the Vickers design team. Ready to exploit its reputation for high-quality workmanship and practical design, Vickers studied many of the Brabazon proposals. By 1945 one of these had been firmed up and designated Brabazon IIB, as

Vickers and Aircraft

As long-standing suppliers of munitions, ships and other hardware to the British armed forces, the Vickers-Armstrongs group of engineering companies had taken an interest in the design and production of aircraft since their military potential had been recognized in the early years of the twentieth century. The company had become involved in early airship designs, mostly for military applications, as far back as 1908. This work led to an interest in also developing aeroplanes.

Initially, aeroplane projects were studied at the Vickers plant at Erith in Kent, with design offices in Vickers House in Broadway, Westminster, London. Eventually a new aviation department was established at Brooklands, near Weybridge in Surrey, in 1915, where a great deal of the early experimental work was undertaken. Brooklands also became home for a Vickers-run civil flying school that was to become well known as a centre for innovation and pioneering efforts.

After peace returned, Vickers continued to concentrate mainly on military projects. The company's work on large military transport aircraft as well as trainers and fighters saw some interwar civilian spin-offs, such as the Vimy Commercial, Vulcan, Viastra, Vellox and Vanguard airliners. However, actual production of all these types was very limited. The all-metal Viastra won a handful of export sales to Australia and was selected to equip the fledgling Royal Flight of the RAF. The others enjoyed either small production runs or were one-off projects which were spin-offs from military contracts. For the most part, military designs took up most of the company's time, a more notable exception being the development of the civil R100 rigid airship.

The Second World War saw Vickers-Armstrongs producing large numbers of Wellington and Warwick bombers, small numbers of which were also produced in modified versions as wartime transports. By its acquisition of the Supermarine Company, in Southampton, Vickers 'inherited' the famous Spitfire fighter, which the company continued to develop throughout the war years. As the war progressed and the Allied victory became more likely, Vickers took more of an interest in the proposed civil products. Studies of more radical conversions of its wartime bomber types eventually led to the proposing of a 'Wellington Continental' airliner. This was to be refined to become the Vickers VC1 Viking, based on the Wellington but incorporating a new fuselage with a spacious passenger cabin, and powered by two Bristol Hercules radial engines.

The 21-passenger Viking entered service with the then fledgling British European Airways (BEA) on 1 September 1946, and also won a number of important export sales to customers in such far-flung regions as the Middle East, India and South America. Although only ever intended as an 'interim' front-line airliner, the rugged Viking and its military versions, the Valetta and Varsity, gave many years of service to their users.

ABOVE: **Based on the Virginia bomber and similar to the Victoria military transport, the 23-passenger Vickers Vanguard served briefly with Imperial Airways on routes to Brussels and Paris from Croydon. Development of the promising design was halted following the loss of G-EBCP on a test flight in 1928, but its name was destined to be revived many years later.** via author

The rather robust Viking proved to be a popular design, attracting orders from many commercial and military customers around the world. via author

a requirement for a 24-seat airliner 'powered by four gas turbine engines driving airscrews'. Another proposal, Brabazon IIA, was for a similar-sized aircraft powered by piston engines. This was eventually to be produced by the Airspeed Company as the AS57 Ambassador.

The Brabazon IIA and IIB specifications were devised with a view to providing an early, yet more sophisticated, replacement for the rather basic Viking. Vickers-Armstrongs' chief designer, Rex Pierson, had appeared before the second meeting of the Brabazon Committee in December 1944, where progress on the Viking and its possible successor were examined. At another meeting, in March 1945, between the Ministry of Aircraft Production (MAP), the Ministry of Civil Aviation and the main airline operators, the British Overseas Airways Corporation (BOAC) and Railway Air Services (RAS), it was concluded that a contract to develop the Brabazon IIB would probably be awarded to Vickers. Soon after this meeting Vickers designers submitted several proposals of their own options for the Brabazon IIB to the MAP. On 19 April 1945 the company was formally instructed to proceed with its Brabazon Type IIB design studies.

Vickers' Initial Offering

The Vickers design office at Brooklands came up with several contenders for the Brabazon IIB design. Two were for 24-passenger aircraft, either pressurized or unpressurized, and a third was for a 27-passenger aircraft, all having a 1,000-mile (1,600km) range. Early options had based the aircraft on an unpressurized Viking airframe powered by four turboprops. The question of the use of pressurization was decided by a study submitted by Rex Pierson in May 1945, which showed the turboprop to be much more efficient at higher altitudes. The options were eventually narrowed down to a pressurized design with a new 'double-bubble' fuselage.

Vickers' first choice of turboprop engine was the Rolls-Royce Dart, the Armstrong Siddeley Mamba or Napier Naiad also being considered in case the Dart, then still under development, failed to live up to expectations. The Mamba was of similar power to the Dart, while the Naiad promised to offer rather more. As presented by Pierson in June 1945, the 24-passenger aircraft, by now designated Vickers VC2, would be able to carry a 7,500lb (3,400kg) payload over a 1,040-mile (1,670km) range, cruising at 297mph (478km/h) at 20,000ft (6,000m). The aircraft's estimated gross weight was 24,500lb (11,100kg), and its double-bubble fuselage would have a cabin 4ft (1.2m) wide, with the floor line at the common chord to the two circular sections. The fuselage would be 63.7ft (19.4m) long, the wingspan 88ft (26.8m) and the wing area 860sq ft (80sq m).

Changes at the Top and on the Drawing Board

Pierson was promoted to chief engineer for all of Vickers-Armstrongs Ltd in September 1945. His place as chief designer was taken by George Edwards, who had previously been the Experimental Works Manager. Edwards took over the general control of the VC2 design until Pierson died suddenly in 1948. From then on, Edwards assumed total technical control of the project.

Ministry of Supply (MoS) Specification 8/46 was issued to Vickers on 17 April 1946, outlining a definitive Brabazon IIB aircraft. The final specification confirmed the Ministry's requirement for:

- A short-to-medium-range transport aircraft powered by four turbine engines.
- A 24-seater with possible conversion to 28 seats.
- Freight capacity to be 274sq ft (25.5sq m).
- Specified noise level not to be more than 60 decibels in the cabin and 70 decibels in the flight deck.
- The working differentials pressure to be 6½lb/sq in (31.7kg/sq m), with 1lb (0.45kg) of fresh air per minute at all heights. There was to be individual cold-air supply to passengers, and humidity was to be controllable between 40 per cent and 60 per cent.
- Emergency oxygen for the crew was required.
- The aircraft was to be capable of carrying a 7,500lb (3,400kg) payload for 700 nautical miles (800 miles/1,290km) at 240kt (275mph/440km/h) at 20,000ft (6,000m). Total fuel capacity was to be for a 1,200-mile (1,930km) range, and

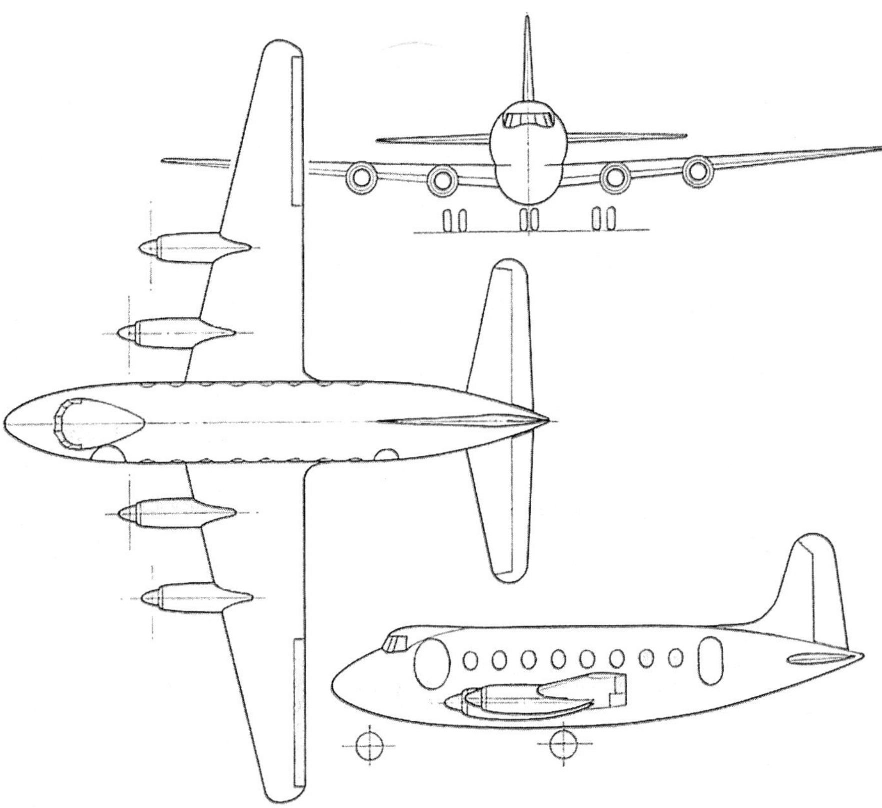

The double-bubble, pressurized-fuselage project showed its Viking origins in the basic design of the tail unit. The distinctive Viscount flight-deck profile was also beginning to emerge. Vickers via author

the aircraft had to be capable of cruising at 30,000ft (9,100m).

- Specified stalling speed was to be 70kt (80mph/130km/h with flaps and undercarriage down, and the take-off distance was to be 1,200yd (1,100m) with all engines operating, but the aircraft also had to be able to take off with one engine cut. The landing run was to be 1,200yd (1,100m).
- Seats had to be readily removable for freight conversion.
- Specified floor loadings: Passengers 100lb/sq ft (488kg/sq m), freight 150lb/sq ft (730km/sq m).
- Operating costs were to be estimated at 2½d per capacity ton-mile, assuming a 3,000hr annual utilization.

However, before the final contract could be signed, significant changes were agreed upon. As a result of consultations with potential airline customers, a need was now seen for a larger 32-seater. The fuselage would be lengthened from 65ft 6in (19.96m) to 74ft 6in (22.7m), with an appropriate increase in wingspan to 89ft (27.1m). This increased the possible payload to the required thirty-two passengers. As, at the time, the Armstrong Siddeley Mamba still appeared to making better progress than the Rolls-Royce Dart, the engine nacelles were designed to take either engine. The higher gross weight of the new version was to be 38,170lb (17,325kg), later increased to 39,500lb (17,930kg).

This much-modified VC2 design was given the Vickers type number 609 and named the Viceroy. The MoS finally ordered two V.609 prototypes in December 1946, to be built at Vickers' experimental works at Foxwarren. A new study of alternative powerplants for the aircraft, in March 1947, saw the MoS confirm its current preference for the Mamba. Nonetheless, less than five months later the Ministry underwent a change of heart, and instructions were issued to Vickers to install Darts, first on just one of the aircraft, and later on the other as well. This change was prompted by significant progress at Rolls-Royce, the company having effectively redesigned and upgraded its original Dart engine. The new version of the Dart made its first flight attached, as an additional engine, to the nose of an Avro Lancaster bomber. Two Darts were also later fitted to a Wellington, as its sole source of power, to great effect. The success of the new Dart prompted the MoS to switch the Viceroy to Dart power, and with confirmation of the eventual engine preference the aircraft was redesignated the V.630, and its name was also changed, to Viscount. This was seen as politically expedient, as India had just been granted independence from Britain and the imperial post of Viceroy of India no longer existed.

BOAC to BEA

Changes were also taking place regarding the primary customer at which the new aircraft was aimed. Originally constituted in 1940, BOAC had been formed as a government-owned airline by the merger of the operations of the two main pre-war British airlines, Imperial Airways and British Airways Ltd. Throughout the war years BOAC had kept the country in physical contact, under great difficulties, with the rest of the Allied world, as well as with some important neutral ports of call.

At the war's end BOAC was able to reopen services to a newly liberated Europe, and a specialist division began operations on 1 February 1946. The new European Division of BOAC took over routes previously operated by No. 110 Wing, RAF Transport Command. A handful of Douglas DC-3 Dakotas, many still in wartime RAF camouflage and with their recently demobbed crews mostly still wearing RAF uniform, were to form the core of the operation. The new division's main base was to

The DC-3 comprised the backbone of the BEA fleet when the airline was formed from BOAC's European Division in 1946. Global Air Image

The RAF station at Northolt, west of London, was adapted to serve as BEA's main base. Not only BEA but several European operators flew into Northolt until the early 1950s, when more facilities were made available at Heathrow. BEA via author

be at Northolt, an RAF aerodrome west of London. On 1 August the European Division was reconstituted and renamed the British European Airways Corporation (BEA), becoming a new government-owned airline in its own right. On the separate emergence of BEA, no fewer than twenty-one DC-3s were in use and, a month later, the first of seventy-five new Vickers Vikings ordered for the carrier entered service.

Doubts at BEA

Even during the changeover from BOAC to BEA, officials at the new corporation were still expressing doubts as to the operational viability of a revolutionary, Dart-powered aircraft. In response to their concerns, Vickers produced studies involving several different engine combinations, some of them even more innovative, including four Naiads, two Naiads, or two Darts inboard and two Nene turbojets outboard (and vice versa).

BEA's choices for a DC-3 and Viking replacement were not confined to the progressively varied versions of the Brabazon IIB designs being offered by the manufacturer in increasingly desperate attempts to keep the airline's attention. The Airspeed AS57 Ambassador, developed from the Brabazon IIA requirement, also had much support at BEA. Not least, it found favour among more conservative elements in BEA's management because of its use of two much more conventional Bristol Centaurus piston engines.

Airspeed versus Vickers

Although no way matching the giant Vickers-Armstrongs concern in size or financial strength, Airspeed Ltd of Christchurch, Hampshire, gave the larger company a lot to worry about in the race for BEA's Brabazon Type II orders. Airspeed had made its name in the pre-war years as a producer of smaller light transport and military training aircraft, such as the Courier, Envoy and Oxford twin-engine types. During the war, in 1940, the de Havilland Aircraft Company had acquired a majority shareholding in Airspeed, though the latter maintained a great deal of independence as a subsidiary company of the larger concern. Despite the company's pre-war preoccupation with smaller designs, some experience with larger airframes was gained by Airspeed during wartime production of the Horsa troop-carrying glider.

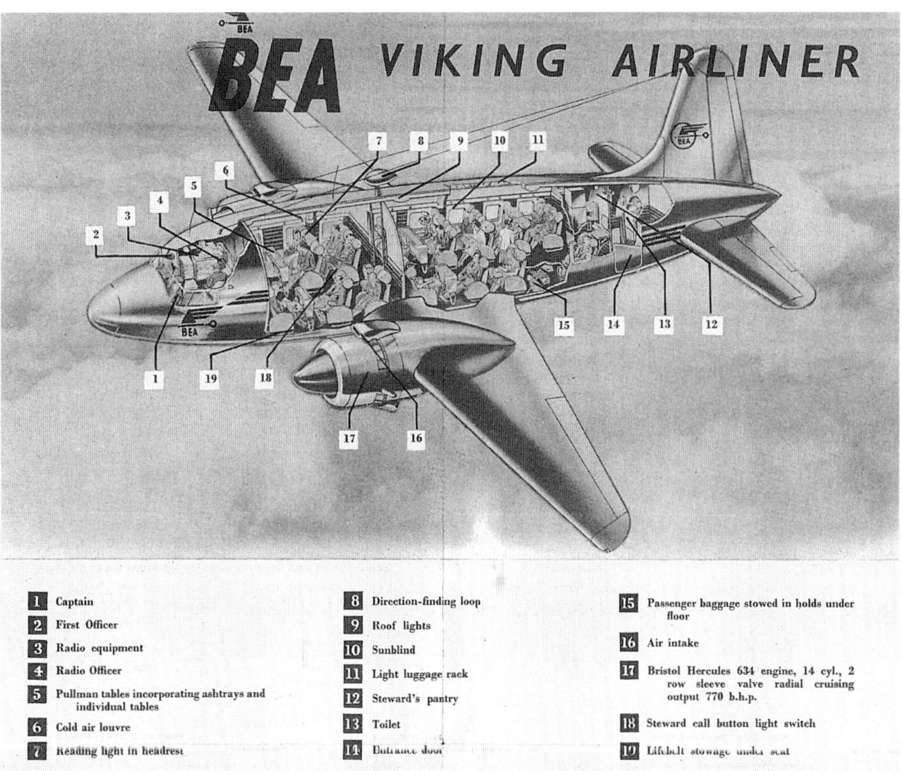

The Viking offered basic but comfortable accommodation for BEA's early passengers on its main routes. Nonetheless, the airline was very keen to introduce a modern replacement to help attract traffic from its rivals. Author's collection

After the war the company continued to concentrate on its established market, producing the Consul light-twin transport, developed from its established Oxford design. All the while, though, Airspeed was working on its own Brabazon IIA proposal. Despite having only limited experience in building larger airframes, Airspeed produced an impressive and very attractive design in the AS57 Ambassador. Originally envisaged as a thirty-seater, powered by two Bristol Hercules, the initial design proposal soon grew, mainly as a result of consultations with the Brabazon Committee and potential operators. The increase in size called for larger engines, which led to the eventual selection of the more powerful eighteen-cylinder Bristol Centaurus. Airspeeds' engineers and designers claimed several important performance advantages for the Ambassador over the Viscount. For example, though the Viscount's 310mph (500km/h) cruising speed was faster than the Ambassador's 282mph (454km/h), Airspeed calculated that this would only result in an 18min saving in overall journey time over an 800-mile (1,290km) routeing. In addition, the Ambassador could carry 15 per cent more payload over 800 miles (1,290km), 21 per cent over 1,000 miles (1,600km) and 30 per cent over 1,150 miles (1,850km). Airspeed also claimed that the Ambassador would require less fuel. The Viscount was estimated by Airspeed to need 10,995lb (4,990kg) of fuel for a 1,000-mile (1,600km) flight, compared with the Ambassador's 6,380lb (2,900kg). This difference was mainly accounted for by the higher fuel reserves required by the turboprop.

Debut

The Viscount versus Ambassador competition steadily increased, both manufacturers trying to meet BEA's requirements as closely as they could. Proposals and counter-proposals were batted back and forth between George Edwards at Vickers, the various government ministries concerned and BEA executives. Following a meeting of the Interdepartmental Civil Aircraft Requirements Committee on 16 August 1947, Vickers even seriously considered BEA's proposal at the meeting for building an interim aircraft based on the V.630 airframe, but with a larger wing and powered by two Centaurus engines. This hybrid design would be capable of being re-engined with four Darts at a later date.

The fuselage of the first V.630 was eventually completed at Foxwarren. Transferred to Vickers' Wisley facility for final assembly, the first complete Viscount was rolled out in June 1948, having been allocated the registration G-AHRF. On the morning of 16 July Vickers chief test pilot, J. 'Mutt' Summers, with J.R. 'Jock' Bryce as copilot, took G-AHRF into the air for the first time. The V.630 Viscount was the forty-third prototype aircraft Summers had taken on its first flight. He commented after the flight that: 'It was the smoothest and best I have ever flown'. The only reported fault after the brief first flight was a faulty fuel-flow gauge.

With only fifteen test-flying hours (albeit very promising hours) in its logbook, G-AHRF was shown off to great effect at the 1948 Society of British Aircraft Constructors' (SBAC) show at Farnborough in September. The aircraft's spirited Farnborough appearance attracted a great deal of press coverage, as well as a degree of initial interest from other potential airline customers. On 20 September G-AHRF made its international debut with a flight to Villacoublay in France.

The unusual, modern lines of the completed Viscount 630 prototype attracted interest as soon as it made its first appearances. Author's collection

'Mutt' Summers and Jock Bryce took G-AHRF aloft on its first flight and saw the Viscount project finally airborne. Author's collection

Specification – V.630

Powerplant:	4 × R.Da.1 Mk502 Dart
Weights:	Empty basic equipment weight 27,000lb (12,200kg); maximum zero fuel weight 36,000lb (16,300kg); maximum take-off weight 45,000lb (20,400kg); maximum landing weight 40,000lb (18,100kg); typical maximum payload 9,000lb (4,100kg).
Dimensions:	Length 74ft 6in (22.71m); span 89ft (27.13m); fin height 26ft 3in (8m); wing area 885sq ft (82.22sq m).
Performance:	Economic cruising speed 273mph (439km/h); maximum cruising speed 300mph (480km/h); range with maximum payload 700 statute miles (1,130km).
Average passenger accommodation:	32 (all first class – high density)

BEA's Challenge

BEA's apparent reluctance to commit itself to either the Viscount or the Ambassador was partly influenced by its own uncertain future. As well as being formed out of the old European Division of BOAC, under nationalization, the infant BEA had also been obliged to take over the operations of ten smaller, previously independent scheduled British airlines. The newly elected post-war socialist government had embarked on mass nationalization of many sectors of the country's commercial activities, and the scheduled airline companies were prime targets. This was to affect the airline industry, insofar as all British scheduled services were only to be operated by one of the three government airline corporations: BOAC, which was to operate long-haul, worldwide services; BEA, which would operate all domestic and European routes; and the British South American Airways Corporation (BSAA).

The last-named, BSAA, had originally been formed as an independent operator but was nationalized under the new regulations before it had began commercial operations. It flew routes from London to the Caribbean and South America, but, after a very turbulent and short existence, marred by numerous accidents and equipment problems, BSAA was eventually taken over by BOAC. One of BSAA's major problems had been the failure of a new British airliner, the Avro Tudor, to live up to its promise. The failure of the Tudor had left BSAA with an uncompetitive and hopelessly uneconomic fleet of 'interim' Avro Lancastrians, converted from the Lancaster wartime bomber, and unpressurized Yorks. BSAA was unable to compete with foreign operators equipped with more modern aircraft, and this led directly to the forced merger with BOAC.

BEA's Inheritance

The ten airlines absorbed by BEA under nationalization were Allied Airways (Gandar Dower), Channel Island Airways, Great Western & Southern Airlines, Highland Airways, Isle of Man Air Services, North Eastern Airways, RAS, Scottish Airways, West Coast Air Services and Western Isles Airways. Of these, Highland Airways, North Eastern Airways, West Coast Air Services and Western Isles Airways were actually dormant by the time of the takeover.

The absorption of the remaining companies still had to be delayed until January 1947 while the complicated details of the integration were worked out. In the meantime the operating airlines continued to fly their services on behalf of BEA. The governments of the autonomous Channel Islands had also tried to retain their own airline's independence, but eventually had been forced to bow to political pressure from the mainland.

Author's collection

The engineering and operations departments of BEA encountered many problems in trying to integrate this 'inherited' fleet with the BEA's DC-3s and Vikings. The airline now found itself the 'proud' owner of two more DC-3s, eight German-built Junkers Ju 52s, thirteen Avro 19s and no fewer than forty-five D.H.89 Rapide biplanes, as well a small collection of mostly highly unsuitable types. The unpopular Ju 52s, which had been passed to RAS as war reparations, and the small, uneconomic Avro 19s were disposed of as soon as possible. These had mostly been based at RAS's main base at Croydon, the original London Airport, in Surrey. BEA eventually transferred all the Croydon services to Northolt.

The absorption of the smaller, domestic carriers had been a complicated affair for BEA, and resulted in the fledgling airline being presented with a meandering, uneconomic network, much of it unconnected with the main route system. Such a network stood little chance of making any money for BEA, especially in financially strapped post-war Britain.

Following nationalization, BEA had tried to rationalize the much-expanded operation, cutting many routes in an attempt to create a viable airline out of the multiple 'shot-gun marriages' forced upon it. Services to Belfast, Bristol, Cardiff, Carlisle, the Isle of Man and Prestwick were either severely reduced or dropped altogether. In addition, an unexpected slump in air travel in 1947–48, following

The Convair CV240 attracted a great deal of interest, winning many orders from airline operators worldwide, as well as in its native USA. Author's collection

the post-war boom, had led to a number of redundancies in BEA and a reduction of the Viking order.

The economic drain on BEA's limited resources caused the airline to examine its future fleet options very closely. Even so, a re-equipment decision was urgently needed. After some initial de-icing problems, which had led to a short period of grounding, the Viking had finally proved itself a sturdy and reliable transport. However, BEA's rivals on Europe's major routes were taking delivery of much more modern types, and the Viking was having increasing difficulty competing. The new Convair CV240, imported from the USA, was proving popular with the newly re-emerging European airlines such as KLM, Sabena and Swissair.

Although its modern lines and turboprop power drew some attention, the Armstrong Whitworth Apollo was far too small to be seriously considered for commercial operation by BEA. Jenny Gradidge

BEA's Shopping Lists

Despite the MoS's improved confidence in the design and its placing of orders for the Dart-powered V.630 prototypes, the airline continued to hedge its bets even a year after its formation. The MoS was also actively supporting and promoting development of Viscount rivals. As well as Airspeed's Ambassador, Armstrong Whitworth in Coventry was developing its own turboprop airliner, the AW.55 Apollo. A 24–30-seat aircraft, the Apollo was eventually cancelled as a commercial project after two prototypes had flown. Its smaller capacity, and disappointment with the Armstrong Siddeley Mamba engines that powered it, finally ruled the Apollo out as a commercial proposition.

Even when the newly refined versions of the Dart started to show significant improvement, BEA continued to delay making any firm commitment to the aircraft, much to the continued frustration of Vickers and George Edwards. The airline was also examining its options for smaller aircraft to operate on the local services it had retained. The de Havilland Dove and Heron, the Miles Marathon and the Cunliffe-Owen Concordia were all contenders for the contract. A large order was actually placed for twenty-five Marathons, though this was later reduced and eventually cancelled altogether. In the end, of all these available options only a handful of Herons were delivered as 'Rapide replacements'. The somewhat primitive Rapide biplanes, once earmarked for early disposal, managed to remain in BEA service, albeit in steadily declining numbers, until the mid-1960s.

Amid all the upheaval of taking on and reorganizing the nationalized routes, as well as trying to develop the mainline airline operation, BEA's management faced a daily struggle to survive and prove the airline was a viable concern. Unless BEA was seen to have made the right equipment choices, it would face severe scrutiny and might well suffer the ignominy of a remerger back into BOAC. Just one expensive mistake could well have proved fatal for the airline's existence.

BEA inherited a sizeable fleet of de Havilland D.H.89 Rapides from the UK operators it was obliged to absorb. Several of these pre-war-designed biplanes were retained in the fleet for another twenty years on some local routes. MAP

V.630 Certification and the V.700

Two days after the G-AHRF's triumphant Villacoublay flight, on 22 September 1948, Vickers' increasingly high hopes for the aircraft were dealt a sudden, severe blow when BEA's management finally signed a £3 million contract for twenty Airspeed Ambassadors. The Ambassador prototype had made its first flight over a year earlier, on

10 July 1947. Vickers seriously had to consider the option of ceasing work on the Viscount altogether. However, with test flying of the first V.630 prototype well under way, work was continued on the project. George Edwards, strongly supported by Vickers Aircraft Division managing director Sir Hew Kilner, managed to keep the Viscount alive, though the aircraft's future was in some doubt for several months after the loss of the BEA order. Nonetheless, the airline still encouraged Vickers to develop the design to meet its requirements, even without placing a definite order.

Despite BEA's apparent preference for piston engines, continuing improvements in the prototype turboprop's performance continued to keep the airline interested. Vickers eventually offered BEA the V.700, a forty-seater, stretched Viscount with bigger wings and powered by a new, more powerful version of the Dart than the R.Da.1 fitted to the initial V.630, which was now available. This higher-rated engine, the R.Da.3, allowed the increase in the aircraft's size, and Vickers was finally confident that it could to offer a design matching BEA's requirements.

The prototype V.630, G-AHRF, received its initial Certificate of Airworthiness (C of A) on 15 September 1949, after 290hr flying and more than 160 flights. Further trials, covering pressurization, the de-icing systems and operation under tropical conditions, followed over the next few months. The pressurization system was tested up to

A large order for twenty of the attractive, yet still piston-powered, Airspeed Ambassadors was placed by BEA in preference to the Vickers V.630 Viscount. MAP

The Jet Viscount

The Ambassador order led to an initial slow-down on work on the second Viscount prototype, still being built at Foxwarren. Intended initially to be powered by four Dart turboprops, like G-AHRF, the incomplete aircraft was fitted instead with a pair of wing-mounted experimental Rolls-Royce Tay jets. The resulting aircraft was to serve as a flying test bed for the new engine, instead of assisting in developing the airliner aspects of the aircraft's original design. In place of its originally allotted civil registration, G-ARHG, the aircraft, now designated V.663, wore the military serial VX217. After final assembly at Wisley it made its first flight, piloted by 'Jock' Bryce, on 15 March 1950.

Only one public appearance was made by VX217, at the SBAC Display at Farnborough in September 1950. Thereafter the aircraft was operated from Seighford in Staffordshire on research flights by the MoS. This unique aircraft was then leased to Bolton Paul Aircraft and used to test its new flying control systems, flying from Defford. Further valuable research and test flying was undertaken for Louis Newmark Ltd and the Decca Navigator Company, operating once again, from 1957, from Seighford.

In 1958, while undertaking a research flight for Decca, VX217 suffered a serious in-flight fire in a wheel bay, following hydraulic failure. A safe landing was made, but the fire had burnt through the main spar and the aircraft was declared a write-off. With only 110hr 15min in its flight log, VX217 was broken up at Seighford during 1960.

The unique V.663 spent most of its existence out of the public eye, making important contributions to aeronautical research and the development of new equipment. Jenny Gradidge

BEA titles and logos were applied to G-AHRF for a number of demonstration and display flights. MAP

Structural Solutions

Although unpressurized, the Viking's semi-monocoque, stressed-skin fuselage design had been used to form the basis of the Viscount's pressurized fuselage. The Viscount's single-spar wing and the use of unbroken hoop frames in the main structure were also design features originally tried on the Viking.

The fact that the Viscount was to be pressurized from the flight deck to the rear of the cabin posed its own problems. The flight deck roof presented particular difficulties at the design stage. The sheer-down angle of the main fuselage structure at a point that far forward dictated that a 'hood' was required to allow any decent view outside for the pilots. As a result, a dome was inserted above where the pilots' heads would be, and faired over. This gave the Viscount its distinctive 'perky' cockpit profile.

The much-commented-on choice of large cabin windows, rather than the then perceived wisdom of much smaller windows in a pressurized fuselage, was controversial. However, Vickers engineer Bill Stephenson had concluded, mathematically, that the large elliptical shape, on the 'neutral hole' principle, was the most efficient at bearing the stress loads. The same formula led to the adoption of elliptical entrance doors and rear freight-hold door.

The design also kept weight penalties to a minimum, as only light reinforcement was needed around the boundary structure on the cabin windows. On early production aircraft all the cabin windows were also fully functioning emergency exits. This was slightly modified on later aircraft, only a few of them being used as such. The fact that there was not a single reported occurrence of a cabin window failure during the following six decades of Viscount operation certainly seems to vindicate Stephenson's calculations.

In stretching the V.630 to produce the V.700 the passenger cabin underwent a fundamental change. In the V.630 it had been structurally divided into two. On the larger V.700 the cabin was unobstructed, the galley being relocated by the forward door, with the washrooms moved to the rear. This offered much greater operational flexibility, enabled the Viscount to attract a wider variety of customers, and allowed Vickers to adapt the aircraft more closely to their needs. The flight deck was laid out for two pilots, and a rear-facing radio officer's position was squeezed in behind them. This was still required in the days before radio equipment was sufficiently developed to allow the pilots to communicate directly with ground stations themselves.

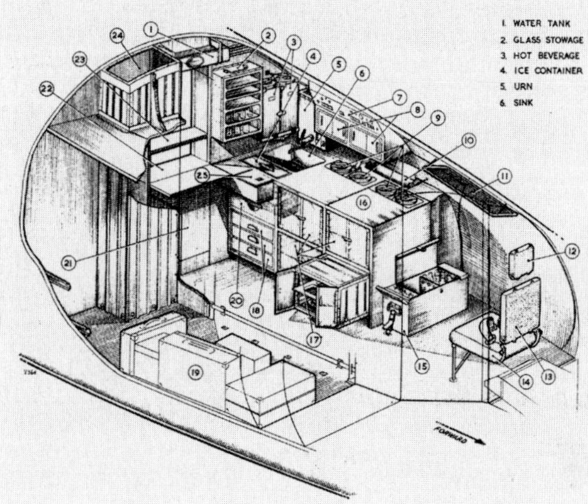

BEA titles and logos were applied to G-AHRF for a number of demonstration and display flights. The forward cabin area, behind the flight deck, could be configured with a well-designed, compact galley, as well as offering extra baggage space and providing access to some of the aircraft systems. Vickers via author

altitudes of 30,000ft (9,000m). The thermal de-icing system was one of the first of its type to be fitted to a civil airliner, and its trials on G-AHRF were actually delayed until January 1950, awaiting sufficiently severe conditions. These were eventually found off the Atlantic coast of Eire, the aircraft being based at Shannon to undertake the research. Although the thermal system worked satisfactorily, the liquid-based systems for the propellers and the windscreen had to be modified owing to problems encountered during the trials. On later production aircraft the propellers were fitted with electrical overshoes and the pump on the windscreen system was improved. The Dart engines were also fitted with electrically heated intakes as a result of data gathered during the de-icing trials.

Then, in contrast, G-AHRF was sent south to Nairobi and Khartoum for tropical trials in June and July 1950. Before leaving for Africa the aircraft made a number of publicity flights in association with BEA in March and April. Although BEA still had yet to place any firm order, G-AHRF carried BEA colours for the tours, which visited eight European capitals and covered 4,400 miles (7,080km).

While the second prototype Viscount had been almost complete when it was modified to jet power, the third aircraft, provisionally registered G-AJZW, existed only as a number of components, and these had been placed in storage when the programme was slowed down. However, these stored parts came in useful when the MoS, in consultation with BEA, ordered a single V.700 prototype, to be powered by four Darts. Because many of the required components already existed and needed only minor modification to form part of the new aircraft, it took only eighteen months to construct the Viscount 700 prototype. Owing to limited space at the experimental plant, the work was transferred from Foxwarren to two separate Vickers-Supermarine factories, one at South Marston, which built the fuselage, and the other at Itchen, where the wings were built. The disparate parts were brought together at Brooklands for final assembly in April 1950, and the first of the larger Viscounts, the V.700, now registered G-AMAV, made its maiden flight on 28 August. Taking off from Brooklands, it landed at Wisley, where the test-flying programme was to be based. The fuselage of the new design was 7ft 4in (2.2m) longer than that of the V.630, and its wingspan was 5ft (1.5m) greater.

Specification – V.700

Powerplant:	4 × R.Da.3 Mk505 Dart
Weights:	Empty basic equipment weight 36,859lb (16,730kg) (40 seats); maximum zero fuel weight 49,000lb (22,240kg); maximum take-off weight 63,000lb (28,600kg); maximum landing weight 58,500lb (26,325kg); typical maximum payload 12,141lb (5,510kg).
Dimensions:	Length 81ft 2in (24.74m); span 93ft 8½in (28.56m); fin height 26ft 9in (8.15m); wing area 963sq ft (89.46sq m); wheelbase 24ft 10in (7.57m).
Performance:	Economic cruising speed 302mph (486km/h); maximum cruising speed 318mph (512km/h); service ceiling 28,500ft (8,700m); range with maximum payload 970 statute miles (1,560km).
Average passenger accommodation:	40–65 (all first class – high density)

Brief Scheduled Debut

A special C of A was issued to G-AHRF on 27 July, shortly after its return from tropical trials. Now in full BEA livery, it operated the world's first scheduled commercial, turbine-powered airline service on 29 July. Operating a normal scheduled BEA flight from Northolt to Paris-Le Bourget, G-AHRF carried twelve guests and BEA chief executive Peter Masefield in addition to fourteen fare-paying passengers. The special VIP guests included George Edwards and Sir Frank Whittle, British inventor of the jet engine. Captains R. Rymer and W. J. Wakelin were the pilots. In gaining his Viscount rating, Capt Rymer became the holder of the world's first commercial licence to operate a civil turbine-powered air transport aircraft.

After this historic inaugural flight G-AHRF operated a further thirty-five scheduled services to Le Bourget, the airline's busiest route, over the next two weeks. On 3 August 1950 BEA finally placed a firm order for twenty V.701 Viscounts, slightly modified versions of the V.700 with a gross weight of 53,000lb (24,000kg) and capable of accommodating forty-seven passengers in a five-abreast configuration. Still on loan to BEA, G-AHRF was switched to the Northolt–Edinburgh domestic trunk route between 15 and 23 August, to carry increased traffic on the service during that year's Edinburgh Festival.

By the time the Viscount was returned to Vickers it had flown 1,815 scheduled passengers. The airline, whose crews had operated the aircraft, had been very impressed by the new type's timekeeping in scheduled service, as well as its reliable serviceability. The favourable publicity generated for both BEA and the aircraft was invaluable to both airline and manufacturer. The passengers lucky enough to find themselves on G-AHRF's flights showed great enthusiasm for the new aircraft with its revolutionary

BELOW: For its debut on the London–Paris route in July 1950, G-AHRF was repainted in full BEA livery. Here, it shares the Northolt ramp with a Swissair CV240 before the first flight. ATPH via author

BOTTOM: Among the VIPs on the first commercial Viscount service were Vickers designer George Edwards (third from left), jet engine pioneer Frank Whittle (third from right, forward row) and BEA's Peter Masefield (furthest up the steps). ATPH via author

powerplant. The comparative smoothness of the flight and quietness of the cabin came as a revelation to regular passengers. It became a common trick on the V.630 flights to balance various items on tables and trays in the passenger cabin to show off the vibration-free ride.

The European demonstration tour and the use of G-AHRF on BEA schedules had shown the day-to-day practicality of the Viscount design, especially in terms of engine reliability and ease of operation compared with the established piston-powered airliners. As well as its quieter, much more comfortable cabin, the Viscount's large oval passenger windows, offering panoramic views even for those seated over the wing, gave rise to much favourable comment.

Early advertisements for the Viscount 700 used modified artists' impressions of the V.630 and photographs of G-AHRF's interior as fitted for its BEA operation.
Author's collection

A New Impetus

The final confirmation of the hard-sought BEA order gave a huge boost to the whole Viscount programme, not to mention the collective morale of Vickers-Armstrongs staff. The increasingly encouraging reports from the flight-test programmes of the two busy prototypes, G-AHRF and G-AMAV, enabled Vickers to build up an impressive portfolio of data to show to more potential customers. The appetite of BEA had been whetted by G-AHRF's encouraging performance on the Paris and Edinburgh routes, and the airline was eager to put the production models into regular service as soon as possible. With both the Ambassador and Viscount on order, BEA was looking forward to finally being able operate a modern, commercially viable fleet.

The Viscount 700, G-AMAV, was soon undergoing a development and flight-test programme similar to that already being undertaken by V.630 G-AHRF. Once it had gained enough flight-test hours, the V.700 had impressed visitors to the 1950 SBAC show at Farnborough when it performed a low-level fly-past with only engine operating. By October 1951 G-AMAV had flown for 250hr, and it was despatched to Africa for tropical trials. The opportunity was also taken to demonstrate the aircraft to interested parties, including airline officials and the local press, in Salisbury, Johannesburg and elsewhere en route. During the trials a very satisfactory low oil consumption of 1½gal per 100hr was achieved, and fuel consumption also returned exceptionally economic figures.

March 1952 saw G-AMAV undertaking icing trials, and the aircraft was awarded a normal C of A, excluding scheduled passenger operations, in June. Later that month a demonstration and sales tour was undertaken, routeing via Malta, Beirut, Bahrein, Karachi, Delhi, Madras, Hyderabad and Bombay to Calcutta, before routeing back to Karachi. The journey home to Weybridge from Pakistan saw the aircraft calling at Baghdad, Bahrein, Beirut, Nicosia, Ankara and Malta. This five-week tour introduced the Viscount to many important and influential airline and government officials. During the rest of the summer numerous flights were made to Cyprus, Gibraltar and Germany. As well as providing valuable data and continuing development and trial services, these trips increasingly involved BEA crew members familiarizing themselves with the aircraft.

Test equipment was often installed in the cabins of both Viscount prototypes, G-AHRF and G-AMAV, during trials, alongside the representative passenger interiors fitted for demonstration work. Author's collection

The Loss of G-AHRF

The flight-test programme suffered a major setback in August when G-AHRF was lost during further trials in East Africa. In the course of a simulated forced landing in the Sudan on 27 August 1952, the aircraft's undercarriage collapsed. Although none of those on board suffered any serious injury, the aircraft was very seriously damaged and it was eventually decided that it was unrecoverable and should be scrapped

BELOW: The V.630, G-AHRF, was despatched on various trials once BEA had returned it to Vickers. On the trials services a mixture of Vickers and airline personnel would usually accompany the aircraft, giving customers' staffs a chance to familiarize themselves with the aircraft. Author's collection

on site. The original, unique Viscount V.630 had been described by many of those fortunate enough to pilot it as a delight to fly and one of the quietest aircraft built among propeller-driven types. The prototype Viscount had managed to accumulate 931hr 50min invaluable flying time for the flight-test programme.

The sad loss of G-AHRF was only a temporary hindrance, as the first two production V.701 Viscounts, BEA's G-ALWE and G-ALWF, had joined G-AMAV on the test programme by early 1953, G-ALWE having first flown in August 1952 and G-ALWF in December the same year. All three aircraft were also being increasingly used for more training and route-familiarization flights for the airline.

Later-version Mk 505 Darts, instead of the Mk 504s fitted to G-AMAV, powered the two production aircraft. These differed from the earlier version of the engine in incorporating a number of improvements added as a result of the test and development programme. Other changes in the new V.701s over the V.700 prototype included significant noise reduction in the forward passenger cabin, achieved by moving the engines 18in (0.45m) further outboard. Otherwise the V.700 and V.701s were virtually identical, both structurally and dimensionally.

The first production V.7015 for BEA supplemented G-AMAN on flight trials after the loss of G-AHRF. Jenny Gradidge

Finally Under Way

The success of the trial passenger flights with G-AHRF, plus the BEA order, gave the Viscount project some much-needed new momentum, and the first production aircraft were starting to emerge from the Weybridge production line in increasing numbers. There was finally a prospect of the pioneering yet much-troubled and continually redesigned Viscount actually having a practical future. Only time would tell whether it would be the hoped-for bright future, or another dead end for British commercial aircraft design.

The Viscount 700 prototype, G-AMAV, prepared the way for the production models of the Viscount, which were finally poised to enter service after several years of design development. Vickers via author

CHAPTER TWO

Up a Gear

The Dart Dakotas

In addition to the considerable flight development work and the engine hours amassed during the test flights of the prototype Viscount airframes, the Dart engine itself was the subject of its own extensive test and familiarization programme. Just using the Viscount prototypes to accumulate the required number of flying hours to enable the engine to be certificated for scheduled passenger services would have been a prohibitively long process. Being a post-war, totally civil-focused project, with no previous military use from which to draw data, the Dart needed to be extensively flown to build up the required operating information. Vital data to give an indication of flight patterns and control techniques for turboprop-powered aircraft in daily airline use was among the important information that was lacking.

To provide this data, and also to give BEA's operational and engineering personnel experience with the revolutionary engine, two of the airline's Douglas DC-3 Dakotas had their original piston engines replaced by two Mk 505 Darts. Field Aircraft Services converted G-ALXN *Sir Henry Royce* and G-AMDB *Claude Johnson* at their factory at Tollerton Airfield in Nottinghamshire. The Dart installation was modelled as closely as possible on that in the Viscount, except for the cowlings.

As the DC-3 was unpressurized, it was not a practical proposition to operate the converted aircraft on passenger services. The high altitudes required for efficient operation of the turboprops would have required the passengers to be given personal oxygen supplies. However, with only the flight deck crew needing to be provided with oxygen, the aircraft could be used on all-freight services. The operation of the aircraft was entrusted to a specially established Dart Development Unit controlled by Capt A.S. Johnson, assisted by Mr R.B. Ferris. The first scheduled freight service with the converted aircraft was operated by G-ALXN on 15 August 1951. Subsequently the aircraft operated all-cargo schedules to Copenhagen, Hanover and Milan for just over a year, until September 1952. They were capable of flying at 202mph (325km/h) at 25,000ft (7,600m) at a normal all-up weight of 28,000lb (12,700kg). This compared to a 'normal' DC-3 performance of 167mph (270km/h) at 7,000ft (2,100m) for the same payload. The experiment was hardly an economic success. The number of operational hours flown by the pair was well below expectations, mostly due to a shortage of qualified crews and engineers. There were also technical difficulties with the new engines which caused delays and cancellations of services. However, these were precisely the kind of problems that the exercise had been designed to expose, enabling them to be solved before the Dart entered scheduled passenger service on the Viscount. By the end of the project G-ALXN had flown 538hr and G-AMDB 668hr in Dart-powered configuration.

As a result of these services and the later 550hr of route-proving flights by G-AMAV and the first two production aircraft, detailed performance charts could be produced for Viscount operations well in advance of the scheduled service entry of the type into daily operations. The Dart Dakotas were reconverted to piston-engine configuration following the end of the trials. Both aircraft continued in BEA service until early 1962, and went on to enjoy new careers with independent operators.

Operation of the two Dart Dakota conversions as freighters gave BEA and Rolls-Royce valuable day-to-day in-service experience of the new engine. via author

Instead of using Northolt, BEA chose to operate its new Ambassadors and Viscounts from the original Northside Terminal at Heathrow, beginning the eventual change of its main London base.
Author's collection

New Home for the New Fleets

Before the new Ambassadors and Viscounts were due for delivery, BEA had decided to develop a new home for them. Northolt was always regarded by the airline as a temporary main London base, albeit fairly long-term. Facilities at the ex-RAF base were quite limited and could not have coped with the imminent expansion. Northolt was already surrounded by suburban sprawl, and there was little hope that the runways could be extended. BEA had already had to scatter much of its engineering operation to other airfields around the country.

The rapidly growing airline desperately needed more room, and in 1949 the corporation's board decided to move the Northolt operations to the much larger Heathrow Airport, to the south. At the time, although the early Heathrow terminal facilities were still rather primitive, there was at least space for a brand-new, purpose-built engineering base for BEA and enough runway capacity to allow for all the airline's current operations and the future expansion plans based on the Ambassador and Viscount fleets. A new purpose-built central terminal complex was being designed and about to be erected which would provide BEA with a spacious, efficient gateway to the capital for its passengers.

Initially only two Viking services a day were scheduled from Heathrow, to Paris/Le Bourget, beginning on 16 April 1951. However, this was only meant as the start. The Ambassadors, and later the Viscounts, were scheduled to be based at Heathrow from delivery, and all remaining Viking and DC-3 services were to be transferred over the next few years.

New Viscount Sales

Despite BEA's new-found enthusiasm for the aircraft, new sales of the Viscount to any other airlines were still slow to materialize. It was to be over a year after signature of the BEA contract before Vickers was able to record any other sales. This frustrating new delay was fairly understandable, however. The world's airlines were still looking very cautiously at the prospect of operating the new propjet or pure-jet airliners, regarding them with a certain degree of suspicion. Both new forms of powerplant had still to prove themselves to many of their prospective customers. However, the next two orders for the Viscount 700 arrived within seven months of each other. In March 1951 Air France placed an order for twelve V.708s, and Eire's national carrier, Aer Lingus, ordered four V.707s in November that year.

With the Viscount, Vickers had introduced a modified type numbering system to distinguish models for different customers. From the Viscount onwards, new designs or modifications involving major structural changes were designated a new basic type number, a block of secondary numbers being used to identify individual customers. BEA's aircraft, the first production model, became the type 701. Subsequent model numbers were based on the sequence in which the aircraft were designed to the customers' specifications. This was not always in the sequence in which they were ordered, sales negotiations not always being finalized, if at all, in the same order that the customers had approached Vickers.

Air France's Viscount order was only part of a major modernization programme upon which the airline had embarked as it rebuilt its sizeable European and worldwide

Airspeed's Woes

After initially beating Vickers to the BEA order, Airspeed's fortunes with its rival Ambassador project took a distinct turn for the worst. The development programme and production schedules were beset by technical problems and production delays. Even on the prototype's maiden flight, on 10 July 1947, problems started. The aircraft, G-AGUA, lost the spring-tab from the centre of its three rudders immediately it took to the air. After a further 50hr of test flying, the bolts holding G-AGUA's port main undercarriage in place failed and the leg dropped down while the aircraft was cruising at high speed, pulling away hydraulic lines in the process. The aircraft was forced to land on its belly, with the port leg still extended and with the starboard leg and flaps inoperable owing to the lost hydraulic fluid. Repairs to the considerable damage to the prototype badly delayed the flight development programme.

Even after the emergence of the second, slightly larger and pressurized prototype Ambassador, G-AKRD, the project continued to encounter disruption and bad luck. On 13 March 1950 G-AKRD sank back on to the runway at Bournemouth Airport during a take-off meant to demonstrate performance during an engine failure. The resulting lower fuselage damage kept the aircraft firmly grounded while repairs were completed. The definitive production prototype Ambassador, G-ALFR, joined the first two prototypes in May 1950, and in July suffered its own first mishap. As a result of a starboard undercarriage failure the aircraft's lower fuselage was damaged on landing, as were the starboard engine nacelle and propeller. Later that year, on 13 November, during overweight landing and centre-of-gravity trials at Airspeed's Christchurch factory airfield, G-ALFR landed too heavily, causing the failure of the upper longeron attachments to both engines, which then promptly became detached from the wings and flew off, continuing on their trajectory ahead of the airliner. The aircraft, transformed into a rather large and ungainly glider, bounced over the fallen engines and actually climbed 40ft (12m) before the highly skilled Airspeed crew managed to land it safely.

As the aircraft continued its troubled development programme, Airspeed's owners, de Havilland, decided that the Christchurch site could be put to more profitable use. Despite advanced sales negotiations being held at the time with Australian National Airways and Central African Airways, de Havilland announced in 1951 that any future plans for developing the aircraft with turboprops were to be scrapped, and that the production line would be closed down after the last BEA aircraft were delivered. The Airspeed Division of de Havilland was later to become The de Havilland Aircraft Company, Christchurch. The former Airspeed factories and offices at Christchurch and Portsmouth survived, later becoming involved in de Havilland military projects such as the Venom and Sea Vixen.

The good looks of the first prototype Airspeed Ambassador belied the aircraft's frustrating technical design problems and other developmental delays.
de Havilland/Airspeed via author

operations. Lockheed Constellations and Douglas DC-4s, soon to be joined by new, larger, Super Constellations, served the long-haul network. For its post-war European and medium-range network Air France had relied on large fleets of converted war-surplus DC-3s and the DC-4s, alongside smaller fleets of France's own 'interim' post-war types, such as the Sud Ouest Languedoc. As part of the modernization programme, in addition to the Viscounts, Air France had also ordered a trio of pioneering de Havilland Comet 1A pure-jet airliners, also from Britain. These were set to enter service shortly before the first turboprops of the Vickers order were due to be delivered.

The Aer Lingus order was also part of a concerted modernization programme. Aer Lingus had been operating for only three years when the war had interrupted its initial healthy growth. Although Eire was a neutral country during the war years, the services of its fledgling national carrier had been severely curtailed and limited to a few politically vital routes to the beleaguered UK. At the end of hostilities the airline had only a handful of operational aircraft, the largest being a single DC-3.

Although it had financial backing from BEA, the UK corporation having inherited a shareholding in the Irish national carrier when it absorbed West Coast Air Services, Aer Lingus endured financial growing pains as it attempted to establish itself in the post-war airline world. Some initial expansion had included the brief introduction of a fleet of Vickers Vikings, but eventually the airline had replaced them with more Douglas DC-3s, which were eventually relied upon to expand the small network from Eire to the UK and Europe. Aer Lingus had also seriously considered the Airspeed Ambassador, one of the prototype Ambassadors having been demonstrated to the airline in 1950.

Longer-ranging ambitions to operate transatlantic services in association with a sister company, Aerlinte, had been frustrated in the late 1940s by political interference. The brand new Lockheed Constellations purchased to operate the new routes to the USA spent most of their time in storage at Shannon, or uneconomically deployed on Aer Lingus services to London and Rome from Dublin, before being sold off when the long-range plans were indefinitely postponed. A number of other unsuccessful routes had also been cut from the network in a rationalization programme. Finding itself resigned to remaining a short/medium-range operator for the foreseeable future, Aer Lingus took a brave step in ordering the Viscount.

Commonwealth Orders

The first sale to a Commonwealth country was confirmed with an order for six Viscounts, later increased to seven, for Trans Australia Airlines (TAA). The airline was still a comparatively new carrier, having been established by the Australian government in the immediate post-war years to compete against established private operators such as Australian National Airways. Growing from a single DC-3 in 1946, the airline soon expanded its DC-3 fleet and introduced larger DC-4s on longer-ranging services. Later, TAA placed new, US-built Convair 240s on busier routes. The Viscount contract was signed in June 1952, the type number V.720 being allocated to the TAA aircraft. The airline was the first to specify the use of external 'slipper' tanks that increased fuel capacity by 290gal (1,315ltr). These, along with extra internal wing tanks, would allow the TAA aircraft to operate the important 1,380-mile (2,220km) Adelaide–Perth sector with an economic payload against the strong headwinds often encountered on the route.

One feature that attracted TAA was the Viscount's promised flexibility. The Australian carrier was keen to be able to operate the new aircraft economically on the shorter services between regional centres, as well as on transcontinental coast-to-coast routes across the country. This would enable TAA to assign one aircraft to operate a service that would previously have been split between a DC-3 or Convair on the intercity flights and a DC-4 on the longer sector.

By this time negotiations were also well advanced for a Viscount order from British West Indian Airways (BWIA). The purchase of the aircraft would be made via BOAC, which had inherited a shareholding in BWIA when it absorbed the assets of the failed BSAA, which had previously operated from the UK to the region. Headquartered at Port of Spain, Trinidad, BWIA operated a wide-ranging route network throughout the Caribbean region with a fleet of Vikings, DC-3s and Lockheed Lodestars. As well as offering a valuable local service, BWIA provided useful connections to and from its catchment area to BOAC's services to the region from the UK and the USA. An order for three V.702s was eventually placed in June 1953, a fourth being ordered in 1954 for 1955 delivery.

Trans Australia Airlines was an early export customer for the Convair CV240, which it acquired for its wide-ranging Australian domestic services. MAP

The Viscount 700 prototype, G-AMAV, wore BWIA's livery following the announcement of the Caribbean airline's order. The BWIA fleet also carried BOAC titles and logo, as many of its services were flown on behalf of, or in partnership with, the parent airline. Vickers via author

North American Breakthrough

Of particular significance was the winning of a contract from Montreal-based Trans-Canada Air Lines (TCA) for no fewer than fifteen Viscount 700s in November 1952. George Edwards, who had personally presented the aircraft's case to TCA's executives in Montreal, had fought hard for this order, the first sale of a major British airliner to an operator in the potentially lucrative North American market. TCA had actually delayed placing orders for available piston-engine types in the class, such as those on offer from Convair and Martin, while it examined Edwards's Viscount proposals. In the meantime, TCA had continued to operate its considerable fleet of DC-3s, supplemented by larger Canadair North Stars, Canadian-built, pressurized, versions of the American Douglas DC-4 powered by British Rolls-Royce Merlin engines.

Viscount versus Convair

Vickers' main competition for the TCA order had come from US manufacturer Convair, based in San Diego, California. Post-war, the larger US aircraft builders had tended to concentrate on longer-haul airliners designed for the more prestigious routes. For the most part they were still relying on well-established piston engines to power their civil aircraft.

Boeing, in Seattle, was then still primarily a military contractor, although it had sold a small number of Stratocruiser airline

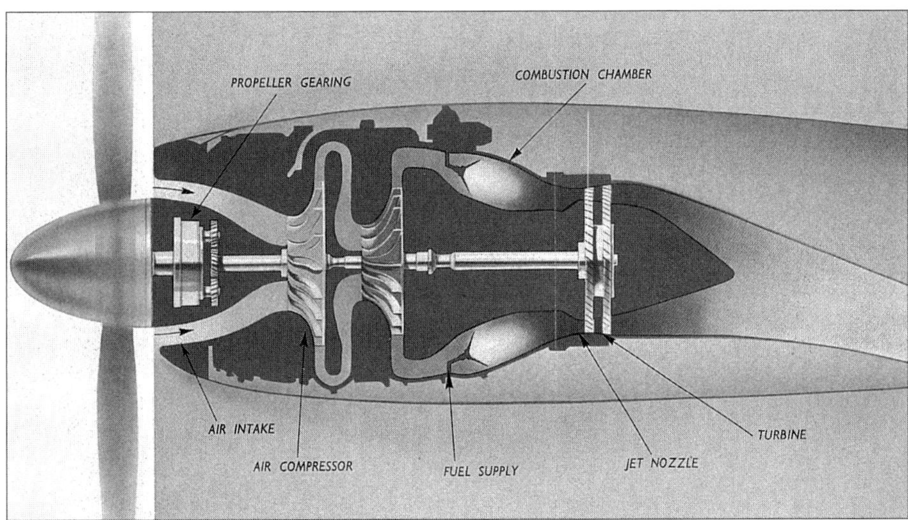

The much-developed and improved Rolls-Royce Dart allowed Vickers to maintain a technical edge over the piston-engined Convairs. Rolls-Royce via author

versions of its KC-97 tanker/transport aircraft and was beginning to develop pure-jet airliner designs by the early 1950s. The Douglas Aircraft Company tended to specialize in larger and more-powerful versions of its piston-powered airliners, intended for the medium- and long-haul markets. Its few short-haul commercial projects failed to get off the drawing board. Lockheed was firmly basing its future on developing its medium-range Constellation design into a larger-capacity, longer-range aircraft.

This left the shorter-range North American market to two smaller US manufacturers, Convair and Martin, of Baltimore. Convair was the clear victor in this particular battle, Martin being dogged by problems with its similar M202 and M404 aircraft. Basically in the same operational, pressurized, forty-passenger, two-piston-engine, short-range class as Convair's CV240, the Martin aircraft eventually sold only in comparatively small numbers. The Convairs, however, achieved respectable domestic and worldwide sales figures.

Responding to the CV240's success, Convair designed a slightly larger, more powerful and generally improved version, the CV340. Entering service with United Airlines in 1952, the CV340 was the Viscount 700's closest piston-powered rival. In 1952, in an attempt to influence any of its customers that might be considering the new turboprop design, Convair produced a study, showing the CV340 to be much more economical to operate than the Viscount. However, Vickers countered with its own study, which took into account the recently increased all-up weight. Adjusting the costs to allow for the advantages of the turboprop, it showed the Viscount to be a better proposition with regard to revenue payload, increased speed and operating costs.

That the Viscount fuselage was 10in (25cm) wider than that of the Convair made a five-abreast configuration much more practical. Even with a 2-3 seating layout the Viscount aisle was half an inch (1.25cm) wider at 17½in (44.5cm), as opposed to the CV340's 17in (43cm). High-density seating arrangements could be accommodated on the Convairs, but only by removing some of the galley and rearranging and reducing the size of the passengers' washroom. The basic Viscount price per aircraft was £235,000, about £15,000 less expensive than a Convair.

TCA Changes

Following the formal placement of the TCA order, G-AMAV later spent several weeks in Canada in early 1953 on cold-weather trials. In positioning for these tests, the prototype Viscount 700 became the first propeller-turbine aircraft to cross the Atlantic. During this evaluation programme the aircraft was operated in very demanding sub-Arctic conditions, its engines successfully starting on occasions after standing idle in temperatures of –40°F for over 12hr. Although extreme, these weather conditions were not uncommon during the long winters on TCA's northern scheduled routes. Some 250 technical modifications were suggested by the airline following the evaluations, and the resulting aircraft; their basic designs adapted to TCA requirements and incorporating the changes, were allocated the type number V.724. The TCA Viscounts were initially equipped to take forty-eight passengers in a four-abreast configuration.

Among the more major changes and modifications incorporated into the basic Viscount design for TCA were:

- A total redesign of the flight deck layout, to accommodate only the two pilots and dispensing with the radio operator's position, which was standard in the earlier models.

The Canadian cold-weather trials undertaken by G-AMAV were useful in developing many of the new, improved, technical features that would be incorporated in the Trans-Canada V.724s and other later models. MAP

- The incorporation of much more American-designed and -produced equipment.
- The air-conditioning scoop on the underside of the fuselage was fitted flush, replacing the original projecting scoop.
- An integral heating system was installed, and the soundproofing further improved.
- The weight of the aircraft was increased to 60,000lb (27,000kg).
- Even more powerful Mk506 Dart engines were installed.

A number of the design improvements specifically incorporated for TCA soon became options or, in many cases, standard design features on later production aircraft. The improved Viscounts offered greater efficiency, flexibility and economy of operation over the earlier versions, and aroused the interest of many more potential customers for Vickers.

The Viscount's fuel and water methanol systems were grouped in the aircraft's wings.
Vickers via author

The Basic Model

Although, at least externally, the Viscount 701s of BEA, the 707s of Aer Lingus, the 708s of Air France and all the other Viscount 700 customer variants to follow were identical, each could be adapted, in its own way to suit its purchaser's needs. The multitude of possible modifications and adaptations were, nonetheless, based on a core design.

The aerodynamic formula for the aircraft was still very much based on the Viking, the wing having a similar taper and the tail surfaces being a refined, developed, version of those of the earlier aircraft, having a distinctive Vickers style and shape. However, pressurization had dictated a circular rather than oval fuselage cross-section. The stressed-skin structure of the wing also betrayed its Viking origins. The wing comprised three sections, a centre section, two inner planes, which carried the engine nacelles, and two outer planes with detachable wing-tips. The flaps and ailerons were metal-covered, each half-span consisting of three sections. When retracted, the double-slotted flaps showed no projections at all, giving exceptional aerodynamic efficiency. On the tailplane and elevators the moveable surfaces accounted for almost half the surface area.

Two groups of eight fuel tanks fed the four Darts. Made to a flexible bag design, the tanks were secured to the inner wing structure to prevent their collapse when empty. A cross-feed pipe, with a shut-off cock, connected both sides. A long-range tank was also fitted, feeding its contents to the other tanks and not directly to the engines. The fuselage was built up with closely-spaced frames, carrying stringers to which the skin was attached. Flush riveting was used on all external surfaces, except at joints in the pressure skin, where mushroom-headed rivets were used. Cabin pressurization was run from the blowers, connected to the engines; 66lb (30kg) of air

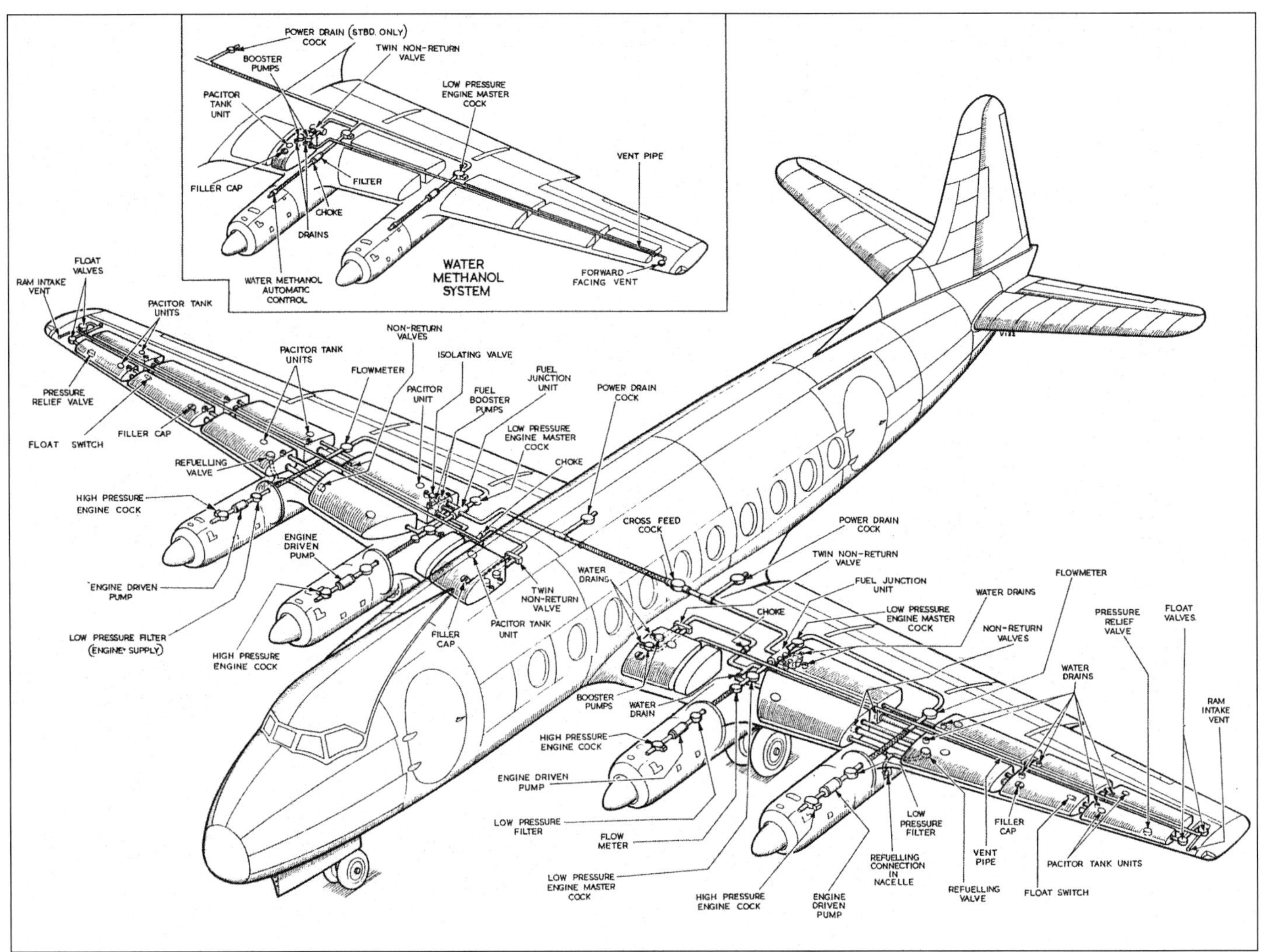

per minute could be delivered at 25,000ft (7,600m). Any altitude between sea level and 5,200ft (1,600m) could be selected for the comfort of the occupants. De-icing of the wing and tail unit was by air heated through heat exchangers.

The twin-wheel undercarriage was designed by Vickers and offered with a choice of Goodyear or Dunlop wheels, anti-skid units and brake plates. Hydraulics operated the raising and lowering of the main and nose undercarriage, the brakes and the nosewheel steering. These systems were duplicated. The nosewheel steering was operated by two small handwheels on the flight deck, one for each pilot.

The electrical system was run from a generator on each engine, stabilized by a carbon-pile regulator which delivered 28V to four 24V batteries. An electrical actuator extended landing lights on the wing, and de-icing lights were also provided to illuminate the wing. In the event of a crash an inertia switch cut out the generator system and isolated a battery, which continued to provide emergency cabin lighting.

Versatility with Simplicity

Three basic passenger-seating layouts were originally devised for the Viscount 700. The original standard four-abreast, forty-seater, a 48-seat layout, still four-abreast but with reduced seat pitch, and another 48-seat arrangement with the original bigger seat pitch but five-abreast seating and a narrower aisle. Other seating variations were soon being proposed. The earliest production models were fitted with galleys at the front and lavatories at the rear. This was later adapted for some customers, being installed the opposite way round, and the forward, main deck, baggage compartment could also be adapted to provide carry-on luggage space. Alternatively it could be deleted altogether to provide space for another row of seats, with the bulkhead moved forward. Combined cargo/passenger loads could also be catered for, by allocating the forward cabin to freight loads, moving the forward bulkheads back and fitting strengthened floor panels forward of them.

As much as possible, the Viscount was designed for swift turn-rounds and ease of servicing. The three cargo-hold doors, one on the upper starboard fuselage serving the rearmost hold, and two others on the lower fuselage, either side of the wing, also on the starboard side, allowed baggage and freight handling to continue while passengers were boarded using one or other of the main doors on the port side. The other main door could be used for galley servicing at the same time, depending on the layout chosen. Also on the starboard side were external servicing connections for draining the lavatory and replenishing the water tank. All the normal aircraft servicing panels were located where they could be reached without the use of ladders or platforms.

The Dart engines' low-slung installation was especially useful for any maintenance required during the turn-round, helping to keep any last-minute technical delays to a minimum. The engines, their mountings and propellers made up interchangeable powerplant units. The whole assembly could be easily removed, either for regular maintenance or for an in-service engine change, though the propellers were usually removed first for convenience and ease of handling.

For less drastic maintenance, the cowling doors were connected and hinged behind the firewall. By releasing toggle fasteners, the top and bottom panels of the nacelles swung up or down respectively and clipped to catches on the wing, exposing the entire engine for servicing or removal. Small

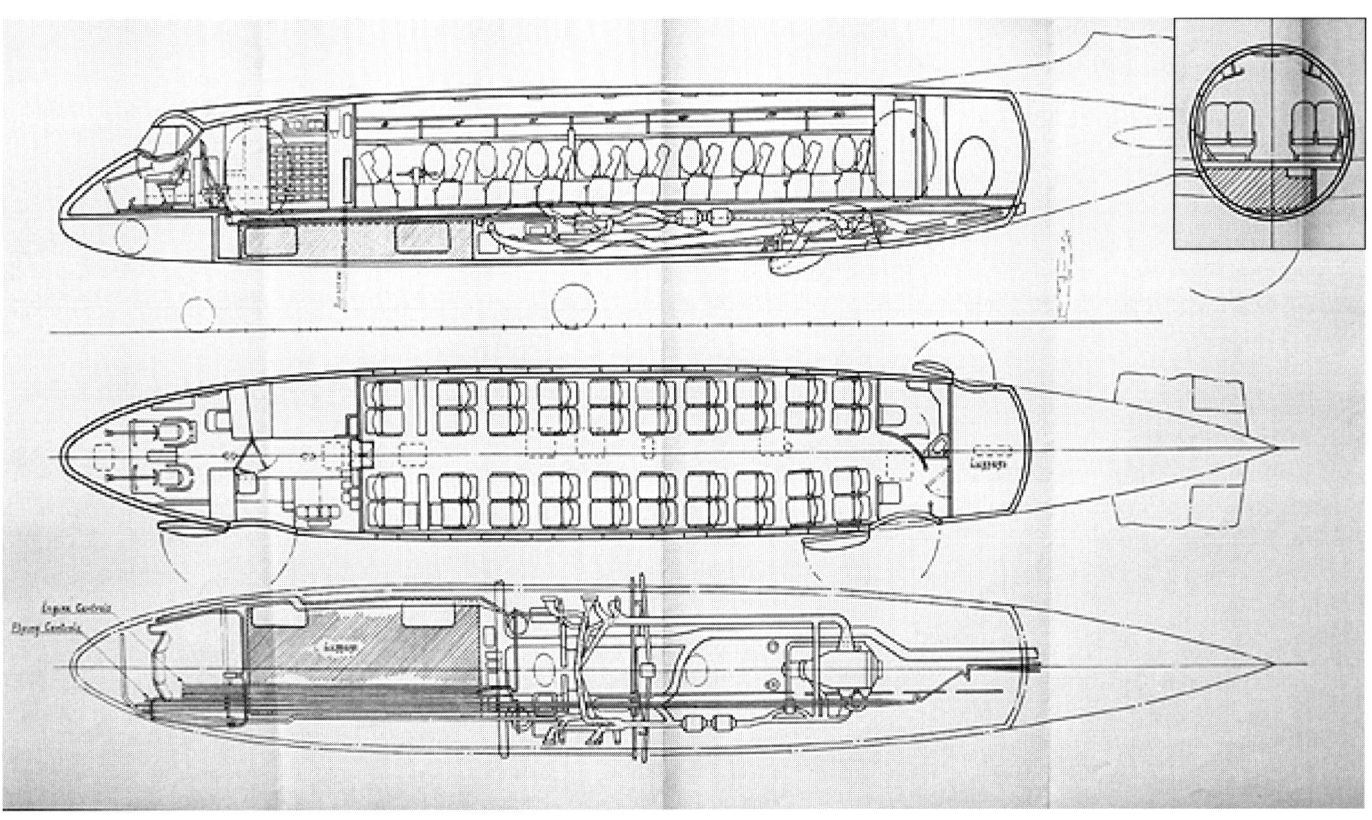

The forty-passenger first-class configuration was just one of several cabin layouts available to Viscount customers. Vickers via author

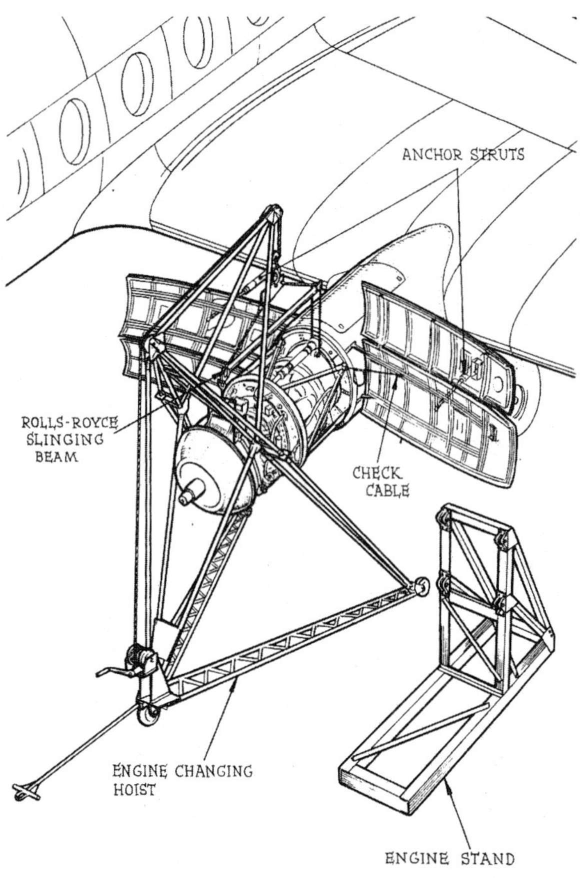

ABOVE: Easy access to the Dart engines for line maintenance, regular servicing or even a complete engine change, was a popular feature of the Viscount design. Vickers via author

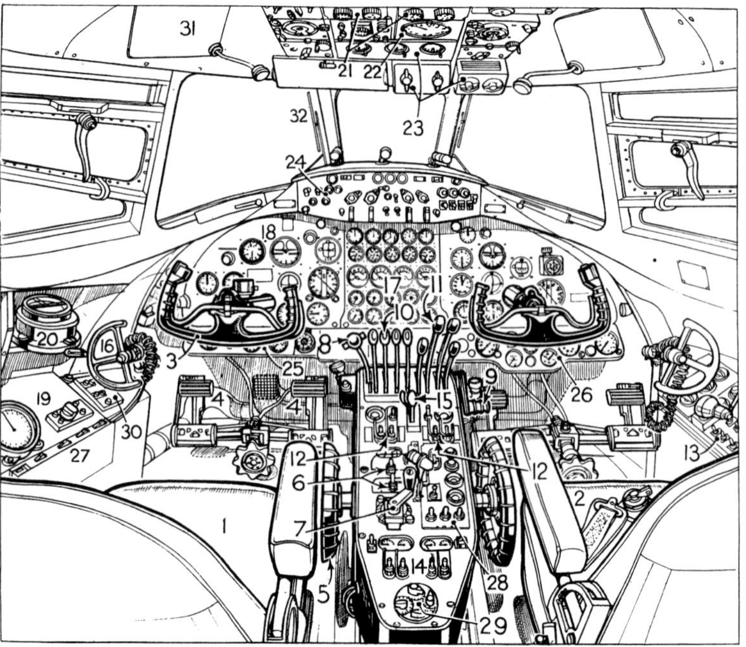

RIGHT: The Viscount's flight-deck layout was only one aspect of the new aircraft with which potential crews had to become familiar during type-conversion training. Author's collection

1. Captain's Seat
2. First Officer's Seat

FLYING CONTROLS
*3. Control Column (including Aileron and Elevator Controls and Handbrake for Undercarriage Main Wheels)
*4. Rudder Pedals (with Toe Brakes for Undercarriage Main Wheels)
*5. Elevator Trim Wheel
6. Aileron Trim Switches
7. Rudder Trim Unit
8. Flap Control
9. Control Locking Lever

ENGINE CONTROLS
10. Throttles
11. High Pressure Fuel Cocks
12. Low Pressure Fuel Cocks
13. Fuel Controls
14. Fuel Trimmers

UNDERCARRIAGE CONTROLS
15. Undercarriage Lever
*16. Nosewheel Steering Wheel

MAIN INSTRUMENTS
17. Engine Gauges
*18. Instrument Flying Panel
19. CL2 Compass Master Indicator
20. Magnetic Compass
21. VHF Radio Control Knobs
22. Automatic Direction Finding Equipment
23. Decca Navigator Equipment

ANCILLARY CONTROLS
24. Panel for Propeller Feathering Buttons, Fire Warning Lights and Switches, Fuel Flowmeters, etc.
25. Panel for Undercarriage Indicators, Flap Indicator, etc.
26. Panel for Fuel Contents Gauges and Rate of Fuel Flow Indicators
27. Cockpit Lighting Controls
28. Automatic Pilot
29. Sperry Zero Reader Controls
*30. Radio Selector Switches

ACCESSORIES
*31. Sun Visor
*32. Windscreen Wiper

*These items are duplicated on port (left) and starboard (right) sides

access panels on the engine nacelles allowed the inspection and checking of items such as the gearbox oil level without having to open the main cowlings. Pressure-fuelling couplings were located on the outboard side of each of the two outboard nacelles, allowing refuelling to be completed in seven minutes. It transpired that oil consumption on the turboprops was negligible, topping-up between flights rarely being necessary.

BEA Preparations for Service

Throughout early 1953, as the prototype and first production Viscounts built up the flying hours to the figure required for full certification, an increasing amount of flying time could be allocated to BEA's crew-training and type-conversion plans. The first production Viscount 701, G-ALWE, spent most of its time, from January 1953, on intensive training and familiarization sorties. It often operated for 10hr a day, with up to thirty landings, many of the training flights being made with only three or two engines operating, in various combinations, as crews learnt to handle the aircraft in as many different conditions and circumstances as possible.

On 22 January G-ALWE set an official speed record from London to Cologne in West Germany, averaging 283mph (455km/h) in unfavourable weather conditions. On another occasion, newly-delivered Viscount 701 G-AMNY operated a London–Geneva proving flight in less than two hours. This compared with Swissair's scheduled time of 2hr 10min using Convair CV-240s. The Viscount's performance was particularly impressive when compared with BEA's previous Viking journey time from Northolt of 3hr 15min.

The Ambassador and Viscount were among the first commercial aircraft for which functional flight-deck simulators were extensively used for pilot training. BEA installed new Decca Navigator simulators for both types, much of the initial crew conversion work being carried out on them. In addition to both aircraft being new and much more modern, in many instances it was the first time that even the most experienced of BEA's pilots had flown a high-altitude, pressurized aircraft. The extensive use of electrical controls and much more modern instrumentation introduced the crews, accustomed to the decidedly more basic comforts of the DC-3 and Viking, to a whole new era of piloting.

Initially, twenty-two experienced BEA captains and twenty-two of the airline's first officers were selected for Viscount training. A remarkable 99 per cent of those eligible to apply for conversion had done so, giving the new Viscount Fleet Captain, A.S. Johnson, previously with the Dart Development Unit, a choice of the best pilots in the corporation. Eight-week ground courses for the pilots included a week studying the Viscount's electronic system at Northolt. That was followed by three weeks at the Vickers Aircraft Servicing School, followed by two weeks with Rolls-Royce, studying engine handling data. A week's revision saw the course ending with a further week on the Decca simulator. Captains then went through 9½hr of type conversion, followed by a flexible period of route flying and further type training before receiving the Viscount endorsement on their licences. First officers received 5½hr of type training before beginning their own route flying to complete their conversion to the Viscount. The aim was to have between ten and fourteen complete crews fully trained and ready to inaugurate services by the beginning of April 1953.

Radio officers, cabin crews, engineers and all the other BEA staff who would soon be involved in the aircraft's operation, all received their own training on the Viscount. The engineers and electricians also attended technical courses at the Vickers Aircraft Servicing School. The Viscount innovations to which BEA's personnel had to become accustomed included the on-board public address system. Cabin crews had to be instructed in its correct use, allowing a much more civilized method of communication with the passengers. At last they would no longer have to shout their safety briefings to make themselves heard above the infernal din of piston engines revving up. As well as operational staff, the airline's sales and marketing force had to be instructed on the aircraft's features and start to sell the Viscount to the travelling public.

Once the Heathrow engineering base was open, the engineering staff soon settled into its efficient new surroundings. The new building was ready by March 1952, and BEA began the mammoth task of moving the Northolt maintenance operation the few miles south to Heathrow. The new base had an area of no less than 458,405sq ft

Ambassador's Rocky Start

The mostly trouble-free nature of the Viscount 701's initial training and route-proving period made a welcome change for BEA when compared with that of the Airspeed Ambassador a year before. The first production aircraft began to be delivered to BEA from Airspeed for training and route-proving flights in September 1951. A period of *ad hoc* schedules followed on the Heathrow–Paris route, the aircraft replacing the Vikings normally assigned to the service.

Unfortunately the initial Ambassadors suffered from numerous technical problems, often centred on their electrical and radio systems. This resulted in them being returned to Airspeed in attempt to cure the faults. At the end of March 1952 six Ambassadors were finally ready to enter full-time scheduled service with BEA, over a year late. By the end of the year the Ambassador, or 'Elizabethan class', as BEA rechristened the aircraft, was operating from Heathrow to Athens, Copenhagen, Milan, Paris, Rome, Stockholm, Vienna and Zurich. The Elizabethan chalked up one particular success with the reintroduction of the prestige Silver Wing service. This daily flight operated between Heathrow and Paris from June 1952, with a 1pm departure from either end of the route. BEA's predecessor, Imperial Airways, had originally introduced the Silver Wing service in the pre-war era.

As with the original Imperial flight, the all-first-class refined cabin service featured gourmet meals. The Elizabethan's passenger capacity was restricted to forty, instead of the more usual forty-seven or forty-nine. The Silver Wing flight was actually slowed to 90min to allow a leisurely champagne luncheon to be served to the elite clientele by three experienced cabin crew. Air France introduced its own rival prestige flight on the Paris–London route, though this was operated by its unpressurized, piston-powered Douglas DC-4s. Named 'The Epicurean', this was also a revival of a pre-war luxury service.

Even on this second attempt the Elizabethan fleet was initially plagued by more technical difficulties. However, solutions were soon found as more experience with the type was accumulated, and the aircraft finally started to leave its teething problems behind. Eventually the Elizabethans built up a popular following with crews and passengers. When the last of the order were delivered, in 1953, they were also to be seen on routes from Heathrow to Amsterdam, Brussels, Cologne, Dusseldorf, Hamburg, Hanover, Malta, Manchester and Nice. Manchester-Birmingham–Paris and Manchester–Dusseldorf passengers also enjoyed the elegant comforts of the new fleet.

THE LUXURY SERVICE TO PARIS
BEA
SILVER WING
BRITISH EUROPEAN AIRWAYS

Author's collection

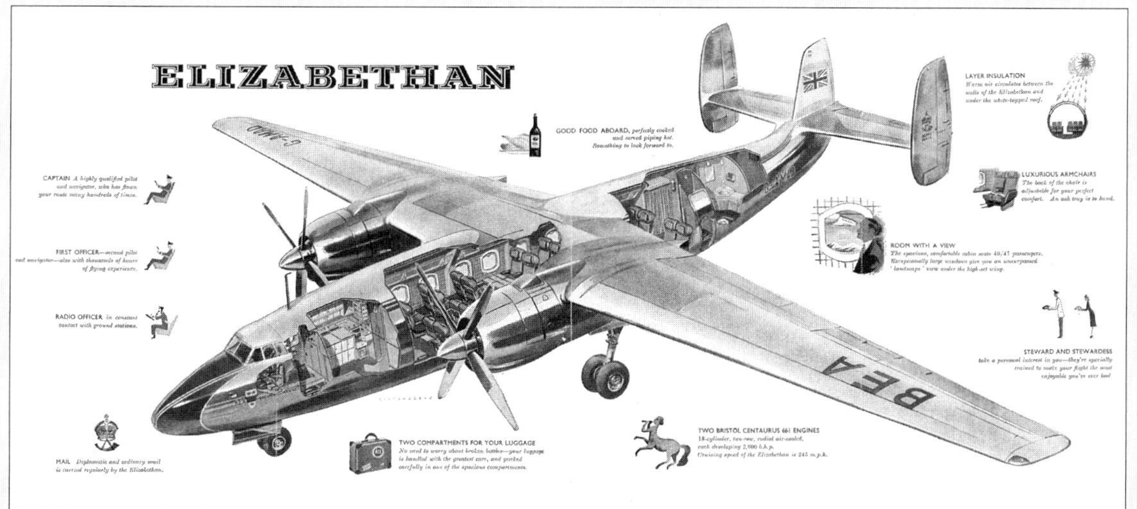

The Elizabethan class offered unprecedented passenger comfort for its day. Despite early technical problems, mostly concerned with its advanced electrical systems, the aircraft soon gained a popular following on many prestige services. Author's collection

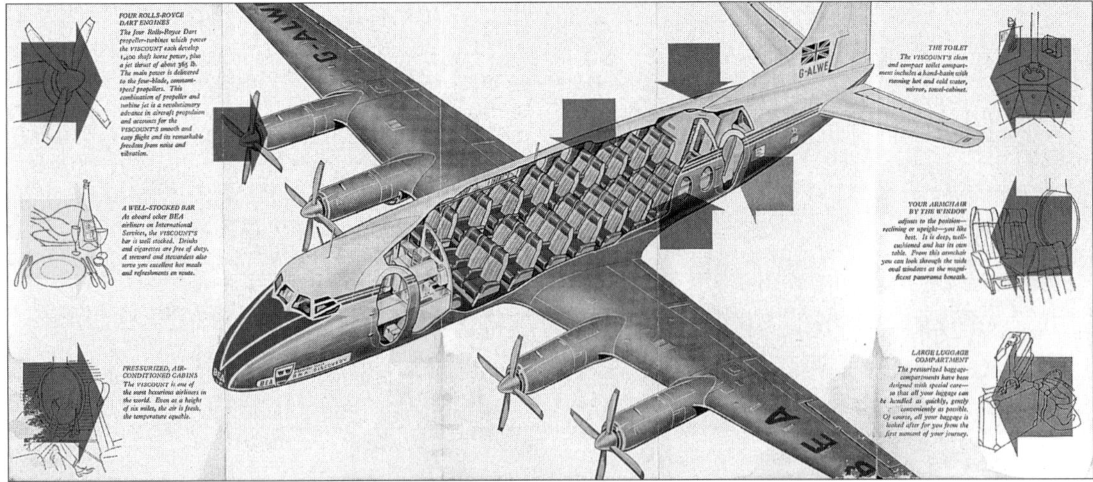

The Viscount 701s were configured with a five-abreast tourist-class cabin for entry into BEA service. However, the seat pitch remained the same as the four-abreast layout, still allowing a great deal of leg room, and the overall effect was still one of spaciousness compared with the Vikings and DC-3s. Author's collection

(42,586sq m), divided into ten aircraft bays. Five of these were ready in 1952, the remaining bays coming into use during 1953. The innovative equipment installed included an engine servicing cradle that could be moved around, with an engine in it, by just one engineer. This, and other, purpose-built new engineering items was designed by Mr J. J. Gibbons, BEA's manager in charge of design and procurement of equipment, and built by Bramber Engineering Ltd. All of the Northolt-based engineering work, except some electrical and instrument workshops, which remained at Northolt for the time being, had been transferred by April 17. Many of the more scattered resources around the south of England were also relocated to Heathrow, greatly improving efficiency.

Happily, despite the intensity of the training and route-proving services, the engineers and technical staff were impressed by the lack of technical problems. The very unfamiliarity of the new engine should have seen many more problems arising daily, but even minor troubles with the fairly unproven Darts, and the aircraft in general, were few and far between.

Viscount or Discovery?

The first three production Viscount 701s were delivered to BEA with a first-class, forty-seat configuration. However, BEA announced that it intended to operate the Viscounts only on new 'tourist-class' services, at fares up to 20 per cent cheaper than the 1952 levels. Subsequently, all the remaining aircraft were delivered in five-abreast, 47-passenger arrangement, and the early aircraft were converted to the new layout before entering full commercial service. Although seating extra passengers, the new configuration was achieved with no loss of legroom, simply by replacing the original four-abreast seats with a 2-3, five-abreast layout. Scheduled service entry was planned for April 1953, and six Viscount 701s were expected to be on hand to begin commercial operations.

In the same way that the Ambassador had been renamed the Elizabethan class, BEA had plans to rename the Viscount the Discovery class. The Elizabethans all carried the names of notable figures from the sixteenth-century reign of Queen Elizabeth the First, and the Discovery class Viscounts were given names of important British discoverers and explorers. This trend had started early in BEA's existence with most aircraft types being 'rechristened' by BEA for its own marketing purposes. Subsequently the Rapides became known as Islander class, the short-lived, unpopular Ju 52s were Jupiters, the DC-3s eventually became Pionairs (or even Pionair Leopard for the freighter DC-3s!) and the Vikings had latterly been renamed Admirals when operated in a new all-tourist-class configuration.

The first of the production Viscount 701s to be delivered, G-ALWE, had been briefly flown back to the Vickers plant at Wisley on 11 February 1953, where the wife of BEA's chairman, Lady Douglas, officially christened it *RMA Discovery* as the flagship of the fleet, RMA standing for 'Royal Mail Aircraft'. The next two production aircraft, G-ALWF and G-AMNY, were named *RMA Sir John Franklin* and *RMA Sir Ernest Shackleton* respectively with BEA, and the succeeding aircraft were all christened in a similar fashion as they were delivered.

The Elizabethans were one of the few instances when the BEA class name actually stuck. The type became known as the Elizabethan, or even 'The Lizzie', almost as much as by its original name, even after BEA ceased using it. In most other cases, especially with the Viscount, the last BEA type to be renamed in this way, the new name was almost universally ignored outside the airline itself. With the Viscount, the aircraft's own fame and reputation from day one almost ensured the quiet dropping of the Discovery classification, even, eventually, within BEA.

Into Scheduled Service

Although it did not attract the publicity of the later scheduled passenger services, the first actual Viscount 700 revenue-earning flight took place on 2 April 1953. On that day the newly delivered V.701 G-AMOG *Robert Falcon Scott*, flew as a substitute for one of the Dart Dakotas on the scheduled London–Rome–Athens–Nicosia route, carrying cargo. More scheduled freight services were operated by G-AMOG over the following weeks, on revenue cargo-carrying flights to Istanbul following a similar route via Rome and Athens, as well as more Nicosia services.

The flight that was to grab most of the media attention, however, left Heathrow at 08.32am on 18 April 1953, the day after the type was granted a full C of A. That morning G-AMNY operated the first scheduled Viscount 701 passenger service, on the Nicosia route, again via Rome and Athens. The flight was crewed by two captains, A.S. Johnson, the Viscount fleet captain, and A. Wilson, with radio officer

ABOVE: Viscount G-AMOG carried BEA's first revenue loads by V.701 in April 1953, on scheduled freight services. BEA via author

J. Whittaker. Attending to the passengers were steward L. Melton and the airline's chief stewardess, Pamela Rome. This flight was actually only a BEA service as far as Athens. On arriving at the Greek capital that afternoon the flight became a Cyprus Airways service onwards to Nicosia, under a charter agreement with BEA. This arrangement had also applied to the previous Elizabethan service on the route. Cyprus Airways operated a small fleet of six DC-3s of its own on local flights from Nicosia to neighbouring Mediterranean and Middle Eastern destinations. Thus, Cyprus Airways was, technically, the second commercial operator of the Viscount.

After G-AMNY opened the Viscount passenger service to Cyprus, the other delivered V.701s soon began earning their keep for BEA on scheduled services. With new aircraft coming down the Weybridge production line, even more BEA passengers could look forward to experiencing a new class of travel on short- and medium-haul routes. The BEA Viscount passenger service inaugurals over the rest of 1953 were as follows:

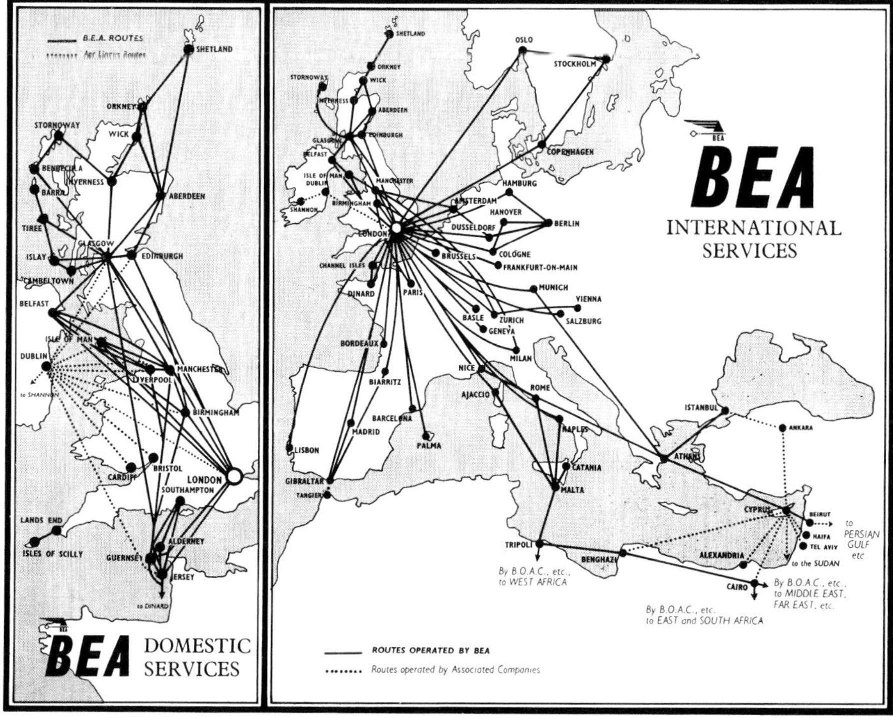

In the 1950s BEA's expanding route system encompassed most of Western Europe and reached as far as North Africa and the eastern Mediterranean, in addition to the airline's extensive domestic network. Author's collection

- 19 April, London–Rome–Athens–Istanbul (G-ALWE)
- 25 April, London–Zurich (G-ALWE)
- 1 June, London–Geneva (G-AMNY)
- 1 July, London–Copenhagen–Stockholm (G-ALWE)
- 17 July, London–Glasgow (G-AMOB) – initially only on an *ad hoc* basis
- 6 October, London–Milan (G-AMNY)
- 6 October, London–Geneva–Milan (G-AMOB)
- 1 November, London–Frankfurt (G-AMOD)
- 1 November, London–Belfast (G-AMOD)

The service from Heathrow to Belfast was a first-class luxury flight along the lines of the London–Paris 'Silver Wing' service. Departing London in the evening, the 'Ulster Flyer' would night-stop in Belfast and operate the morning flight to Heathrow. Similarly scheduled, first-class Viscount services were later introduced on flights to Glasgow as 'The Clansman' and to Edinburgh as 'The Chieftain'.

Typical of the time savings that were to become standard on routes on which the Viscounts replaced earlier, slower aircraft was the Heathrow–Frankfurt route. The Viscounts cut over 50min off the Viking's schedule from Northolt. The reduced flying times were of great importance where the comparatively primitive Vikings, and even the much more modern Elizabethans, had been losing the commercial battle for passengers against some of the European national carriers operating modern US aircraft such as the Convairs and DC-6s. The introduction of the Viscount brought a rapid increase in BEAs' percentage share of the market on services to Switzerland and Scandinavia in particular.

Elizabethan Reshuffle

As the new Viscounts took over many of the BEA Elizabethans' initial services, the Elizabethans, in turn, took on new routes from Heathrow that had previously been operated by the Vikings from Northolt. The Elizabethans opened a Heathrow–Manchester service to provide the northern city with access to worldwide connections from Heathrow, and were also seen more on important routes to Belgium, Germany, Italy and the Netherlands.

Elizabethans also replaced Vikings on busier routes on BEA's West Berlin-based German Internal Service. At that time, only aircraft of British, American or French airlines could operate domestic flights from West Berlin, and BEA maintained a busy out-station at Tempelhof, the downtown airport. The Elizabethans increased their presence on services to Malta, taking over Viking routes from the Mediterranean island to Cairo via Tripoli and Benghazi. As the process continued the Vikings were gradually withdrawn, and by the beginning of 1954 only eighteen remained in use at Northolt. BEA already had plans in hand to dispose of the last survivors and move all remaining London services to Heathrow by the autumn.

Bigger Yet

As the Viscount accumulated operating hours, new data and research allowed the Dart engine to be even further developed and modified to increase its power and

Vickers' initial proposal for a stretched Viscount for BEA was an impressive design. Author's collection

efficiency. Early in 1952 Rolls-Royce had proposed the R.Da.5, an uprated version of the Dart capable of producing 1,690ehp for take-off. Inevitably, Vickers looked at options for employing the new engine in future developments of the Viscount, and eventually came up with a much-enlarged design, the Viscount 800.

In the V.800 the extra power available from the more powerful engines was to be used to carry an increased revenue load over shorter stages. With the fuselage stretched by no less than 13ft 3in (4m) and the gross weight increased to 65,000lb (29,500kg), the aircraft would be capable of carrying sixty-six passengers in a standard configuration. Higher-density layouts were also designed for up to eighty-six seats. BEA decided this would be ideal for its high-capacity, shorter-range services to European cities such as Amsterdam, Brussels, Dusseldorf, Nice, Paris and Zurich, and the busier domestic routes to Belfast, Edinburgh and Glasgow. An initial order was placed for twelve of the larger aircraft, designated the V.801 for BEA. The new contract was signed at the official christening of G-ALWE *Discovery* at Wisley on 11 February 1953.

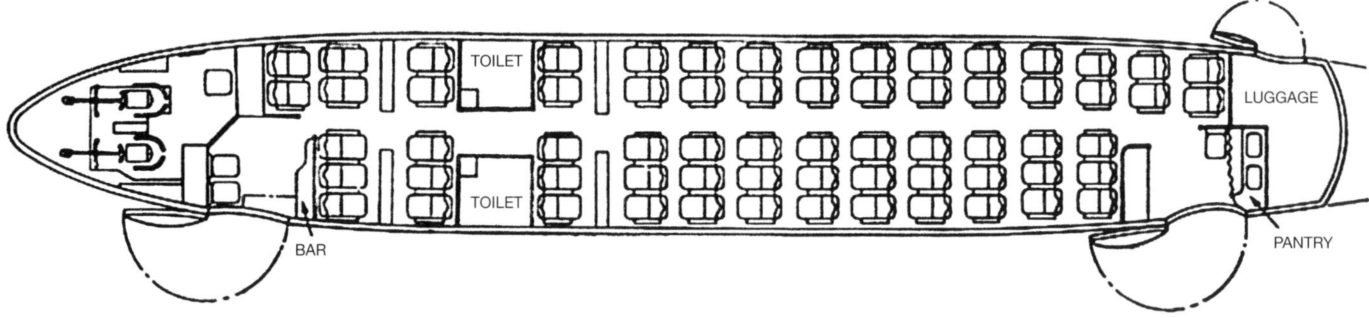

A 68-passenger configuration was one option for the Viscount 800 offered to BEA. Author's collection

Following its construction at Weybridge, the first Air France V.708 made its maiden flight in March 1953. Air France

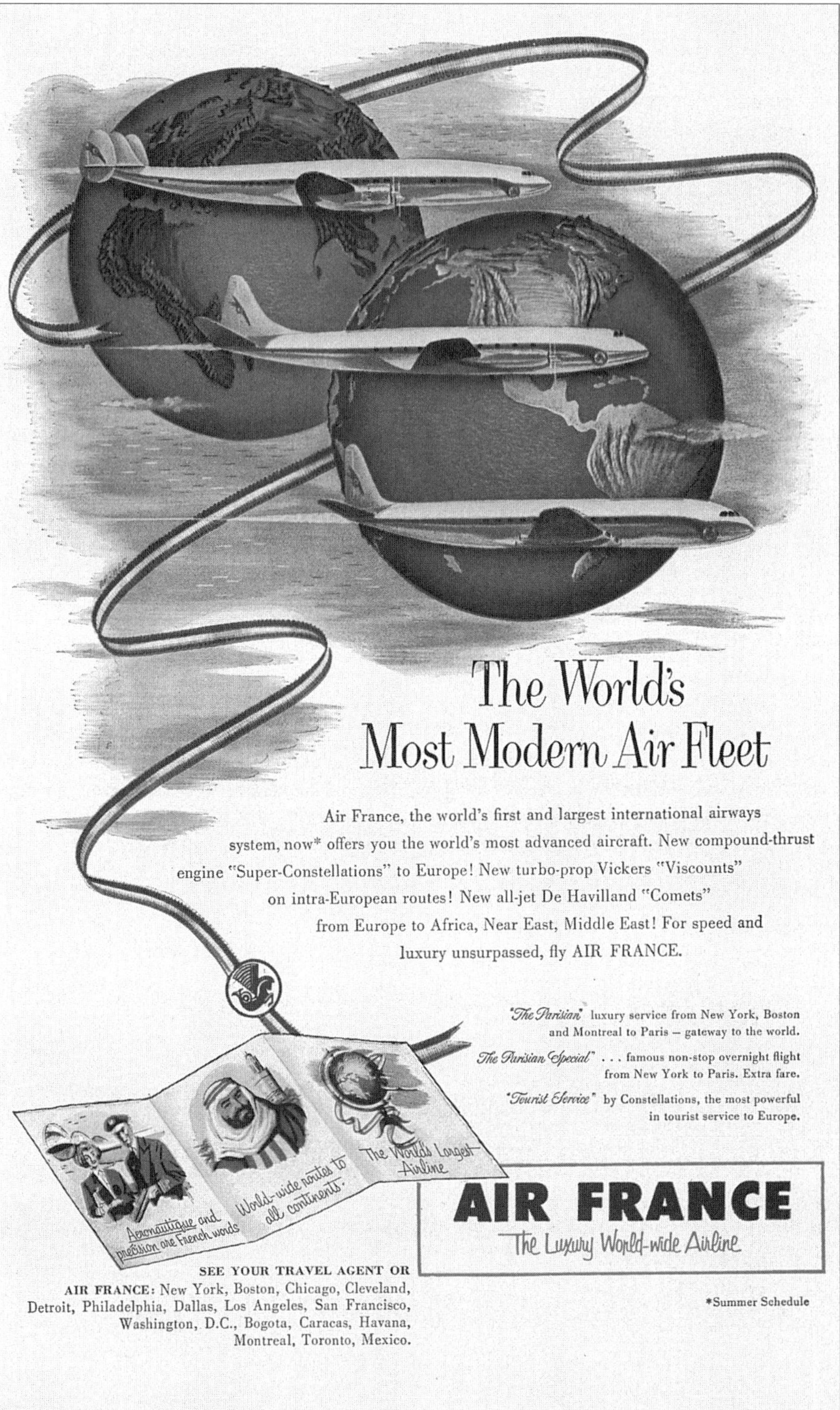

With its new Viscount turboprops and Comet jets operating alongside state-of-the-art Lockheed Super Constellations, Air France was able to boast one of the most modern airline fleets in scheduled service. Author's collection

Exactly a month later, on 11 March, the first V.708 for Air France took to the air for the first time. The first three Air France Viscounts were delivered in May, and entered service on the Paris-Orly to Istanbul route, via Milan, Rome and Athens, in August, and to London from Orly in September. The Viscounts replaced Lockheed Constellations on the Istanbul service and, as the fleet grew in numbers, the Viscounts were also introduced on more European services. Viscount flights were operated from Orly to Geneva, and to Vienna via Zurich, mostly replacing DC-4s. On the London route, demand was soon such that frequencies from Orly were doubled to ten a day, and a direct Nice–London Viscount route was opened.

To the Future?

With the remaining Air France and Aer Lingus Viscount 700s making their way down the production line, as well as the remaining BEA V.701s, the order book was looking healthy. A number of potential customers were close to signing their own orders and, in anticipation of this, Vickers decided to open a new Viscount production line at Hurn Airport, just outside Bournemouth in Dorset. The company already leased a factory at Hurn from the government, which was being used to produce the Varsity, a modernized, military version of the Viking with a tricycle undercarriage. In December 1953 work began on establishing a Viscount production line alongside the Varsity one, the latter eventually to be ousted by more Viscount production.

The end of the 1953 summer season saw the Viscount 700 established in daily scheduled service, with more customers due to take delivery. Iraqi Airways had signed up for three V.735s in July, and the Indian Air Force for two VIP-configured V.723s in November. The remarkably trouble-free entry into service had already attracted the attention of other airlines, and Vickers' sales team was busy working on new orders to fill the Weybridge and Hurn production lines.

The year had been wonderful for the company and its new prize product. Yet one more triumph was set to finish off the year. It remained to be seen whether Vickers would continue to build on its successes.

CHAPTER THREE

More Worldwide Success

G-AMAV's Grand Adventure

As if it was not enough to be the first definitive model of a potentially great line of airliners and the first turbine powered airliner to cross the Atlantic Ocean, the V.700 prototype was destined to carve yet another niche for itself in aeronautical history.

As part of the celebrations marking 1953 as the centenary of the founding of the city of Christchurch, New Zealand, the ambitious residents and the Royal Aero Club organized an air race from London to Christchurch. Recognizing the immense publicity potential of the race, BEA placed an entry, proposing to operate one of its new Viscounts on the 12,500-mile (20,100km) course.

Initially the airline planned to use its appropriately registered Viscount 701 G-AMNZ. The aircraft had been named *James Cook*, after the famous British nautical explorer who had discovered New Zealand. However, as the race approached, BEA found that it could not spare the aircraft from commercial service without causing major disruption to its schedules. As well as the unprecedented success of the Viscount's introduction, a surge in traffic to the UK had been inspired by the spectacle of the Coronation of Britain's new monarch, Queen Elizabeth II. BEA had taken the opportunity to use its shiny new fleets of modern Elizabethans and Viscounts to carry many of the VIPs and dignitaries into London. The rise in traffic made the temporary withdrawal of G-AMNZ unacceptable.

All was not lost, though. With Vickers' co-operation, a successful request was made to the MoS, which was still the official owner of G-AMAV, for the Viscount 700 prototype to be loaned to BEA to replace G-AMNZ in the event. This came as a great relief to the organizers for, in addition to the possibility of losing BEA's entry, there had already been a number of other withdrawals, and the race might have had to be cancelled owing to the much-reduced field.

Under Starter's Orders

The remaining contestants in the race were gathered in the new central terminal area at Heathrow on 8 October 1953. The tunnel connecting the new complex had recently been completed, and the central ramp area was ready enough to host the race, though the terminals and other buildings were still under construction. This inconvenience did little to deter the several thousand spectators gathered to watch the start of the race. Adding colour to the otherwise sparse location were several 'hospitality' caravans, including those of sponsors such as Dunlop and Shell-Mex. There were five English Electric Canberra military jets competing in the speed section, three from the RAF and two from the Royal Australian Air Force (RAAF). Also competing, in the handicap section, which included G-AMAV, were a Handley Page Hastings transport aircraft, *Trade Wings*, of the Royal New Zealand Air Force (RNZAF), and Douglas DC-6A *Dr Ir. M. H. Damme* of KLM, Royal Dutch Airlines. The KLM aircraft would be carrying a party of sixty-four young emigrants to a new life in New Zealand during its participation in the race.

The Viscount was repainted in full BEA colours for the race and named *RMA Endeavour*, after Capt James Cook's famous ship. The aircraft had worn an experimental version of BEA's then-new livery ever since its first flight and throughout the subsequent flight-test, training and route-proving trials. It was later painted in Vickers' own colours, and even wore BWIA livery for a while, including its appearance at Farnborough. For the race, *Endeavour* wore the current BEA livery and was given the official racing number 23, which it carried on its tail, and special 'London–New Zealand Air Race' stickers on its nose and rear fuselage. In addition, it had large 'Vickers Viscount' titles on its lower fuselage.

The BEA crew consisted of the airline's chief executive, Peter Masefield, as team manager, pilot-in-command Capt W. 'Bill' Baillie, pilots Capt A.S. Johnson and Capt Stanley E. Jones, chief radio officer I.A. Dagleish, radio officer E.H.S. Barstow and navigation officer R.H. Chadwick. Also on board were two representatives from Vickers, E.W. Walker and R. Shaw, and, from Rolls-Royce, another Stanley Jones.

For its participation in the London–New Zealand Air Race G-AMAV once again took up BEA livery, this time wearing the full version. Jenny Gradidge

ABOVE: Both Britain's RAF and the Royal Australian Air Force entered English Electric Canberras in the speed section of the race. Jenny Gradidge

A Handley Page Hastings of the Royal New Zealand Air Force completed the trio of aircraft comprising the air transport section of the race. Jenny Gradidge

These last three were to act as flight engineers. The Deputy Minister of Civil Aviation, John Profumo MP, was to act as steward throughout the flight as a crewmember, as was BBC reporter Raymond Baxter. Unrequired seats had been removed from the Viscount and four large fuel tanks fitted in the cabin, increasing the fuel capacity to 2,900gal (13,160ltr) and giving the aircraft a potential non-stop range of over 3,500 miles (5,600km).

Even with the extra fuel capacity allowing longer legs between time-consuming refuelling stops, the strict handicap formula applied by the Royal Aero Club meant that *Endeavour* had no chance of winning in its class. Nonetheless, every effort was to be put into putting-up a 'good show' and completing the race in as fast a time as possible. The team had put months of hard work and planning into the event, backed by many others behind the scenes, from both the airline and the manufacturer. The worldwide publicity that stood to be gained for the airline, the aircraft and its revolutionary engine was of inestimable value.

The Off!

Before they departed, the Duke of Gloucester inspected the participating aircraft and their crews, accompanied by Lord Brabazon of Tara. *Endeavour* was the first aircraft to be toured by the VIPs, escorted by Peter Masefield and Capt Baillie. Once these formalities were dealt with, the flight personnel and ground crews busied themselves with getting the aircraft under way. The Viscount's turn to take-off finally came at 16.30, ten minutes after the KLM DC-6A. Captain Jones was in command for the first section of the epic flight. The crewmembers were to operate a rota system of two hours' duty each on the flight, turn and turn about, except for Chadwick and Profumo, who had to grab their chances of rest when they could. The Hastings and the five military jets then followed *Endeavour* into the air. On departure from London the Viscount was carrying 2,850gal (12,940ltr) of fuel, and its all-up weight was 62,000lb (28,140kg).

In the transport section, the DC-6A was scheduled to stop at Rome, Baghdad, Karachi, Rangoon, Djakarta, Darwin and Brisbane, and the Viscount at Bahrein, Colombo, Cocos Island and Melbourne. The DC-6A, carrying a commercial load and not provided with any extra fuel capacity like the Viscount, was forced to make more en route refuelling stops. The crew of the RZNAF Hastings intended to route via Athens, Shaibah and Masirah to Colombo, then onwards to Australia and home to New Zealand.

Endeavour reached Bahrein after a marathon 10hr 10min overnight non-stop flight from Heathrow. With the aircraft eventually cruising at 30,000ft (9,000m), the 3,200-mile (5,150km) sector was flown at an average speed of 310mph (500km/h). The Viscount's very swift 14min turn-round and refuelling at Bahrein set the pace for the rest of the contest. Even the DC-6A had managed a creditable 20min turn-round at Rome, with its seventy-four occupants all to be dealt with by the authorities. At 03.06 in the morning G-AMAV left Bahrein for its next stop, Colombo in Ceylon. The sector was flown in 8hr 3min, averaging 310mph (500km/h) at 25,000ft (7,600m).

The Viscount's four Darts continued to give little cause for concern throughout their ordeal, despite being abused on long sectors through tropical conditions, followed by speedy turn-rounds at the refuelling stops. *Endeavour* spent barely 19min on the ground at Colombo and was soon on its way to Cocos Island in the middle of the Indian Ocean. Meanwhile, *Trade Wings* had encountered technical problems when it reached Colombo, and the Hastings was forced to drop out of the race. This left just the KLM DC-6A and the Viscount in the handicap section. One of the RAAF Canberras also retired during the race, at Cocos Island, but the remaining military jets in the speed section continued to leave the more sedate transport aircraft in their wake.

Just successfully navigating to Cocos was a major achievement for the navigator, Chadwick. The tiny island had been unfavourably described as a lagoon surrounded by a runway. It should also be borne in mind that this was accomplished in an era when astro-fixes and the navigator's personal skill with a sextant and a pencil and ruler were vital. There was no satellite navigation available at the flick of a switch. One of the comparatively shorter legs, the flight from Colombo to Cocos Island took just 6hr 24min, averaging 310mph (500km/h) at 22,000ft (6,700m). The Cocos Island turn-round took 22min before the aircraft took off again, this time with the continent of Australia as a slightly larger target.

End in Sight

The west coast of Australia was sighted just as the second dawn of *Endeavour*'s adventure broke in front of the aircraft. Favourable winds allowed a non-stop run into Melbourne, the flying time from Cocos Island being 10hr 15min at an average air speed of 350mph (560km/h). This translated to a ground speed 405mph (650km/h), and the aircraft had cruised at 35,000ft (10,600m) on this sector.

The last leg, from Melbourne to Christchurch, a comparatively short 'hop' of 1,580 miles (2,540km), was flown in 4hr 42min. *Endeavour* crossed the line at Christchurch Airport with a flourish, executing a low-level flypast before finally landing, with Baillie at the controls. The Viscount was the fourth aircraft to cross the finishing line, the four remaining Canberras, not surprisingly, having landed hours before. The DC-6A followed 9hr after *Endeavour*, but was still awarded the first prize, on handicap, in the transport section.

Viscount G-AMAV had flown the 12,365 miles (19,895km) of the race in an elapsed time of 40hr 43min, of which 39hr 38min had been spent in the air. The Rolls-Royce Dart turboprops had completed 125,000,000 revolutions without having given a moment's cause for concern on the entire trip.

This was far from the end of *Endeavour*'s odyssey. After a short break the aircraft and its crew were off again, this time on a more leisurely full demonstration tour in the area before heading homewards. The Viscount routed via Wellington and Auckland, back to Melbourne. Once in Australia, calls were made at Launceston, Adelaide, Canberra, Sydney, Brisbane and Darwin before departing to Singapore. Colombo, Delhi, Bahrein, Nicosia and Rome were also visited by G-AMAV before it finally returned to the UK. Throughout the journey *Endeavour* was demonstrated to potential customers, attracting a great deal of interest from airlines and operators all along the route. From the time it left London to its return to Weybridge, the most serious technical problem encountered with G-AMAV was a single burst tyre.

Viscount G-AMAV wore race number 23 in the competition, as well as several other stickers displayed over its basic BEA livery. via author

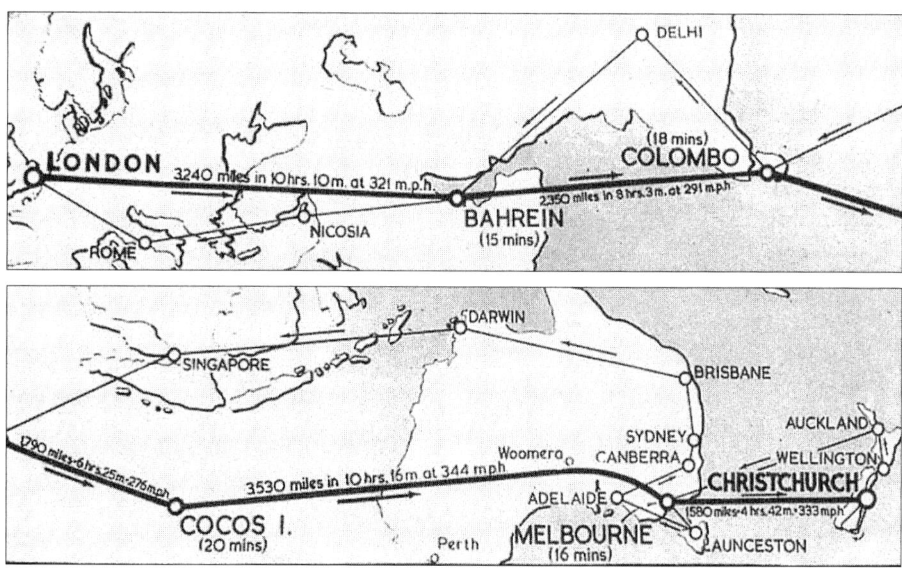

The marathon excursion of G-AMAV to New Zealand and back brought the Viscount to the attention of many potential customers throughout the journey. via author

Changes to the 800

While G-AMAV was making its dramatic dash to New Zealand and the more leisurely return tour, serious misgivings were being voiced about the new, much larger V.801. As the enlarged design was refined and probable performance data examined, it was becoming clear that it would actually be slower than BEA's V.701s. The current version of the Dart would need more power to be able to maintain the higher speeds with the larger aircraft. The corporation was also having second thoughts regarding the capacity, recent projections having indicated that it might be too large for the expected traffic on many of the routes for which it was being designed.

Consequently the aircraft was remodelled and refined to match BEA's now-perceived needs much more closely. In February 1954 the original order for the V.801 was cancelled, but immediately replaced by one for twelve V.802s, the modified version. Options were also taken out on a further ten. The V.802 was officially named Viscount Major to emphasize its increased capacity, but the name did not stick and the 'Major' suffix was soon forgotten.

Although the fuselage was not to be as stretched as that of the original V.801, only 3ft 10in (1.2m) being added forward of the wing compared with the Viscount 700s, the rear pressure bulkhead was moved over 5ft (1.5m) to the rear. This greatly increased the useable cabin area, allowing up to seventy-one passenger seats in high-density layouts, though BEA envisaged using a less-cramped configuration. The proposed BEA seating included provision for sixteen first-class seats and thirty-seven tourist-class passengers in the rear section. An extra passenger window was added at the rear on each side to serve the extra seat row, and more passenger seating was available in the forward, stretched area of the cabin. The galley and forward bulkhead were to be mounted on rails, permitting an adjustable-sized freight compartment and offering a great deal of flexibility, dependent on commercial traffic requirements. The tailplane incidence would also be revised to allow for the aerodynamic effects of the longer fuselage.

The most noticeable difference, apart from the longer fuselage, was the redesigned cabin doors. The initial 800/801 proposal originally used the oval design, but this had been proving a problem to open, and keep open, against a high wind. Instead, the V.802s were given a new, sideways-opening rectangular door that lay flat against the fuselage when fully opened. The forward door was enlarged to 5ft by 4ft (1.5m by 1.2m) to allow bulky items to be loaded through it during cargo operations. The cabin floor was strengthened to be capable of bearing 150lb/sq ft (732kg/sq m), instead of the more normal 100lb/sq ft (488kg/sq m), to allow more freight to be carried in the main cabin. In the BEA aircraft the Short Brothers and Harland-designed seats could be quickly and easily folded flat against the cabin wall, permitting very swift changes from all-passenger to all-cargo, or even mixed, configuration. The rear entry door was of a more conventional size, but was also rectangular. An extra door was added to the rear fuselage, on the starboard side, to facilitate galley or toilet servicing away from the loading of passengers, and could also be used to embark passengers if required.

The more powerful Dart R. Da.6 Mk510, rated at 1,740ehp, was developed from the earlier engine variants for the larger aircraft. It would be able to offer cruising speeds of 325mph (520km/h), even with an all-up weight of 64,500lb (29,275kg). This was much more respectable than the now-cancelled V.801's estimated speed of less than 300mph (480km/h).

Eire Introduction

Aer Lingus took delivery of their four Viscount 707s in March and April 1954. They were soon put into service, initially on routes to London, Paris and also to Amsterdam via Manchester, and Frankfurt via Manchester and Brussels. As experience accumulated, the new aircraft were soon also seen on other important routes.

The ultra-modern Viscounts were an undoubted improvement over the comparatively primitive Douglas DC-3s and Bristol Freighters that had comprised Aer Lingus's fleet until their arrival. The Bristol aircraft were fully convertible from all-cargo to passenger configuration, and when carrying passengers were known as Wayfarers. However, although they were extremely useful in being able to operate a variety of services, including combined passenger/cargo flights where traffic called for it, they were highly unpopular, being even noisier than the DC-3s and much slower.

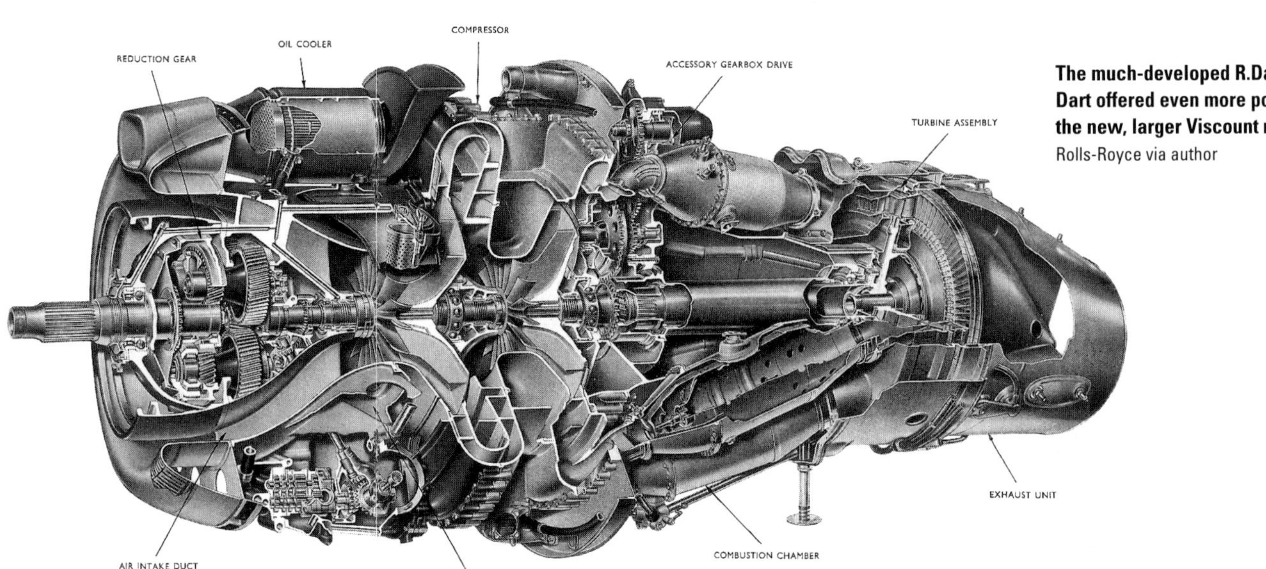

The much-developed R.Da.6 Mk510 Dart offered even more power for the new, larger Viscount models.
Rolls-Royce via author

LEFT: The Aer Lingus Viscounts brought a significant upgrade in comfort for the Irish carrier's passengers. Jenny Gradidge

Prior to Aer Lingus taking delivery of its Viscounts, BEA had provided a great deal of assistance in training the Irish airline's personnel, in addition to the already extensive training and conversion programmes offered by Vickers. Once licensed on the aircraft, senior Aer Lingus pilots served as crewmembers on BEA Viscount flights to build up experience on the type. A number of Aer Lingus engineers also spent time at BEA's new Heathrow Engineering Base.

As well as the scheduled services, the Aer Lingus Viscounts were used on a number of services to the Roman Catholic shrine at Lourdes, in southwest France. For these flights the cabin could be converted to carry fourteen stretcher cases, a large number of the pilgrims being physically disabled. In addition to the stretchers, thirty-five other passengers could be accommodated in standard seats. The conversion from the normal passenger layout to the specialized Lourdes configuration could be achieved in 90min. In their first year of Aer Lingus service the Viscounts carried over 50,000 passengers. They managed to average a very healthy 75 per cent load factor, even with their much-increased capacity over the smaller DC-3s and Bristol Freighters.

TAA's Success

Trans Australia Airlines' introduction of the Viscount was initially marked by tragedy. The first aircraft delivered, VH-TVA *John Batman*, named after the founder of Melbourne, was lost in a training accident during a three-engined take-off at Mangalore Aerodrome, Victoria, on 31 October 1954. Of the eight occupants, three were killed in the accident. The second aircraft, VH-TVB *Gregory Blackland*, was delivered in late November and

ABOVE: Aer Lingus was quick to promote its new modern fleet members, emphasizing the Viscount's speed and comfort. Author's collection

Following the early loss of its first Viscount in a training accident, TAA had to await the arrival of VH-TVB to resume its preparations for turboprop operations. via Bob Turner

Only a few months after full scheduled operations were introduced, TAA's Viscount services were returning impressive traffic figures. Author's collection

The first of what was to become a healthy stream of export Viscounts that made their way over the Atlantic to North American customers was TCA's CF-TGI. Vickers via author

enabled the disrupted training programme to be resumed.

Once the third aircraft, VH-TVC *John Oxley*, arrived, TAA was ready to open scheduled Viscount services with the two aircraft on 18 December. It was the first airline outside Europe to fly the Viscount commercially, initially operating them in a comfortable forty-seat, four-abreast configuration. By January 1955 190 commercial flights had accounted for 390 flying hours for the pair, and the average load factor was a staggering 94 per cent. Two more aircraft were in service by March, when an average utilization of 11hr per day was becoming common.

Although they were an undoubted success on the busy short/medium-haul runs between Australia's bigger east-coast cities, the Viscounts speed advantage was especially significant on longer routes, such as Melbourne–Adelaide–Perth. The extra fuel capacity provided by the optional slipper tanks, plus additional tankage for an extra 230gal (1,044ltr) built into the inner wing of the V.720s, came into its own. The carrier's main rival was Australian National Airways, which operated much larger, long-range DC-6s against the Viscounts on the longer transcontinental runs. However, the turboprops were consistently shown to be taking passengers away from the piston-powered competition wherever they appeared on TAA's network.

Canadian Triumph

The end of 1954 saw the first of the TCA Viscount 724s, CF-TGI, being ferried across the Atlantic to its new owner at Montreal. Upon arriving in December the aircraft embarked on the now-familiar round of training and route-proving flights. Encouraged by the resounding success of the earlier Viscount operators, TCA had placed a follow-up order for no fewer than thirty-six more of the type. These aircraft, their own extra improvements earning them the new designation Viscount 754, had been ordered in August 1954, two months before CF-TGI had even made its first flight.

The delivery flight left the UK on 8 December and routed from Weybridge to Prestwick, then onwards to Keflavik, Bluey West, Goose Bay and on to Montreal, arriving on the 12th. On this epic delivery flight, Vickers' Jock Bryce and Capt G. Lothian of TCA piloted the aircraft. George Edwards, who had worked so hard for the TCA order, was also on board.

The first North American scheduled turbine-powered-airliner service was flown on 1 April 1955, from Montreal to Winnipeg, by a TCA Viscount. Other domestic routes were soon included in the Viscount network as more aircraft joined CF-TGI after making the trek from the production line at Weybridge to their new home in Canada. For the most part the

Viscounts replaced the TCA fleet of locally-built, but notoriously noisy, Canadair C4M North Stars on busier routes, or even the smaller, long-serving Douglas DC-3s.

In addition to the TCA domestic route network, the Viscount enjoyed a significant success on the cross-border flights to the USA. On the Montreal and Toronto services to New York business was so brisk that the frequencies were doubled from three each, as previously flown by the North Stars, to six. Between April and December 1955 passenger boardings from Toronto to New York flights increased by 31 per cent southbound and 34 per cent northbound. The Montreal to New York route was even more successful for the Viscount, boardings increasing by an incredible 64 per cent southbound and 69 per cent northbound!

The TCA aircraft were competing directly with major US airlines operating Convairs and Douglas DC-6s. Other US points soon included on TCA's Viscount network included Boston in the east, Chicago in the Midwest, and Seattle was served from Vancouver. It took only 134 days for TCA to carry its 100,000th Viscount passenger, by which time only fourteen aircraft of the order had been delivered. In the first year of operations, TCA Viscounts carried 470,000 passengers, with a load factor of over 80 per cent.

One TCA Viscount unwittingly demonstrated the design's ruggedness only fifteen months after the Canadian airline had put its new turboprops into service. On 9 July 1956 one of the Viscounts was en route from Chicago to Toronto, cruising at 18,000ft (5,500m), when it suddenly lost its starboard outer propeller, debris from which also damaged the inner engine and caused a fire. Although the engine fire was soon extinguished, more debris had smashed its way into the cabin, killing one passenger and injuring five others. Despite the sudden depressurization when the cabin was punctured, no further damage or structural failure resulted, though an emergency descent was immediately initiated. The pilots skilfully managed to control the aircraft with the two remaining engines, and a successful landing was made at Windsor, Ontario.

More 'Americanization'

The TCA order attracted a great deal of attention from the media, but the next transatlantic Viscount order caused a mild sensation. Vickers had found a customer in the heartland of commercial aviation production, where no British, or even European airliner had been sold before – the USA.

The initial order that caused all the fuss, albeit for just three Viscounts, came from Washington D.C.-based carrier Capital Airlines, the contract for the three V.744s being signed in June 1954. These aircraft were to be powered by the Dart 506. The icing on the cake came two months later, when Capital signed another contract, this time for no fewer than thirty-seven V.745s powered by the more-powerful Dart R.Da.6 Mk510 being developed for the forthcoming V.802s for BEA. The new engine would give the Viscount 700s to which it was fitted greater speed and range, and allow higher operating weights.

The Viscount 700s with R.Da.6 Mk 510s were redesignated Viscount 700Ds, and the improvements helped to attract interest from even more prospective customers. New paddle-blade propellers were fitted to the higher-rated engines, as they had a revised reduction-gear ratio that reduced propeller tip speed. The wing spars were strengthened, to cope with the short stages and frequent landings on Capital's busy network. A great many modifications had to be made to the design to achieve US certification. Nineteen of these had already been met by the changes already made to the TCA aircraft for Canadian certification, but further measures required that a fuel jettisoning system be added. A pipe projecting from the trailing edge of the inner wing was fitted to facilitate this

The 'Americanization' of the new Viscount variant included yet more US technical and radio equipment being fitted as standard, over and above the many changes and modifications already made for TCA. The TCA and Capital Viscount cabins were also fitted out with a much brighter, more modern style of interior furnishing, designed to appeal to the more sophisticated North American taste.

Capital also required that its V.745s could be fitted with weather radar, and the redesign of the nose to accommodate it added a further 8in (20cm) to the aircraft's length. A freon-based air-conditioning system and a combustion-style cabin heater for use on the ground, as in the TCA aircraft, was to be fitted, as were hydraulically operated integral airstairs giving quicker turnarounds and less dependence on ground equipment. In December 1954 another order for a further twenty V.745s was placed by Capital, bringing its total number of Viscounts on order, including the initial three 744s, to sixty. The Capital order, worth in the region of $67 million in total, was the greatest single post-war dollar earner for Britain at the time.

Specification – V.700D

Powerplant	4 × R.Da.6 Mk510 Dart
Weights	Empty basic equipment weight 37,918lb (17,211kg) (40 seats); maximum zero fuel weight 50,168lb (22,771kg); maximum take-off weight 64,500lb (29,275kg); maximum landing weight 58,500lb (26,325kg); typical maximum payload 12,250lb (5,560kg).
Dimensions	Length 81ft 10in (24.94m); span 93ft 8½in (28.56m); fin height 26ft 9in (8.15m); wing area 963sq ft (89.46sq m); wheelbase 24ft 10in (7.57m).
Performance	Economic cruising speed 325mph (520km/h); maximum cruising speed 335mph (540km/h); service ceiling 27,500ft (8,380m); range with maximum payload 1,330 statute miles (2,140km).
Average passenger accommodation:	40–65 (all first class – high density).

Capital's Story

At the time of its historic Viscount orders, Capital Airlines was one of the USA's larger regional carriers. Its network spread over the eastern USA, south to Alabama and west to the Great Lakes and Minnesota. Florida was served by an 'interchange' arrangement with Miami-based National Airlines.

The airline could trace its lineage back to 1928, when a pioneering carrier, Clifford Ball Inc, owned by a Pittsburgh-based businessman Clifford Ball, started flying for the US mail between Pittsburgh and Cleveland via Youngstown. Initially using a fleet of Waco 9 biplanes, the company soon purchased Fairchild FC-2 monoplanes, with accommodation for four passengers. In 1929 Pittsburgh to Washington services were begun, using slightly larger Fairchild 71s that could accommodate six passengers.

Following a change of owner the airline was renamed Pennsylvania Airlines, and

Following the merger of Pennsylvania Airlines and Central Airlines, the newly formed PCA relied a great deal on the ten-passenger Boeing 247 for many of its routes. Author's collection

all-metal Ford Trimotors were introduced in 1933. A year later Pennsylvania bought out Kohler Aviation Corporation, and added its route from Milwaukee to Detroit, via Muskegon, Grand Rapids and Lansing. This one move almost doubled the route miles of the company at a stroke. Cleveland and Detroit were linked by a new route extension, merging the two original networks.

However, in 1934, a new competitor began operations from Pittsburgh, when Central Airlines opened a rival Washington–Pittsburgh–Akron–Cleveland–Detroit route. A fares war ensued, and the two airlines also fought to match each other with duplicated frequencies. Central eventually leased ex-American Airlines Ford Trimotors to upgrade its equipment from its original Stinsons. Pennsylvania responded by replacing its Fords with then-ultra-modern Boeing 247s. Central then promptly replaced its Fords with a fleet of more modern versions of their original Stinsons, A-model tri-motors that could match the Boeing's speed. Finally, however, both managements recognized that the competition was potentially ruinous for both airlines. An agreement was reached in late 1936 and the two carriers were merged to produce Pennsylvania Central Airlines (PCA), with effect from 1 November that year.

PCA Becomes Capital

Following the merger of the two arch rivals, PCA entered an unprecedented period of growth. The original main route was extended to the southeast from Washington to Norfolk, Virginia. Important new services were added to Baltimore and Buffalo from Pittsburgh, and both Chicago and Sault Ste Marie were reached via new routes from Detroit. By 1939 new 21-passenger Douglas DC-3s were being introduced, with six in use, alongside the thirteen 247s, by 1940. The system was expanded southwards in late 1940, with new routes to Birmingham, Alabama. In December 1941 the corporate head office was moved to the new National Airport serving Washington, D.C. With this expansion outside the original Pennsylvania catchment area, the airline's name was regarded as too parochial, and soon it was being promoted as 'PCA – The Capital Airline'. Post-war, more DC-3s arrived and were joined by a new fleet of DC-4s. By 1948 a new interim PCA-Capital Airlines name had been phased through Capital Airlines-PCA to become just Capital Airlines.

Routes were extended to New Orleans via Mobile and to Atlanta via Asheville in 1948, the Midwest services having been extended to Minneapolis-St Paul the year before. Also in 1947, Capital had introduced a new style of 'Air Coach' services, whereby low-fare, no-frills services were offered over the company's routes at night, when the aircraft used would otherwise have been idle. Capital was the first US carrier to introduce this new class of air travel, which proved an immediate success.

Carmichael, Capital and the Viscount

This profitable 'Air Coach' was the brainchild of Capital's newly appointed president, J.H. (Slim) Carmichael. Previously the airline's chief pilot, Carmichael had also served as operations manager, vice-president operations and executive vice-president. Taking up the post in late 1947, he faced spiralling costs and declining passenger loads.

Under Carmichael's careful management, Capital's financial situation improved enough to allow the introduction of a fleet of modern Constellations in 1950. These brought a new standard of comfort for Capital's customers, offering pressurization and speed, and boasted a forward 'Cloud Club' lounge area for in-flight relaxation, complete with club chairs. By 1954 Capital was operating twelve Constellations, twenty-five DC-4s and twenty-five DC-3s, and was ranked fifth among US domestic carriers.

The decision to buy the fleet of Viscounts was based on the recommendations of a task force sent over by Carmichael to evaluate the new turboprop. Capital had already looked closely at the available US options for re-equipment, but was unable to find anything meeting its requirements. The task force looked closely at data supplied by Vickers and BEA, eventually deciding that the Viscount offered the flexibility needed to operate profitably on the airline's varied network. With its mixture of short regional flights and longer services between major cities, a commercially viable competitor to the larger airlines' equipment was vital.

At the signing of the first contract, at Weybridge, Carmichael praised the happy personal relationships that he and his task force had built up with Vickers during the evaluation and sales negotiations. He also praised BEA for freely supplying operational data on the Viscount, based on its own experience as an operator of the aircraft. The British airline had actually been persuaded to give up three delivery positions on the production line 'in the national interest', to allow the V.744s to be supplied earlier than would otherwise have been possible.

First Independent Order

In the early 1950s the remaining British independent airlines were kept firmly in their place by the nationalization of scheduled UK services, only being permitted to operate *ad hoc* and contract charter services. Although there was work available and money to be made, the competition was intense, and it could be a very lean existence. The ban on independents operating schedules was eventually relaxed with the introduction of 'Associate Agreements', whereby the private airlines were permitted to operate scheduled services that the corporations had no interest in serving.

One major source of revenue for the charter companies at the time was trooping contracts, issued by the military authorities for the carriage of servicemen and their families to the far-flung parts of the British Commonwealth, where UK forces were still charged with keeping the peace. Among the busiest routes were the ones serving the Mediterranean islands of Malta and Gibraltar, both still heavily garrisoned with bases for all three armed services. One holder of a government contract to carry forces personnel and their dependants to the islands was Hunting-Clan Air Transport (HCAT).

Based at Bovingdon, near London, HCAT had originally been formed as Hunting Air Transport shortly after the war's end. Initially flying various light aircraft, the company soon graduated to larger types, such as the DC-3, and ordered a fleet of new Vikings from Vickers. A varied programme of *ad hoc* and contract charter services was flown throughout Europe and to the Middle East and Africa. Trooping contracts soon formed a large part of Hunting's portfolio, as were a network of scheduled services based at Newcastle, for which the company operated as an 'associate' of BEA.

Author's collection

A very successful low-fare 'Colonial Coach' service was also opened from Bovingdon to East Africa in 1952, in partnership with another independent, Airwork Ltd, using both companies' fleets of Vikings. The Clan Line shipping group purchased a major shareholding in Hunting in October 1953, the company name being changed to Hunting-Clan.

In May 1953 HCAT made a brave move, becoming the first UK independent airline to order the Viscount when it signed a contract for three V.732s. It had hoped to introduce the Viscounts on the African services, but BOAC objected to the independent being allowed to fly such modern equipment in competition against it. Consequently, the trusty Vikings continued to operate the longer routes. Instead, when the three Viscounts, G-ANRR, 'RS and 'RT, were delivered to HCAT in May and July 1955, they were placed in service on the trooping runs to the Mediterranean.

The V.732s were laid out in a 53-passenger configuration, their seats all being rearward facing as required for military contract work. They also appeared briefly on the scheduled service network from Newcastle to Scandinavia and London, in an attempt to encourage higher loads on routes that had returned disappointing figures when flown by DC-3s. Unfortunately the trooping contracts were due to end in September, and were not renewed. The scheduled routes from Newcastle were not busy enough to support the costs of operating the larger aircraft, and HCAT was forced to look elsewhere for gainful employment for its Viscount fleet.

Wanted, a Good Home

The trio of HCAT Viscounts soon found a home with Middle East Airlines (MEA), based at Beirut. The Lebanese carrier was an associate company of BOAC, which had a shareholding in MEA. Although BOAC Associated Companies had already placed an order for Viscounts on MEA's behalf, these aircraft, improved 700D versions, were not due for delivery until 1957. The sudden availability of the HCAT aircraft allowed MEA to bring turboprop comfort to its routes much earlier than planned. Operated on a long-term lease from HCAT, the Viscount 732s joined a fleet of DC-3s on the busier regional routes from Beirut. Almost overnight, the Viscounts turned MEA from a small regional operator to a major international carrier. They were also eventually introduced on new, longer-ranging services reaching European cities, and in due course were used to extend the MEA network east to India and Pakistan.

Hunting-Clan was forced to find new homes for its expensive, under-used Viscounts when the initial trooping contracts were not renewed. MAP

Leasing-in the HCA Viscounts allowed Middle East Airlines to modernize its fleet several years earlier than it had originally planned. Global Air Image

Iraqi Airways' Viscounts were a feature of the Baghdad-based fleet for many years, operating on both international and domestic services. Jenny Gradidge

Originally built as G-AOCC for Airwork, CU-T605 was sold to Cubana before delivery. Jenny Gradidge

Iraqi Airways, also based in the Middle East, put the first of its three V.735s into service in late 1955, and they replaced Vikings on the more important routes. The turboprops were initially used on routes from Baghdad to Egypt, Iran (then known as Persia), Jordan and Syria. As with MEA, the Iraqi Viscounts were also to be found later on new services linking the Middle East to Europe. The first three V.739s, for Misrair, Egypt's national airline, were also introduced around the same time, supplementing and eventually ousting an ageing fleet of Vikings and French-built Languedocs.

Cubana's Lucky Break

Hunting-Clan's partner on the African services, Airwork, had also placed an order for Viscount 700s, in the hope of operating them on the 'Colonial Coach' flights. A contract for a similar sized fleet of three V.755Ds was signed, with delivery expected in December 1955. When BOAC blocked the use of the Viscounts, Airwork had no other options for operating the now-redundant aircraft. The Viscounts were still under construction, and Airwork was lucky enough to find another airline, Havana-based Compania Cubana de Aviacion, commonly shortened to Cubana, already interested in the Viscount and willing to take over the contract in order to obtain early delivery. Cubana wanted the Viscounts to replace ageing DC-4s, and even its more modern Constellations, on regional routes to the mainland USA, where they failed to attract traffic from competing US carriers such as Pan American and National Airlines.

Another operator that passed on its Viscounts to another carrier was Fred Olsen Air Transport, the aviation wing of the famous Norwegian shipping company. The airline operated a variety of aircraft on behalf of the parent company, ferrying its ships' crews and cargoes around the world, as well as performing general *ad hoc* and contract charters. Originally ordering two Viscount 736s, Fred Olsen did not take delivery itself, leasing them out instead to BEA as G-AODG *Fridtjof Nansen* and G-AODH *Roald Amundson*. The aircraft were delivered directly to BEA in December 1955. In keeping with BEA *Discovery* class policy the aircraft were named after explorers, but this time Norwegian ones.

BEA Incidents

BEA's leasing of the Fred Olsen aircraft was partly the result of the temporary loss of one of its V.701s at the beginning of the year. Viscount G-AMOK *Sir Humphrey Gilbert* was scheduled to operate the London–Rome–Athens–Istanbul service on the morning of 16 January 1955, but had been delayed by fog. When it was finally cleared to taxi in the bad visibility, the aircraft inadvertently turned on to the wrong runway, No 3, which had been closed to allow for the building of Heathrow's new central terminal area. As 'OK sped down the disused runway it ran into stored equipment, builders' huts, a steel barrier and even a pile of cast iron.

Luckily it was a Sunday, and few construction staff were in the area. Although the Viscount shed its undercarriage and both port engines, and ruptured its fuel tanks, there was no post-crash fire. Only the captain and one passenger were injured. Severely damaged, 'OK was transported to Cambridge, where the aero-engineering company, Marshalls rebuilt it for BEA. Returned to the airline in 1958, 'OK was redesignated a V.701X.

Capital's Unveiling

The early successes of TCA's Viscounts on routes into the USA from Canada were merely a prologue to the impact the aircraft made on Capital's US domestic services. As usual, and in keeping with the importance of the order, Vickers offered the airline a great deal of assistance in preparing its crews, engineers and all other staff who would come in contact with the Viscount during daily operations. Capital itself, under Carmichael's enthusiastic guidance, was determined that the introduction of the first non-US-built airliners into commercial service, scheduled for July 1955, would go as smoothly as possible. Rolls-Royce engine test cells were installed in the airline's maintenance facilities, and a Viscount flight-deck simulator was a welcome addition to the training programme, enabling even more of Capital's crews to be ready for the new aircraft.

Capital Airlines promised its customers unheard-of comfort and numerous innovations with its new fleet of Viscounts. Author's collection

Pre-introduction advertising for the new Viscounts saw cities served by Capital bombarded by the airline's publicity machine. The very act of importing an airliner into the USA, the undisputed world industry leader in airliner production, had attracted a great deal of attention already, not all of it favourable. To a certain extent Capital found itself having to justify the choice of the British aircraft to its very vocal US critics, notwithstanding the clearly advanced nature of the new form of propulsion, which offered speed and comfort levels which none of the US manufacturers could match at that time.

Overall, the aircraft was introduced as a 'New Concept in Flight'. A whole campaign was built around the Viscount, with advertising, mobile exhibitions and intensive staff awareness training all playing their part.

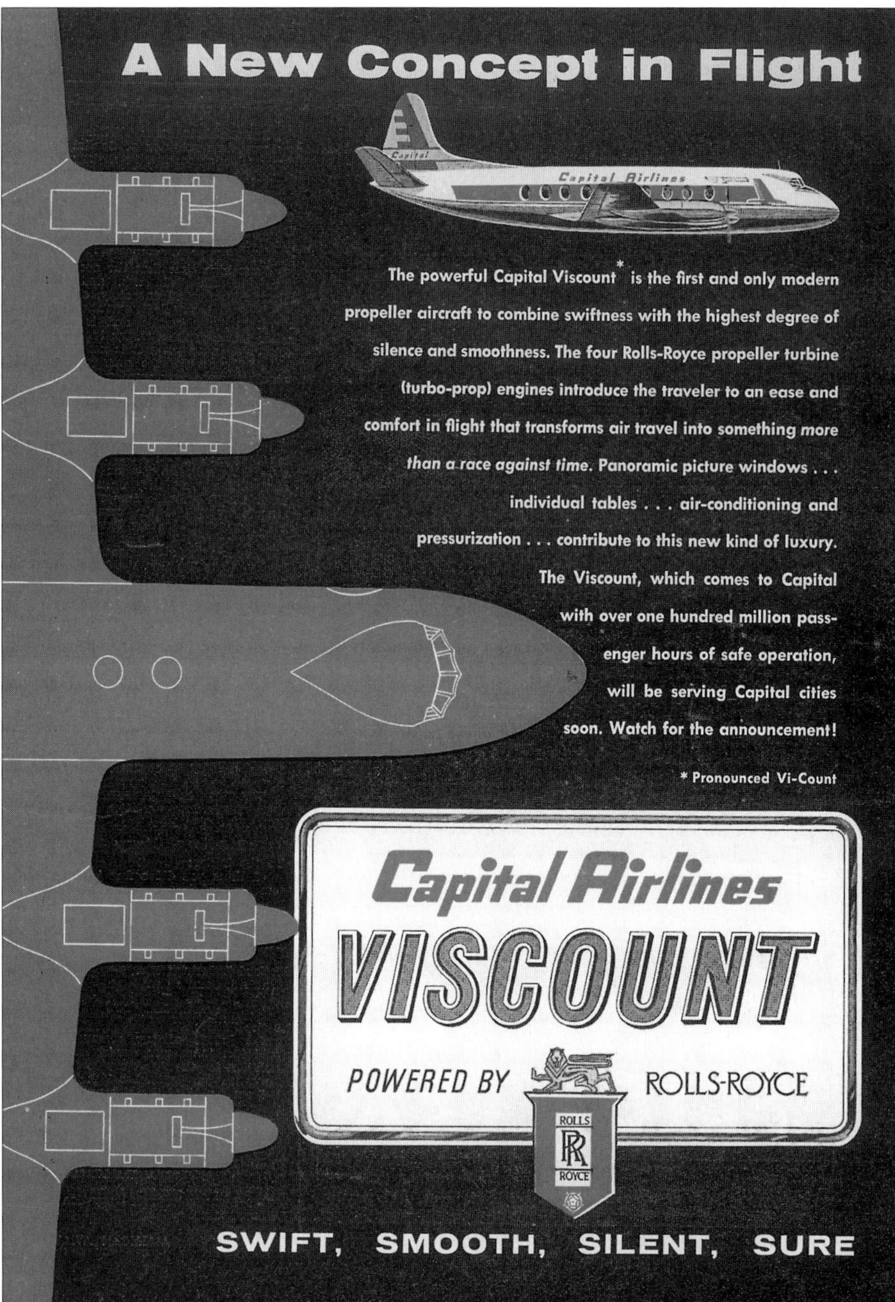

Capital based its Viscount introduction on an advertising campaign heralding 'A New Concept in Flight'. Author's collection

The distinctive whine of the Dart engine was promoted as 'The New Sound in the Air', and advertisements pointed out the swift and smooth nature of Viscount travel. A 45ft (13.7m) trailer containing a full-scale Dart engine and a cutaway section of the new Viscount interior toured cities on Capital's network.

The interior, remodelled by designers in the US Butler Zimmerman Company, was said to offer 'a quiet elegance, a passengers plus that no other aircraft can claim'. The floor was carpeted in dark green, the sides of the cabin were trimmed in beige vinyl, and the ceiling was pale green. The seat units were upholstered in beige cloth, contrasting with plaid curtains. Modern amenities for the passengers, 'at their fingertips', included individual ashtrays, light switches and fresh-air louvres, folding seatback tables and hostess call-buttons, all serving every seat. With the buffet and galley located at the rear, a convenient carry-on luggage storage area was installed by the forward entry door. As well as the light snacks more usual on Capital's short-range network, the galley was capable of producing hot meals for the longer sectors.

No stone was left unturned in promoting public acceptance of the Viscount in Capital service and in creating a strong desire among potential Capital passengers to fly in the aircraft. Reservations agents were even encouraged to answer calls by saying: 'May I make a reservation on the Viscount for you?'. Reservations and ticket agents were also briefed on the history of Vickers, the aircraft and its revolutionary engine, all comparatively unheard of in the USA, to enable them to answer their customers' queries about the new fleet member. To supplement and add impact to Capital's own campaign, a number of other linked companies also became involved in advertising the forthcoming Viscount services. Not surprisingly, Vickers and Rolls-Royce ran a number of complimentary Viscount advertisements in US newspapers and magazines. Tie-in advertising was also arranged with Viscount suppliers such as Shell Oil, Dunlop Tires and Bendix Radio.

A 23min film entitled *A New Concept in Flight* was made available for both staff and public viewing. In addition, an employees' handbook was also published, covering all aspects of the Viscount and explaining why Capital had chosen to operate it. Numerous booklets, such as *Talk About the Viscount* and *Tinkering with the Turbine*, were produced and widely distributed to help educate and inform the public and the industry. The employee handbook encouraged every one of Capital's 4,500 employees to become 'a Viscount Salesman by performing his job in the most efficient manner. Once a passenger rides in the Viscount, he will be sold on its swift smooth, silent and sure performance. You, as a Capital employee, must sell the passenger on Capital's NEW CONCEPT IN FLIGHT, the Viscount Service.'

The Capital Debut

The first of the V.744s, registered N7402, made its maiden flight, from Hurn, on 14 May 1955. Following the transatlantic delivery route already established for the TCA aircraft, it arrived in Washington on

Viscount operations began at Capital with the introduction of a trio of Viscount 744s, followed by the bulk of the order in the shape of a later version, the V.745.
United Archive

BELOW: Patricia Nixon christened the first Capital Viscount at the airline's Washington base, assisted by 'Slim' Carmichael.
United Archive

15 June, followed by the second aircraft, N7403, on 9 July. Present at the arrival of the first aircraft was newly-hired Capital aircraft and engine mechanic Joseph P. Noto:

> I had chosen to go to work for Capital rather than other airlines because Capital was known to be getting the Viscount soon, and would be the first in the USA with the turboprop. Within a few days of my hiring, a brand-new shiny Viscount appeared in our hangar at Washington National Airport, the main base where most of the maintenance was done. The aircraft was N7402, and generated great excitement and envy among other airline people.

In a christening ceremony at the airline's Hangar 3, at Washington National Airport, the aircraft was formally introduced to the press and Capital's employees, and US vice-president Richard Nixon addressed the 2,500 persons present. The vice-president's wife, Patricia Nixon, christened N7402, accompanied by 'Slim' Carmichael. As well as serving on the vital crew-training and operational-familiarization programme, the aircraft operated a number of press and travel-industry demonstration flights around the airline's routes. The last of the three V.744s, N7404, arrived on 23 July, and full scheduled services were able to begin three days later.

The very first scheduled US-based turbine-powered airline service opened on 26 July 1955, with two daily First Class flights between Washington and Chicago. As elsewhere in the world, the high passenger loads attracted by the Viscounts soon saw the frequency increased to three a day, and then up to six, with some of the extra services making a traffic stop at Pittsburgh. The large order for V.745s started to arrive from Hurn in November 1955 and Viscounts were soon also serving cities such as Norfolk, Detroit and Cleveland. The first nine V.745s were still powered by Mk 3 Darts, like the V.744s, but the full 745D versions with Mk 6s soon followed. Other points on the network were added as quickly as the aircraft could be delivered and put into service. In 1956 non-stop Philadelphia–Chicago, Philadelphia–Detroit, Detroit–New York and Chicago–New York Viscount services were introduced, and the airline extended its Viscount network south to include Atlanta, Mobile and New Orleans.

As Joseph Noto observes, the Viscount's reliability soon became legendary:

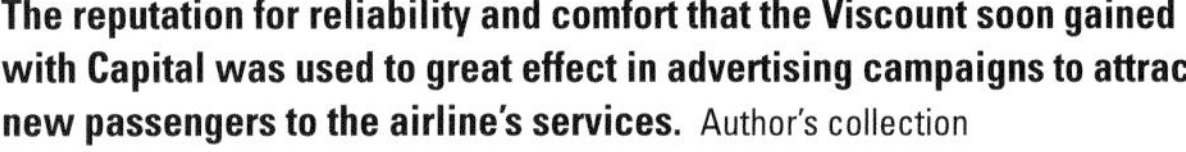

The reputation for reliability and comfort that the Viscount soon gained with Capital was used to great effect in advertising campaigns to attract new passengers to the airline's services. Author's collection

As the 1950s progressed, the sight of airline passengers boarding or disembarking from Viscounts became increasingly common worldwide. United Archive

The engines were superb, the latest state of the art. They required so much less routine maintenance than piston engines and seemed trouble-free and completely dependable. My life as a line mechanic became much easier. For instance, piston engines used oil by the bucket, much of which wound up dripping from the cowling. Oil was added to the engine by climbing out on the slippery wing, often wet, slippery or icy, with a 5-gallon can of thick oil, which was much thicker in winter. By contrast, after flying all day, a one-quart can per engine was all the Dart needed.

Also, in cold conditions, piston engines were run-up several times during the night to keep their oil warm enough to enable starting for morning departures. Then, after coaxing them to life, a careful run-up was needed before flight, often involving some ignition problems such as 'mag drops', fouled plugs etc. It took some skill to get the piston engines started in cold or wet weather.

But no matter how cold or how long since the last run, starting the Dart was no trick. Press the start button, open the fuel lever and your engine was running, and the throttle could be advanced immediately. Most big pistons were limited to only operating a few minutes at take-off power, and then power had to be reduced. In contrast, the Dart throttle could be pushed to the stops and left there throughout the climb.

A rival airline had a hangar near ours where its DC-7 was checked nightly after a round trip Washington–Chicago–Washington run. The DC-7 left Washington at the same time each morning as our Chicago-bound Viscount, so a race became customary. Although the DC-7 was probably a bit faster in a long cruise, the Viscount could pull ahead in a long climb without risking engine problems at maximum power. All night, mechanics for the rival carrier could be seen hard at work on their DC-7 engines, changing spark plugs or even cylinders and checking oil screens for metal fragments that could foretell an engine failure. As the number of engine failures on the struggling DC-7 built up, the FAA [Federal Aviation Administration] ordered changes in the departure schedules to prevent the race.

Up and Running

The Viscount was becoming a common sight at many airports throughout the world as the 1950s passed their meridian. The bustling assembly lines at Weybridge and Hurn were busy fulfilling the contracts being brought back from around the world. Nonetheless, new Viscounts were soon to be seen, with the larger 800 well on its way. The Viscount's success had turned the thoughts of the design office staffs to a whole new, even bigger turboprop airliner for the 1960s.

CHAPTER FOUR

Viscount to Vanguard

Global Expansion

The forthcoming arrival of the stretched new Viscount models far from heralded the immediate end of the original, shorter-bodied Series 700s. Indeed, with the improvements made to the aircraft after the 'Americanization' of the design for Canadian and US customers, the aircraft was attracting even greater numbers of potential new customers. Between 1955 and 1958, Viscount 700s were seen around the world in the colours of an increasing variety of operators, large and small.

In 1955 carriers as diverse as BWIA in the Caribbean, Iraqi Airways, MEA and Misrair in North Africa and the Middle East and Butler Air Transport of Australia were taking delivery of their first aircraft and starting to enjoy the success of earlier operators. The first of BWIA's four aircraft was introduced on thrice-weekly first-class services between New York and Bermuda, in co-operation with BOAC and in direct competition with US airlines such as Eastern Air Lines and Pan American. The Viscount's flying time of 3 hours was half an hour less than that of the Lockheed Constellations used by BWIA's rivals, and traffic was soon being taken from the other carriers. Further south, the Viscounts also operated from the Bahamas to Miami and New York from Nassau. The success of the V.702s BWIA had leased from BOAC was such that BWIA decided to order its own aircraft, and placed orders for four V.772s, later, improved models of the Viscount 700 to replace three of the early-model V.702s.

Misrair's three-strong Viscount 739 fleet, which contributed to the replacement of Vickers Vikings and French-built Languedocs, saw the Egyptian airline expand its services throughout North Africa and to Europe and the Middle East. The Suez Crisis of 1956 cut this expansion short, though. One of the Viscounts, SU-AIC, was actually destroyed by the RAF in a raid on Almaza on 1 October. However, post-Suez, Misrair soon re-established its network, initially using the two surviving Viscounts, with extra aircraft acquired to help rebuild the airline.

The two-crew 'Americanized' Viscounts, such as those supplied to Capital Airlines, had a much more modern flight-deck layout. United Archive

In September 1955 a pair of Viscount 747s was delivered to Vickers's second Australian Viscount customer, Sydney-based Butler Air Transport (BAT). Founded by pioneer Australian airline owner Arthur Butler, BAT had established a successful

ABOVE: The success of the V.702s leased by BWIA from BOAC led to orders for later versions for the Caribbean network.
Jenny Gradidge

LEFT: Butler Air Transport introduced turboprop airliner service to several smaller Australian towns and cities, as well as on routes linking the more important population centres.
Jenny Gradidge

BELOW: The first Central African Airways Viscounts began making their way down the Vickers production lines in 1955–56.
Jenny Gradidge

regional network throughout the state of New South Wales with a fleet of DC-3s and smaller aircraft. Serving both the larger cites and more 'outback' areas, the airline had made a point of getting involved with the local communities it served.

Originally BAT had ordered the first pair of Viscounts and then taken options on four more. However, only the initial pair was delivered, the first entering service in September 1955. They were soon achieving high utilization figures, the average of 9hr 8min a day being a record for the Viscount world-wide. The 1956–57 financial year was the first to see both Viscounts in service, and BAT was able to report a £28,997 profit, compared with a loss the previous year.

On 1 May 1956 Central African Airways (CAA) took delivery of the first of an order for five V.748Ds, fitted with weather radar and slipper tanks to give extra range. The aircraft also had de Havilland propellers fitted to provide better take-off performance under difficult African conditions. The British Colonial governments of the nations of Northern and Southern Rhodesia and Nyasaland jointly owned CAA. As well as linking the three African nations, CAA also flew to neighbouring countries. Its fleet of Vikings also operated a long-range, low-fare route from Salisbury to London, along the lines of the HCAT/Airwork Safari service. The Viscounts soon ousted the Vikings from the Zambezi service to London, flying via Ndola, Entebbe, Khartoum, Wadi Halfa, Benghazi and Rome. They also operated flights to Mozambique and Mauritius, as well as proving a great success on the busier local and regional routes to such places as Bulawayo, Durban and Johannesburg.

The V.759D TF-ISU *Hrimfaxi* never actually entered commercial service with its original owner, Hunting-Clan Air Transport, eventually being delivered to Icelandair in March 1957. via Bob Turner

Hunting-Clan Again

Hunting-Clan Air Transport made another bid to operate Viscounts on its own increasingly popular Safari services to Africa, but, although it took delivery of the two V.759s G-AOGG and G-AOGH in November and December 1956, permission was still withheld and the airline was again forced to dispose of the aircraft, as it had with the three V.732s it had earlier leased to MEA. This time the two aircraft were sold on, rather than leased out, both being delivered to Icelandair in March and April 1957. They were soon placed into regular service, operating from Reykjavik to Copenhagen, Glasgow, Hamburg, London and Oslo. The Icelandair Viscounts' first four months saw an incredible 40 per cent increase in traffic and an average 75.5 per cent load factor, compared with 58.4 per cent carried the same time the previous year. Although one was lost in an accident on approach to Oslo in 1963, the survivor served Icelandair for its entire life, finally being scrapped in 1970.

The three V.755Ds originally ordered by HCAT's partner on the Safari flights, Airwork, were delivered to Cubana in 1956. Introduced on services to Miami and Veredo Beach from Cuba, they were soon rebuilding Cubana's market share on these routes, where its older equipment had been suffering in competition with American carriers. Cubana also put the Viscount into service on busier domestic routes from Havana to bigger cities on the island. Within three months the traffic increase was nearly 120 per cent over the Constellation's performance and the load factor percentages were swiftly climbing towards the high 80s.

Unfortunately, two years later, the first of Cubana's Viscounts became one of the earliest victims of terrorist hijacking. On 1 November 1958 CU-T603, en route from Miami to Varadero, was taken over by a group of five hijackers, one of whom replaced the captain at the controls. Rerouted towards Oriente Province, near the base of revolutionary leader Fidel Castro, the pilot was unable to land because the airstrip was unlit. Rapidly running out of fuel, the Viscount was eventually ditched in the sea off the Cuban coast, bringing about the deaths of all but three of its twenty occupants.

More Power

The faith of BEA in the as-yet-unbuilt enlarged V.802 was emphasized by its placing of an extra order for ten more in May 1955, before the first of the new version had flown. Encouraged by the success and popularity of its initial 701s, BEA was anxious to acquire more examples and build up its turboprop operation. At the same time as it placed the second V.802 order, BEA ordered an extra V.701 to replace an Elizabethan written off in a forced landing near Dusseldorf the previous month.

On-going development of the Dart engine saw Roll-Royce offering the even more powerful Mk 520, which had three turbine stages and offered increased shaft horsepower, with a potential take-off thrust of 1,890ehp. In early 1956 BEA ordered nineteen Mk 520-powered Viscount 800s, designated V.806. The airline planned to introduce a two-class configuration on these aircraft, which were otherwise identical to the V.802s.

The Vickers sales team clinched the first export sale of the Viscount 800 a month after BEA's second V.802 order, when KLM Royal Dutch Airlines placed a £2million order in June 1955 for nine Viscount 800s, designated V.803s, for use on their busier European services. Hitherto, KLM had been a faithful Convair customer, taking

The Viscount 'Major' Emerges

The first stretched Viscount 802 'Viscount Major' for BEA was assembled at Weybridge in 1956. Its fuselage had been built at the new Viscount production plant at Hurn, which was now responsible for all V.700 series production as well as manufacturing the fuselages for all Viscount variants. Initially Hurn had been designated to produce the larger production runs, such as the Capital and TCA orders. After extra manufacturing space was built at Weybridge, this arrangement was altered so that Hurn took over all Viscount 700 production and Weybridge was responsible for Viscount 800 series assembly. All Viscount fuselages, though, were built at Hurn, and the wings were built by Saunders-Roe, a Vickers subsidiary on the Isle of Wight. The first V.802 fuselage was moved to the Weybridge production line for final assembly in April. Orders for all Viscount variants had now exceeded 300 aircraft, for numerous customers, civil and military, all over the world.

No separate prototype V.802 was built. Instead, the first of the stretched Viscounts to fly was the first production model, G-AOJA, named *Sir Samuel White Baker* by BEA. It first took to the air on 27 July 1956, taking off from Weybridge. After being put through its paces for 55min, G-AOJA landed at Vickers's flight-test base at Wisley, where it would be based for the V.802's development and certification programme. The aircraft made its public debut two months later in September, being exhibited at Farnborough.

The second V.802 was rolled off the production line later that month, followed by two more in November. The first Viscount 802 to be officially delivered to BEA was G-AOJD *Sebastian Cabot*, on 11 January 1957, two more, G-AOJC *Robert O'Hara Burke* and G-AOJE *Sir Alexander Mackenzie*, arriving later that month. The airline introduced the V.802 into commercial service on 13 February, when G-AOJD carried forty-seven passengers from Heathrow to Glasgow. Two days later, 'JD was used for the first international service of the type, a Heathrow–Amsterdam schedule. The Paris route saw its first Viscount 802 on 18 February. As the production aircraft were steadily delivered to BEA, the larger aircraft were also placed in service on flights to Belfast, Copenhagen, Dublin, Dusseldorf, Frankfurt, Geneva, Hamburg, Nice and Zurich by the end of the summer. For the most part, the V.802s replaced V.701s which, in turn, began to oust Elizabethans. The Airspeed aircraft were already earmarked for replacement as more Viscounts arrived, the small size of the fleet and the piston-powered aircrafts' less-economic operating costs having sealed their fate. The first five of the Elizabethans left BEA in 1957, though the remaining aircraft continued in service until 1958.

Among the improvements enjoyed by the V.802's passengers was a more modern looking décor, with new-style overhead luggage racks, fluorescent strip lighting and a redesigned galley and bar unit ensuring them an even higher quality of cabin service. The washrooms were redesigned as well, most of the changes for the better resulting from the experience of BEA and other operators with the earlier models. The V.802 also heralded the use of a two-pilot flight deck for BEA's Viscounts, the superfluous radio officer finally being replaced by more modern communications equipment.

Final assembly of the V.802s was completed at Weybridge, though many components were constructed at other plants throughout the company.
via Bob Turner

delivery of CV-240s and eventually replacing them with the slightly enlarged CV-340s to operate their short/medium-haul network from Amsterdam. However, the extra capacity offered by the Viscount, as well as the technical superiority of the more modern turboprop, tempted the airline away from the US supplier. The carrier had seen its market share on services to the UK drop when it had been up against BEA's Viscounts, and it was anxious to redress the balance.

The more powerful Dart Mk 520 also found favour on more V.800s that were sold to UK independent airlines Transair Ltd and Eagle Aviation. In 1955 the two carriers ordered three V.804s and two V.805s respectively. Both independents were heavily involved in a variety of charter contracts for civil and military customers, and the extra power of the new version of the Dart was expected to be of use in operating from some of their more obscure, far-flung destinations. As well as its extensive civil and military charter contracts, Eagle also planned to use its aircraft on their expanding network of scheduled services, under the name of its wholly-owned scheduled service subsidiary, Eagle Airways. Eagle's small scheduled network was operated from its home base of Blackbushe to the southwest of London, and also from Manchester. The company had great ambitions to expand from both bases.

New Zealand's national domestic operator, New Zealand National Airways Corporation (NZNAC), signed up for three V.807s in November 1955. The airline's then-current flagship on its major routes was the DC-3, and the Viscount represented an impressive leap in progress. The first Viscount 700 operator, after BEA, to order the V.800 was faithful customer Aer Lingus, which ordered six V.808s in May 1956. The Aer Lingus Viscount 808s were intended for the busier runs to the UK and Europe, where capacity was of more importance than longer range. They would initially operate alongside the earlier V.707s, which would then be redeployed to bring Viscount service to more of the Irish carrier's routes.

More Power

Rolls-Royce's never-ending development of the versatile Dart soon led to yet another version, the Mk 525, being offered. The new engine could actually have produced a very creditable 2,100ehp for take-off, but this would have been far too powerful for the Viscount airframe. Nonetheless, a de-rated version offering a 'mere' 1,990ehp could be used on the Viscount; its spare power making it ideal for use at 'hot and high' airfields, for instance, in warm and/or mountainous regions. In either of these conditions an aircraft's effective take-off power could be greatly reduced by thinner air, especially in a more humid atmosphere, and more available take-off power was very welcome. Earlier remedies to this problem with other airliners had entailed the fitting of small rocket or jet engines to the lower fuselage, to provide an extra burst of thrust during the take-off run. Although this was an effective, if not to say spectacular, answer, it was hardly an ideal solution.

Several potential Viscount customers operating aircraft in this environment had been forced to reconsider once they examined the performance figures for the earlier Viscount/Dart combinations. Although Vickers was keen for their business, the Viscounts then on offer were geared more towards short, high-density inter-city routes and were not suitable for similar load-carrying over longer distances and at higher speed. There appeared to be a definite niche for a Viscount 800-sized aircraft capable of economic operation under these complex conditions.

Rolls-Royce met Vickers's new requirement by giving the Mk 520 a recalibrated fuel control unit, increased flame temperature and modified controls with an additional pitch stop for the propeller. With new Dowty propellers giving greater efficiency and increasing relative thrust, the Mk 525 offered a greatly improved take-off field performance. This allowed the use of shorter runways, or higher payloads and/or fuel loads for greater range. The braking system could also be enhanced to permit landings at more-restricted airports.

The stretched production Viscount 800 airframe formed the basis of the new version, a number of the load-bearing components in the aircraft being strengthened to allow for higher stresses involved in the more demanding kind of daily flying envisioned by customer airlines. The wing construction, especially the spars and ribs, was strengthened, as was the fin and rear fuselage to help cope with the increased load. The rudder power was increased, larger deflections being obtained by adjusting the forward balance of the controls. In addition, the nacelles and mountings also had to be modified to take the larger, more powerful engine.

Launch Orders

The new sub-type, designated the Viscount 810, soon attracted a great deal of interest from around the world. Vickers was especially pleased when the first airline to place an order turned out to be yet another US-based carrier, Continental Airlines, then headquartered at Denver, Colorado. Continental signed up for fifteen Viscount 812s, straight off the drawing board, in December 1955. Continental's route network was varied, with larger DC-6s and DC-7s serving major transcontinental routes from the Great Lakes and Midwest to the West Coast. On more regionally oriented, local services in the western half of the USA the airline was operating a mixture of Convair CV340s and CV440s, the latest version of Convair's twin. In addition, a small fleet of faithful, if ageing, DC-3s was still operated. Denver airport was 5,000ft (1,500m) above sea level, located in an area having both hot summers and freezing winters, and close to the Rocky Mountains; the very conditions that had inspired the design of the V.810.

More orders for the V.810 soon followed. Interestingly, these mostly came from new

Specification – V.800

Powerplant:	4 × R.Da.6 Mk570
Weights:	Empty basic equipment weight 41,200lb (18,700kg) (71 seats); maximum zero fuel weight 55,000lb (24,960kg); maximum take-off weight 64,500lb (29,275kg); maximum landing weight 58,500lb (26,325kg); typical maximum payload 13,700lb (6,220kg).
Dimensions:	Length 85ft 0in (25.91m); span 93ft 8½in (28.56m); fin height 26ft 9in (8.15m); wing area 963sq ft (89.46sq m); wheelbase 28ft 8½in (8.75m).
Performance:	Economic cruising speed 310mph (500km/h); maximum cruising speed 335mph (540km/h); service ceiling 27,500ft (8,380m); range with maximum payload 690 statute miles (1,110km).
Average passenger accommodation:	53–71 (all first class – high density)

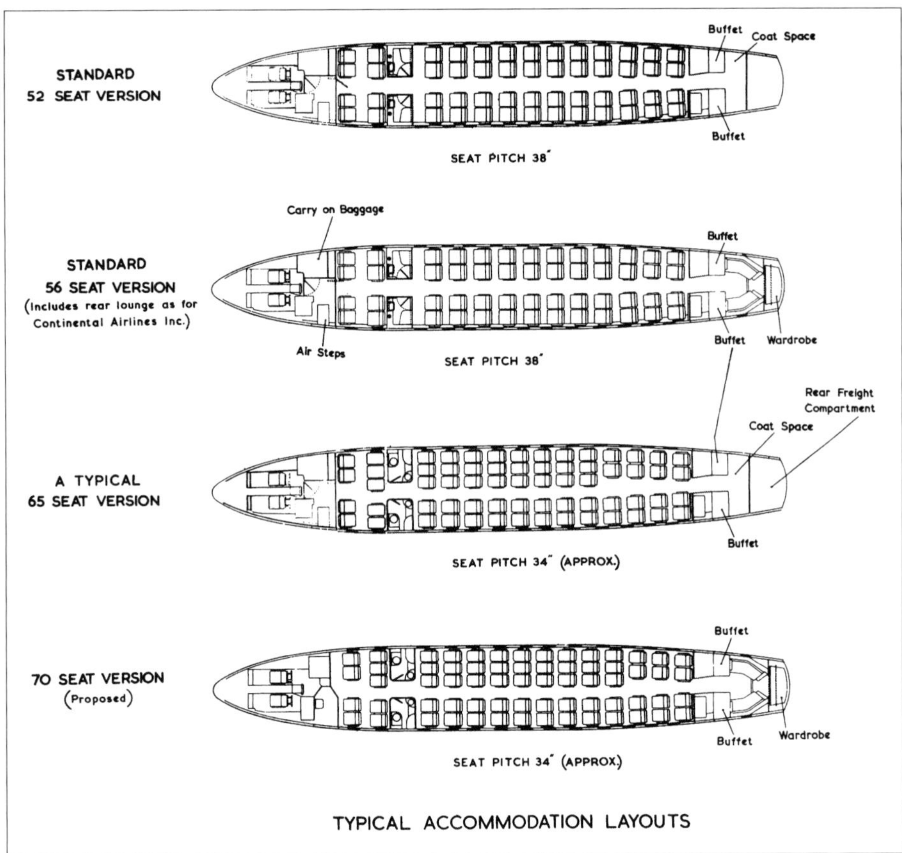

ABOVE: Cabin seating options for the Viscount 810 included all-first-class arrangements with a rear lounge and an all-economy seventy-passenger version. Vickers via author

BELOW: The more-powerful, hybrid V.806/810 G-AOYF took to the air for the first time in August 1957. Vickers via Bob Turner

Viscount customers, rather than V.700 operators. South African Airways (SAA) signed up for seven V.813s in March 1956, and this was followed by an order for three V.815s from Pakistan International Airways (PIA) in May, and one for nine V814s from West Germany's Lufthansa in June. Both PIA and SAA operated services into more remote, 'hot and high' airports on their networks. In addition they operated busy inter-city routes in more populated areas. These routes were also earmarked for modern Viscount service in place of the Convairs and DC-3s operated by PIA and the Constellations, DC-4s and DC-3s flown by SAA on their regional routes. Lufthansa, which had only just restarted operations with Convair 340s after being forbidden to operate since the defeat of Germany in 1945, planned to use the aircraft to expand its busy domestic and European routes. Plans were also in hand to operate the Viscounts to points in the Middle East and the Mediterranean from West Germany.

A Hybrid V.806/810

A great deal of the test flying for the V.810 structural modifications and the Dart Mk 525 was carried out by the long-suffering V.700 prototype, G-AMAV. With its engines uprated 'AV was successfully flown at speeds of up to 400mph (645km/h) on several occasions, with no significant

The first production Viscount, G-ALWE, met a tragic end at Manchester in 1957. Jenny Gradidge

problems. However, there was a need for a more representative aircraft on which to try out the new components fully. Consequently the airframe that was originally to have been the first production Viscount 806, G-AOYF, was built to the new Viscount 810 structural standards as the sole V.806A. Wearing dual Viscount 806/810 titles, G-AOYF first flew on 9 August 1957. Therefore the second V.806, G-AOYG *Charles Darwin*, was the first actual production V.806 to fly, on 4 October.

In September G-AOYF was despatched to South Africa for tropical trials, with a special clearance to operate at weights up to 69,000lb (31,300kg). Initially the trials proceeded to plan, but on 20 October G-AOYF was badly damaged at Johannesburg during a simulated emergency landing. The 'simulation' went very wrong when an even-heavier-than-intended landing caused the starboard undercarriage to collapse, severely damaging the starboard wing and engines. Although, fortunately, none of the occupants was badly injured, the aircraft was considered far too seriously damaged for on-site repair. Its battered remains were ignominiously shipped home by sea to Weybridge, where Vickers would decide its fate.

More Losses at Home

It was not only on experimental test flying that Viscounts came to grief in 1957. On 14 March the first production V.701, G-ALWE, was lost when it crashed on approach to Manchester at the end of a BEA flight from Amsterdam. The aircraft struck a house close to the airport, killing two of its occupants, as well as all twenty on board the aircraft. An investigation revealed that a 9/12in bolt on the No 2 starboard flap unit had failed owing to metal fatigue. This caused the aileron on the starboard wing to lock, and the aircraft entered a shallow right descending turn with a steep bank angle. In this uncontrollable configuration, the aircraft's starboard wing-tip struck the ground and the Viscount careered into the house before bursting into flames.

At the time more than 180 Viscounts were in service and had accumulated 500,000 flying hours between them. Of this, 150,000hr had been flown by BEA and, in the process, BEA alone had carried over two million passengers in its Discovery fleet. Before the fatal flight, 'WE itself had logged 6,900hr and made 3,450 landings. Many of the older Viscount 700s were temporarily grounded for inspection of all suspect bolts, and examined for evidence of fatigue. Thirty-three bolts were found to show signs of minor fatigue in the inspection of over 100 aircraft.

Later the same year, on 23 October, BEA lost another aircraft. The first production Viscount 802, G-AOJA, crashed during an attempted overshoot at Belfast in bad weather. The accident was not the fault of the aircraft this time, being accredited to a fatal combination of bad weather and pilot error. Nonetheless, it still claimed the lives of the five crew and two staff passengers on board. Much luckier were the two crew on V.802 G-AOHP, which suffered a triple engine failure as it approached Copenhagen during a cargo flight on 17 November. Crashing short of the runway, the Viscount was written off, but the crew escaped serious injury. Extra V.806s were ordered to replace these aircraft.

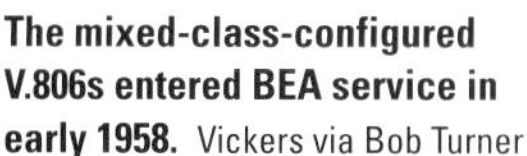

The mixed-class-configured V.806s entered BEA service in early 1958. Vickers via Bob Turner

Despite the loss of G-AOYF, the rest of the Viscount 806's certification programme was as trouble-free as those of the earlier versions, and BEA took delivery of its first aircraft, G-AOYH *William Harvey*, on 23 December. This aircraft was used for the first commercial flight of the new type, on 27 January 1958, a Heathrow–Amsterdam service. The mixed-class V.806s replaced the Elizabethans on the Silver Wing service to Paris, and were also scheduled to operate on flights to Copenhagen, Geneva, Nice, Oslo, Stockholm and Zurich. The last branded Silver Wing service on the Paris route was operated by V.802 G-AOHU *Sir George Strong* on 30 April 1958, and on the next day, 1 May, BEA carried its three-millionth Viscount passenger. As more V.806s arrived at Heathrow, the last operational members of the Elizabethan fleet were finally withdrawn, the type flying its last BEA operation, a Hanover–Cologne/Bonn–Heathrow service, on 30 June 1958.

Worldwide 800s

Aer Lingus began supplementing its V.707s with the first of its V.808s on its high-density, shorter-range routes. When first introduced, the longest regular Viscount 808 service was Shannon–London, at 378 miles (608km). The V.803s of KLM were much further ranging, offering 'Swift, Smooth, Spacious, Sure' Viscount service, as the airline marketed it, on many of its European services from June 1957. The Dutch aircraft were usually operated in a mixed-class, 53-passenger layout, with thirty-eight tourist-class seats forward and fifteen first-class seats in the rear. When required, the cabin could also be converted to a 63-seat all-tourist configuration.

The delivery flight of NZNAC's first Viscount 807, in December 1957, was the longest to date. Scheduled services began on 3 February 1958, over the Christchurch–Auckland route. Despite offering twice the available seats of the DC-3s previously used on the trunk services, the three Viscounts were soon carrying 40 per cent more

TOP: The larger Viscount 808s wore Aer Lingus's distinctive new green-topped livery on delivery for use on the airline's shorter but busier routes. via Bob Turner

ABOVE: The Viscount 803s of KLM Royal Dutch Airlines were introduced on the airline's hectic European route network. via Bob Turner

passengers and operating at 75 per cent load factors. Other important New Zealand cities, such as Palmerston North and Wellington, soon saw Viscounts replacing DC-3s on busier flights, with similar dramatic increases in traffic.

Transair's two Dart Mk 520-powered V.804s entered service on military trooping flights from the UK to Gibraltar, Libya and Malta in October 1957. Transair was based at the old Croydon Airport, south of London, from where it operated a large fleet of DC-3s on scheduled services to the Channel Islands and Northern France, as well a large programme of *ad hoc*, contract and inclusive-tour holiday flights.

The short grass runway at Croydon was totally unsuitable for the Viscounts, and Transair was already planning to move its entire operation further south, to Gatwick Airport in Sussex. At that time Gatwick had been selected for development as London's second airport, and was being completely rebuilt, with a new runway, terminal and hangar complex. Until Gatwick was ready, Transair based its Viscounts at Heathrow. Its V.804s had fifty-eight rear-facing seats, as required for trooping flights. The layout also included a 'mother's room' and a four-cot nursery, which had been included specifically to cater for the large numbers of Service families carried on the military charters. The Transair aircraft were also chartered by Air France during 1958 to operate scheduled flights from Heathrow to Paris and Nice.

The 'Real' 810

Two months after G-AOYF had come to grief, on 23 December 1957, the first proper V.810 model made its maiden flight at Weybridge. Painted in Continental's livery, the Viscount 810 prototype, G-AOYV, completed the type's flight-test and development programme without any more hitches. Until Continental's own

The economy cabin of KLM's Viscount 803s provided a bright and welcoming environment. First-class passengers were accommodated in the rear section. via Bob Turner

ABOVE RIGHT: The introduction of the Viscount was a giant step forward for New Zealand's domestic airline, NZNAC, both technically and in greatly increasing the available capacity over that of the DC-3s previously operated. Jenny Gradidge

RIGHT: Transair's V.804s were initially based at Heathrow while refurbishment of their new home at Gatwick was completed. MAP

Specification – V.810

Powerplant:	4 × R.Da.7/1 Mk525 Dart
Weights:	Empty basic equipment weight 43,200lb (19,600kg) (71seats); maximum zero fuel weight 57,500lb (26,100kg); maximum take-off weight 72,500lb (32,900kg); maximum landing weight 62,000lb (28,140kg); typical maximum payload 15,000lb (6,800kg).
Dimensions:	Length 85ft 8in (26.11m); span 93ft 11in (28.62m); fin height 26ft 9in (8.15m); wing area 963sq ft (89.46sq m); wheelbase 28ft 8½in (8.75m).
Performance:	Economic cruising speed 350mph (565km/h); maximum cruising speed 365mph (590km/h); service ceiling 27,000ft (8,230m); range with maximum payload 1,275 statute miles (2,050km).
Average passenger accommodation:	56–80 (all first class – high density)

BELOW: Continental Airline's first Viscount 812s completed all US certification and crew training in time for a May 1958 entry into scheduled service. via author

BOTTOM: The Viscount enjoyed a comparatively trouble-free introduction into service with Continental, and soon settled down into reliable daily service throughout the wide-ranging route network, from the Midwest and the Rockies to the Pacific Coast. Jenny Gradidge

aircraft were delivered, Vickers leased an ex-Capital V.744 to the airline for a month for crew training. The vital US Federal Aviation Administration (FAA) type certification was awarded to the aircraft on 22 April 1958, allowing deliveries of the first aircraft to Continental Airlines in May. On 28 May the airline became the second US carrier to operate the Viscount.

Continental initially operated the Viscounts in an all-first-class, 52-passenger configuration, in a very comfortable 2-2 layout. The interior trim and decor were skilfully redesigned on the Viscount 812 so that an effective 4in (10cm) greater cabin width was obtained. A forward eight-seat cabin was located between the two-crew flight deck and the forward washrooms. Behind the main cabin was the galley, and behind that there was a small four-seat lounge lit by two small windows. This new feature was similar to the popular lounge areas already found on the airline's larger DC-6s and DC-7s used on the longer trunk routes. On the Continental Viscounts it occupied the area more usually used as a rear main-deck baggage compartment or washrooms. Forward-folding airstairs were also fitted to the new aircraft.

Marketing the aircraft as the Viscount II, to distinguish it from Capital's earlier Viscount 700s, the airline initially placed its new turboprops in service on its Chicago–Kansas City–Denver–Los Angeles route. This was the Viscount's first appearance on US domestic scheduled services in the western half of the country. As well as coping with the difficult conditions at Denver, the fleet was required to operate in demanding temperatures and other arduous weather conditions at airports the airline served in the southwestern states. Even though the aircraft was operated in a reduced-capacity, first-class configuration, Continental found that the Viscount was able to break even on most of its routes at a 38 per cent load factor.

Within eight months the Viscount IIs were accounting for 43 per cent of the total first-class travel of all the competing airlines between Chicago and Denver, and 46 per cent between Denver and Los Angeles. In 1958 Continental increased its passenger boardings by over 90 per cent at Chicago and 67 per cent at Los Angeles, compared with the previous year. In the Viscount's first full year of operation it was estimated that use of the aircraft added a further $4 million to the airline's revenue.

The Boston-based Northeast Airlines' Viscounts were mostly kept busy on the northern half of the company's network, ranging from Canada and New England as far south as Washington and Virginia, but were also used on longer services to Florida before jets replaced them. Global Air Image

Boston-based Viscounts

Another US airline also found itself able to introduce Viscounts in 1958. Northeast Airlines of Boston, Massachusetts, successfully negotiated with Vickers for an order for ten V.798Ds in the previous year. These aircraft were originally part of an option for fifteen that Capital had been unable to take up, as it had begun to suffer serious financial problems. Northeast's own financial position was not that healthy either, as it operated a predominately short-haul, fairly uneconomic network.

Nonetheless, Northeast had been awarded a number of important trunk routes in the region, as well as receiving authority to extend its network south to Florida in an effort to strengthen its operating base. The airline was keen to obtain more modern equipment than the DC-3s, Convairs and DC-6Bs it was operating at the time. This, it was hoped, would give the comparatively small airline a competitive edge over the larger carriers operating rival services in the area.

Northeast had recently cancelled an order for five UK-built Bristol Britannia turboprops, following difficulties not only in getting finance for the order but also due to obstacles encountered when attempts were made to get the Britannia certificated for US registry. A complicated finance deal for the Viscounts, and their engines, was finally agreed with the assistance of the Irving Trust Company of New York, between Northeast, Vickers-Armstrongs and Rolls-Royce in July 1957. With the aircraft already in an advanced state of construction, the first delivery was quite swift, taking place the following March, and all ten aircraft were in service by February 1959.

Originally introduced on the Boston–New York trunk route, the Viscounts saw the airline's load factors rise by as much as 60 per cent in some cases. The type was soon seen on services to other larger cities on Northeast's regional network, such as Philadelphia, Portland and Washington, as well as the important longer-range routes to Florida, serving Jacksonville, Miami and Tampa. Northeast also operated an international service to Montreal, Canada, from New England, and the introduction of Viscounts brought greatly increased frequencies and load factors in response to increasing passenger boardings.

VIP and Corporate Viscounts

With the early government and military orders for VIP Viscounts from India and South Africa, later followed by Brazil and Pakistan, the aircraft was soon to be seen carrying important political and military personages in different parts of the world. This helped promote the aircraft to the airlines in the region. Indeed, the Indian Airlines Corporation (IAC) did not order its initial fleet of five Viscount 768Ds until after the country's air force had taken delivery of its aircraft. Later, IAC acquired a further nine Viscounts for use on domestic and regional routes throughout the sub-continent.

Britain's Royal Family were early users of the Viscount, beginning with HRH Princess Margaret, who flew to Oslo in BEA's G-AMOB in May 1953. From then on BEA was regularly chartered for official royal visits, and the Royal Family repeatedly used BEA's scheduled services for personal travel. The royal patronage was often matched by government charters on official business, and many leading British politicians of the day were frequently seen patronising BEA, both on charters and on normal scheduled services.

Once the Viscount had made its mark as a VIP transport as well as a commercial airliner, the comparatively new corporate flying market started to take an interest. Use of private large transport aircraft by companies and individuals was still a comparatively novel concept in the mid-1950s. Pre-war, only a handful of airliner-size aircraft were operated privately. A large number of war-surplus aircraft, especially the versatile DC-3, were converted after the hostilities ended. Once flying on the scheduled airlines for business became more common, a number of the larger industrial and commercial concerns found that having their own transport aircraft started to make financial sense. Where regular trips by a number of personnel were required, operating a private service started to look economical when compared with repeatedly buying airline tickets. A dedicated aircraft could be scheduled to meet the company's specific needs, as opposed to those of the airlines, and staff time was used more efficiently.

The US Steel Corporation was an enthusiastic executive aircraft operator, with a large fleet of DC-3s ferrying executives and personnel throughout the USA and surrounding countries. It ordered three Viscount 764Ds in June 1955, to be equipped with VIP interiors, extra belly and slipper fuel tanks and integral airstairs. At about the same time the Standard Oil Corporation

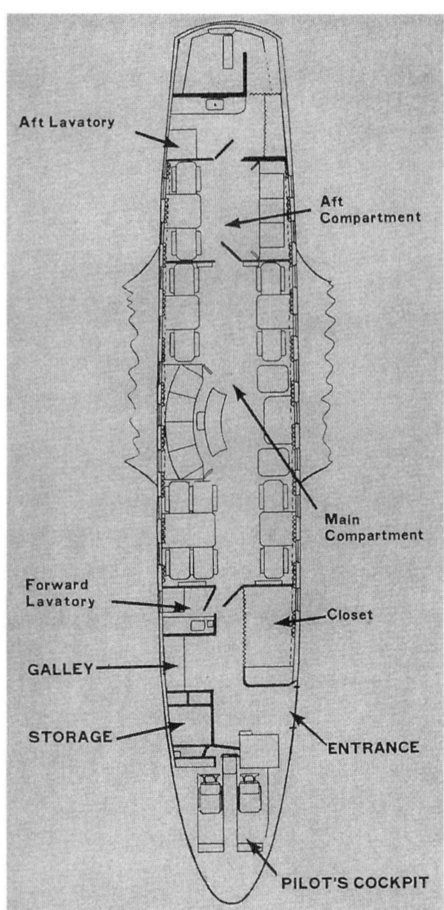

ABOVE: Britain's Royal Family used Viscount services for many official and private journeys. via Bob Turner

BELOW AND RIGHT: The Victor Comptometer Corporation of Chicago operated a well-equipped Viscount as a VIP transport, travelling conference room and valuable sales tool. Author's collection

ordered a similar Viscount 765D, which was delivered in February 1957.

A single Viscount 763D had been ordered by the Hughes Tool Corporation for use by its eccentric millionaire owner, Howard Hughes, and Vickers duly completed the aircraft ready for delivery in 1956. However, after the aircraft had been sitting at Weybridge for a while, instructions arrived from the American company that the Viscount was to be stored away from any other aircraft and not to be approached by anyone. Although far from happy with the arrangement, Vickers complied with its customer's wishes, and the aircraft was untouched for a further ten months. By 1959 Vickers was getting increasingly concerned about the state of the aircraft, and insisted on being allowed to inspect it. The Vickers engineers discovered that over £55,000 work would have to be done on the Viscount to bring it back to standard, and Vickers initiated steps to regain legal possession. Eventually Hughes was persuaded to return ownership of the aircraft in July, and it was sold on to Central American airline TACA International Airways of Honduras.

The Vanguard

Although BEA had subsequently declined the original version of the stretched V.800 in favour of the more modest V.802 option, the airline had remained in active discussion with Vickers with a view to producing an even larger Viscount version. The airline stated that it wanted the aircraft to be in service by 1959, and that it was to be bigger, faster, and to exhibit a 10 per cent improvement in economics over even the latest, improved Viscount models.

Initial studies still centred on a much more developed Viscount variant, with a new model, the V.850, eventually being proposed in an effort to meet BEA's requirements. The V.850 would have been further stretched to a length of 95ft (30m) and powered by 2,500hp Dart R.Da.8s. However, as the airline refined its own ideas for the aircraft, a very different design proposal began to emerge.

The role of the proposed new type came in for much discussion within BEA. One side of the argument had the aircraft being designed with the airline's longer routes to the eastern Mediterranean more in mind. A requirement to fly the 1,500-mile (2,400km) London–Athens route non-stop was proposed for this concept. Vickers saw the commercial possibilities of this medium-range version of the aircraft as a turboprop replacement for the large numbers of medium-range DC-6/Constellation class piston-powered airliners then in service around the world.

Other factions in BEA, however, wanted more emphasis placed on the new design economically serving the airline's core short-haul network from the UK. They envisioned a 100-passenger aircraft with a 500-mile (800km) commercial range and improved economics over 200-mile (300km) sectors. A much-improved freight capacity over the Viscounts was also seen as very desirable in the shorter-range option. The improved cargo-carrying capacity would help on some of BEA's highly seasonal European and domestic passenger routes by providing extra revenue-earning potential in the winter months, when passenger numbers were traditionally much lower.

A Merging of Ideas

Eventually BEA determined that the short-range option best served its future needs. The airline's chief executive, Peter Masefield, wrote to George Edwards at Vickers, giving BEA's requirements, on 15 April 1953. A 370kt (425mph/680km/h) cruising speed, 100-passenger capacity, 1,000-mile (1,600km) range with a 350-mile (560km) diversion reserve and a large freight hold was requested. These initial thoughts were refined and generalized into five basic requirements for the aircraft:

- It must have better economics than anything else then available or even in prospect.

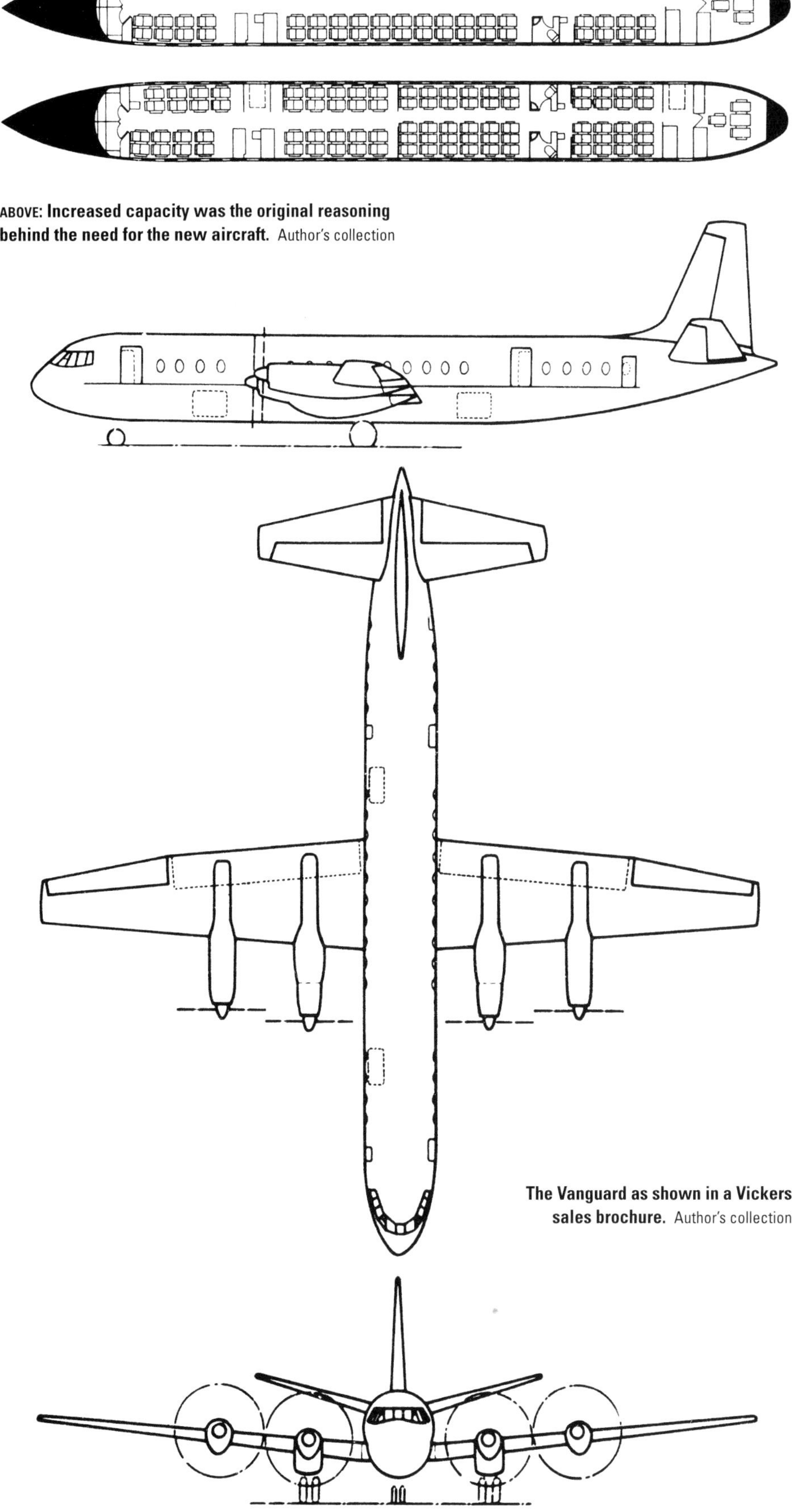

ABOVE: Increased capacity was the original reasoning behind the need for the new aircraft. Author's collection

The Vanguard as shown in a Vickers sales brochure. Author's collection

- It must be big enough to handle the amount of air traffic to be expected six years hence.
- It must be fast enough to compete successfully with any possible challengers on its own routes.
- It must have better 'customer appeal' than any likely US-built rival.
- It must be available for service by 1958/1960.

By pure coincidence TCA had been having similar thoughts, and a letter from the Canadian carrier arrived on George Edwards' desk at Vickers on the same day. It outlined TCA's own requirements for an aircraft with transcontinental capability, as well as the ability to supplement their Viscounts economically on shorter routes, carrying sixty passengers at a gross weight of 72,000lb (32,680kg).

Vickers designers saw the possibility of meeting the needs of both airlines with one new aircraft, and began work on a new V.870 project, which soon overtook and replaced the V.850. While the V.850 had still been a Dart-powered venture, the much larger V.890 called for even more power. Rolls-Royce had a likely new turboprop engine, the RB.109, under development, and the design proceeded with this powerplant in mind. The pure turbojet was also considered, but was eventually dismissed as there was still no jet engine available that was deemed suitable for economic short-haul operations.

The Options

More than sixty design proposals were produced. These varied from propjet to pure-jet, straight-wing to swept-back, and most combinations in between. This number was soon whittled down to five, all turboprop powered. One area where BEA and TCA had shown greatly differing preferences was in the possible position of the wing. Following the very favourable passenger reaction to the high-wing Elizabethan, BEA was very keen that the V.870 would also have this feature. Combined with the already popular large Viscount windows, the unobstructed view of the passing scene from the passenger cabin would have been unprecedented. On the other hand, TCA was concerned that a high wing would have been difficult to de-ice properly and clear of snow in the harsh Canadian winter conditions.

It was BEA's stated requirement for increased cargo-carrying that finally clinched the choice. To provide this, a high-wing aircraft would have needed an impossibly extra-long fuselage, as well as a long, cumbersome and very heavy undercarriage. Instead, the designers proposed a deeper, double-bubble fuselage, with a passenger cabin in the top half and large, low-slung baggage and cargo holds forward and aft of the midsection to which the wing would be attached. The low wing also offered much easier maintenance and refuelling.

At a meeting with BEA on 13 April 1955 the five remaining proposals were finally narrowed down to one, the Scheme 16A version of the V.870. This was for an 88-passenger aircraft with a cruising speed of 425mph (680km/h) at 25,000ft (7,600m) and, originally, with a 1,000-mile (1,600km) range, though it was accepted that 500 miles (800km) would be sufficient for most of BEA's needs. Once BEA had agreed to the basic design, Vickers began improving the specifications to attract other airlines.

The Orders

Changes during project development saw the range increased to 2,500 miles (4,000km) with the addition of wing tanks. The payload was increased to 21,000lb (9,500kg) and the passenger capacity grew to ninety-three. The cargo capacity was,

Eventually satisfied with the final proposal, BEA felt confident enough to place a production order for the Vanguard. Author's collection

The Vanguard eventually emerged as a potentially impressive aircraft. via author

for its day, a very generous 1,300cu ft (36cu m). The alterations were sufficient to warrant another change of type number, to V.900, the BEA version being designated V.901. By the time the gross weight had been finalized at 135,000lb (61,275kg), the type number was V.950, with the BEA aircraft designated V.951. Vickers and BEA signed a contract for twenty aircraft, now named Vanguard by the airline, on 20 July 1956. Service entry was planned for 1960.

Although TCA had been instrumental in encouraging Vickers to produce the Vanguard, the Canadian carrier had taken little part in the design developments up to the time that BEA signed the order. The new production specifications were examined by TCA and, although they represented a great improvement on the earlier options, they were actually found to be wanting. With full load and tanks, the freight and mail capacity would be insufficient to meet TCA's needs. Vickers was informed that a greater payload would have to be available if TCA was to consider placing an order. Vickers countered this objection by coming up with a design having an increased gross weight of 142,000lb (64,450kg), all but 1,000lb (4,500kg) of this being increased payload. After further negotiations TCA finally signed a $67.1 million order for 20 Vanguards on 31 January 1957. Its improved model was designated V.952. Options were also taken out on four more aircraft, three of which were eventually converted to firm orders.

Very interested in the improvements made for TCA, BEA contacted Vickers with a view to having its own aircraft built to the same standard. By then, however, the first six BEA Vanguards were already being built and could not be economically modified on the production line. Nonetheless, in July 1958 the airline persuaded Vickers to allow it to modify its order to cover the six V.951s already under construction, while the remaining fourteen would be built to the new specifications and redesignated V.953s. The V.952/V.953s' increased weights would allow a passenger capacity of up to 139.

The Viscount Glory Years

One of the busiest years for the Viscount production lines was 1957, with both V.700s and V.800s rolling off the Weybridge and Hurn production lines in the colours of numerous operators. As usual, the spread was wide. New operators that year included Hong Kong Airways, Indian Airlines Corporation, KLM, Linee Aeree Italiene, Lloyd Aereo Colombiano, New Zealand National Airways, Philippine Airlines, TACA International Airlines, Transair and Union of Burma Airways.

Both BWIA and MEA took delivery of their more modern version Viscount 700s, passing their original older models back to their owners when the leases ended. Fred Olsen Air Transport also took delivery of new aircraft, in the shape of four V.779Ds. The Norwegian shipping company operated them on a variety of charter services, as well as continuing to lease them out frequently to other carriers short of capacity. The two Fred Olsen V.736s that had been

RIGHT: The Viscount 772 joined BWIA's V.702s on the Caribbean and Western Atlantic network. via author

BELOW: Middle East Airline's later model V.754Ds, such as OD-ACU, began to replace the leased Hunting-Clan V.732s in 1957. Jenny Gradidge

BOTTOM: Finally able to introduce faster Viscounts in place of ageing Vikings on their Safari Service, Airwork and Hunting-Clan saw an immediate rise in traffic once the new aircraft were in operation. Jenny Gradidge

leased to BEA, G-AODG and G-AODH, had been returned to their Norwegian owner in March and April 1957 and then immediately leased on to MEA and BWIA as OD-ACR and VP-TBY respectively. They returned to the UK later that year and were finally sold, via BOAC Associated Companies, to Airwork Ltd.

Hunting-Clan had reclaimed its V.732s at the end of their lease to MEA, and the two partners were finally permitted to introduce Viscounts on their scheduled UK–Africa colonial coach-class Safari services in January 1958. Both airlines had also ordered V.800s, planning to replace the V.700s with the new aircraft on the scheduled services, which were now being operated from Heathrow. The Safari service had been popular when operated by the old Vikings, but passenger loads soared with the introduction of the Viscounts.

The main East and Central routes were to Salisbury, via Rome, Benina, Luxor or Wadi Halfa, Khartoum, Entebbe, N'dola and Lusaka. The Nairobi service operated over a similar routeing, and a West African Safari route also operated to Accra via Lisbon, Las Palmas, Bathurst and Freetown. The chance to exploit the greater range, higher speeds and much more comfortable ride of the Viscounts over the Vikings saw the en route 'night-stops' ending for the passengers, except for a brief stay at Las Palmas on the Accra flights. Instead, the Viscounts continued through after refuelling and changing crews, if required, at the intermediate stops. Hunting-Clan also flew a scheduled London–Gibraltar flight with its Viscounts.

Asian Arrivals

The Indian Airlines Corporation (IAC), created by the nationalization and merger of several independent domestic operators, had been in existence for only two years when it placed its first Viscount order in 1953. Its network covered a vast amount of territory throughout India and also reached into neighbouring countries. Operations were centred on three main bases, at Delhi, Calcutta and Bombay, and before the arrival of the Viscounts the fleet consisted mostly of DC-3s and DC-4s, with a large fleet of Vikings also taking much of the workload.

Deliveries of the five V.768Ds initially ordered began in August 1957. Most of the aircraft actually started their delivery flights from Heathrow, where they had been based briefly for crew training. They entered services on the main trunk routes, such as Delhi–Calcutta, Delhi–Bombay and Delhi–Hyderabad–Madras. As usual, the Viscounts started to make their mark with increased traffic, generating more revenue. Passenger loads increased by 41 per cent, with an average 72 per cent load factor in less than two weeks after the Viscounts entered service. On the Delhi–Bombay route load factors were often over 90 per cent, and the success of the Viscounts led directly to lobbying by passengers for the introduction of increased frequencies on the Delhi–Calcutta service.

The Indian Airlines' Viscounts were operated throughout the subcontinent on domestic and regional services. Jenny Gradidge

Union of Burma Airways (UBA) used its three Viscount 761s to replace its DC-3s, previously used on international routes. Services were operated from Rangoon on established routes to Bangkok, Hong Kong and Singapore. The previously fortnightly Rangoon–Bangkok–Singapore service was replaced by a weekly Viscount flight, and a new Viscount route to Djakarta was also opened by UBA with great success.

As well as BWIA and MEA, BOAC Associated Companies also had an interest in Hong Kong Airways (HKA). The airline had originally linked Hong Kong with many points in mainland China, as well as regional points in the area, with a fleet of DC-3s. But HKA's network had then been decimated by the rise of Communist China, which had cut off all links to the British Colony. However, HKA continued to serve busy routes to the Philippines, Japan and Taiwan from Hong Kong. A pair of V.760Ds were delivered in January and February 1957 and soon put to work. The Viscount's reputation for reliability could have been hard-pressed in such a small fleet, but a remarkable 99 per cent regularity was achieved. In eighteen months, of

The pair of Viscounts operated by Hong Kong Airways gained a remarkable reputation for reliability, especially considering their high utilization. via Bob Turner

LEFT: Once improvements had been made to local airports, the PAL Viscount network was expanded to include several important domestic points. Jenny Gradidge

BELOW: Vickers was now able to offer a full family of turboprop airliners, ranging from 40- to 139-seaters, depending on customer requirements. Author's collection

Now! 3 different Vickers turbo-props for higher profits on routes up to 2,500 miles!

VICKERS VISCOUNT 700

VICKERS VISCOUNT 810·840

VICKERS VANGUARD 900

turbo-prop VICKERS VISCOUNT

VICKERS-ARMSTRONGS (AIRCRAFT) LTD., WEYBRIDGE, ENGLAND

Member Company of the Great Vickers Group.

1,260 flights scheduled, only nine were delayed or cancelled, mostly due to adverse weather in the typhoon season.

Another regular Viscount visitor to Hong Kong from 1957 was Philippine Air Lines (PAL). The first of its two V.784s was delivered in May 1957 and placed in service on the Manila–Hong Kong route. The second aircraft was leased out to TACA in Central America while improvements were made to airports at the more important Philippine regional cities that the carrier intended to serve on domestic services. In the meantime, the solitary first aircraft was soon achieving a highly creditable 8½hr daily utilization.

While on lease to TACA, the second PAL Viscount was operated on an intensive six-day schedule that included flights to Guatemala, Managua, Mexico City, New Orleans and San José from San Salvador. The introduction of the Viscount into scheduled service had been spearheaded by a large publicity campaign, promoting 'New Wings Over Middle America'. Proving extremely popular with TACA's passengers, the aircraft managed to average 2,400 miles (3,860km) a day, and during the year-long lease only three flights were cancelled. The V.784 was returned to PAL when TACA's own aircraft was delivered, the first of many to be acquired and operated by the carrier over the next eighteen years.

A New Future Beckons

With the Viscount established as a technical and commercial success, and the Vanguard taking shape, Vickers was looking forward to a prosperous end to the 1950s. Yet, even as new customers continued to sign up, rivals abroad were finally finding their feet. The Vickers turboprops would soon face some serious competition.

CHAPTER FIVE

The New Competition

More Turboprops

For several years after its entry into service, in 1953, the Viscount had enjoyed a unique position as the only turboprop airliner available to commercial operators. The aircraft's contemporary turboprop rivals, such as the Armstrong Whitworth Apollo and the Airspeed/de Havilland Ambassador turboprop proposals, had failed to attain production status. The 1954 withdrawal of the de Havilland Comet pure-jet airliner, following unforeseen structural failures, had left the Viscount as the only turbine-powered commercial airliner in service. From 1954 to 1957, if an airline wanted to offer anything resembling jet comfort, the only choice was the Viscount.

When another British turboprop airliner design did finally make a belated appearance, it was never intended to be a serious Viscount rival. Another Brabazon Committee-sponsored design, the Bristol 175 Britannia, powered by four Bristol Proteus engines, was designed with BOAC's worldwide services in mind. Plans had been made to put the aircraft into service in 1955/1956, but protracted icing problems with the engines delayed full airline services with the Britannia until 1957.

While the Britannia was designed for long range, the next turboprops to appear were intended for more local services than the larger Viscount and Vanguard category of aircraft, with a short-field performance that put them firmly in the 'DC-3 replacement' class. The reliable pre-war Douglas design's rugged nature and economy of operation still ensured it a place in many airline fleets, large and small, but the 1936 design was twenty years old, and a number of manufacturers around the world sought to develop a viable modern substitute for the several hundred DC-3s still in service at that time.

The first main turboprop contenders for the 'DC-3 replacement' market eventually appeared in Europe, Britain's Avro and

ABOVE: The V.745Ds ordered by Capital continued to be produced in a steady flow from 1955. Delivered in 1957, N7462 was lost in 1960 when it suffered multiple engine failures after encountering severe icing conditions shortly after taking off from Richmond, Virginia. All forty-six passengers and four crew perished. via Bob Turner

RIGHT: Aer Lingus took delivery of the first production Fokker F.27s in 1958. US-built versions produced under licence by Fairchild had entered service shortly before. MAP

The Handley Page Herald later had its four piston engines replaced by two Rolls-Royce Dart turboprops. via author

Avro's robust, twin-Dart-powered 748 was to remain in production with Hawker Siddeley and British Aerospace for over twenty-five years. via author

The 'Local Service Viscount' was proposed with high-density, ultra-short-haul operations, especially in the USA, firmly in mind. Vickers via author

Handley Page companies, and Fokker of the Netherlands, coming up with very similar designs during the mid-1950s, all of which were eventually to be powered by two Darts. Handley Page's aircraft, the Herald, was originally designed to be powered by four Alvis Leonides piston engines, the prototype originally flying in this form in August 1955. However, that November the similarly sized, 44-passenger Fokker F.27 Friendship flew for the first time, powered by two Darts. Handley Page realized that it faced the prospect of an originally healthy order book disappearing overnight in the light of the Dutch aircraft's obvious technical superiority, and decided to redesign the Herald to be powered by a pair of Darts.

This cost Handley Page valuable time, and the project never regained its momentum. Most of the original orders were still lost, and Dart Herald sales failed to live up to the aircraft's promise. Fokker's F.27 fared much better, with steady sales over many years. The Dutch design was also built under licence in the USA by Fairchild, this version actually being the first to enter service, with West Coast Airlines of Seattle, in September 1958. European-built Friendships entered service with Aer Lingus that November. The original version was increased in size and updated, and Fairchild even built a stretched version, the FH-227. The much-delayed Dart Herald did not enter service until 1961. As well as Aer Lingus, a number of other Viscount operators ordered F.27s in order to bring turboprop services to smaller cities and less-dense routes where the DC-3 had previously reigned supreme.

The last of the trio to appear was the British-designed 48-passenger Avro 748, another twin-Dart-powered aircraft, which first flew as late as June 1960. Unlike the previous two aircraft, the 748 sported a low wing instead of a high wing, and it was aimed even more at regional and even rough-field operations than were the F.27 and Herald. Avro was later merged into Hawker Siddeley, and thereafter the aircraft was marketed as the HS.748. Although it enjoyed more success and longevity than the Dart Herald, it still found itself well outsold by the Friendship.

The Vickers Regional Option

Reacting to much the same perceived 'DC-3 replacement' markets as Handley

Page and Fokker, Vickers attempted to offer its own solution to the regional aircraft market's requirements. The company proposed a much-modified Viscount 700 in January 1958, to be designated V.790. The needs of the local service operators, flying shorter-range services, were to be accommodated by incorporating extra strengthening already developed for the Viscount 810. This permitted higher landing weights and much faster cruising speeds at lower altitudes.

The aircraft would be much more suitable for operations over shorter, 100-mile (160km) stage lengths, where there was call for more capacity than the 21–36-seat DC-3 could provide. Seating could be increased by redesigning the interior, only one toilet being provided and only basic galley facilities being needed on the shorter flights. Four-abreast seating for forty-eight passengers, or five–abreast for up to fifty-nine to sixty-five, was offered, galley facilities being completely dispensed with in the denser configurations. A curious mixture of four- and five-abreast seating was also offered in some configurations.

Cabin pressurization was to be reduced, to 4.5lb/sq in (0.33kg/sq cm), instead of the more usual 6lb/sq in (0.42kg/sq cm), in view of the lower altitudes at which the aircraft would mostly be flown. To facilitate quick turn-rounds on multi-sector flights, forward airstairs were to be fitted as standard, and it was expected that the No 4 engine would be kept running to provide start-up power for the other three. Brakes would be applied to the stationary propellers on the other engines, to prevent dangerous windmilling during the turn-round servicing and loading. The earlier-version Dart R.Da.3 Mk506 was to be used, being much lighter than the later models and already well proven in service.

The proposed new 'local service Viscount' was presented to a number of airlines around the world, but especially to regional carriers in the USA. Vickers even organized a 'Local Service Carrier Jamboree' in 1958, in which top executives from nine US local airlines were flown to the UK and introduced to the Viscount 790 project. The presentation also included a VIP demonstration flight in one of BEA's new V.802s, which was also considered suitable for US local operations. Delivery was offered for mid-1959. However, no sales materialized for the V.790 or V.802 as a result of the 'Jamboree' or any of the Vickers sales team's other efforts.

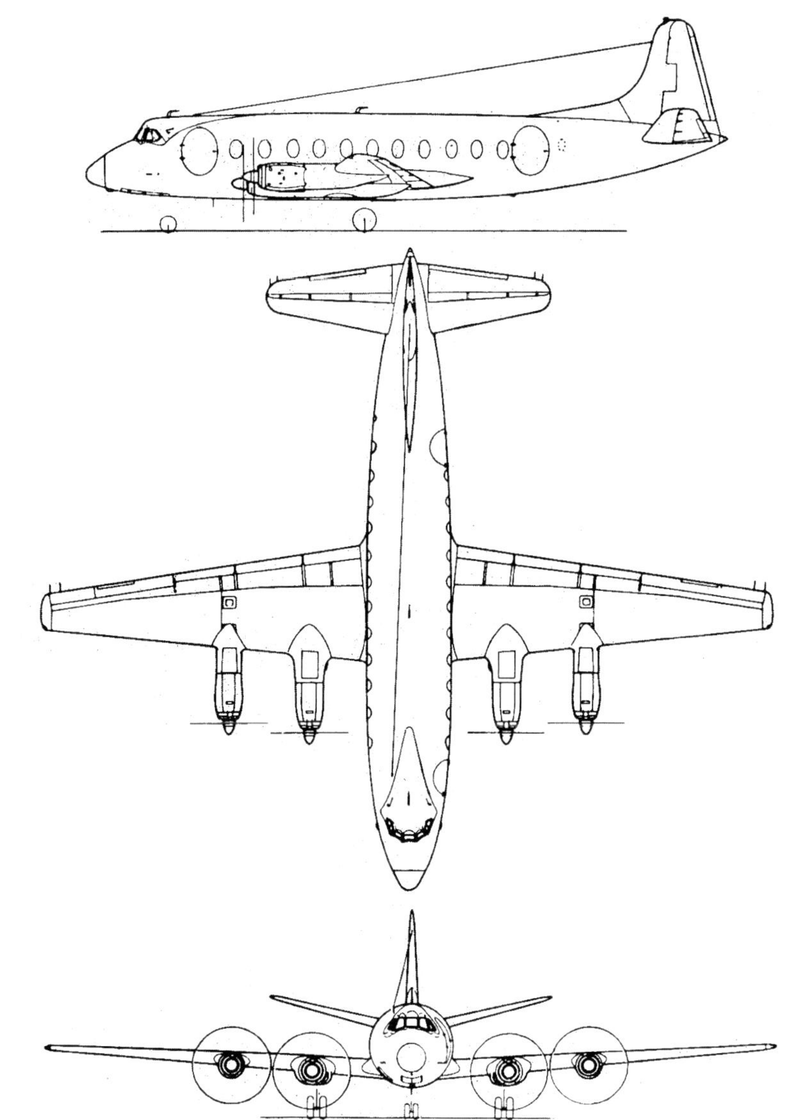

54–59 seat version

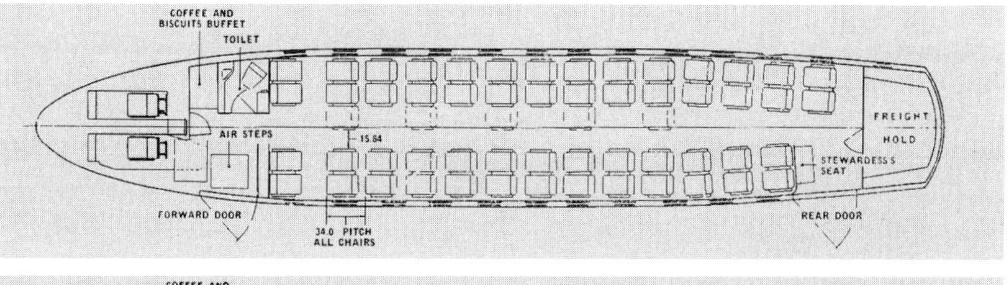

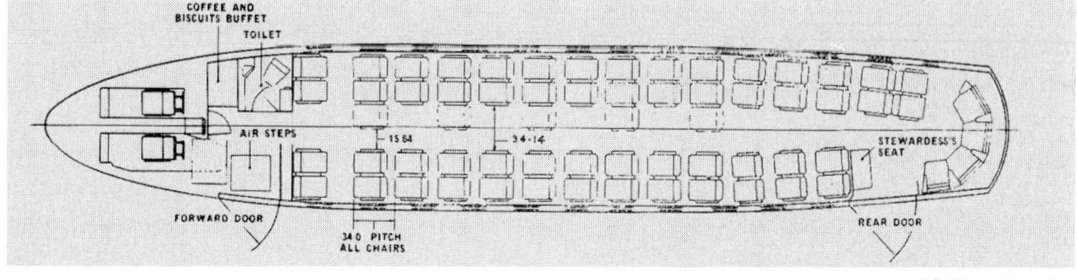

60–65 seat version

Proposed cabin arrangements (above) in the local service Viscount (top) included an unusual mixture of 2-2 and 2-3 seating, as well as the option of a rear lounge area. Vickers via author

The Convair Turboprops

The main US rival to the Viscount had remained the piston-powered Convair series. Gradual improvements had led to the development of the CV340 and CV440 models, which, although still piston-engined, had achieved very respectable sales figures, not only in the Americas but worldwide.

While the Convairs' performance was still not able to match that of the Viscount in terms of speed, the progress made had produced a very capable aircraft. In service, the actual block-to-block flight times were certainly close to those of the Viscount, and improvements in cabin amenities and soundproofing had produced almost as comfortable a ride for the passengers. In response to the imminent arrival of the Viscount with Capital Airlines, Convair proposed a turboprop-powered, stretched version of the CV340 as early as 1955. Ironically, the new design would have been fitted with four Rolls-Royce R.Da.7 Darts. Designed to specifications drawn up by American Airlines, the 'Model 15', as it was known, was not pursued after little interest was shown by the airline.

New turboprop Convairs were eventually produced, but not by the parent company. Canadair, in Montreal, produced a version of the CV340/440 under licence, which was powered by two British-built Napier Eland turboprops. The CV540, as the new Eland version was designated, was ordered by a number of airlines, most of which cancelled their orders when Rolls-Royce acquired control of Napier and decided to discontinue the Eland programme. In the end, only Allegheny Airlines in the USA and Quebecair in Canada operated the CV540 commercially. A large number of the military version, the CL-66B, were produced for the Royal Canadian Air Force.

Even so, a number of CV240, CV340 and CV440 airframes were successfully converted from piston-engine to turboprop power, especially during the 1960s. These had either Rolls-Royce Darts or US-built Allison engines, which were produced by Convair's associate, General Motors Corporation. The Dart and Allison-powered turboprop Convair conversions remained popular with regional airlines, especially in the USA, and large numbers of these aircraft served in both commercial and military roles around the world for many years.

Vickers had hoped to sell the Vanguard to Hong Kong-based Cathay Pacific Airways, but the airline ordered the rival Lockheed L-188 Electra. CPA via author

The Soviet Union's Ilyushin Il-18 turboprop was produced in large numbers. Similar in size and performance to the Vanguard and Electra, it was successfully operated by Aeroflot and several other carriers around the world. via author

Many of the potential US customers simply regarded the four-engined Viscount as too sophisticated for their smaller operations. They preferred to consider either the new smaller twin turboprops, or even the large numbers of post-war piston-engined designs such as the Martins and Convairs then starting to come on to the secondhand market, as replacements for their DC-3s. At one point the major US operator Trans World Airlines (TWA) considered ordering a fleet of V.790s to replace its Martin 202s and 404s, and the designation V.795 was reserved. Unfortunately TWA decided not to proceed and, instead, replaced its Martin aircraft with Lockheed Constellations that had been displaced from international routes by larger Super Constellations.

Vanguard Rivals

Given the success of the Viscount, it is perhaps surprising that US airliner manufacturers showed little interest in producing a direct rival, particularly after the large Capital and Continental orders. However, by the time the Viscount was making a name for itself with Capital, three of the largest airliner producers, Boeing, Convair and Douglas, were already putting all their efforts into constructing the USA's first pure-jet commercial airliners. All three had resolved that they would bypass the turboprop option altogether. Notwithstanding this, their long-standing co-rival, the Lockheed Aircraft Company, went in a totally different direction and decided to put all its eggs firmly in the turboprop basket.

Still regarding the pure jet transport as unsuitable for operations over short inter-city stage lengths, Lockheed had also proposed its own design in response to the

American Airlines earlier specifications for a turboprop airliner. Lockheed was encouraged by American to develop its original, smaller, proposal into the L-188 Electra, which in due time was to be ordered not only by American but by several other larger carriers in the USA and worldwide. Of similar size and performance to the Vanguard, the Electra was powered by four Allison 501 turboprops, and entered service in January 1959 with American Airlines and Eastern Air Lines, which had placed firm orders in 1955. Although its use as an airliner was limited by the advent of the short-haul jets, the Electra has managed to survive far longer than the Vanguard by virtue of the very successful production of a military version. The Lockheed Orion early-warning and maritime patrol aircraft, developed directly from the Electra, remained in production long after the last Electra airliner left the Lockheed factories.

Russia's answer to the Vanguard and Electra, the Ilyushin Il-18, also entered scheduled service in 1959. Similarly designed for high-capacity, economic operations, the Il-18 four-engine turboprop could carry 75–110 passengers. Several hundred were produced for Russia's state airline, Aeroflot, which operated them on both intercity and transcontinental services throughout the Soviet Union for many years. However, although it was a very successful aircraft, sales outside the communist bloc were very limited, apart from a number of exports to allied countries.

New Jet Threat

As early as the mid-1950s, de Havilland was well on its way to bringing back the Comet in a much-enlarged and strengthened form. Even Vickers was working on long-haul, pure-jet designs for BOAC. In the USA, Boeing had been flying the prototype of its Model 707 jet airliner since 1954, and Douglas was not far behind with its own first commercial jet, the DC-8. These were all intended for long-range flights, though the initial versions were really only medium-range aircraft and would usually have to make refuelling stops when operated on long-range flights.

Yet, by the time the first Vanguard was taking shape on the Weybridge factory floor, the jet-versus-turboprop picture was changing. There were also new pure-jet designs on the way, solely intended to operate economically on short- and medium-range services. In Europe, France's Sud Aviation was building the SE-210 Caravelle short-haul jet and de Havilland was considering a short-haul version of the Comet for BEA. Even before producing its own turboprop design, the Soviet Union had enjoyed a spectacular propaganda coup, putting its own Tupolev Tu-104 jet airliner into regular service as early as 1956. Even Convair was designing its own medium-range jet, the CV600, later redesignated CV880.

Although the original Comet models had been in service for barely two years, the airlines that had operated them had been very satisfied. Load factors on routes on which the handful of early Comet 1s had been operated had soon been in the high-80-per-cent range, in spite of their having offered only an all-first-class service. Although structurally flawed, the first Comets had shown the enormous potential for commercially successful jet-powered airliner services.

Just as the Comet and Viscount were making their joint revolutionary presence felt in terms of high speed and comfort, cheaper economy- and tourist-class fares became available in the early 1950s, giving air travel a tremendous boost when the post-war travel boom was starting to slow down. The increased availability of the cheaper fares and the early introduction of the turboprop Viscount on many of the new economy-class services showed that a combination of jet speed and lower fares had the potential to change the face of airline travel. Consequently the next generation of pure-jet airliners, both long- and short-haul, were designed from day one with at least a generous percentage of their capacity devoted to the lower-fare-paying passenger.

Jet Glamour or Turboprop Economy?

Nonetheless, doubts still lingered in many airline boardrooms as to the economic viability of pure jets on short-haul services, especially on routes of less that 500 miles (800km), such as most of those between the European capitals and in the high-density US east coast regions. Even the developed jet engines still had comparatively high fuel consumption, especially on short sectors with little cruise time at altitude. High fuel consumption during holding periods at low altitudes while awaiting their turn to land at busier airports was also widely regarded as a potential financial drawback for short-haul jets.

The prospect of jet aircraft operating on rival airline services on its longer-range routes was one of the factors that led BEA to have its later Vanguards built to the revised TCA standard, geared towards more versatility on shorter, high-capacity intercity routes. For its further-reaching services to the eastern Mediterranean and Middle East, originally earmarked for the first Vanguard design options, BEA was finally forced to

BEA relied heavily on its Viscount fleet right through the mid–late 1950s. Global Air Image

begin to look seriously at pure-jet design options. By the late 1950s numerous British companies, such as Avro, Bristol, de Havilland and Hunting, were already presenting jet airliner design proposals to BEA.

However, the airline's management still firmly held the view that the fleet of turboprop Viscounts and Vanguards would offer economic operations on most of BEA's shorter routes for many years to come. It was presumed that, because the jets would offer only minor point-to-point time savings on the shorter intercity flights, the travelling public would choose the cheaper fares available on turboprops rather than jet speed. As it transpired, this was a rather naïve assumption, and the theory was soon overtaken by events. The sheer glamorous, popular marketing appeal of pure-jet travel soon far outweighed purely economic considerations.

The reliable Viscounts of KLM were a common sight throughout the airline's European network until the mid-1960s. via author

Viscount Customers and the Electra

For the time being, though, Vickers, BEA and TCA continued to regard the Vanguard as the more practical, economic large-capacity option for intercity and medium-range routes, at least for the foreseeable future. However, the Vanguard soon found itself struggling to make much of an impact on the new airliner market. As well as many of the prospective customers keeping a weather eye on the promised new short-haul jet projects, the Vickers aircraft was up against the impressive might of the US aircraft industry in the shape of the very similar Lockheed L-188 Electra.

Vickers might have reasonably expected a few more of the previous Viscount operators to favour the Vanguard, but most of these potential customers were soon seen to be waiting for jets or going to Lockheed. One major factor in Lockheed's favour was the ability to promise earlier delivery of the Electra. With the commercial life of the larger turboprops possibly being limited by the forthcoming arrival of the next generation of jets, the airlines wanted to get as much productive life out of the aircraft as possible.

Two original Viscount operators who were to select the Electra over the Vanguard were KLM and TAA. Although TAA had taken delivery of two larger V.816s in 1959, to operate on the busier routes alongside their already successful Viscount 700s, their own 68-passenger Electras soon followed. The Electras entered service in July, to complete TAA's Jetline fleet, as it was now marketed. The airline had actually favoured ordering Caravelles, but the Australian government pronounced that it felt that many of the country's airports would be unable to cope with the more sophisticated aircraft, and blocked the order. The V.816s had arrived closely after the delivery of TAA's second Viscount 700 order for seven V.756s. Two of the V.756s had been fitted with low-pressure tyres to allow operation from rougher runways than the earlier Viscounts and allowing the extension of TAA turboprop services to even more Australian cities.

The pair of 'Super Viscounts' joined TAA's smaller Viscount 700s on busier inter-city routes in eastern Australia. Jenny Gradidge

Ansett Inherits the Viscount

Australian National Airways (ANA), the original private-enterprise rival to government-owned TAA, had been struggling financially and was taken over in 1957 by Ansett Airways, a much smaller operator. Ansett's founder, Australian airline pioneer Reg Ansett, had seen the opportunity to create a merged airline that could take on TAA much more successfully. The Australian government, also keen to see a more stable national airline industry, encouraged the merger. Through the ANA takeover Ansett acquired a small shareholding in Butler Air Transport (BAT), and set about attempting to absorb the smaller carrier into the larger enterprise.

Butler had continued to expand its regional operations throughout New South Wales, operating a pair of Viscounts alongside its original DC-3s. A small fleet of Ambassadors was also operated for a while. These had been bought secondhand from BEA and, although they offered much-needed extra capacity, they were not really suited to BAT's outback style of operation, and were eventually returned to the UK. Still holding a sizeable number of the shares in the airline he had founded, Arthur Butler resisted the takeover by his contemporary

and old adversary, Reg Ansett. Sadly, Butler's generosity in initiating a pioneering employee shareholding scheme backfired when Ansett managed to persuade enough of the BAT staff to sell their shares at a premium rate, and Arthur Butler was finally forced out of the company in 1958.

With the takeover, Ansett-ANA inherited the BAT Viscounts, which it was initially reluctant to keep. The two aircraft were put up for sale, being among the first Viscounts to be offered on the secondhand market. However, commercial pressure on the Ansett-ANA fleet of Douglas and Convair piston types from TAA's Viscounts not only led to retention of the ex-BAT Viscounts, but also caused the airline to acquire more turboprop aircraft. Four new

ABOVE: The 'De luxe' Ansett-ANA V.832s were operated on several high-profile routes to major cities. Jenny Gradidge

LEFT AND BELOW: Ansett-ANA promoted the high standard of passenger comfort and facilities offered on its V.832s as the 'Golden Jet Service'. Author's collection

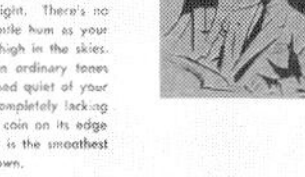

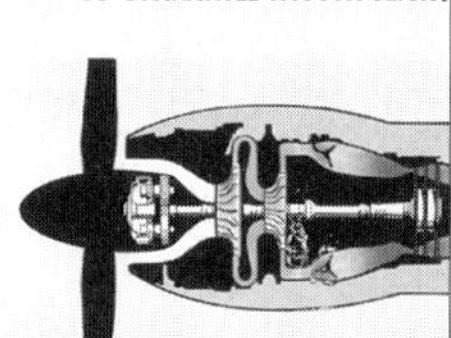

V.832s were ordered by Ansett-ANA for 1959 delivery, these being placed into service alongside four Lockheed L-188 Electras, finally putting Ansett-ANA on a much more equal footing with TAA as far as equipment was concerned.

In December 1959 KLM's Electras followed the carrier's smaller Viscounts on to intra-European and Middle East services. As well as serving on the longer runs to the Middle East, once the whole fleet of twelve was delivered the Dutch airline's Electras even operated as far as Singapore from Amsterdam for a while, albeit with a number of stops en route. The turboprop Viscounts and larger Electras complemented one another quite well on the KLM network, allowing much of the airline's piston-powered fleet to be retired from its European services by the early 1960s.

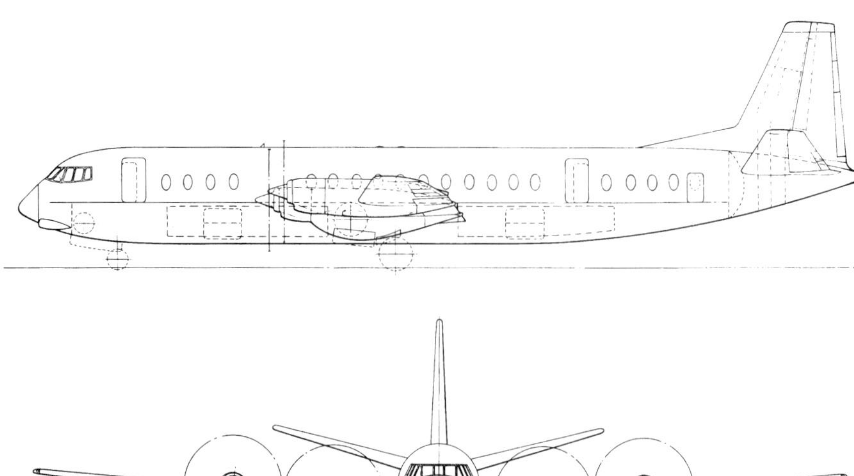

Vanguards Take Shape

As the prototype and first production Vanguards made their way down the line at Weybridge it was becoming clear that the aircraft was no mere 'scaled-up' Viscount. Although it certainly drew much from the earlier design from which it had been developed, it was a very different aircraft.

Aerodynamically and structurally, the Vanguard incorporated well-established, orthodox fail-safe and multi-load-path design principles. The new double-bubble fuselage structure followed Vickers practice developed from the Viking days, being built up from longitudinal stringers attached to hoop frames by shear cleat brackets, the skin being flush-riveted to the stringers. One of the few structures to survive from the original Viscount, the passenger cabin windows, were of the same large elliptical pattern that had proved so popular, embodying identical stress-free, neutral-hole capabilities.

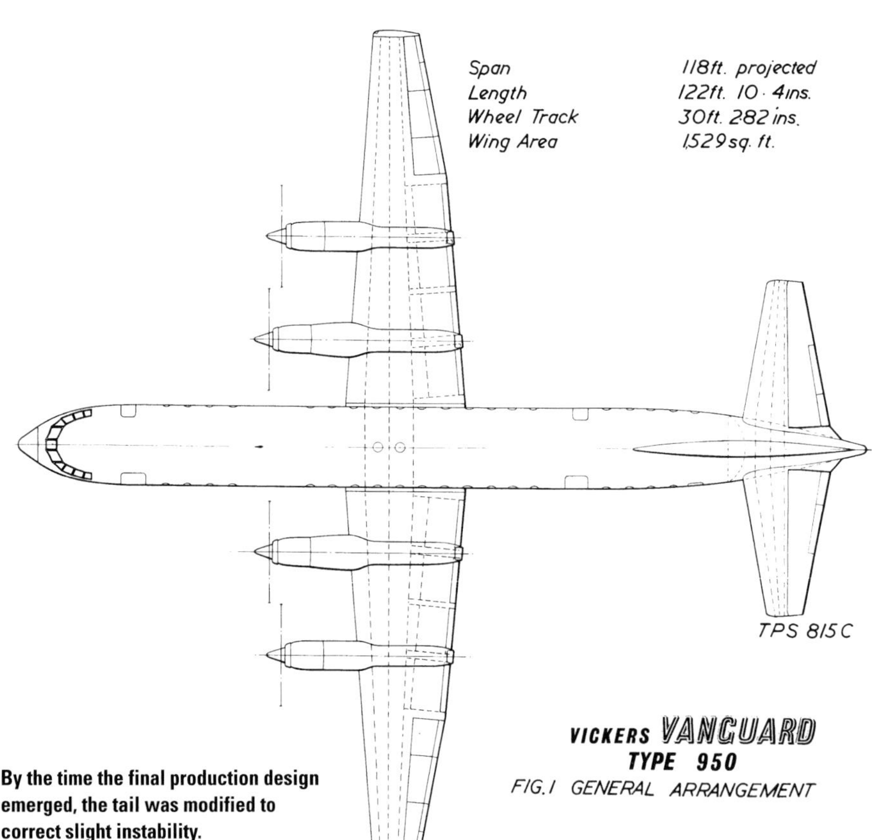

By the time the final production design emerged, the tail was modified to correct slight instability.
Vickers via author

The wing structure, however, was a new concept. It was made up of skin panels machined from solid billets of light alloy, with spanwise stiffeners. This new method of construction was not only faster and more cost-efficient, it also avoided concentrated stress by maintaining the wing profile with closely spaced ribs which acted as link members between the machined skin panels and spanwise shear webs. In effect, the completed wing structure became a homogeneous torsion box. The entire box structure outboard of the centre section was sealed to serve as an integral fuel tank. The total wing area was 1,527sq ft (142sq m). The tailplane had a marked dihedral angle, inherited from the Viscount, to keep it clear of the jet residue efflux and aid directional and longitudinal stability.

The Vanguard's large fin was originally faired into the fuselage with only a small aerodynamic fillet. This was later replaced by a larger dorsal fin that was added to correct a slight rudder instability. The Viscount 810 prototype, G-AOYV, still flying in full Continental Airlines livery, was fitted with a scaled-down version of the redesigned Vanguard tail and used for aerodynamic and de-icing trials. For the de-icing trials the aircraft was also fitted with a large rig to spray water on the tailplane to simulate icing conditions.

Testing the Tyne

The new Rolls-Royce RB.109 engine, designed for the Vanguard, was eventually to be redesignated RTy1 Tyne. From the original 2,750shp of the RB.109, the RTy1 was further developed to provide 4,000shp for the prototype and first production V.951s for BEA, and an impressive 4,500shp for the V.952s for TCA and V.953s for BEA. As with the Dart, the untried Tyne engine was to be extensively flown on specially converted test-bed aircraft, this time using a pair of Airspeed Ambassadors. A total of 16,000hr of flying was needed, with at least 400hr normal running without any failure required before the Tyne could be certificated for use on a commercial aircraft.

The ex-second prototype Ambassador, G-AKRD, was converted in 1957, and an ex-BEA aircraft, G-ALZR, in 1958. The former was no stranger to test flying, having been almost continuously used for such work since its Ambassador prototype flight-test days. It had been used for the de Havilland Propeller Division's projects, and later to test the Proteus engine for the Bristol Britannia programme. Based at Hucknall, Rolls-Royce's own test airfield, the Ambassadors were to be flown by a team comprising both Rolls-Royce and senior BEA pilots as part of the development and evaluation programme. As well as providing much-needed extra pilot hours, this arrangement would enable the BEA pilots to gain invaluable experience of the Tyne before operating it in daily service when the Vanguards came into service.

The test programme was designed mostly to be flown in 3½hr sectors, to simulate the kind of services on which the engine would be used once it was powering Vanguards. After take-off an Ambassador was required to climb on full power to 5,000ft (1,500m), then climb at more conventional power settings to a height of 25,000–30,000ft (7,600–9,000m), where it would cruise for approximately an hour. This would be followed by 30min of low-level flying, usually 1,000ft (300m) above sea level, the aircraft then being taken back up to the cruising level for the remainder of the sortie. However, the test programme for the much more complex, two-stage Tyne would not proceed in as trouble-free a manner as the Dart certification had.

On one occasion a Rolls-Royce engineer, attempting to rectify a rough-running problem reported by the BEA pilot on start-up, managed to restart the engine without checking the correct supplementary throttle settings. Before the crew had a chance to do anything about the error, the engine promptly seized completely and ejected most of itself, in the form of white-hot molten metal, on to the ramp. A number of other less-serious, but still annoying, technical problems arose which were, after all, precisely what the test programme was designed to reveal. Nonetheless, the resulting delays in the engine certification threatened to disrupt Vanguard production.

At least the BEA crews were getting plenty of experience of single-engine flying as more problems presented themselves for correction, usually at the least-convenient moments. The crews also found themselves rewriting the manual regarding relighting the engines at altitude, which was proving to be an unpredictable process in itself. Weather delays in the UK in the early part of 1958 caused the whole programme to be decamped to benefit from the more reliable Mediterranean sun of Malta during April and May, in the hope of making up some of the lost flying time. One by one, the Rolls-Royce engineers and designers tackled the Tyne's quirks and problems. The aircraft and crews returned to the UK in June, and eventually, thanks to a fine summer, the prototype Tynes finally reached their 1,600hr target and the engine was certificated for normal use.

The second Airspeed Ambassador prototype, G-AKRD, was equipped with Tynes for the engine's intensive development programme for Rolls Royce. Jenny Gradidge

One notable improvement over the Viscount was the addition of a very powerful 28V DC electrical system. This had sufficient capacity to allow the aircraft to be totally self-reliant for start-up power at airfields lacking their own external starter equipment. The Vanguard also boasted a much more spacious flight deck than the rather claustrophobic one on Viscount, and could be arranged to be operated by two- or three-pilot crews. The flying controls were manually operated, with aerodynamic balancing.

Getting the Vanguard into the Air

The prototype V.950 Vanguard, G-AOYW, was rolled out at Wisley on 4 December 1958 and began a series of engine runs. Unfortunately, in the course of one of these runs two bearings seized on one of the four Tynes, causing a rather dramatic catastrophic failure. As a precaution, all four engines were returned to Rolls-Royce for detailed investigations, leaving G-AOYW stranded and engineless at Wisley. Much more importantly, the maiden flight was delayed for vital weeks.

Rolls-Royce eventually pronounced that a blocked oil line had caused the double bearing failure in the rogue Tyne engine. Soon G-AOYW was again fitted with four engines, and the ground-running trials were resumed. These proceeded without further serious incident and, on 20 January 1959, Vickers senior test pilots Jock Bryce and Brian Trubshaw made their preparations for the Vanguard's first flight.

The Weybridge runway was only 3,600ft (1,100m) long, which was rather short for an aircraft as large as the Vanguard. Bryce

The first landing of the Vanguard prototype, G-AOYW, was made at Wisley after its well-satisfied pilots had extended the initial maiden flight. Author's collection

and Trubshaw had to plan to take on the minimum fuel load for the brief flight to the Vickers test airfield at Wisley, just under 3min flying time away. With no other crew members, engineering or flight-test staff carried, a comparatively light all-up weight of 95,000lb (43,100kg) was achieved. A high-speed taxi was also undertaken, proceeding directly on to the runway once clearance was given, so that take-off speed would be reached as soon as possible. At about 16.00hr, before a large crowd of Vickers workers, G-AOYW became airborne for the first time.

Following the historic first flight, G-AOYW embarked on a programme of test and development flights. Author's collection

Specification – V.950

Powerplant:	4 × R.Ty.1/506 Tyne
Weights:	Empty basic equipment weight 86,800lb (39,400kg); maximum zero fuel weight 122,500lb (55,600kg); maximum take-off weight 146,500lb (66,500kg); maximum landing weight 130,500lb (59,235kg); typical maximum payload 37,000lb (16,790kg).
Dimensions:	Length 122ft 10½in (37.45m); span 118ft 0in (35.90m); fin height 34ft 11in (10.64m); wing area 1,529sq ft (142.04sq m); wheelbase 40ft 6¼in (12.35m).
Performance:	Economic cruising speed 420mph (675km/h); maximum cruising speed 425mph (685km/h); service ceiling 30,000ft (9,150m); range with maximum payload 1,350 statute miles (2,170km).
Average passenger accommodation:	97–139 (all first class – high density)

The first production model Vanguard, G-APEA, made its first flights wearing the classic BEA colours, and also originally had the early tail configuration. via author

The original plan, simply to position the aircraft directly to Wisley, was quietly forgotten as Bryce soon gained a feel for the Vanguard in the air. A tendency for the throttles to 'creep back' was noticed, but Trubshaw was easily able to monitor this. Bryce decided to extend the 'ferry flight', with 'YW remaining airborne for about 20min. When the aircraft finally began its descent into Wisley some buffeting was noticed when the flaps were deployed. Moreover, when reverse pitch was applied on landing, the ailerons thrashed about fairly violently and Bryce had great difficulty in keeping them under control. These were regarded as minor problems that could easily be fixed during the flight-test programme and, to add a touch of first flight bravado, Bryce and Trubshaw taxied the aircraft in reverse down the runway for a short distance after landing, to get back to a taxiway turn-off.

Building up the Hours

The prototype soon started the daily round of development and test flights required for the Vanguard to be certificated for airline use. By 28 January a grand total of 10hr 45min had been accumulated on eight sorties. Problems with the Vanguard's stalling characteristics took up a lot of the development team's time. A variety of combinations of spoiler strips, wing fences and vortex generators were tried to overcome what could be rather violent rolling, and even inversion, at the stall. Over 2,000 stalls were induced on 'YW, mostly in the expert hands of Brian Trubshaw, before the right combination of modifications was found. Engine noise and vibration levels in the passenger cabin proved to be a major problem, the powerful Tynes making their presence much more felt than the Darts on the Viscount. Although steps were taken to rectify this, the Vanguard never attained the standards of the earlier Viscount in this respect. On the plus side, high-speed handling proved to be excellent and, apart from the initial stalling problems, the Vanguard proved to be a stable and easy aircraft to handle for its size.

The first of the production V.951s, G-APEA, joined the sole V.950 in the test programme following its own maiden flight on 22 April 1959. The second production Vanguard, G-APEB, first flew on 23 July and also joined the trials at Wisley. Although 'EA was finished in the traditional red and white BEA livery of the

1950s, its lower fuselage was painted grey instead of being the usual natural metal. In contrast, 'EB was rolled out resplendent in the airline's brand-new 'Red Square' image, which was being introduced at the time. The Vanguards were assigned individual names, continuing the usual tradition of BEA. The flagship, 'EA, was named *Vanguard* and the other aircraft were given names of famous British naval ships, such as *Bellerophon*, *Ajax*, *Leander*, *Valiant* and *Swiftsure*. Sadly, the glossy new livery did not make allowance for painting the names on the outside of the aircraft. Instead, they were featured inside, in the passenger cabin.

On 6 March G-APEA flew to Hamburg for BEA, then on 3 June it went to Brussels for demonstration to Sabena, the Belgian national carrier. The next day the aircraft was similarly shown to Alitalia in Rome, and was also flown to Paris. On all these demonstration services the aircraft set up new speed/distance records. In July, wearing Vickers Vanguard titles applied in place of BEA's, 'EA was despatched to Canada, where TCA was finally able to see its new type. Later transatlantic crossings saw G-APEA getting as far south as the Caribbean, with demonstration flights to BWIA in Bermuda and Trinidad, although these were slightly marred by engine problems caused by contaminated fuel.

Tropical Trials

From October to December G-APEB was in Africa, completing a series of tropical trials to examine the Vanguard's characteristics at 'hot and high' airfields. Under the command of Brian Trubshaw and fellow test pilot Richard Rymer, with Vickers flight test manager Joe Leach and a staff of Vickers technical and sales personnel on board, 'EB was initially flown to Khartoum, with a technical stop at Rome. The Vanguard remained in the Sudan, completing a series of trials, for ten days, then carried the team south to Johannesburg for a 38-day stay.

The trials were mainly focused on measuring take-off and landing distances and climb rates, and developing handling techniques under the harsher conditions. A number of demonstration flights were also made to prospective customers wherever the aircraft stopped en route. Given the history of tropical trial mishaps with the Viscounts, with the losses of both G-AHRF and G-AOYF during their own trials in Africa, no doubt there was some

After gaining Vickers Vanguard titles, G-APEA was used for a number of demonstration flights to potential customers. Author's collection

BELOW: The visit of G-APEA to Canada aroused a great deal of interest from TCA staff and crews anxious to examine the company's latest purchase for its fleet. Author's collection

ABOVE: The early Vanguards carried BEA's new black-and-red colours far from the airline's European territory while on the manufacturer's development, demonstration and certification flights. via Jon Proctor

LEFT: While the production aircraft ranged worldwide, G-AOYW tended to remain closer to home for its own development flights. Vickers via author

trepidation among the Vickers teams on the tour. Happily 'EB broke the jinx, the only serious incident occurring at Johannesburg, when all the tyres burst during a heavy landing. This caused a certain amount of damage to the hydraulic pipes in the undercarriage and the undercarriage doors. The aircraft was consequently grounded for several days while the necessary spares were flown out to South Africa.

At the end of the South Africa-based trials, G-APEB left Johannesburg on 6 December and headed north for Salisbury, Rhodesia. During the next day, two test flights and a demonstration flight for Central African Airways were carried out. On 8 December the aircraft was flown to Nairobi to complete one more demonstration and three test flights over the next two days. The Vanguard flew to Cairo via Khartoum on 11 December, and made three more demonstration flights before continuing on to Beirut the same evening to end a busy day.

On 12 December the second of three planned demonstration flights from Beirut brought more drama when the port undercarriage refused to lower. For nearly an hour Trubshaw and Rymer tried several unconventional methods to free the leg, including pulling the aircraft up sharply to try and dislodge it. In the end Trubshaw had to go into the cabin and lift floorboards, in view of the commercially important clientele, and try to lower it by pulling on various cables and rods! He was eventually successful, and 'EB landed safely. The cause was traced to a bolt that had worked loose and jammed the undercarriage door. Applying a smooth lining material to the doors solved the problem, and the Vanguard's return trip to Wisley, via Nice and Gatwick, was uneventful.

Proving Flight Problems

Two more early production V.951s, G-APEC and 'ED, joined the Wisley flight-test programme after they completed their own initial post-production flights in October and December 1959, respectively. A transatlantic trip was made by G-APED to give further demonstrations to BWIA, including a number of short inter-island services to show the Vanguard's suitability for the Caribbean airline's network. At this time BEA senior training captains were given instruction on the aircraft by Vickers at Weybridge and Wisley, and at Roll-Royce's factory in Derby. From February 1960 BEA began using some of the available flying hours for crew training and a handful of route-proving flights.

The route-proving programme increased significantly in March, when G-APED was used by BEA for a more intensive

The first TCA V.952, CF-TKA, took to the air for the first time in May 1960. via author

simulated schedule to test the aircraft's performance under normal airline conditions. These mostly took place over the Paris and Brussels routes from London, and the early results were so promising that BEA confidently began to plan for full service introduction in time for the beginning of that summer's peak traffic period, on 1 July. The route-proving flights also began to reach further afield, with trial services to Athens, Benghazi, Dusseldorf, Gibraltar, Malta, Nicosia, Stockholm and Zurich, the destinations being chosen to provide a wide variety of operating and weather conditions. For these flights the aircraft was furnished in a 100-passenger configuration with a mixture of 2-3 and 3-3 seating. On 21 May CF-TKA, the first V.952 for TCA, made the short hop from Weybridge to Wisley on its maiden flight. On the same day, TCA announced it was increasing its order by three, to a total of twenty-three Vanguards.

Unexpected and potentially serious problems with the Tyne engines caused a temporary halt in the certification and customer crew training programmes. Author's collection

Then, just when everything seemed to be going so well, the Vanguard programme suddenly encountered significant problems. Within weeks of the planned inauguration of scheduled flights, during a proving flight to Athens, one Tyne suffered a dramatic failure. Some of its turbine blades were blown out through the engine cowling. A handful of similar enforced shutdowns of Tynes on the other flying Vanguards had already been experienced. Only a few days earlier one had been shut down in flight on a Beirut–Athens sector, as an aircraft was returning from a demonstration to Iraqi Airways in Baghdad. All route-proving and training flights were immediately halted by BEA and Vickers until the cause of the failures could be determined.

During the ensuing bench tests another Tyne suffered a near-identical failure, and it was not too long before Rolls-Royce identified the source of the problem as an incorrectly applied heat treatment on the forgings in the compressor discs during production. However, this was discovered too late to save BEA's planned July entry into service, and the slowly growing number of completed aircraft remained grounded until modified Tynes were made available to enable the delayed certification programme to continue.

The Vanguard's Return

By October 1960 modified Tynes were finally available to be installed in V.950 G-AOYW and V.951 G-APED, and the flight-test programme resumed in earnest at Wisley. New engines were also fitted to G-APEE within the month and, more than 200 flying hours later, on 2 December, the Vanguard was finally awarded its full C of A. Immediately, 'EE was positioned to Stansted Airport, where BEA's Vanguard crews were given a refresher course. Both BEA and TCA also made considerable use of newly delivered simulators to speed conversion and refresher training. Soon, G-APEF joined 'EE at Stansted to complete the refresher training and, once enough BEA Vanguard crews had been licensed, G-APEF inaugurated the long-awaited Vanguard service with a Heathrow–Paris flight on 17 December.

Viscounts to the Rescue

The loss of the Vanguard's capacity was a major blow to BEA's plans for the summer season of 1960. A big sales drive had been in full swing since the beginning of the year, successfully selling a large number of the promised Vanguard seats. Much of the busy sales effort had been directed at the new, heavily promoted, off-peak, low-fare services to which the Vanguard would have been ideally suited, with its ability to carry large passenger volumes economically. Plans had been made for no fewer than seven daily Vanguard flights over the popular London–Paris route alone, but providing an equivalent number of Viscount seats called for up to twelve rotations with the smaller aircraft. In an attempt to cover the shortfall, BEA indulged in some serious juggling of its available aircraft, especially the Viscounts.

Fred Olsen's V.779, G-APZP, was one of several aircraft drafted in to fill the gaps in the schedules left by the undelivered Vanguards. Jenny Gradidge

A number of Viscounts that had been operating scheduled freight services were quickly returned to passenger configuration to take up some of the capacity shortage. To replace these aircraft on some of the cargo flights, BEA chartered ageing Avro York freighters from Dan-Air Services Ltd of Gatwick. Dan-Air was also contracted to operate its fleet of Ambassadors (ironically all ex-BEA Elizabethan fleet aircraft) on many of BEA's scheduled London–Jersey passenger services.

Two more Viscounts, both V.779s, were leased from Fred Olsen Air Transport again, repeating the similar arrangement of 1955–57. The two aircraft, LN-FOH and LN-FOM, re-registered G-APZP and G-ARBW, differed sufficiently from the rest of BEA's Viscount fleet regarding equipment and flight-deck layout to make it awkward to schedule the regular Viscount crews without expensive re-training and conversion. A solution was found in confining the leased aircraft to the London–Paris route and simply converting the now idle Vanguard-trained crews to operate the two aircraft during their spell with BEA.

Despite the delays, Vickers was still able to deliver the first production TCA Vanguards in time for their scheduled inaugural services in February 1961. via Jon Proctor

On 19 December 'EE entered scheduled service with a Heathrow–Zurich flight, followed by a Heathrow–Geneva service that afternoon. The aircraft then remained at Geneva until 22 December before positioning empty to Dusseldorf and operating a scheduled passenger service from there to Heathrow. The first UK domestic Vanguard service was operated by 'EF over the Heathrow–Glasgow route on 20 December. On these initial flights the two Vanguards were substituted for Viscounts over the busy Christmas period. This *ad hoc* use of the Vanguards continued over the festive season, the aircraft being put into service in their own right on 22 February 1961, again on the London–Paris route.

Canada Bound

The Vanguard delivery schedule to TCA had been less critically disrupted by the aircraft's temporary groundings due to the Tyne's problems. The Canadian airline's own time-scale had called for a 1 February 1961 entry into service, and the first delivery from Vickers, V.952 CF-TKD, was able to be completed on 7 December 1960, once new engines were available. Among the crew operating the delivery flight was Capt George Lothian, TCA's superintendent of flying, the first TCA pilot to have been licensed to fly the Viscount, and Richard Rymer of Vickers, the world's first commercial pilot to be certificated on the V.630 Viscount.

Until 'KD had been delivered to Montreal, TCA had been sending crews to Wisley for Vanguard conversion training. This training could now be continued in Canada, and a concentrated programme of refresher courses for TCA's Vanguard crews provided enough personnel for a series of proving and demonstration flights. The TCA Vanguards were approved for two-pilot operation in Canada. Conversion training comprised a month at ground school, 25hr on the simulator and a further 15hr flight training. The initial crew training was completed successfully, leading to full scheduled service entry for the Vanguard on 1 February as planned. The demonstration flights also allowed TCA ground crews to familiarize themselves with the aircraft as it would be operated in daily service. On one occasion during the demonstration tours, at Toronto, a full load of ninety-six passengers was disembarked and another full load of ninety-six boarded in a highly creditable seven minutes!

TCA passengers were able to enjoy scheduled Vanguard service a full three weeks before BEA's.
Air Canada via Bill Mellberg

By 1 February four Vanguards, CF-TKC, 'TD, 'TF and 'TG, had been already been delivered to TCA, and a fifth, 'TE, was about to make its transatlantic delivery flight from Wisley to Montreal. The two inaugural TCA scheduled Vanguard V.952 flights were operated on the transcontinental multi-stop services, from Montreal to Vancouver via Toronto, Winnipeg, Regina and Calgary, and from Toronto to Vancouver via Winnipeg, Saskatoon and Edmonton, and were flown by CF-TKD and CF-TKC respectively.

The Canadian carrier had actually beaten BEA into placing the aircraft into scheduled service, as opposed to *ad hoc* and substitute services, by a full three weeks. As more Vanguards made their way to Canada the aircraft were placed in service on more services throughout the country, and also on the busier cross-border flights to the USA. In April the Vanguards made their first scheduled appearances on TCA's popular tourist routes from eastern Canada to Bermuda, the Bahamas and other island resorts in the Caribbean.

The economy of the high-capacity Vanguards allowed TCA to introduce 35 per cent fare reductions on these routes, which greatly boosted traffic. The arrival of the Vanguards also saw the final demise of the increasingly unpopular piston-powered Canadair North Stars, the last of which was withdrawn from TCA service on 30 April 1961.

The BEA V.951s and V.953s were given different configurations, only the original six V.951s, G-APEA to G-APEF inclusive, having first-class seating. The V.951s were equipped with thirty 2-2-abreast first-class seats in the rear cabin and eighty-nine 3-3-abreast economy-class seats in the forward areas. The later V.953s, benefiting from their increased permitted all-up weights, were configured

Viscount Prototypes Move On

The much-travelled Viscount 700 prototype, G-AMAV, made its final flights for Vickers in October 1960, and was placed in storage at Wisley. The aircraft still had a comparatively low number of flying hours, 2,160, but had been structurally modified so much that it was no longer economically feasible to convert it for resale. However, a productive use was later found for G-AMAV's fuselage, when it was employed on engine installation trials for the BAC One-Eleven short-haul jet airliner. The battered remains were finally donated to the Stansted Fire School in 1963.

The V.810 prototype, G-AOYV, was luckier. Following de-icing tests fitted with a scaled-down Vanguard tailplane, it was converted to a V.827 and sold to the Brazilian airline, Viacao Aerea Sao Paulo (VASP) as PP-SRH. VASP had already taken delivery of five V.827s in 1959 for use on its extensive domestic network. No fewer than sixty flights a week were scheduled by the airline over its busiest route, between Sao Paulo and Rio. One of the Viscounts was lost later that year in a tragic mid-air collision with a Brazilian Air Force North American AT-6. It was replaced by PP-SRH, delivered in October 1960.

The increasing use of the high-capacity Vanguards brought a welcome improvement in standards of comfort and service to the busier domestic routes. Author's collection

By mid-1961 both BEA and TCA were operating complementary fleets of Viscounts and Vanguards over their networks. Author's collection

in an all-economy 132-seat layout, all 3-3 abreast. The TCA V.952s were delivered with a forty-six-seat 2-2 first-class section in the rear cabins and fifty economy seats, still only 2-3 abreast, forward.

The two distinct BEA Vanguard configurations were each allocated to very different routes to suit the vagaries of particular marketing needs. The first-class accommodation on the V.951s was only required internationally on the flights to Paris; in fact only the first-class passengers received a meal or even bar service on this brief flight. However, these first production aircraft were otherwise mostly assigned to domestic flights to Belfast, Edinburgh and Glasgow, on which there was a high percentage of important business travellers expecting first-class service to be available. The all-economy-configured V.953s were also assigned to the Heathrow–Manchester domestic flights, as well as operating most of the remaining Vanguard routes.

Established Jet Competition

When the BEA and TCA Vanguards did finally begin scheduled service, the much-hyped arrival of widespread jet airline travel, on short- as well as long-haul services, had already taken place. BEA's new Vanguards were already facing direct competition from Air France's Caravelles on the route to Paris, these having been introduced into service in 1959. Thus the shiny new Vanguards arrived on an international airline scene where many passengers already regarded them as old-fashioned. Consequently they would have a struggle to prove themselves in a hostile environment, relying heavily on their much-vaunted economic abilities to make money where jets would struggle to survive.

CHAPTER SIX

Soldiering On

Towards the 1960s

Vickers had already decided to close its Vanguard order book after the last order for three extra aircraft from TCA. The sales tours and demonstrations had produced no more firm orders. High hopes of sales to Viscount customers such as Central African, BWIA, Iraqi Airways and Philippine Air Lines were frustrated by the airlines declining the bigger Vanguard as unsuitable for their networks, or preferring to await the new jets. The Viscount had continued to roll off the established production lines even as the Vanguard made its stuttering progress towards full commercial service. As the new decade approached, the world's original turboprop airliner still managed to find new followers among airliner operators around the globe. However, a number of potentially lucrative Viscount orders that appeared very promising had stumbled at the last hurdle.

Lost Orders

In addition to its V.805 contract, Eagle Aviation had ordered three more-powerful Dart 525-powered Viscount 821s for trooping and charter work within Europe, for delivery in the beginning of 1959. A contract was also negotiated with the Fred Olsen Line for the lease of two V.736s as an interim measure until the larger aircraft were delivered. The lease of the Fred Olsen aircraft would ensure that Eagle was equipped to inaugurate a substantial trooping contract from the Air Ministry, for which the airline was negotiating. This would have provided most of the work for the new aircraft, but Eagle was unsuccessful and the new trooping contract was never signed. The financial package to purchase the aircraft was dependent on the trooping flights guaranteeing a certain amount of revenue and, as this could no longer be relied on, Vickers reluctantly agreed to the cancellation of the order on 19 July 1957.

What would have been an important export order for Dart 525-powered Viscounts was cancelled the following year. Oakland-based California Eastern Airways (CEA) operated a large fleet of DC-4s and Lockheed Super Constellations on supplemental and contract charter services, mostly for the US military. In November 1956, in an attempted change of direction, CEA applied to operate full scheduled services. Two routes were proposed, from Dallas to Los Angeles or San Francisco, authority for both direct and multi-stop flights being applied for.

The airline had been impressed by the Lockheed Electra turboprop, but had been unable to secure sufficiently early delivery positions. To satisfy the authorities that it was fit to operate the new routes, CEA was required to have suitable aircraft available to operate the service in 1958. After a visit

Cubana's Viscount 818, CU-T622, was delivered in August 1959, by which time the Viscount production line was starting to slow down. via author

to Weybridge a letter of intent was lodged with Vickers by CEA's management on 19 November 1956, covering possible orders for up to eleven Viscounts. This was to include possible orders for an unspecified number of the V.840 version. In 1957 the letter of intent was converted to a contract for confirmed orders for eight V.823s for 1958 delivery. The licensing hearings dragged on until early 1958, though it did look as though CEA would be successful. However, on 7 April 1958 the recommendation surprisingly went against CEA and the routes were awarded to Continental Airlines. Legal appeals were unsuccessful, and CEA was forced to write to Vickers on 11 August, explaining it had no choice but to cancel the order.

Atlantic Adventures

Even as the airlines of the world were busy throwing the glamorous new jets into service as quick as the manufacturers could deliver them, the Viscount was still finding useful niches. The two Eagle Airways Viscount 805s were instrumental in pioneering whole new markets on both sides of the Atlantic for their owner.

Despite the disappointing loss of the V.821 trooping contract, Eagle's first Dart 510-powered V.805, G-APDW *Enterprise*, was still delivered in late 1957, resplendent in a stylish new maroon and grey livery. It was operated both on scheduled and charter services for the first few months of 1958, from Eagle's main base at Blackbushe. The arrival of the second Viscount, G-APDX *Good Fortune*, heralded the departure of the first aircraft across the Atlantic to Bermuda.

Now reregistered VR-BAX, this Viscount was to work for a newly established Eagle subsidiary, Eagle Airways (Bermuda). Eagle's founder and chairman, Harold Bamberg, had realized that there was an opening for flights to Bermuda, where the now jointly operated BOAC/BWIA service was evidently not properly exploiting the potential market. On 2 June 1958 VR-BAX opened the new daily Eagle Airways (Bermuda) scheduled service from Bermuda to New York. The Eagle Viscount flight was up against not only the combined might of BOAC/BWIA but also Eastern Airlines and Pan American. Nonetheless, the new Eagle flight still proved very popular, attracting nearly 10,000 passengers in 1958.

The UK company's second Viscount remained in the UK and was used for a network of tourist-class scheduled services to Belgium, Germany and Scandinavia being built up from the northern city of Manchester. Although regulations still heavily favoured BEA and BOAC, the situation had greatly eased for independent airlines developing their own networks of scheduled services. Bamberg was very keen to see the Eagle group expand into more scheduled markets, and sought every opportunity to do so. In Eagle's case these were to be flown by the UK-based Viscount from both Blackbushe and Manchester, alongside Eagle's already established fleet of Vikings. The Vikings were also operated on a handful of scheduled services from Heathrow. In addition, the Viscount operated from the midlands to Spain on a weekly Birmingham–Palma tourist service.

A fleet of DC-6As had been acquired for operation on worldwide charter services. Bamberg wanted to deploy them on low-fare schedules from the UK similar to the Hunting-Clan/Airwork African flights but operating, instead, over the Atlantic to Bermuda and the Caribbean, and ultimately to the USA, as well as eastwards to Singapore and Hong Kong. Eagle applied for licences for a number of such services, and also campaigned vigorously for the establishment of a 'VLF' (very low fare) class of low-frequency, long-range services in competition with BOAC. The opposition to the plans from BOAC was sufficient to see the concept blocked for the time being, but Eagle's busy DC-6As did operate a number of charter flights to Bermuda and the Caribbean, which helped further strengthen the company's presence and general influence in the region.

Although Eagle's new Bermuda-based services to New York were proving a great success, the passenger figures for the European schedules were much less encouraging. At the beginning of 1959 Viscount G-APDX was re-registered VR-BAY and sent out to join 'AX in Bermuda. The European services were drastically cut back and the surviving flights reverted to Viking

After only a few months of European operations, G-APDW became VR-BAX in preparation for the inaugural Bermuda-based schedules. via author

The airline's second Viscount 805, G-APDX, was used alongside Eagle's numerous Vikings during 1958. Jenny Gradidge

operation. In contrast, the two Viscounts embarked on a major expansion of the Bermuda operation, new services opening to Baltimore, Montreal and Nassau. The Nassau service was soon extended to Miami under the name of yet another new Eagle company, Eagle Airways (Bahamas) Ltd, on whose behalf the Bermuda-based aircraft operated over the new route.

G-APDX became VR-BAY for the Eagle (Bermuda) operation and was a regular visitor to US and Canadian cities on the popular island routes. via author

Far-Ranging Viscounts

The long-standing partnership arrangement between BEA and Cyprus Airways was taken a step further from January 1958, when the British carrier took over all of the Cyprus airline's operations, two Viscounts under charter replacing the increasingly uncompetitive DC-3s. Cyprus Airways had considered ordering its own small fleet of Viscounts from Vickers, but decided in favour of expanding the charter arrangement on economic grounds. Still in full BEA livery, they were rotated regularly with the BEA UK-based fleet when they returned for scheduled maintenance at Heathrow. The Nicosia-based Viscounts took the BEA flag much further east than before, being operated on Cyprus Airways services to Bahrain, Doha, Kuwait and Tel Aviv from Nicosia, as well as on the established routes in the region and the joint BEA/Cyprus route to London.

January 1958 also saw Turkish Airlines (THY) place the first of its 48-passenger Viscount 700s, one V.754D and four V.794Ds, into service. The new aircraft greatly expanded the airline's presence in the area, THY having operated mostly on domestic and regional flights with a fleet of DC-3s until the Viscounts arrived. As well as connecting the larger Turkish cities on domestic flights and linking Istanbul and Ankara to regional points such as Adana, Beirut and Nicosia, the Viscounts inaugurated new longer-ranging services into Western Europe. The Magic Carpet Route, as it was marketed, operated from Ankara via Istanbul, Vienna and Frankfurt to London three times a week. The Viscounts also flew another Frankfurt service, from Ankara via Istanbul, Athens and Rome.

The use of the Viscount on the longer services from Turkey to points such as London and Frankfurt saw THY joining Iraqi Airways, MEA and Misrair in using the turboprops on important longer routes where they were competing against much larger aircraft. Misrair actively expanded its Viscount fleet, purchasing two second-hand V.754Ds from HCAT in July 1959 and taking delivery of a new V.739B, SU-AKW, the airline's eighth, in April 1960. Later that year Misrair was merged with Syrian Arab Airlines and renamed United Arab Airlines.

THY Turkish Airlines used its Viscounts to expand its operation with far-ranging new routes, encompassing both Europe and the Middle East. THY Turkish Airlines

Under African Skies

A new long multi-stop Viscount service between Africa and Europe was inaugurated in June 1959, when Airwork Ltd began operating one of its newly delivered V.831s on behalf of Sudan Airways on the Blue Nile route from Khartoum to London via Cairo, Athens and Rome. Registered in the Sudan as ST-AAN, the Viscount was flown by Airwork crews and the service was Sudan Airways' first major international route. Airwork itself had been operating its first two V.831s on the Safari Service to Africa, alongside HCAT, since the beginning of that year.

The end of 1958 and beginning of 1959 also saw the entry into service of South African Airways' (SAA) fleet of seven V.813s. Initially operated in a 52-passenger configuration, the aircraft were originally placed into service on Johannesburg–Cape Town and Johannesburg–Salisbury routes. They replaced DC-4s and Constellations on first-class services, the older aircraft being reconfigured in all-tourist-class layouts and reassigned to low-fare flights. As the turboprop fleet was delivered, the Viscounts were soon deployed on most of the major domestic services within South Africa, as well as some of the more important regional routes to neighbouring countries and territories. Within seven months of their introduction a loss of £35,600 on the domestic routes had been turned round to a £138,219 profit.

Ghana Airways began operations in late 1958, shortly after the country gained independence from the UK in 1957. The airline was established in partnership with BOAC, replacing the Ghanaian portion of the West African Airways Corporation (WAAC), which had previously operated airline services for Ghana and Nigeria. The new airline's own small fleet comprised a pair of DC-3s and a pair of de Havilland Herons, flown on local routes. As it had previously done for WAAC, BOAC supplied leased aircraft, originally Boeing Stratocruisers and later Britannias, from its long-haul fleet for international flights to Europe and the UK.

A major long-term expansion plan saw an order placed for three Viscount 838s in April 1960. The Viscount order was only part of the 'master plan', later orders also being placed for ambitiously large, not to mention uneconomic, fleets of Russian-built Antonov An-12 and Ilyushin Il-18

ABOVE: The Blue Nile scheduled service from Khartoum to Europe was operated on behalf of Sudan Airways by an Airwork V.831, re-registered in the Sudan especially for the new venture. Jenny Gradidge

BELOW: The use of Viscounts enabled South African Airways to bring its domestic and regional operations back into profit. via SAA

turboprops, and Vickers VC10 jets. Delivered in the autumn of 1961, the Viscounts were operated on important local services from the capital, Accra, both within Ghana and on routes throughout the West African coastal region.

Joining Forces and Moving Home

Airwork's busy Viscounts were rapidly becoming the company's only active airliner fleet members. After their replacement by Viscounts on the Safari schedules, the Vikings were progressively withdrawn from charter work owing to their advancing age and increasing lack of commercial credibility. Airwork's fleet of equally ageing Handley Page Hermes 4s was disposed of after the company lost valuable trooping contracts to the Far East, which had been the fleet's main source of income. A worthy attempt to develop a scheduled all-cargo network, including transatlantic routes, had proved an expensive failure, and the increasingly beleaguered airline was having trouble finding a new direction.

Airwork had already become a major shareholder in Transair, and the day-to-day operation of the Airwork Viscount fleet was increasingly transferred to the subsidiary. Transair finally completed its long-awaited move to Gatwick Airport when the rebuilt airport was opened in 1958. One of Transair's Viscounts, inbound on a trooping flight from Gibraltar, was the first commercial aircraft to land after the reopening. The airline had spent £250,000 on building a new administration and maintenance centre at Gatwick. The new complex included a hangar capable of taking up to three aircraft and equipped with a special Viscount maintenance dock, with retracting 'pits' that could lower the aircraft to enable it to be worked on without the need for ladders, steps or platforms.

The Transair/Airwork Viscounts were soon returning average annual utilization figures in the region of 2,500hr per aircraft. As well as operating the trooping flights and the Safari Service, the aircraft were also increasingly used on inclusive-tour charters to holiday resorts. In addition to its Viscounts, Transair continued to operate a substantial fleet of DC-3s on scheduled services to the Channel Islands, a busy network of contract newspaper charters, and its own programme of inclusive-tour and *ad hoc* charters.

While older members of the Airwork fleet were being retired and disposed of, the new Viscounts were kept busy on the Safari services to Africa. Jenny Gradidge

The HCAT Viscount fleet, now reduced to the three newer V.831s following the sale of the surviving pair of Viscount 732s to Misrair, was engaged on trooping flights around Europe and to the Mediterranean, as well as on the East and West African scheduled services. The other V.732, G-ANRR, had been written-off in a tragic fatal crash during a test flight on 2 December 1959, following scheduled maintenance. All five occupants were killed when the aircraft came down near Frimley in Surrey, the cause being traced to incorrect assembly of the elevator spring tab mechanism during the aircraft's recent major check. However, the inclusive-tour charter was also starting to feature in HCAT's Viscount programme, the V.831s operating flights to many Mediterranean resorts from both Heathrow and Manchester.

Hunting-Clan still operated a handful of remaining Vikings on charter work, and was flying a pair of DC-6As on both passenger and cargo work, the latter including a scheduled Africargo all-freight service to East Africa. On several occasions the DC-6As were substituted for Viscounts on the Safari Service. Although the big Douglas was quite capable of operating the route in longer stage-lengths, all the scheduled Viscount en route stops were made on these flights.

Bristol Britannias were delivered to HCAT in 1959 for trooping and other charter contracts, as well as for possible future use on the Safari Service. They were also operated briefly for CAA, replacing that carrier's Viscounts on the Zambezi route from London to Salisbury, many of the previous refuelling stops now being dropped in favour of a quicker journey. At the end of this contract CAA replaced the HCAT aircraft with aircraft leased from BOAC, initially more Britannias and later Comet 4 jets, and the CAA Viscounts were confined to regional services within Africa.

The successful rationalization of the Airwork group's Viscount operations eventually led to moves being made to merge Transair and Airwork with HCAT, with which Airwork had been so successfully co-operating for some years. As well as Transair, Airwork had also acquired control of independent operators Air Charter, Morton Air Services and Bristow Helicopters. Air Charter operated worldwide trooping and *ad hoc* charter flights from Stansted Airport with DC-4s and Britannias, and also flew scheduled cross-Channel car ferry services from Southend under the name of Channel Air Bridge, using Bristol Freighters and Aviation Traders Carvairs. Morton flew scheduled and charter services to Europe and the Channel Islands from Croydon, later moving to Gatwick, and Bristow was involved in a worldwide operation of helicopter contract charters.

Encouraged by the government, which was becoming keen to see a stronger independent airline industry and establish a viable 'second force' UK competitor to BEA and BOAC, the three airlines finally came together in July 1960 under the new name of British United Airways (BUA), with an operational headquarters to be established at Gatwick. The aviation-based holdings of the major shareholders were eventually

The HCAT Viscount fleet was used on an increasing amount of charter work, both military and civil, in addition to the Safari services. via Bob Turner

brought together under a new company, Air Holdings Ltd. The chairman and founder of Air Charter, Freddie Laker, was appointed managing director of the new airline operation, which comprised the air transport interests of Airwork Ltd, HCAT and British & Commonwealth Shipping, which owned 50 per cent of HCAT.

As it transpired, it would take a few years for all the disparate parts of BUA to be brought together at Gatwick. The Air Charter and HCAT Britannias, and the DC-4s, continued to operate most of their trooping services from Stansted for some time, and the DC-6A cargo service to Africa continued to operate from Heathrow. Morton Air Services continued operating its own fleet of de Havilland Doves and Herons separately under its original name for some years, though some of its busier Gatwick scheduled routes were to be transferred to BUA. The specialized cross-Channel car ferry service continued to be operated separately by Channel Air Bridge from Southend with Bristol Freighters and Carvairs. In contrast, however, the new airline's Viscounts were soon gathered at the new base at the Surrey airport, the last of the ex-HCAT aircraft moving over from Heathrow by the autumn to join the Transair/Airwork fleets.

Route Switch

Upon the new airline's formation, the resulting BUA Viscount fleet comprised two V.736s and three V.804s from Transair, two V.831s originally delivered to Airwork and the three ex-HCAT V.833s, plus the single Airwork V.831 operated on behalf of Sudan Airways. The BUA Viscounts continued to operate the schedules to Africa and an increasing number of European destinations, as well as numerous trooping and inclusive-tour charters to the Mediterranean area. In addition to BUA's own Safari services, extra flights were now operated in association with BOAC, CAA and East African Airways, jointly marketed as the low-frequency/low-fare Skycoach service. The Viscounts, Britannias and DC-6As flew a number of the BUA-operated Skycoach services from Heathrow, as well as from Gatwick.

The low-cost schedules to Africa continued to grow in popularity. After twelve months under the new BUA management they were returning loads sufficiently high to justify the use of the larger Britannia, which took over the flights from Gatwick from 2 October 1961. The displaced Viscounts were immediately redeployed on a large trooping contract BUA had been awarded, to carry 11,000 military personnel and their families per month from both Gatwick and Manchester to bases in West Germany. The most frequently served bases included Dusseldorf, Frankfurt, Gutersloh, Hanover and Wildenrath.

More BEA Associates

In addition to the Cyprus Airways charter arrangement, BEA had a similar agreement with another associate, Gibraltar Airways, more usually known as Gibair. For some years BEA had supplied one of its DC-3 Pionairs to operate Gibair's scheduled services from Gibraltar to Tangier and Madrid. From 1958 the DC-3 was replaced by a BEA Viscount, still in full BEA livery as with the Cyprus lease. Viscounts 802s were also operated by BEA on behalf of Portuguese national airline TAP on a joint, thrice-weekly Lisbon–Heathrow service, one of which called at Oporto en route. The aircraft were flown by BEA crews and carried small TAP stickers by the passenger doors. A shareholder in the Malta Airline, BEA had provided aircraft for all of its services, which connected Malta with North Africa,

The BEA Viscounts were often equipped with suitable stickers over their basic livery when operating on lease on behalf of Malta Airline on its Mediterranean network. Jenny Gradidge

as far as Cairo, and with Italy, for some years. The Viscounts followed on from earlier Vikings and Elizabethans on the joint services, which were operated by aircraft totally in BEA livery, though Malta Airline stickers were frequently applied.

British European Airways had also been a shareholder in Alitalia (full name Aerolinee Italiene Internazionali) since 1946, when valuable technical assistance was provided to help establish the new post-war Italian carrier. Originally two major airlines were established in Italy. Linee Aeree Italiane (LAI), in which US carrier TWA held an interest, operated a number of European services and routes to the USA. Alitalia, too, operated within Europe, but also to South America, and both airlines operated from Italy to the Middle East.

Two batches of Viscount 785Ds were ordered by LAI to supplement its Convairs and DC-6Bs. The first order, for six aircraft, was placed in May 1956, and was followed by a second, for four, in January 1957. Shortly after the first six were delivered to LAI the two airlines were merged in an attempt to stem mounting losses and rationalize the Italian airline system.

The combined carrier took on the name of Alitalia, in whose colours the last four aircraft of the LAI order were delivered, and was soon operating the Viscounts on many

The Gatwick Experiment

BEA had also been present when the rebuilt Gatwick opened for business. To relieve increasing congestion, BEA decided to transfer the operation of most of the Heathrow–Jersey and all the Heathrow–Guernsey flights to Gatwick.

Being further south, and thereby closer to the Channel Islands, as well as enjoying the benefit of a high-speed train link direct to central London, the new airport was very suitable for the island flights. Douglas DC-3 Pionairs flew all the Guernsey services, and a mixture of Pionairs and Viscounts operated to Jersey.

Several aircraft of the BEA fleet were on hand when the airport was officially opened by HM Queen Elizabeth II on 9 June 1958, and the corporation confidently made plans to transfer more continental and domestic schedules to Gatwick in due course. In 1959 two new Viscount services were opened from Gatwick, to Dinard in northern France and to Hanover via Cologne. Although the seasonal route to Dinard continued to be operated from Gatwick until 1963, the Gatwick–Cologne–Hanover service failed to attract profitable loads and was dropped at the end of October 1959.

Unfortunately the move proved to be nothing like as popular as BEA had hoped. A number of influential voices in the Channel Islands were less than impressed by the apparent 'downgrading' of 'their' service to what was perceived as a less-prestigious airport. In those early days at Gatwick, connecting services, especially to domestic points, were almost nonexistent, and transfer passengers were obliged to make a laborious road journey between the two airports. Despite the BEA operations at Gatwick attracting a number of profitable handling contracts from visiting carriers, and providing a very useful emergency handling service when BEA and BOAC aircraft were diverted due to bad weather at Heathrow, the overall concept of transferring a number of flights to Gatwick was a commercial failure.

When load factors failed to come up to expectations, BEA became less enthusiastic about the use of Gatwick, and the operation was soon drastically reduced to a handful of Viscount services. via author

Gatwick was given another chance in the summer of 1961, with a daily service from Paris-Le Bourget, operated by a Viscount. The aircraft was actually a Birmingham-based aircraft, which operated a busy daily Birmingham–Glasgow–Birmingham–Le Bourget–Gatwick–Le Bourget–Birmingham–Glasgow–Birmingham schedule. Unfortunately the traffic loads to and from Gatwick were again disappointing and the service was not renewed after the summer season. Gradually BEA quietly transferred most of the European and Channel Island flights back to Heathrow by the end of 1961, though a single daily flight from and to Guernsey was to survive for many years as the airline's only scheduled flight from Gatwick.

routes from Milan and Rome to Barcelona, Brussels, Dusseldorf, Frankfurt, London, Madrid, Munich, Vienna and Zurich. In addition, night tourist flights were operated from Rimini and Venice to London several times a week in the summer, and the Viscounts were flying most of the major domestic services between Milan, Naples, Rome and Venice. The 'adopted' Alitalia Viscounts were so successful that ten more originally intended for Capital Airlines were purchased from Vickers at the end of 1960, shortly followed by two ex-Northeast Airlines V.798Ds.

Alitalia not only retained the LAI Viscounts, but also expanded its fleet with extra new and second-hand aircraft. Alitalia via author

BEA Modifications

Many of BEA's V.701s were modernized with some major adaptations from 1958 onwards. The changes were originally implemented to make the aircraft more suitable for use on the West Berlin-based German Internal Services. The aircrafts' flight decks were updated and converted for two-pilot operation, dispensing with the radio officer position, as had already been done on the later model V.802s and V.806s. The cabins were reconfigured to carry 60–63 passengers in lightweight seats, and the toilets, galleys and bar units were also rearranged and updated to more modern standards. Forward airstairs were fitted to speed up turn-rounds and, most noticeably, a new large oval cabin window was cut into the rear starboard fuselage to accommodate the extra passenger rows in the higher-density layout.

After proving themselves an operational success on the German routes, the modified V.701s were introduced on several UK regional and domestic services, including many of the Channel Island routes. From 1959 a number of the BEA V.802s were also operated in high-density configurations, with capacity increased from fifty-eight to sixty-six, or even as high as seventy-one if all but the most basic catering equipment was removed. These aircraft were operated on scheduled routes where new low-fare excursion and night-tourist rates had been introduced and had substantially increased demand. Although BEA was not yet operating whole-plane inclusive tour charters in the same way as the independent airlines, a great deal of the passenger capacity on many routes to Europe and the Mediterranean was already being sold to travel companies at inclusive tour rates for use on holiday packages.

The last new Viscount to be delivered to BEA, V.806 G-APOX *Isambard Brunel*, arrived on 11 April 1959. This was, in fact, the substantially rebuilt and reregistered V.806A development airframe that had been badly damaged at Johannesburg during flight trials. Its delivery made up a grand total of seventy production Viscounts to be purchased by the corporation from Vickers, plus the V.630 and V.700 prototypes, which had been operated by BEA 'on loan'. In addition, seven other Viscount 700s of various marks were leased in by BEA from other sources at different times between 1955 and 1961 to cover temporary shortfalls.

Following its Hong Kong Airways service, Viscount 760D 9M-ALY was also leased by Malayan Airways from BOAC, from 1959 to 1963. Jenny Gradidge

Viennese Overture

In much the same way that West Germany had been forbidden to operate its own airline services in the immediate post-war years, Austria had also been forced to rely on foreign carriers to link it to the world's commercial air networks. However, in 1957 permission was given for the country to establish its own air transport carriers. As a result, two fledgling airline companies were established as potential national airlines, Air Austria and Austrian Airways. Before any operations began, the two rivals were merged under the name of

The Wanderers

The ever-nomadic Viscount 700s owned by BOAC Associated Companies continued their travels throughout the late 1950s and early 1960s. Following their replacement by new V.772s, three of the four BWIA V.702s owned by BOAC Associated Companies were passed on for operation by another airline in which BOAC held shares, Kuwait Airways, during 1958/59. The fourth V.702 was retained by BWIA and continued to operate alongside the new V.772s. A V.776D was also leased in by Kuwait, in 1958. Originally built for Capital, but not delivered, the aircraft had been leased out to Aer Lingus from May–June 1958 as EI-AJW, then to BEA from July to August as G-APNF. It was then sold to British International Airlines for lease to the Kuwait Oil Company, and operated by Kuwait Airways.

British International was originally jointly owned by BOAC Associated Companies, BEA and HCAT, and was eventually fully merged with BOAC Associated Companies in a rationalization exercise. As well as operating on Kuwait's own service in the region, the aircraft were flown on joint services with Bahrain-based Gulf Air. The V.776D was later reregistered in Kuwait as 9K-ACD. Throughout their time on lease to Kuwait Airways the V.702s operated with British registrations, which they adopted on returning from the Caribbean, as G-APTA, G-APOW and G-APPX.

The HKA pair of BOAC Associated Companies aircraft were also on the move in 1959. Although the Viscounts had proved a great success on HKA routes, the tiny airline's route network was very restricted and, even with the high loads the Viscounts traditionally attracted, the company had great difficulty in making its restricted network earn any profits. There was very little prospect of this situation changing, and an agreement was reached whereby rival Hong Kong carrier Cathay Pacific Airways would take over the airline. Cathay was in the process of introducing new Lockheed Electra turboprops, and had no use for the Viscounts.

As BOAC also had an interest in Malayan Airways, which operated a large fleet of DC-3s, it transferred the Viscounts to Singapore to operate on the busier routes. Another of Malayan's shareholders, Qantas, supplied Constellations for operation over the airline's only longer route to Hong Kong. Initially one of the V.760Ds was registered in Singapore and the other in Malaya, though both eventually operated under Singapore registry. First introduced on the Djakarta route, the aircraft were later also operated on the important Singapore–Kuala Lumpur service, as well as busier flights to the Borneo Territories, supported by the DC-3s. Within a very short space of time 95 per cent loads were regularly being achieved by the Viscounts.

Kuwait Airways operated a number of leased Viscounts on its services around the Middle East, including ex-BWIA V.702 G-APDW, belonging to BOAC Associates. Jenny Gradidge

Austrian Airlines and, with the assistance of SAS, Fred Olsen, Rolls-Royce and Vickers, the new carrier laid plans for the opening of international air services from Vienna in 1958.

No fewer than four Fred Olsen Viscount V.779Ds were supplied to begin services. Fred Olsen Air Transport also supplied eight pilots, including the chief pilot and a number of engineers to support the aircraft. At 08.30 on 31 March 1958 the first Austrian Airlines scheduled flight, OS201, left Vienna for London Heathrow. The four leased V.779Ds quickly established Austrian Airlines as a major new European carrier and soon extended the airline's network throughout the region. The Fred Olsen aircraft were eventually replaced by six new V.837s, which entered service in early 1960. The V.779Ds were returned to Fred Olsen as soon as the larger aircraft were delivered from the UK. Nonetheless, two second-hand V.745Ds were acquired from Vickers by Austrian Airlines in January 1961 to join the larger V.837s.

On their return from Austria, two of the quartet, as already mentioned, were leased to BEA to help cover the capacity shortage caused by the delayed Vanguard deliveries. The other two were also immediately leased out again, this time to SAS. Although SAS had previously considered a Viscount order of its own, an unacceptably long wait for delivery had caused the loss of the potentially important order. Even so, SAS's own capacity shortage led it to lease two V.779Ds in 1960, followed by the other two V.779Ds in 1961 on their return from the BEA lease. The aircraft were mostly operated on services within Scandinavia, and were all eventually sold by Fred Olsen to Indian Airlines at the end of the SAS contract.

BEA and TCA Go Jet

BEA had been forced to address the vexing problem of the up-and-coming competition from Caravelles and other new jets that would be flying for their rivals long before the Vanguards arrived. The airline had actually placed a fleet of de Havilland Comet 4Bs into scheduled service on its longer routes to the Mediterranean and Eastern Europe in April 1960. Originally responding to an enquiry from Capital Airlines, de Havilland had offered the US carrier the Comet 4A, a stretched version of the Comet 4, which Capital had ordered with a view to introducing them on its network alongside the Viscounts already in service. The Capital order eventually fell through, but the redundant Comet 4A was further developed into the 4B for BEA.

Although not really suited for shorter flights, the BEA Comets also saw some service on routes from London to Paris, and other nearer European capitals. The airline regarded this as a stopgap measure until the next-generation British-built jet designed specifically for BEA's short-haul services arrived. This was the de Havilland Trident, due to be delivered in 1964. Trans-Canada had also entered the pure-jet age before its first Vanguards arrived

The leased Viscount 700s were eventually replaced by new, larger, V.837s bought new by Austrian Airlines from Vickers. Global Air Image

After being leased to BEA as G-ARBW, Fred Olsen's V.779D LN-FOM was awarded a new leasing contract with SAS. The aircraft carries both registrations here, shortly before delivery from London to Scandinavia. via author

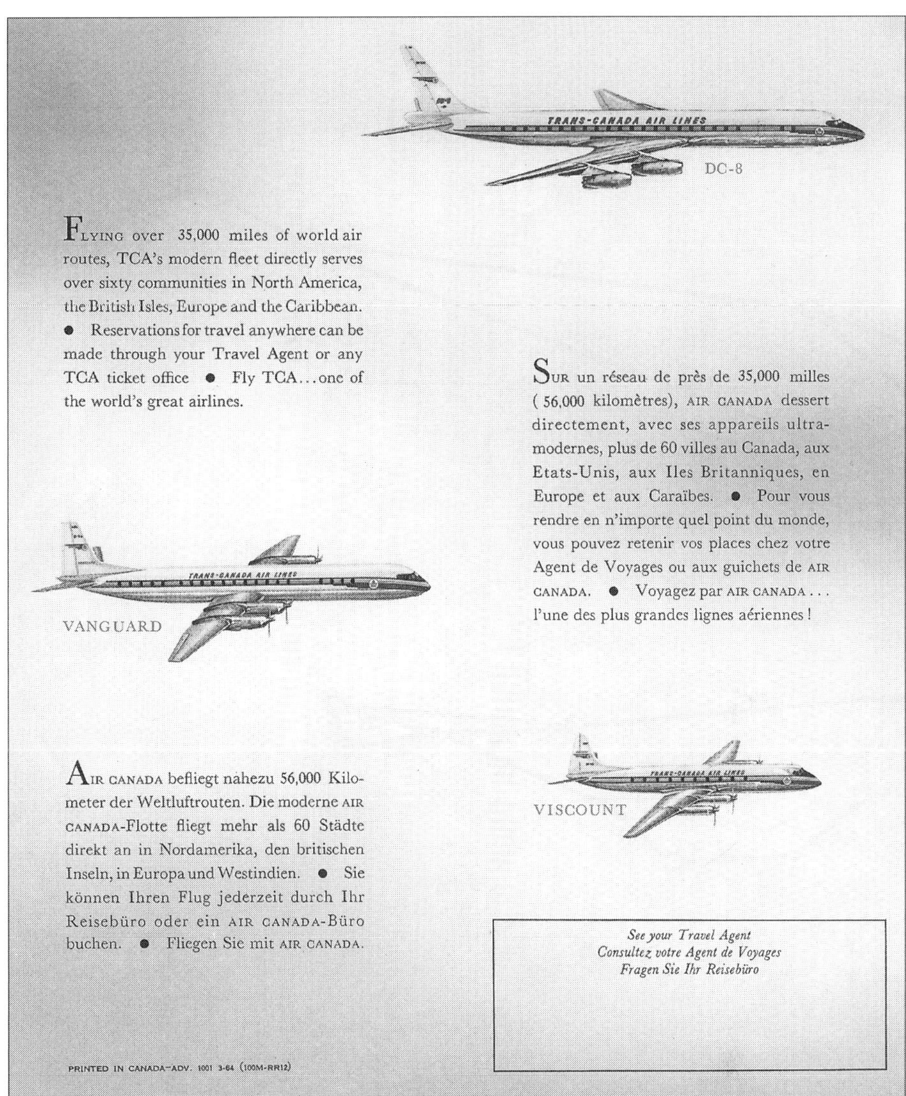

The Rolls-Royce powered DC-8s of TCA operated on long-haul services while the turboprop Viscounts and Vanguards were assigned to the regional services. Author's collection

from the UK, having begun operations with the introduction into service of US-built DC-8s in April 1960.

The magical glamour of the jets had even replaced the turboprop in Vickers' affections. In the mid-1950s the company had started working on several designs for long-range jets for BOAC. A very promising design, for BOAC, eventually did take shape as the VC10, and the first of this new generation were being built at Weybridge as the last of the Vanguards were making their way down the production line.

Final Vanguard Deliveries

The last of BEA's V.953 Vanguards, G-APEU, was delivered to Heathrow on 30 March 1962. The last aircraft of the initial TCA order, CF-TKW, first flew on 6 June 1962 and was retained by the manufacturer for further research into the aerodynamic issues that had arisen in service, and for ongoing flight tests on the still-troublesome Tynes. As a result, 'KW was not delivered to TCA until 3 April 1964. The first TCA Vanguard built, CF-TKA, was also retained by Vickers for a while, taking part in further tropical trials at Nairobi in May 1960, eventually being delivered to Montreal in November 1961.

The Tyne had continued to give concern, the early Vanguard operations of both airlines unfortunately being marked by frequent unscheduled engine changes. While the operating experience was built up there was already a short period, initially as low as 400hr, between the mandatory scheduled maintenance overhaul engine changes. Further operational day-to-day familiarization did eventually see this increased to 1,000hr during 1962.

Work also continued in an effort to decrease the amount of annoying noise and vibration experienced in the passenger cabin, especially in the forward areas. An early attempt at resolving the problem saw a selection of 5 degrees of flap, which seemed to offer some relief. More in-depth research by Vickers, Rolls-Royce and de Havilland, which manufactured the propellers, resulted in further trials and

Vickers Becomes BAC

As Vickers was battling to overcome the delays in getting the Vanguard into service, the company itself was undergoing major changes to its basic organization. The British aircraft industry had continued to fight a losing battle for orders against the giant US manufacturers in the post-war years. Even the largest British companies had barely the production capacity of some of the US aircraft-builders' bigger subcontractors and suppliers. The simple fact that British manufacturers were having to put so much energy into competing against each other for the comparatively small orders for the tiny home market was a major factor in their comparative lack of success.

As most of even the most innovative British designs eventually failed to live up to their promise (the Viscount being one of the few exceptions), it became clear that some sort of rationalization was needed, to create a more viable industry that was better equipped to compete on the world stage. Extensive consultations between the industry and government bodies eventually resulted in an agreement to create two large companies by the merger of most of the then-current airframe builders.

By March 1960 Hawker Siddeley had been merged with de Havilland and Blackburn Aircraft under the Hawker Siddeley name, still operating under private ownership. A new government-owned company, the British Aircraft Corporation (BAC) was formed to take over the aircraft design and manufacturing divisions of Vickers-Armstrongs (Aircraft), the Bristol Aeroplane Company and English Electric Aviation.

Under the leadership of Sir George Edwards, who was appointed managing director of BAC, the new corporation soon set about developing a new family of jet airliners, among its many projects. The VC10, originally from Vickers, was being built for BOAC's worldwide long-range network. In May BAC also took over Hunting Aircraft Ltd, from whom it inherited a promising new design, the Hunting 107, which was being developed as a second-generation short-haul jet airliner. This was eventually developed further and materialized as the BAC One-Eleven, being openly marketed by the corporation as a jet replacement for the Viscount.

The flexible, economic Vanguard made a significant commercial contribution on a variety of short- and medium-haul passenger routes with BEA. via author

flight-testing. Eventually, the addition of extra weight to the tailplane structure and refinements to propeller synchronization and synchrophasing were introduced in an effort to secure a longer-term solution. Although these measures all helped to some degree, the Vanguard never completely lost its reputation as a noisy aircraft in which to fly.

BEA Vanguard Deployment

The first of the BEA V.953s, G-APEG, entered service on 18 May 1961 on the Heathrow–Paris service. By the time the 1961 summer season was in full swing, both versions of the new BEA Vanguards were operating internationally from London direct to Gibraltar, Madrid, Milan, Paris and Malta, with other Malta services operating via Naples, Palermo or Rome. On the UK domestic services the Vanguards were operating no fewer than four flights a day from Heathrow to both Belfast and Glasgow, as well as twice a day to Edinburgh, alongside the established Viscounts. The Vanguards were first scheduled on the London–Manchester domestic route on 1 November, and this service was to become the backbone of BEA's Vanguard operation for many years to come.

As well as the Vanguard problems, BEA's Comet 4Bs had also experienced some delivery delays, and BOAC Britannia 312s and DC-7Cs were chartered in to help to cover the shortfall by operating from London to Copenhagen and Nice (Britannia) and to Frankfurt and Zurich (DC-7C) in early 1961. Even when the Vanguards began to be delivered, on-going technical difficulties saw the BOAC DC-7Cs being seen again on BEA services between June and August, this time operating four flights a day between Heathrow and Paris.

By the summer of 1962, though, BEA at last had its full complement of Vanguards in service. The Tynes had started settling down, the longer periods between maintenance allowing the aircraft to spend more time in the air, earning money, and less in the engineering bays. Nonetheless, the Vanguard's initial problems meant that the aircraft made a £2 million loss in the 1961/1962 financial year.

Despite the arrival of the high-profile Comet 4B jets, the turboprop Vanguards and Viscounts still formed the bulk of the airline's fleet and therefore most of the revenue earning capacity. Of the 796 pilots employed by BEA in April 1962, 213 (80 captains and 133 first/second officers) were assigned to the Vanguards and 358 (192 captains and 166 first/second officers) were assigned to the Viscounts.

The Vanguards were very conspicuous on the busier trunk domestic services from London Heathrow. They operated all five daily flights to Belfast, increasing to seven after 1 June, the eight flights daily to Glasgow and all five services to Edinburgh. The busy Manchester route was shared between the Vanguards and Viscounts, the Vanguards flying five services a day in the week and two at weekends. On Saturdays in the summer a Vanguard was also used to replace a Viscount on the midday service from Heathrow to the Isle of Man.

The Night Tourists

The Belfast, Edinburgh and Glasgow frequencies included nightly 'off-peak' services with much-reduced fares. Departures from Heathrow were scheduled for 23.30hr (Belfast), 23.40hr (Glasgow) and 23.50hr (Edinburgh), with reciprocal flights leaving the three cities at similar times. Traffic growth on the domestic routes was very impressive, passenger traffic to Belfast increasing by 16 per cent, and to Glasgow by 21 per cent. The cargo-carrying capabilities the aircraft were also put to good use, BEA seeing a 20 per cent rise in freight carried on the Scottish services and a staggering 66 per cent increase on the Belfast route.

Once the early technical problems were solved, the Vanguard settled down into reliable day-to-day operations. For several years it was actually the largest aircraft in the BEA fleet, its passenger capacity being higher than that of most of the early jets operated by the corporation. Steve Williams' collection

Until 22 April 1962 the Vanguards shared the Paris-Le Bourget route with Comets. The London–Paris flight was flown in partnership with Air France, which was operating piston-engined Super Constellations and Caravelle jets to Paris-Orly. However, the Comets were transferred to other services for the summer and the Vanguards operated all eight daily BEA flights. These included an 'off-peak' service at the height of the summer season that left Heathrow at 22.00hr.

The economy of the Vanguard's operation came to the fore in BEA's promotion of the cheaper 'off-peak' fares. Being the biggest aircraft in BEA's fleet at the time, the Vanguard's ability to carry sizeable loads of passengers at low cost was vital for the success of the night tourist services. Of the ten weekly Vanguard flights from Heathrow to Palma, only three were daylight services, the remainder being night tourist-class 'off-peak' flights. Similarly, four of the six Heathrow–Gibraltar Vanguard services and three of the five Heathrow–Milan Vanguard flights were 'off-peak' night operations. All of the Vanguard summer services to Barcelona were 'off-peak' night flights, and three weekly Vanguard night tourist flights from London to Venice supplemented three other similar flights by Viscount.

Malta was the furthest point on BEA's Vanguard network, with flights operating via Naples, Palermo or Rome, as well as non-stop. The Palermo service was actually the first direct scheduled air link between the UK and Sicily. Once again, the handful of daytime Vanguard services was outnumbered by the night tourist operations. Four of these were 04.00hr departures from Heathrow, three via Rome and one via Palermo. Three of the six weekly flights via Naples to Malta were 'off peak' 21.10hr departures, the other three leaving just after midday at a much more civilized hour, though for a much higher fare.

Settling in with TCA

The early TCA Vanguard experience was slightly marred on 2 April 1961, when CF-TKG was forced to make a night belly-landing at Montreal. An undercarriage door had become entangled with one of the legs, preventing its proper deployment. None of the occupants was hurt in the successful emergency landing, and the aircraft was soon repaired. Although the rest of the Vanguards were temporarily grounded for inspection of their undercarriages, all were back in service by 4 April. The airline suffered another Vanguard landing mishap nearly a year later when the undercarriage of CF-TKO collapsed on landing at Antigua on 30 March 1962. The aircraft had struck a mound just before touchdown and, in the heavy landing which followed, the undercarriage collapsed. Fortunately, again, there were no serious injuries to those on board and the damaged aircraft was repaired and returned to service.

The cargo-carrying capacity of the Vanguard was soon proving just as useful on TCA's routes as it had to BEA in Europe. Previously, the airline had employed ex-passenger-carrying Canadair North Stars, converted for all-cargo work, on transcontinental freight flights between Toronto and Vancouver, via Winnipeg. The airline had found that the Vanguard was capable of carrying the equivalent of a North Star's cargo load, 16,000lb (7,260kg), in its hold, in addition to a full complement of passengers and their luggage, over the same routes.

Trans-Canada had been disappointed with the Vanguard's early problems, especially when compared with the Viscount's easy introduction. Nonetheless, the TCA

Constellation Reprieve

One outcome of the Vanguard's early Tyne engine problems was the delay in TCA retiring the last of its Super Constellations. The airline had initially planned to withdraw all its remaining Lockheeds as they fell due for major maintenance when enough of the Vanguard fleet was in service to enable TCA to replace them. The new Douglas DC-8 jets had already replaced the Super Constellations on the transatlantic and transcontinental networks, and their retirement would make TCA an all-turbine operator, with a fleet comprising the Viscount and Vanguard turboprops and DC-8 jets. Not only would it be an all-turbine airline, but it would become an all-Rolls-Royce-powered airline with the departure of the Super Constellations. Darts and Tynes powered the Viscounts and Vanguards, respectively, and the US-built DC-8-40s had Rolls-Royce Conway 509 turbofans.

Unfortunately, the Tyne's early reliability problems meant that a number of the Super Constellations, now regarded as obsolete by TCA, had to be given expensive overhauls to keep them in service on routes meant for the troubled Vanguards. By February 1962, however, most of the Super Constellations were finally retired from full scheduled services, their last domestic route being to St Johns and the last international services to Barbados, Bermuda, Port of Spain and Trinidad. Four were still retained for a while, however, as back-ups, mostly for the benefit of the Vanguards. Their number was later reduced to two and by 1963 the last pair were finally sold off.

Several of TCA's Lockheed Super Constellations gained a reprieve from retirement thanks to the Vanguard's initial technical problems. Aviation Hobby Shop

LEFT: As well as serving on much of TCA's domestic network and on extremely busy routes to the USA, the airline's Vanguards were also used for some longer trips south to the Caribbean. via author

Vanguards had found themselves a useful niche between the established, smaller Viscounts and the new DC-8s, sharing the operation of different routes with both types. As well as the transcontinental multi-stop services, frequent services over the intercity network in the east, and flights out to the Maritime Provinces, the Vanguards also proved useful on the cross-border services to the northern USA, alongside the Viscounts, and on the longer vacation routes to Florida, the Caribbean and Bermuda, supplementing the DC-8s. In practice it soon became apparent that the seat-mile costs of the Vanguard were lower than those of both other types, even over such a wide variety of services. By 1963 the seating capacity on TCA's Vanguards had been increased to 109 by reducing the available first-class accommodation and increasing the ratio of economy-class seats, thereby making better use of the aircraft's load-carrying and economic abilities.

New Horizons

By the time the Vanguard fleets of BEA and TCA were finally establishing themselves, the last of the Viscounts to roll off the production lines were also settling in with their owners. Nonetheless, many of the original Viscount operators were beginning to realize that their once-ultra-modern aircraft finally needed to be replaced by more modern types. The patience of the airlines which had shunned the Vanguard, and even the later Viscounts, in favour of the next pure-jet generation was about to be rewarded. Within a couple of years many new operators would be taking advantage of the availability of secondhand Viscounts, and finding new markets and opportunities where they could be put to good use.

TRANS-CANADA AIR LINES—FIRST IN THE UNITED STATES WITH NEW VICKERS VANGUARDS:

SERVICE FROM NEW YORK AND CHICAGO TO TORONTO BEGAN JUNE 15th.

From the home of the Viscount comes—

VANGUARD— "TCA introduced this aircraft on its transcontinental routes on February 1, 1961, and is looking forward to its progressive use on all its more important services"—TCA President, Mr. Gordon McGregor.

VANGUARD—Now flying across Canada for TCA . . . serving the United States from New York and Chicago.

VANGUARD— World's only second generation turbo-prop airliner.

VANGUARD— More than ten years engineering and over 3,000,000 Viscount hours built in.

VANGUARD— Carries over one hundred passengers plus four and a half tons of freight.

VANGUARD— Wider seats, inner-wall radiant heating, large picture windows.

VANGUARD— Built-in ramps and new rapid baggage handling.

For further details contact British Aircraft Corporation (U.S.A.) Inc., 399 Jefferson Davis Highway, Arlington, Washington, D. C.

VANGUARD

VICKERS-ARMSTRONGS (AIRCRAFT) LTD., WEYBRIDGE, SURREY, ENGLAND. A COMPANY OF

BRITISH AIRCRAFT CORPORATION

100 PALL MALL, LONDON S.W.1., ENGLAND

RIGHT: Viscount 702 G-APPX was used to much sunnier climes before its return to the UK in 1969. It had previously served with BWIA, MEA and Kuwait Airways during its years with BOAC Associated Companies. Its final years were spent leased-out to BMA and Air International before it was withdrawn from use in the mid-1970s. Steve Williams collection

BELOW: Originally delivered to Central African Airways as VP-YNA, Viscount 748D 7Q-YDK remained in Africa with Air Malawi and Air Zimbabwe. It is now on display at the Zimbabwe Air Force Base at Thornhill. via author

BOTTOM: Viscount 802 G-AOHH served both BEA and BA from 1956, until it was scrapped at Leeds in 1976. Bill Sheridan Collection

LEFT: Union of Burma Airways' trio of Viscount 761Ds formed the national carrier's front-line equipment from late 1957. Operated by UBA and Burma Airways until 1972, XY-ADG was eventually broken up in Zaire in 1991. Bill Sheridan Collection

BELOW: Fred Olsen Air Transport's colourful Viscounts spent much of their time leased out to other carriers. Viscount 779D LN-FOM was eventually sold to Indian Airlines Corporation in 1962. It enjoyed a nine-year career based on the subcontinent before it was scrapped in 1971. Aviation Hobby Shop

BOTTOM: The red-topped Viscounts of Cambrian Airways could be relied upon to brighten up an airport terminal on the dullest day. Here, two of the Welsh carrier's Viscount 806s share the Liverpool ramp in 1973. Steve Williams collection

TOP: **Viscount 806 'Freightmaster' G-BLOA started its varied life as G-AOYJ with BEA in 1957. It was later leased to Cyprus Airways, transferred to Cambrian and was then absorbed into the BA Regional fleet. After sale to BAF it spent time leased to Manx and Guernsey Airlines before its conversion to all-cargo configuration.** Aviation Hobby Shop

ABOVE: **Iranian Viscount 784D EP-AHB was operated from Tehran on both airline and private Royal and government transport missions between 1958 and 1966. It was later operated by Air Rhodesia, and was shot down by revolutionary terrorists in 1979.** via author

BELOW: **Channel Airways acquired the remaining Continental Airlines Viscount 812 fleet in 1966, operating them on its extensive scheduled and inclusive-tour charter network.** Bill Sheridan Collection

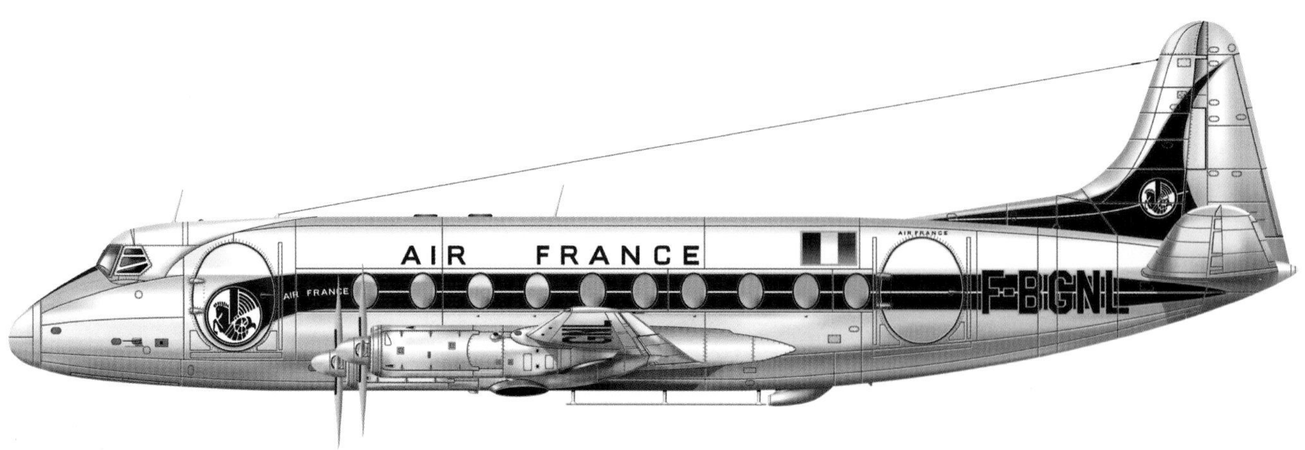

Air France V.708 F-BGNL, built in 1953, was only the second of hundreds of Viscounts to be exported during the type's production run. The aircraft was later lost in a forced landing in Devon while with UK charter operator, Alidair, in 1980.

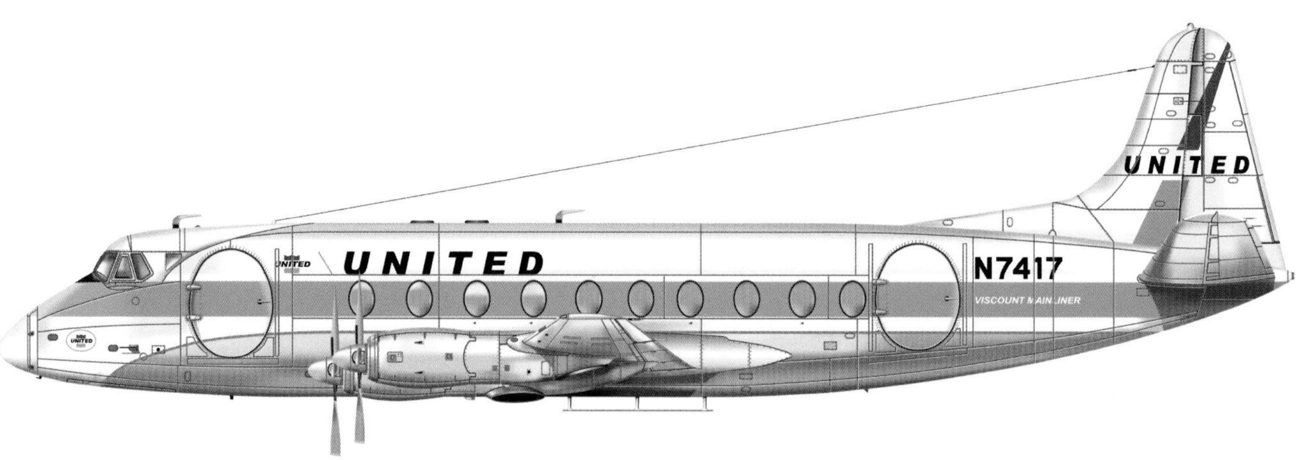

The 'Americanized' Viscounts were equipped with larger, more powerful versions of the Rolls-Royce Dart engine, as well as incorporating several other improvements over the original design. United acquired 1956-built N7417 in the Capital Airlines merger, keeping it in service until 1968.

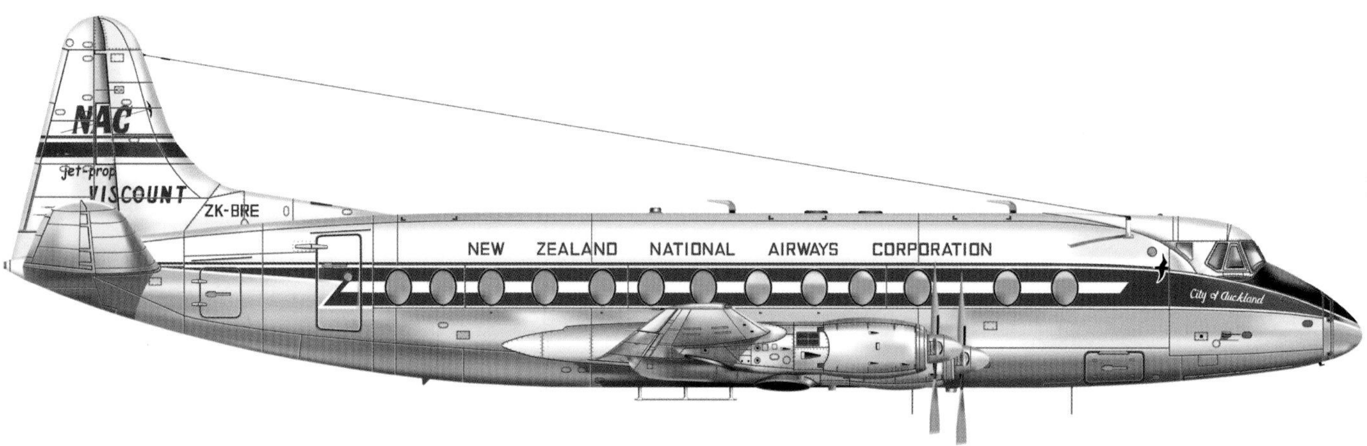

The stretched Viscount 800s were developed to offer higher capacity for shorter sectors than original models. ZK-BRE was operated by NZNAC from 1959 to 1974 and was eventually scrapped in the UK in 1982.

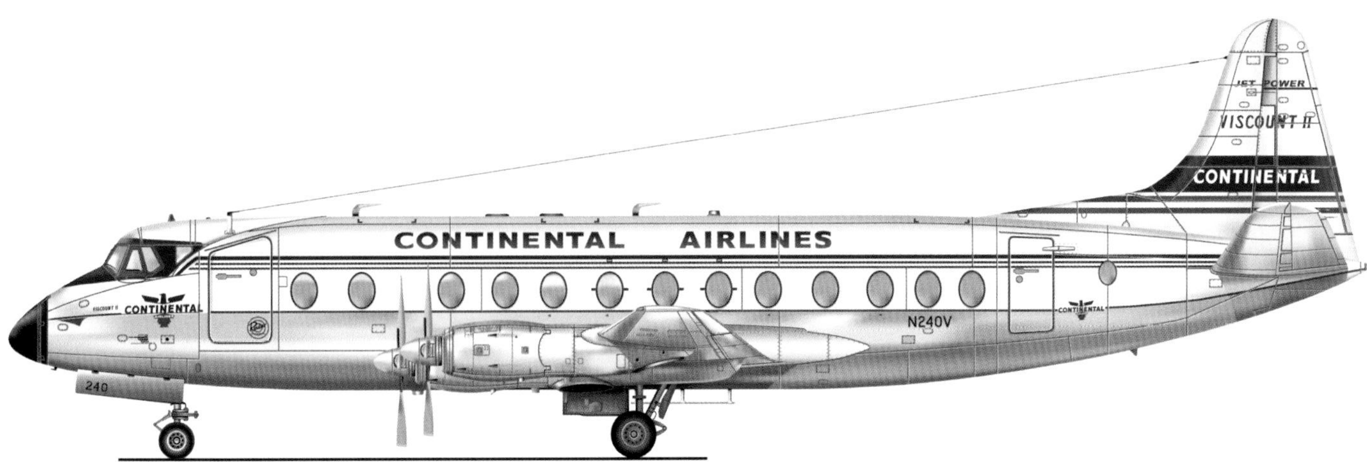

Continental introduced their 'Viscount II's into scheduled service on their western US network in 1958. Their first V.812, N240V, was sold after only two years with the airline, becoming an executive transport for Tenneco.

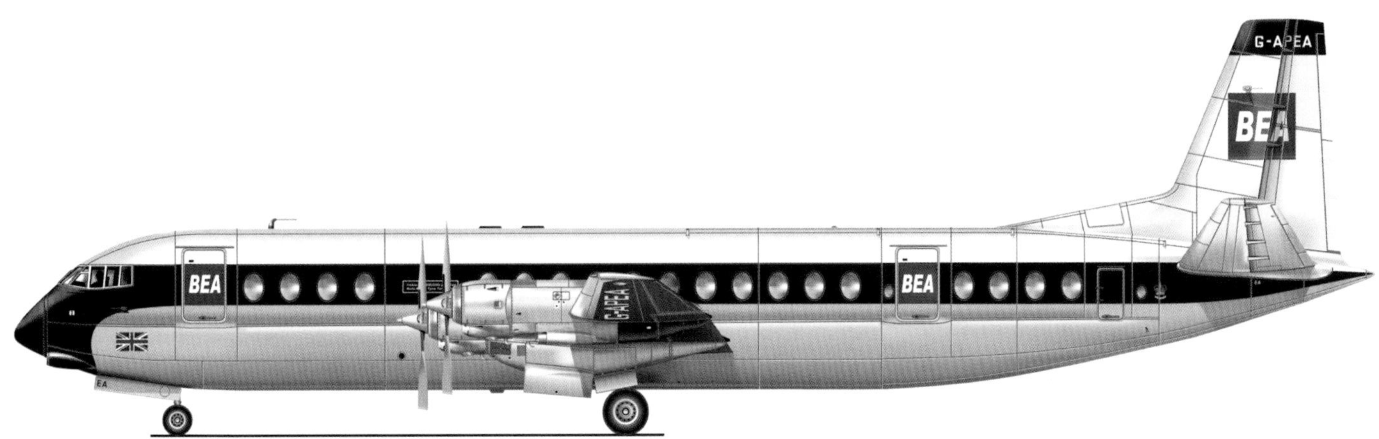

G-APEA, the first production Vanguard, spent its entire commercial career with British European Airways. Delivered in 1961, 'EA was finally withdrawn from service and broken up at Heathrow in early 1973.

Europe Aero Service repainted their last three passenger-carrying Vanguards in the airline's updated livery in 1979. F-BTOV, which had been the last Vanguard built, in 1962, went on to operate the world's last Vanguard passenger services, while based in Indonesia with Merpati Nusantara, in 1987.

TOP: Viscounts served the popular Channel Island routes from the mainland UK and Europe for over forty years. Here, a British Airways-Northeast V.806 and a BMA V.813 share the Jersey ramp on a summer's day in 1974. Malcolm L. Hill

ABOVE: After spending just three years in airline service with Ghana Airways from late 1961 to early 1965, Viscount 838 XT661 spent the next twenty-eight years on experimental work with UK-based research agencies. Steve Williams collection

LEFT: Brazilian carrier VASP operated both new and secondhand Viscounts on its busy network. The airline's first Viscount 827, PP-SRC, was delivered in 1958 and was not disposed of, to Paraguay's PLUNA, until 1975. Aviation Hobby Shop

ABOVE: British United retained several of its Viscount 800s long enough to repaint them in the stylish sandstone and blue livery in the late 1960s. Viscount 833 G-APTC was lost in a training accident just ten days after delivery to its next owner, Arkia of Israel, in 1969. Bill Sheridan Collection

RIGHT: Built in 1960, Austrian Airlines Viscount 837 OE-LAK *Johann Strauss* was eventually withdrawn and stored by its last operator, TAC of Columbia, in 1980. Bill Sheridan Collection

BELOW: British Airways Vanguard 951 G-APEI found a new home with Indonesia's Merpati Nusantara Airlines as PK-MVD. Aviation Hobby Shop

Merchantman G-APET was operated as a freighter for twenty years of its thirty-year commercial life. Bill Sheridan Collection

ABOVE: **Air Traders' freighter Vanguards and single Merchantman operated from Northern Europe to Africa and the Middle and Far East on their wide-ranging cargo charters.** Bill Sheridan Collection

BELOW: **The careers of the Vanguards operated by Invicta International were marked by mixed fortunes. Here, G-AXOY starts up on the Basle ramp, not far from the mountains where its sister ship, G-AXOP came to grief.** J.B. Urech via Bill Sheridan Collection

CHAPTER SEVEN

New Adventures

Capital's Uncertain Future

Although the Viscount was undoubtedly a commercial success in Capital Airline's service, reflecting well for both carrier and manufacturer, Capital's eventual fate threatened to tarnish the aircraft's reputation. While the airline's network linked many important cities and population centres, it was mostly composed of uneconomic short stages, averaging 300 miles (480km). The airline was serving almost as many small cities as large ones, and it was virtually impossible to make money on such a restrictive system, however popular the Viscounts were. Capital was even denied the option of dropping the loss-making services, as it was required to serve the less-populated cities in order to qualify for valuable mail subsidies. Less-economic aircraft, such as the Constellations, DC-3s and DC-4s, were also still in service, their high operating costs chipping away at whatever profits the Viscounts were making.

Attempts had been made to modernize the fleet even more, by placing orders for fifteen extra Viscounts, five Electas and ten de Havilland Comet 4A jets, in 1956. These plans were foiled by a lack of financial backing for the contracts, which led to the orders being cancelled. Had they been delivered, Capital's Comet 4As would have been among the first jets on US domestic service, and would have given Capital another publicity coup. The extra Viscounts were in advanced states of manufacture when the contract was cancelled. Fortunately, Vickers soon found new customers for the aircraft, selling them on to the likes of Northeast Airlines and Alitalia.

Although its large fleet of Viscounts was distributed between several bases throughout Capital Airlines' network, Washington D.C. was the company's headquarters and a major centre of operations. United Archive

A five-week mechanics' strike grounded Capital in 1958, causing further financial pressure. To add to the airline's woes, between 1958 and 1960 it was unfortunate enough to lose five aircraft, four Viscounts and a Constellation, in high-profile fatal accidents. Financial losses continued to build up, despite operating profits, owing to heavy interest payments and other administrative costs. The airline made a $3,210,355 loss in 1957, a small $213,262 profit in 1958 and a loss of $1,757,425, in 1959. By May 1960 Vickers was owed $34 million in outstanding repayments, and felt obliged to file a foreclosure suit in the US courts to regain the money. Eventually, Vickers was persuaded to take back no fewer than fifteen of the remaining Viscounts as an interim settlement while Capital attempted to come up with a survival plan.

Merger Plans

In an effort to strengthen the network, between 1958 and 1960 Capital managed to gain more non-stop authority on its routes from the East Coast to the Great Lakes cities and expanded services from the Great Lakes area to Florida. In addition, the airline was finally given permission to drop several unprofitable cities from the network. Eleven DC-6Bs were leased-in from Pan American to provide more capacity in place of the cancelled Viscounts, and two Viscount 812s were also leased in from Continental Airlines. The V.812s flew with Capital titles over their Continental livery from December 1958 to March 1959, based at Washington. A new image was also revealed with the arrival of the DC-6Bs, the traditional eagle logo being replaced by a smarter, more modern design. Unfortunately it was becoming increasingly clear that these measures were a case of too little, too late.

As a result of the Vickers threat of foreclosure, which would certainly have resulted in the closing down of Capital, the airline began urgent merger talks with United Air Lines (UAL) in May 1960. These followed approaches that had been made by UAL's management. United was one of the few airlines that was strong enough to consider taking on Capital's considerable debts. The merger would give UAL access to Florida and the southern USA, as well as giving it increased presence in the East Coast and Great Lakes regions. An official announcement, proposing the merger, was made in July 1960, and both boards of directors approved the proposal in August. Further approval was obtained from the airline's stockholders in October, and final government approval came from the US Civil Aeronautics Board in April 1961.

Only a handful of the Viscounts carried the restyled Capital livery. United Archive

In the meantime, UAL and Capital had already become closer operationally, United leasing two of its Boeing 720s to Capital from 23 January 1961. The 720s, recently introduced, medium-range versions of the 707, were operated on Capital routes to Florida from Pittsburgh and Cleveland, and to Atlanta and New Orleans from New York. On 1 June UAL assumed responsibility for the assets and remaining liabilities of Capital Airlines, and the first of the Viscounts to be repainted in UAL colours was rolled out at Capital's Washington maintenance base the same month. For the next few weeks the two airlines continued to fly their networks as separate organizations, but on 1 July the two operations were merged into one and the sale of Capital to UAL was finally completed.

At the time of the merger Capital was still flying the two Boeing 720s (leased from United), three DC-3s, ten DC-4s, eleven DC-6Bs (leased from Pan American) and forty-seven Viscount 745Ds. The last of the Constellations had been retired

BELOW: The ex-Capital Viscounts remained valued members of United's operational fleet for a number of years after the merger. United Archive

The Viscount and Capital's Downfall

How much of a factor the Viscount was in the failure of Capital to survive independently has been a topic of debate down the decades since the United/Capital merger was completed. There was a great deal of speculation in the US media 'blaming' the use of Viscounts for Capital's losses. A closer examination of Capital's financial history, however, totally refutes this theory. The simple fact was that the Viscounts were the only fleet members that were actually making any sort of profit for Capital. The Viscount's high profile had enabled Capital to grow, despite its problems, to be the fifth-largest US scheduled airline in terms of passengers carried and the sixth-largest in terms of passenger miles flown.

By the end of the 1950s Capital's Viscounts faced strong competition from other US airlines in the form of the later turboprops, and even early jets on many of the important longer sectors. Unable to introduce new aircraft of its own because of its restricted financial commitments, Capital attempted to fight back by reducing passenger capacity on the Viscounts to forty-four to make the aircraft more comfortable and attractive to passengers. This also allowed the now lighter aircraft to operate at higher speeds over the longer sectors, such as the non-stop routes to Florida and Georgia. However, this reduced potential profitability by simply removing the opportunity to earn the revenue from the lost seats, and Capital's passengers were still being lured away to the larger Electras and DC-8 and 707 jets of its rivals. The higher speeds also resulted in much higher maintenance costs as the aircraft were pushed closer to their performance limits.

The Capital management's early decision to place such a large order for the V.745D was almost certainly a major source of later problems. The large monetary outlay badly overstretched the airline's ability to keep on top of ever-mounting interest charges. A smaller initial fleet of Viscounts would have given Capital much more flexibility in planning its later orders, and it would have enabled the airline to match the emerging market requirements more closely. This would have allowed more-advanced aircraft, either the more economic larger Viscounts or even the much-desired Comets and Electras, to be acquired to allow the airline to maintain its competitive edge.

At its peak the Capital Airlines Viscount fleet was returning an average load factor of 80 per cent, compared with a system-wide average, taking other aircraft types into account, of only 58 per cent. The break-even load factor on the Viscount was 52 per cent. This is hardly the record of an aircraft that many US newspapers and rival aerospace industry giants had still tried to claim as the reason Capital had failed to survive. The fact that UAL not only chose to retain the Viscounts, but also expanded the fleet and continued to operate them for several years, shows that Capital had picked the right aircraft.

Financial problems prevented Capital from finalizing its many attempts at completing modernization plans, and contributed to the retention of ageing, loss-making Constellations and DC-4s alongside the more profitable Viscounts. United Archive

in 1960. Pre-merger, United was already operating a huge fleet of over 200 airliners, including recently introduced French-built Caravelles. Of the Capital fleet, only the Viscounts had a long-term future with the enlarged carrier, the DC-3s, DC-4s and DC-6Bs soon being disposed of or returned to their owners. The Viscount 745Ds went on to be operated very successfully on UAL's short-haul services, mostly over the old Capital network. In fact the Viscounts were so successful that United promptly started negotiating for the recall of six of the returned Capital aircraft from Vickers. The new, combined operation effectively made UAL the largest commercial airline in the western world at that time.

New Lives for the V.744s

The three Viscount 744s supplied as stop-gaps to Capital until its V.745Ds were delivered in sufficient quantities enjoyed varied fortunes both before and after returning to Vickers.

The third V.744 delivered, N7404, had been involved in a very serious heavy landing accident at Chicago's Midway Airport on 20 February 1956. During the approach to Chicago at the end of a flight from Detroit, malfunctioning propeller control switches caused the aircraft to sink beyond the pilot's control and strike the ground on a taxiway, 400ft (120m) short of the runway. The hapless Viscount finally came to a halt after skidding along on its belly for over 1,600ft (490m). Fortunately, none of the five crew or thirty-seven passengers on board was seriously hurt.

At the time of the accident N7404 had accumulated 1,541 flying hours in the nine months since its first flight, in June 1955. The remains of the Viscount were salvaged by Vickers and returned to the UK. The fuselage was used to build a 'new' V.757 for TCA, registered CF-THJ, which was delivered back across the Atlantic to TCA on 30 May 1957 and flew successfully for its new Canadian owner for many years.

The remaining two aircraft of the trio, N7402 and N7403, were eventually returned to Vickers in February 1958. They took up new UK registrations as G-APKJ and 'KK, the latter being leased out to Continental Airlines until the end of March, purely for crew training duties pending the arrival of its own V.812s. After returning to Vickers at Weybridge, both were initially earmarked for resale to LAV of Venezuela, to expand its fleet of three V.749s. This contract was never finalized, and instead of going to LAV, the pair of V.744s were eventually leased to All Nippon Airways (ANA) of Tokyo and delivered to Japan in July 1960. Formed by the merger of several local carriers in the early 1950s, ANA soon grew with Japan's mushrooming post-war economy, and ordered no fewer than nine V.828s for 1961 delivery.

Following its return to Vickers, the first V.744 spent time leased to All Nippon Airways as G-APKJ. All Nippon Airways

After crew training, the V.744s entered limited scheduled service on ANA's domestic Japanese network. All went well for nearly a year, until G-APKJ was written off in a heavy landing at Itama on 12 June 1961. Its remains were sold to Ansett-ANA and scrapped for spares. After the first three Viscount 828s had been delivered to ANA, G-APKK was returned to Vickers in October 1961 and delivered to the Empire Test Pilots' School (ETPS) at Farnborough in early 1962. Given the military serial XR801, it was used for advanced training, being joined by another Viscount, V.745D XR802, later that year. This second aircraft had also initially flown with Capital, and had been leased to Northeast Airlines in 1961. Apart from a navigation station installed in the forward cabin, the ETPS Viscounts retained their original Capital passenger interiors. An extra seat was also installed on the flight deck, in view of the almost constant instructional flying for which the Viscounts would be used. After more than ten years of busy flight-training operations, both aircraft were finally sold for scrap in 1972.

Fleet Shifts

While UAL had decided to hang on to its newly acquired ex-Capital V.745Ds for the foreseeable future, other longer-established users of the type were already making plans to dispose of their early-model Viscounts.

Aer Lingus was among the first of the original Viscount customers to decide to part with their aircraft. The introduction of the first production Fokker F.27 Friendships on less-dense services soon left the four original Viscount 707s redundant, though the larger V.808s remained in service on more important routes. Aer Lingus had proposed converting the V.707s to a pure freighter configuration with the fitting of large cargo doors, but this was never proceeded with. Instead, the four were sold on, two going to Tradair Ltd, a Southend-based UK charter operator, and the other two being sold to Eagle Airways (Bermuda) Ltd.

Still a comparatively new operator, Tradair had been operating a fleet of Vikings from Southend on both inclusive-tour and *ad hoc* charters since 1958, and had also moved into limited scheduled services when a route from Southend to Maastricht in the Netherlands was approved. Rapid expansion had seen seven Vikings in service for the summer of 1959, most of the popular resorts around Europe and the western Mediterranean being visited by the fleet. The entry into service of the two ex-Aer Lingus Viscount 707s, EI-AFV and EI-AGI, reregistered G-APZB and G-APZC, was planned to be in time for the busy 1960 summer season. With their arrival Tradair hoped to able to offer holiday charters to points that were much too distant for the unpressurized Vikings to serve easily, such as the Canary Islands or the eastern Mediterranean.

Eagle Evolves

The two remaining V.707s, EI-AFW and EI-AFY, became VR-BBJ and VR-BBH respectively and were assigned by Eagle Airways to its Bermuda-based subsidiary's operation in early 1960. On 21 March, shipping company Cunard announced it had bought a 60 per cent shareholding in the Eagle companies, and thenceforth all of

The Empire Test Pilots School operated a pair of Viscounts on its unique training and research services for ten years. Jenny Gradidge

ABOVE: Maritime Central Airways' sole Viscount was sold shortly before Eastern Provincial absorbed the company. Jenny Gradidge

LEFT: The Bermuda and Nassau-based services of Eagle Airways' subsidiaries were promoted heavily in the USA. Note the early 1960 use of 'British Eagle' titles, though these would not be used by Bamberg's airline operations for another four years. Author's collection

the airline operations were conducted under the name of Cunard Eagle Airways. It was hoped that the Cunard name and influence would help to further Harold Bamberg's ambitions for a transatlantic scheduled service, and licences were sought for new routes from the UK direct to the USA by Cunard Eagle, as well as to Bermuda and the Caribbean. The first of what was to become a large fleet of Britannias arrived in 1960, and this was used to open a Heathrow–Bermuda–Nassau–Miami scheduled service, linking the main divisions of the Cunard Eagle operation. During 1961 the Bermuda-based Viscounts operated a twice-daily service to New York and four flights a day to Miami via Nassau.

In April 1961 the ex-Aer Lingus aircraft were replaced at Bermuda by two more secondhand Viscount 700s, VR-BBL and VR-BBM, both ex-Cubana V.755Ds that had been displaced at Havana by later-model Viscount 818s. The V.707s returnedto Europe, where they took up the UK registrations G-ARKH and 'KI. Cunard Eagle was now headquartered at Heathrow, following closure of the airline's original base at Blackbushe. Cunard Eagle operated the now Heathrow-based Viscount 707s within a mixed fleet of DC-6s, Britannias and a few surviving Vikings, on scheduled and charter services.

The arrival of the Viscount 700s in Bermuda saw Eagle dispose of its two original V.805s. Eagle's first Viscount, VR-BAX, was sold to Canadian airline Maritime Central Airways (MCA), and was introduced on its longer services to Gander, Goose Bay and St Johns from Moncton, New Brunswick, from June 1959. A moveable bulkhead enabled the cabin to be converted to a variety of passenger/cargo configurations, depending on local traffic demand. However, MCA only flew the aircraft for just over two years before selling it on to Aer Lingus in early 1962. Shortly afterwards MCA was absorbed by Eastern Provincial Airways, another Canadian independent airline. The other Eagle Airways Viscount 805, VR-BAY, had already gone to Aer Lingus in early 1960 as part of the deal to acquire the V.707s. On their arrival in Eire, Aer Lingus had both aircraft converted to V.808 standard by replacing their original Dart Mk 510s with more-powerful Mk 525s.

French Moves

Air France's fleet of twelve Viscount 708s had suffered only one serious incident since entering service in 1953. On 12 December 1956 the first V.708, F-BGNK, crashed after entering a steep dive during a training sortie from Paris-Orly to Reims, killing all on board. The surviving eleven aircraft continued to operate throughout Air France's European and North African network. Reconfigured from the original 48-seat layout to a 63-passenger configuration, the aircraft maintained an excellent reputation for reliability and serviceability that outshone the other aircraft in the fleet.

The arrival of the Caravelle short-haul jet in 1959 saw the beginning of Air France's withdrawal of the Viscounts, the first three being disposed of in 1960. These aircraft, F-BGNL, 'NM and 'NN, were sold to a new UK airline, Maitland Drewery Aviation, in June 1960, becoming G-ARBY, G-ARER and G-ARGR respectively. Maitland Drewery had originally been a small air-taxi company, and had expanded into inclusive-tour and *ad hoc* charter operations in early 1960, with a pair of Vikings based at Gatwick. Early success with the Vikings had encouraged the company to examine more modern alternatives. At a time when the vast

The Paris-based Viscount 708s of Air France enjoyed an impressive, relatively trouble-free record before an expanding fleet of Caravelle jets replaced them. via author

majority of inclusive-tour airlines in the UK were still flying old, unpressurized, piston-powered aircraft such as the Viking and DC-4, Maitland Drewery hoped to put itself in the forefront of the industry by pioneering the use of more up-to-date equipment.

Another UK operator took delivery of an ex-Air France Viscount in early 1961. Originally reserved for sale to a new Danish airline, Danish Air Charter, which failed to begin operations, F-BGNS was sold instead to Starways Ltd, based at Liverpool, becoming G-ARIR. Then operating DC-3s and DC-4s, Starways had built up a large scheduled network from Liverpool, including busy trunk services to Heathrow and Glasgow, as well as flying a number of inclusive-tour services from Liverpool and Manchester. The Viscount was first used on the inclusive-tour network to the Mediterranean from May 1961, and made its first appearance on the important scheduled route to London in July.

In 1962 Air France leased out two more Viscounts, this time to its associate company, Air Vietnam. Until Air Vietnam was formed in 1951, Air France had operated all of the airline services in what had been one of France's colonies in South–East Asia. Even in the 1960s Air France still retained a 33 per cent shareholding in the local carrier. Domestically, Air Vietnam was operating several DC-3s and a single DC-4. On the more important regional routes to Bangkok and Hong Kong, the Viscounts replaced Air France Constellations.

The livery worn by G-ARIR with Starways was heavily influenced by that of its original operator, Air France. via author

Maitland Drewery Disappointment

The lofty ambitions that Maitland Drewery and Tradair had for their Viscounts were to prove difficult to realize. After conversion and maintenance work by Marshall's of Cambridge, Maitland Drewery's first Viscount, G-ARBY, was positioned to Gatwick on 27 August 1960. Unfortunately, although the Vikings enjoyed a busy summer of charter services, work for the new Viscount seemed harder to find. Much of the revenue flying that did take place was often sub-charter work, undertaken on behalf of other airlines. The second Viscount, G-ARER, arrived at Gatwick on 1 October and was then despatched to operate holiday charters from West German cities for the next two weeks. While 'BY spent the Christmas period, from 16 December to 2 January 1961, in West Germany, 'ER operated only a small programme of charter flights from Gatwick and Birmingham to Lyons and Palma during this period.

The Vikings were disposed of in March 1961, and Maitland Drewery concentrated on trying to find charter contracts for its mostly idle pair of Viscounts, while the third aircraft, G-ARGR, remained at Cambridge awaiting conversion. Although business picked up a little during April and May, with the two operational Viscounts flying charters from both Gatwick and Berlin, the long-term prospects were not bright. A more reliable source of work was finally found in late May, when Maitland Drewery signed an agreement to lease out two of its three Viscounts to another British independent airline, BKS Air Transport Ltd.

Named using the initials of its three founding directors, Messrs Barnaby, Keegan and Stevens, BKS had originally been based at Southend as a prosperous charter operator in the early 1950s. However, it later began developing a scheduled network based at Newcastle and Leeds in the north of England, in addition to its established charter work. By 1960 one of BKS's more successful routes was the trunk

Enter Air Inter

Lignes Aeriennes Interieures was originally formed as a 'paper' company in 1954, intending to operate domestic services within the borders of metropolitan France and to the Mediterranean island of Corsica. However, no commercial operations were undertaken until March 1958, when several seasonal routes were opened under the name of Air Inter. The fledgling operation used a variety of aircraft, all leased in from Air France (Constellations), Airnautic (Vikings) or TAI (DC-3s and DC-6Bs). Sadly, financial results in the first year were quite disappointing and 1959 saw a much more limited network being operated, Air France Constellations being used for weekly Paris–La Baule and twice-weekly Paris–Dinard flights.

Similar limited seasonal operations were undertaken in 1961. In the spring of 1962, however, Air Inter took delivery of Air France's last five Viscount 708s, having received a government loan to enable it to establish full airline services as a domestic scheduled operator in its own right. The use of leased aircraft was impractical if the service was to be a sustained one, though Air France Constellations were also used alongside the Viscounts for some months. With its own fleet, Air Inter began a new, year-round, scheduled operation, the Viscounts operating services from Paris-Orly to Biarritz, Clermont Ferrand, Grenoble, Lille, Lyon, Nantes, Perpignan, St Etienne, Strasbourg and Tarbes. Routes were also opened from France's second largest city, Lyons, to Lille, Nice, Toulon and Toulouse. In addition, Calvi in Corsica was linked to Marseilles and Nice. Daily utilization was very high, and the aircraft were soon claiming the highest number of airframe hours for their type.

One of the Viscounts, F-BGNV, was lost in a crash on approach to Lyons from Lille on 12 August 1963, killing all twenty occupants. To replace this aircraft, and also to allow expansion, not only were the two Air Vietnam aircraft transferred to Air Inter on their return from lease, but four V.724s were purchased from TCA in 1964.

The first Air Inter Viscounts, which came from Air France, were soon joined by several ex-Canadian examples. Jenny Gradidge

Maitland Drewery's high hopes for its Viscounts were increasingly frustrated because suitable and profitable work for the turboprops was slow to come forward. Jenny Gradidge

domestic service from Newcastle to London Heathrow, mostly operated by the airline's fleet of ex-BEA Ambassadors. The Viscount lease was a six-month contract, under which Maitland Drewery operated the aircraft in BKS livery using its own flight-deck crews.

Newcastle Bound

The first Viscount to be delivered to BKS Air transport was G-ARER, on 29 May, when it positioned to Southend to be resprayed in BKS colours. After repainting, the aircraft entered service on Maitland Drewery charter flights from Gatwick over the weekend of 3–4 June, before flying its first BKS schedule from Heathrow to Newcastle on 6 June. On 11 June G-ARBY joined BKS, still in Maitland colours, but was returned to its owners on the arrival of G-ARGR on the 20th. The latter aircraft had finally been restored to flying condition for the BKS lease following an extended period of storage since its arrival from Air France.

The two aircraft soon settled down to a much busier working pattern, operating BKS's scheduled services alongside the Ambassadors during the Monday–Friday operations, from Newcastle to Bergen, Dublin and Jersey, as well as on the commercially important route to London. At weekends the Viscounts flew inclusive-tour charters from Newcastle and Southend for BKS, and a weekly Gatwick–Perpignan charter on behalf of Maitland Drewery. At the end of June 'ER was operated briefly by BKS on scheduled services for Jersey Airlines, from Jersey to Gatwick and Bournemouth. At that time Jersey Airlines was suffering a capacity shortage, as the delivery of its new Handley Page Dart

BKS Air Transport took delivery of its first leased Viscount 708, from Maitland Drewery, in May 1961.
Aviation Hobby Shop

Heralds had been delayed. When 'ER returned to BKS it was replaced by Viscount 754 OD-ACU, which was leased in by Jersey Airlines from MEA.

Viscount G-ARBY undertook very little commercial flying for Maitland Drewery for the rest of 1961, mainly serving as a back-up when the Newcastle-based aircraft needed maintenance. For some of the time 'BY was based in Copenhagen for the training of SAS Viscount crews, which was undertaken by Maitland Drewery pilots.

Although the six-month Viscount operation was a success, BKS found itself in severe financial difficulties by the end of the 1961 summer season. Many UK independent operators shared these economic problems at the time, and a number of high-profile bankruptcies in the air-charter industry during the year had done little to boost confidence among the airline's creditors. As a result, BKS Air Transport was placed under receivership on 30 November, though the airline did manage to continue operating. The extra expense of renewing the Viscount leases was out of the question, however, and both aircraft were returned to Maitland Drewery during November 1961.

New Leases

Maitland Drewery did not undertake any more commercial operations in its own name with its Viscounts. Instead, a new lease was arranged for the aircraft with Silver City Airways Ltd. Owned by British Aviation Services, Silver City intended to operate the V.708s from Manston Airport, Kent, on its cross-Channel Silver Arrow scheduled service to Le Touquet, which was directly linked to French Railway services into the heart of Paris. The Viscounts replaced Handley Page Hermes, which, as well as operating the brief cross-Channel hop to Le Touquet, were also used on longer charters to Europe. Plans were also being made to extend the Le Touquet service to more UK cities, such as Birmingham, Blackpool, Glasgow, Leeds and Newcastle, using the new Viscounts alongside DC-3s already in use by the airline's Northern Division, which operated scheduled services throughout the north of England.

Viscount crew training for Silver City began in early 1962. However, before the aircraft could enter service British Aviation Services sold Silver City Airways to Air Holdings, the owners of BUA. As a result, the Maitland Drewery Viscounts were delivered to BUA, joining the already established Gatwick-based Viscount fleet. Consequently, the UK terminal for the Le Touquet Silver Arrow service was transferred from Manston to Gatwick. The Hermes were also moved to Gatwick, from where they continued to operate their European charter work in Silver City colours, being withdrawn at the end of the summer of 1962.

Silver City also operated car ferry services across the English Channel, similar to BUA's Channel Air Bridge. In fact Silver City had pioneered this sort of operation in the late 1940s. The two car ferry systems were merged as a new division, British United Air Ferries. At about the same time Air Holdings also acquired Jersey Airlines, and the Jersey-based operation was merged with the Silver City Airways northern services to form British United (Channel Island) Airways. Configured in a high-capacity layout, the V.708s were used on BUA's expanding European scheduled network. As well as the thrice-daily Le Touquet Silver Arrow service, other routes from Gatwick, such as schedules to both Genoa and Rotterdam, were served by the new leased Viscounts, which were later bought by BUA.

Tradair Troubles

Financial problems had also plagued Tradair's attempts to operate its new pair of Viscounts. Commercial operations with the aircraft began on 12 February 1960, when G-APZB flew a Southend to Copenhagen charter. G-APZC's first revenue flight was on 19 February, operating a charter from Stansted to Nice. For the next few months the aircraft operated several *ad hoc* charters around Europe, and were often also chartered as substitute

Tradair's Viscount 707s found an early source of revenue in operating schedules on behalf of BEA from Heathrow. Jenny Gradidge

aircraft by scheduled airlines, making several appearances on the Heathrow–Manchester route flying on behalf of BEA. The airline hoped to fly the two V.707s on new holiday charters from Southend to Casablanca and Seville, as well as introducing them on the scheduled Southend–Maastricht route.

Unfortunately the anticipated new business for which the Viscounts were originally bought was not forthcoming, and Tradair was unable to find enough work to keep both aircraft occupied. Consequently 'ZC was leased out to Kuwait Airways, leaving Southend en route to the Middle East in June. Although 'ZB was successfully operated on several inclusive-tour and subcharter contracts, most of the airline's operations for the summer of 1960 were still undertaken by the fleet of Vikings.

The return of G-APZC saw both Viscounts in use with Tradair, alongside the Vikings, for the 1961 summer season. However, the airline was affected by the same turndown in holiday and charter traffic that had affected BKS's profitability. In addition, Tradair's ambitions to operate more scheduled services were proving difficult to realize. In November an official receiver was appointed in an attempt to stave off bankruptcy. Although the airline was permitted to continue limited operations, one early decision of the receivers was to withdraw the Viscounts and put them up for sale.

The company managed to survive the winter and was able to operate inclusive-tour flights with the Vikings for the 1962 season. The Vikings also opened new scheduled all-cargo services to Malmo in Sweden, and plans were made to build on this by opening more scheduled freight flights to France, Germany and Switzerland. One more contract was found for the Viscounts, though, G-APZC being brought out of storage in June to operate on BEA's German Internal Service, from West Berlin. From 1 July the aircraft operated several times a day on flights to Frankfurt, Hamburg and Hanover. Three months later 'ZB replaced 'ZC in Berlin for a brief period at the end of the contract. However, on its return to Southend 'ZB was sold, and on 21 November the V.707 was delivered to Liverpool and its new owner, Starways, joining its original V.708, G-ARIR.

Tradair's financial state remained precarious, and by the end of 1962 negotiations had begun for the sale of the company to another Southend-based airline, Channel Airways. Channel operated a fleet of Vikings, with DC-3s and Doves, on charters as well as a number of scheduled routes to the Channel Islands, Belgium, France and the Netherlands. From 31 December 1962 Tradair Ltd became a subsidiary of Channel Airways, and its fleet of seven Vikings and the remaining Viscount, 'ZC, were transferred to the newly combined operation. The Viscount was Channel's first turboprop aircraft and, when painted in its new owner's livery, was proudly promoted as the 'Golden Viscount 707'.

Leaving BEA

Notwithstanding the increased use of the larger V.802 and V.806 Viscounts, and the imminent arrival of BEA's Comet and Vanguards, the pioneering V.701s were still well used by the corporation as it entered the 1960s. The new decade got off to a less-than-encouraging start for the original Discovery Class fleet when G-AMNY was damaged beyond repair at Malta on 5 January 1960. At the end of a flight from London the aircraft suffered a total loss of hydraulic pressure. In an unfortunate chain of events the effect of a fractured hydraulic pipeline was combined with an incorrectly fitted non-return valve, which should have prevented the loss of pressure but only compounded the

'Golden Viscount 707' G-APZC was the precursor of what would eventually grow into Channel Airways' substantial fleet of turboprops. Aviation Hobby Shop

situation. As a result, there were no steering or braking controls available and the crew were unable to prevent 'NY colliding, at speed, with the Malta control tower. Although the unlucky Viscount was badly damaged, none of the forty-six passengers and five crew was seriously injured.

Among the V.701's busiest services in 1960 were the Berlin-based German services and the routes to the Channel Islands from the UK mainland. Viscounts had served the larger island of Jersey for some time, but the neighbouring island of Guernsey refused to provide a hard runway until 1960, so the smaller airport remained the domain of BEA's DC-3s. Eventually the government of Guernsey was made to realize that they ran a serious risk of losing valuable holiday trade if BEA and other airlines were unable to upgrade their equipment. The first Viscount to use the new hard runway at Guernsey, on 1 August 1960, was V.701 G-AOFX *Sir Joseph Banks*. However, the Viscount 701s were initially restricted to forty-four passengers, as one end of the runway was still unfinished.

The late arrival of the Vanguards ensured that the Viscount 701s were kept busy during 1961. By the beginning of 1962, though, once the Vanguards had finally settled down in service, the lower-capacity Viscounts had become surplus to requirements. The last of the BEA V.701s were taken out of service on 31 March 1962, and the whole fleet was put up for sale. By the time they were withdrawn the Viscount 701s had flown over six million of BEA's passengers. They were finally replaced by the Viscount 802s and 806s, which, in their turn, had been displaced on more important routes by Vanguards and Comets.

Disposals

In August, after a brief period of storage, ten of BEA's V.701s were sold to VASP. The Brazilian airline had enjoyed great success with its new V.827s, and was very interested in expanding its turboprop operations and replacing its remaining piston-engined fleet. Originally VASP had ordered a new stretched version of the Dart Herald, but problems and delays in the Herald programme had led the airline to cancel its order and acquire the ex-BEA Viscounts instead. Once refurbishing and other maintenance work was completed, the aircraft were delivered to Brazil during 1963.

The remainder of BEA's V.701s eventually found new homes a little closer to their roots. In 1958 BEA had bought a third share in a Cardiff-based independent, Cambrian Airways. The Welsh carrier had been operating a network of scheduled flights with DC-3s and Herons, unfortunately incurring heavy financial losses in the process. Even with the much-needed injection of capital from BEA the situation was dire, and the airline was all but closed down during the winter of 1958–59 while restructuring took place. Operations began again in early 1959, BEA leasing three of its Pionair DC-3s to Cambrian.

Brazil's VASP was an enthusiastic customer for BEA's redundant Viscount 701s. Originally G-AOFX *Sir Joseph Banks*, PP-SRS made its UK–Brazil delivery flight in August 1962. Jenny Gradidge

Steady expansion followed the fresh start, and in 1963 BEA agreed the transfer of all its Liverpool-based Irish Sea services to Cambrian. The routes had proved increasingly unprofitable for BEA, but it was hoped that Cambrian's lower costs would turn them around and make them more viable. The routes concerned were from Liverpool to Belfast, both direct and via the Isle of Man, from Heathrow to the Isle of Man, both direct and via Liverpool, and from Manchester to the Isle of Man. Five BEA Viscount 701s were acquired to operate the new network. In addition to its established Cardiff headquarters, Cambrian opened new Viscount bases at Heathrow, Liverpool and Manchester, initially flying one aircraft from each once the enlarged network was fully operating.

Although the handover of the Irish Sea routes from BEA did not take place until 1 April 1963, the first of the Viscounts, G-AMOP, was delivered as early as 6 January for crew training. The first commercial flight by a Cambrian Viscount, a charter carrying Welsh rugby supporters from Cardiff to Edinburgh, was operated on 3 February. The Viscount's first scheduled service for Cambrian was operated on 20 February over the Cardiff–Bristol–Dublin route. The airline's maintenance facilities were expanded to accommodate the new aircraft, a £70,000 extension being built at the Cardiff base and the number of engineering staff being doubled from seventy-five to more than 150 by 1964.

The remaining four aircraft had all been delivered by June, and were introduced on Cambrian's busier established services to the Channel Islands and Paris, as well as the new Irish Sea network. In early 1964 the Viscounts also introduced a new Heathrow–Cork schedule, and frequencies were increased between Heathrow and Liverpool. As well as the scheduled services, the arrival of the Viscounts allowed Cambrian to enter the inclusive-tour charter market. By 1963 the travel industry had started to recover from the traumas of 1960/61 and was experiencing growth. The main contractor for Cambrian's inclusive-tour programme was a locally based operator, Hourmont Travel, which chartered the Viscounts for flights to Mediterranean resorts from Cardiff, Bristol and Exeter. These were mostly flown at weekends or at night, when little scheduled flying was undertaken.

BEA's overpainted livery formed the basis of Cambrian's first Viscount colours.
via author

Channel Expansion

Ex-Aer Lingus V.707 G-APZC was Channel Airways' sole Golden Viscount for only one summer season. The only other four-engined aircraft in Channel's fleet at the time was an 88-passenger DC-4. In the summer of 1963 'ZC carried only 17,035 of Channel's grand total of 258,739 passengers, logging 711 flying hours. Most of 'ZC's flying in 1963 was concentrated on the Southend–Jersey scheduled service, alongside the airline's smaller Vikings and DC-3s. In addition, the Viscount occasionally appeared on other scheduled routes from Southend to Guernsey, Ostend and Rotterdam, as well as some charters.

In January 1964 Channel Airways took delivery of ex-BEA V.701 G-AMOA, the first of seven Viscount 701s that Channel had bought to expand its turboprop services. The seven were the last of BEA's V.701 fleet to be sold. As well as joining G-APZC on the established scheduled services during the summer of 1964, the Viscounts also flew a greatly expanded inclusive-tour charter programme from Southend and Manchester that took the Viscounts to France, Italy, Spain and Switzerland.

One distinguishing feature of Channel's Viscount operation was the high-capacity configuration, up to seventy-one passenger seats being crammed into the Viscount 700s. This was just about acceptable on the short hops over the English Channel from Southend, some sectors taking less than half an hour, but some rather stiff-legged passengers must have emerged from the Viscounts at the end of longer-ranging inclusive-tour charter flights. In addition, Channel Airways also started to lease out its spare Viscount capacity to other airlines, providing a new source of revenue for the company.

Cunard Bows Out

Cunard Eagle Airways' services from Bermuda had continued successfully, 15 per cent of the market from New York going to the Viscount operation. The much larger

Ex-BEA Viscount 701s joined Channel's original 'Golden Viscount' to expand the Southend-based fleet.
Jenny Gradidge

Author's collection

DC-6As also operated some of the New York flights when traffic demand required it. The company had also finally been successful in gaining authority to open a scheduled London–New York service, and ordered a pair of Boeing 707s to operate the important new route. Unfortunately BOAC objected strenuously to the award and was successful in having the licence revoked on appeal.

This was just before the first of the Boeings was due for delivery and, rather than have the aircraft idle, it was registered to Cunard Eagle (Bermuda) and operated on the schedule from London to Bermuda and Nassau in place of Britannias, as well as being used on some of the Bermuda–New York services. However, much to the annoyance of Harold Bamberg, who was still managing director, the Cunard management had rapidly become disillusioned with the idea of running an airline and began negotiations with BOAC to sell off the transatlantic and Bermuda-based services.

In June 1962 a new company, BOAC-Cunard, was formed to take over the Atlantic and Caribbean operations of BOAC and Cunard Eagle, and the second Boeing 707 was delivered directly to BOAC. Although Cunard Eagle continued to fly the transatlantic routes until the end of September, the Bermuda-based Viscount services had ceased on 9 September. The two V.755Ds were ferried to Heathrow, where they were re-registered G-AOCB and G-AOCC. Now an all-European-based airline again, the surviving portion of Cunard Eagle started to rebuild under Bamberg's guidance, flying scheduled and charter services with the Viscounts, Britannias and DC-6As.

On 14 February 1963 Bamberg bought back Cunard's remaining holdings, and on 9 August the airline's name was changed to British Eagle International Airlines. Ironically, a month before the name change, the two Viscount 707s were sold to BOAC Associated Companies for operation back in the Caribbean by Bahamas Airways, in which BOAC held a financial interest. With Bahamas the V.707s joined the three BOAC Associated Companies V.702s that had been transferred to Nassau after their Kuwait Airways service. In November Bamberg signed a co-operation agreement with Starways Ltd, which effectively meant that Starways would be taken over by British Eagle on 1 January 1964. A new subsidiary, British Eagle (Liverpool), was formed to operate the Starways network.

With the takeover, a number of important routes were inherited, including the trunk route from Liverpool to London, direct and via Chester, as well as from Liverpool to Cork and Glasgow, both direct and via Blackpool. Although the majority of the Starways employees were transferred to British Eagle (Liverpool), the airline's fleet, which consisted of the two Viscounts, three DC-3s and three DC-4s, was not included in the agreement. British Eagle supplied Britannias and Viscounts for the Liverpool operation from 1 January 1964. Aviation Overhauls, a company owned by the Starways directors, retained all the ex-Starways aircraft.

The V.708 G-ARIR was withdrawn from use by Starways before the takeover and returned to France, being sold to Air Inter in November 1963. Starways' other Viscount, V.707 G-APZB, was operated until 31 December and then remained out of service until it was leased to British Eagle in the summer of 1964. At the end of the lease 'ZB was sold to Channel Airways in November and reunited with its old Aer Lingus/Tradair stable-mate, G-APZC. British Eagle also leased-in four of Channel's ex-BEA V.701s during 1964, at least one of them carrying Starways titles over the British Eagle livery for a while.

With the sale of the Atlantic network, the V.755Ds were moved to London and placed on the UK register.
Jenny Gradidge

The last of the Viscount 700 series, Misrair/United Arab Airlines' SU-AKW was lost in an unexplained crash into the Mediterranean off the island of Elba, in September 1960. The V.739B had been delivered less than a month previously. Jenny Gradidge

All Nippon Airways' fleet of busy Viscount 828s featured several unique innovations, including television for passengers' in-flight entertainment. Jenny Gradidge

Viscount Production Slows Down

By the early 1960s most of the production capacity at Weybridge was dedicated to Vanguards and the first of the VC10s, and during 1962 Hurn was gearing up to produce the new BAC One-Eleven short-haul passenger jet. However, both factories were involved in producing the last few Viscounts. Deliveries of new aircraft for 1960 included the last Viscount 700, a V.739B for Misrair, in April. Also delivered in 1960 were the six V.837s for Austrian Airlines and a single V.816. This was one of a pair originally ordered by Trans Australia but later cancelled. The first aircraft of the two was completed as a V.836 executive aircraft for the Union Carbide Corporation of the USA, becoming N40N.

The first three aircraft of the ANA order were delivered in 1961. The second of these, JA8202, was the last Weybridge-built Viscount, all the remaining aircraft being built at Hurn. The sixty-passenger ANA aircraft were certainly among the most innovative as far as passenger facilities were concerned, being fitted with television sets in the hat-racks! The aircraft were first introduced on services from Tokyo to Osaka and Sapporo, later being assigned to other important regional routes such as Osaka–Kashi and Osaka–Miyazaki. Traffic growth was such that ANA's frequencies were reaching up to thirty a day from Tokyo to Osaka by 1963.

The last NZNAC Viscount 807 was delivered in May 1961, the same time as the remaining V.816, also built at Hurn, which had made its maiden flight in January. This V.816 was completed as a V.839 VIP aircraft. Registered EP-MRS, it was originally delivered to the Iranian Government, later being operated by Iranair. By a curious coincidence both of these undelivered TAA V.816s were to meet up again in their later careers. In 1964 both aircraft were purchased separately for use by the Royal Australian Air Force (RAAF). Used for VIP flights in executive configuration, the RAAF Viscounts carried Australian Government ministers and heads of state until they were replaced by new BAC One-Elevens at the end of 1969.

Last Viscounts off the Line

The last V.814 for Lufthansa and the last V.838 for Ghana Airways were completed at Hurn in late 1961. The German aircraft, D-ANAF, was delivered in January 1962, followed by five of the remaining six ANA Viscounts, which were delivered to Tokyo that year. A surprise last-ever Viscount order for six V.843s from Machimpex, the government-operated import/export organization of the People's Republic of China, followed the last ANA aircraft after it was delivered in February 1963. The six aircraft ordered by Machimpex were to be operated by the People's Republic's government-owned airline, Civil Aviation Administration of China (CAAC). Since the Communist Revolution in the late 1940s, China had operated a fleet of mostly Russian-built aircraft, such as Ilyushin Il-14s, on a rather limited civil airline service. The Viscount order was the first order given by Communist China to a Western aircraft manufacturer.

The USA, which had still not established diplomatic relations with the People's Republic, objected vehemently to the sale of the Viscounts to Communist China, and refused to allow any US-built equipment, such as radios and electrical systems, to be installed on these aircraft. Even non-American subsidiaries of US companies were forbidden to supply anything for the order and, as a result, only British equipment was installed on the V.843s. The aircraft were finished in a neutral livery, devoid of distinctive markings other than a UK registration, to negate any diplomatic

ABOVE: Lufthansa's Viscount 814s were introduced on services as diverse as domestic West German and regional European routes and further-ranging services to the Middle East and North Africa. Lufthansa via Jon Proctor

The Viscounts of CAAC enjoyed leisurely utilization on the Chinese airline's domestic services throughout the People's Republic. via author

problems during delivery flights, which were flown by UK pilots. After a night stop under guard at Hong Kong, the Viscounts were flown to nearby Canton in the People's Republic and placed under military jurisdiction. Only then were they painted in CAAC's livery and given Chinese numerical registrations.

One of the first CAAC Viscounts flew a single UK-based mission before its delivery. On 20 August V.843 G-ASDS ferried BAC/Hunting executives from Luton Airport to Hurn to witness the prototype BAC One-Eleven's maiden flight. The last two CAAC Viscounts, and the very last of the 436 Vickers-Armstrongs/BAC Viscounts to be built, were ferried to Canton during 1964, arriving in February and April respectively.

One curious aspect of the CAAC Viscount operation was that, unlike other airline operators, which ordered spares on an 'as required' basis, the acquisition of spares was restricted to a single order per year. As a result, if a serious fault developed, an aircraft might spend a considerable time out of service awaiting parts. However, the annual utilization of the Viscounts is believed to have been extremely low, even at its height, so the absence of one or two aircraft from the fleet did not cause too many scheduling problems.

Into the World

The end of Viscount and Vanguard production was far from the end of the story for either type. The swift dispersion of the early production Viscounts, once their initial owners had decided to sell them on, showed that there were plenty of customers willing and eager to operate them. Some of the hopeful candidates would certainly be comparable to Maitland Drewery and Tradair, in that no amount of enthusiasm would be able to make up for a lack of either managerial expertise or even plain luck. However, others would survive long enough to add their own chapters to the tale.

CHAPTER EIGHT

Fresh Tasks

Busy Workhorses

The day of the turboprop on major commercial airline routes may well have been perceived by many to have passed even before the Vanguard had entered service, and certainly by the time Viscount production had slowed to a halt. The Viscount had at least enjoyed a halcyon era when it was the latest novelty in air travel. By the time the Vanguards appeared the turboprop had lost much of its prestige in the eye of the travelling public, and was regarded, at best, as a reliable but rather unglamorous workhorse and, at worst, as downright old-fashioned. It was a fate shared by the Vanguard's more numerous contemporary rival, the Lockheed Electra. In fact, some of the Electras operated by US trunk carriers such as American and Eastern, spent only a few years with their original owners before finding themselves on the secondhand market once they became surplus to requirements as yet more short- and medium-range jet airliners appeared on the scene.

At that time, Viscounts were still to be seen on diverse services, linking United and Continental's smaller cities to their major US hubs, and ferrying business travellers and holidaymakers in Europe with smaller independents and major national carriers alike. They also operated as the

ABOVE: Long after the more glamorous jets arrived, the well-maintained Viscount 802s and 806s of BEA continued to carry thousands of passengers a year. BEA via Jon Proctor

BELOW: Uruguay's national carrier, PLUNA, became a long-standing Viscount operator, using them on both regional international routes and domestic services. The first pair of V.769Ds, including CX-AQO, arrived in 1958. Jenny Gradidge

high-profile flagships of Venezuela's LAV Aeropostal and Uruguay's PLUNA in South America. The ex-British imperial enclaves around Africa, the Far East and Australasia, while possibly having been influenced by their governments in their initial choice of the Viscount, found plenty of reasons to keep the aircraft in service on their networks, not least the type's intrinsic economical operation and passenger appeal. The Vanguards might never be able to gain such diversity in their use, not least because of the smaller numbers sold, but they would still make their own mark on the history of the airline industry.

Sturdy, Stately Vanguards

Even though the lack of sales meant that the Vanguard programme brought Vickers a huge financial loss, the aircraft was still able to make money for its operators. Once the early problems were solved, the forty-three production aircraft were doing exactly what they were designed to do. They were kept busy carrying large, economical, commercial payloads of passengers and cargo on high-density routes, safely and with minimal fuss.

One unnamed pilot's affectionate comment on the Vanguard was soon to be echoed among many of the aircraft's crews. 'This aircraft doesn't just go places, it proceeds!' The very size of the Vanguard certainly gave an impression of stateliness, and passengers felt that they were travelling in an aircraft of considerable substance and strength. This could be deceptive, though, as the aircraft could still provide as sprightly a performance as any Viscount, given the right conditions. Care had to be taking in taxying, for instance, as the long fuselage was prone to pitching when turning at speed on the ground, which could result in the passengers in the rearmost seats having the rather uncomfortable feeling that they were being swung sideways.

Pilots were very appreciative of the spacious flight deck as a place of work, with the control wheel adjustable to the individual's needs and useful touches such as a retractable side-table and storage space to hand for briefcases. Two seats were provided behind the two main pilots' seats, as well as a small jump seat. Even when all five were occupied, the space did not feel overcrowded and all the occupants could get up without getting in each other's way. Visibility from the flight deck was excellent, the 36sq ft (3.3sq m) of glazing providing a panoramic view. Forward vision was such that the horizon could still be seen in the steepest climb. To the rear, the outer leading edge of the wing could be seen up to the outboard engines. Cabin crews were equally impressed with their working area. The two spacious galleys, forward and mid-cabin, allowed them to provide a full service efficiently, quickly and easily to the large number of passengers that could be accommodated, even on shorter flights.

Rocky Mountain Drama

The sturdiness of the Vanguard's basic construction was shown to good effect on 6 May 1963, over the Rocky Mountains. Trans-Canada Vanguard 952 CF-TKV was en route from Vancouver to Edmonton as flight 502, cruising at 21,000ft (6,400m), when it encountered sudden severe clear-air turbulence. Unfortunately the two violent bursts of turbulence encountered did not give all the cabin crew or seventy-one passengers time to return to their seats after the 'Fasten Seat Belts' sign was illuminated. Caught in a severe downdraft, the Vanguard fell nearly 1,000ft (300m) before control was regained.

Twenty-five of those on board, including the three flight attendants, were injured in the incident, and one passenger regrettably died of a heart attack. However, once the aircraft was landed safely at Edmonton it was found to have escaped any structural damage other than a few loosened seats and damaged cabin fittings. Engineers calculated that the stresses involved could easily have ripped the wings away from a less sturdily built aircraft. In fact, a similar 'mountain wave' had caused a TCA Canadair North Star to crash in December 1956, killing all the occupants.

TCA Viscount Disposals

The arrival of the Vanguards led to some of TCA's Viscounts being withdrawn and disposed of from 1963. As well as the sale of four to Air Inter already mentioned, a single aircraft was leased to Transair of Winnipeg. Transair (which had no connection with the previous British Viscount operator of the same name) had purchased a number of 'prairie' routes that TCA had found uneconomical to operate. These were operated from Winnipeg to Brandon and Regina, and from Prince Albert to Saskatoon and Regina. The routes, two DC-3s and the Viscount lease were purchased from TCA for a single Canadian dollar! The Viscount was CF-TGI, the first TCA Viscount built, and it would serve Transair reliably for a number of years.

Two more of the early-model TCA Viscounts were eventually acquired by a US company, William C. Wold Associates, in partnership with Timmins Aviation Ltd of Montreal. Wold had also handled the sale of the four aircraft to Air Inter, and had plans to offer executive conversions of Viscounts for under $60,000. The conversion work would include complete overhauls of the airframes and engines, installation of a new executive interior and exterior painting to the customer's requirements, pilot and maintenance training, as well as full after-sales and spares support.

In the end, though, only two executive Viscount conversions were completed. In 1965 Wold acquired CF-TGJ, which had originally been sold by TCA to Maverick Equipment Ltd in 1963. The other, CF-TGN, was sold by TCA to Canadian Schenly, also in 1963, and sold on to Wold in 1964. After being modified to V.744 standard by Timmins and given interior refits, the two aircraft were delivered to executive customers in the USA.

Trans-Canada's first Viscount, CF-TGI, was transferred on a long-term lease, to become the new flagship for Winnipeg-based Trans Air in 1963. via author

TCA to Air Canada

On 1 June 1964 Trans-Canada Air Lines changed its name to Air Canada. The new name was not only simpler and contributed to a more up-to-date image, it also had the advantage of being linguistically neutral, and was acceptable to both Canada's English- and French-speaking communities. For some time the airline had been referring to itself as 'Trans-Canada Air Lines – Air Canada' in advertising material, in preparation for the change. Introduced at the same time was a modern red-and-white livery that was soon applied to the fleet of DC-8s, Vanguards and remaining Viscounts.

One of the Viscount 757s, CF-THT, was lost within days of the name change when, on 13 June 1964, it landed short at Toronto, fortunately with no serious injuries among the forty-four on board. This was the third loss in the Canadian Viscount fleet. On 10 November 1958 V.724 CF-TGL had been written off while parked at the terminal at New York when a Seaboard & Western Super Constellation crashed into it after it becoming uncontrollable during take-off on a cargo flight. Luckily the two TCA pilots were the only persons on board, and they escaped unharmed. Another V.757, CF-TGY, was written off after it struck a water tower on approach to Toronto on 3 October 1959, again with no serious injuries to the thirty-eight passengers and crew.

ABOVE: Air Canada's smart new modern livery made its first appearance on the turboprop fleet of Vanguards and Viscounts in 1964.
Air Canada via Bill Mellberg

BELOW: Despite selling a number of its Viscounts, Air Canada continued to operate a sizeable fleet on local services, including the 1958-vintage V.757 CF-THN.
Jenny Gradidge

Busy Canadian Turboprops

The Viscounts that remained with Air Canada were still kept busy working across the huge country, even though they were increasingly confined to shorter, more provincial routes after the Vanguards replaced them on the longer-ranging services. The TCA/Air Canada Viscounts were actually introduced on routes to a number of cities not previously served by the type, and a repeat of the rise in passenger figures that had occurred nearly a decade before was soon noted.

The Vanguard's use on the longer routes to the Caribbean was soon curtailed, the airliner being confined to the low-season services, as the DC-8s operated the peak-season flights. Closer to home, though, the Vanguards were still to be seen on the high-density intercity services, offering round-the-clock schedules, alongside Viscounts, between the main eastern Canadian cites of Montreal, Ottawa and Toronto, as well as linking numerous other points throughout Canada. On the cross-border service to the USA in the mid-1960s Vanguards still flew most of the schedules from Montreal and Toronto to New York, making four and seven flights a day each, respectively. Three daily Vanguard flights also operated from Montreal, via Toronto, to Chicago, and there were daily Toronto–Detroit and

After only five years in passenger service, V.952 CF-TKK was converted by Air Canada to the unique 'Cargoliner' configuration. via author

Halifax–Boston Vanguard services. One of the most demanding of the Air Canada domestic flights to be operated by the Vanguards was a daily service from Toronto to St Johns, Newfoundland, with no fewer than seven stops en route.

In December 1966 Vanguard CF-TKK was withdrawn from passenger service and converted to all-freighter configuration. All of the interior cabin fittings, including airstairs, were removed, and the passenger windows were blanked off. Although not fitted with a main deck cargo door, the aircraft was still capable of carrying a very respectable freight load of up to 42,000lb (19,000kg). Now dubbed the Cargoliner, 'KK was put into service on Air Canada's cargo and mail services across the length of Canada, and performed very satisfactorily as a dedicated freighter for several years. However, no further cargo conversions were undertaken by Air Canada on any of its remaining Vanguards.

Aussie Swaps

On the other side of the world, the two main domestic Australian carriers also continued to operate their Viscount fleets throughout the continent. Both had also ordered fleets of Dart-powered Fokker F.27s to operate thinner routes alongside the larger Viscounts and Electras.

The Airlines Equipment Act had come into effect shortly after Ansett's takeover of Australian National Airways, in an effort to bring more stability to the Australian airline market. It had been decided that a certain degree of standardization was called for between Ansett-ANA and TAA, in both equipment and service regularity. As a result, TAA was forced to hand over three of its Viscounts to Ansett-ANA, and reluctantly received two DC-6Bs, which it did not really want or need, in return. The aircraft were swapped under a lease/charter arrangement and operated in the receiving airline's colours, though at least one of the Viscounts is reported to have appeared in a joint TAA/Ansett-ANA livery.

One of the ex-TAA V.720s, VH-TVC, was lost on 30 November 1960 while on lease/charter to Ansett-ANA. After taking off from Sydney it encountered unexpected turbulence after entering a thunderstorm and crashed into Botany Bay. The turbulence was so violent that the starboard wing failed, and the aircraft broke up in flight before crashing into the sea, killing all on board.

Towards the end of the Viscount's commercial days in Australia, Ansett-ANA leased three of its V.700s, one V.720 and two V.747s to MacRobertson-Miller Airlines, a subsidiary company based at Perth in Western Australia. The aircraft served on routes up the west coast of the continent, such as Perth–Port Headland–Darwin, with an average journey time of more than three hours per sector. Arriving in September 1968, the trio suffered a tragic loss on 31 December when the V.720, VH-TVB, crashed while flying from Perth to Port Headland, with the loss of all thirty-one on board. The aircraft had suffered structural failure in the wing, and the accident led to a temporary grounding of all the remaining V.700s in Australia. The incident undoubtedly quickened the disposal of the Australian Viscount fleets as, although the ban was eventually lifted, the release applied only to the V.756Ds. The V.720s and V.747s remained grounded and were soon disposed of.

The lease/charter arrangement continued until both airlines had introduced short-haul jets, in the form of US-built Boeing 727s, and this heralded the first disposals of the older Viscounts in both fleets. However, until smaller McDonnell-Douglas DC-9 jets, which had also been ordered, were delivered to replace them, the Viscount 810s continued to operate over a decreasing number of shorter routes to smaller Australian cities for a few more years.

Originally VH-BAT with Butler, Ansett-ANA's VH-RMO was operated by MacRobertson Miller Airlines, an Ansett subsidiary, during 1968. Jenny Gradidge

Swinging Through the Sixties

Even after its early V.701s were disposed of, BEA continued to make heavy daily use of its Viscount 800s. When the jets arrived in the form of Comets and, from 1964, Hawker Siddeley Tridents, the Viscount was still proving its worth on a variety of scheduled services around the UK and European network. In 1963 the type was even used to open a new trunk UK domestic route, a direct daily Aberdeen–Heathrow service being inaugurated. This was the first direct link from Aberdeen to the UK capital for some years. In the 1950s a DC-3 service had been flown between Aberdeen and London, stopping at Edinburgh, though this was later dropped as uneconomic. The Viscounts flew the new non-stop service in two hours, initially operating the northbound sector from London in the evening, night-stopping and flying the southbound service from Aberdeen in the morning. So successful was the new service that it was later modified with the addition of an extra London–Aberdeen service, operating in the early afternoon, the return sector providing an evening departure to London. This was modified once again in 1966, the earlier of the two London–Aberdeen flights being rescheduled to operate in the morning. The aircraft then operated scheduled services around BEA's Scottish internal network during the day, before returning to London in the evening.

Viscounts became even more common on the Scottish local services from November 1966, when BEA decided to replace its trio of Dart Heralds. These had originally been bought especially for the Scottish network, which was based on Glasgow. The Heralds had replaced BEA's last operational DC-3s in the region on scheduled flights to the Highlands and Islands, but the Herald's much smaller capacity had still prevented much profit being made on the Scottish network. The Dart Herald's better runway performance over the Viscount, the main reason for obtaining the three aircraft, had been greatly negated by recent airport improvements that allowed the introduction of the bigger, and hopefully at least slightly less uneconomic, Viscounts. With the Viscounts now serving more remote points among the Scottish Highlands and Islands, such as Benbecula in the Outer Hebrides, the aircraft were fitted with extra-powerful batteries so that they could operate at airports lacking some of the more advanced basics, such as a ground power unit for start-ups.

Viscounts were also used for the introduction of a new non-stop flight from London to West Berlin, opened in 1964. Previously, passengers either had to change to or from the German Internal Service at Cologne, Hanover or another German city, or the aircraft would make an en route stop. The Viscount operated the daily service in two-and-a-half hours, leaving London at 11.25hr, and left West Berlin, to return to Heathrow, at 15.45hr.

Shortly after this, BEA began facing serious jet competition on the West German services in the shape of Boeing 727-100s introduced by Pan American on its own Berlin-based routes. Replacing Pan American's ageing DC-6Bs, the Boeing tri-jets were an immediate hit with the West German public and BEA's revenue loads from the city plummeted. The British airline had no immediate plans to introduce jets, suitable British-built aircraft being some years away. In an effort to win back some of the lost traffic, Berlin-based Viscount 800s were reconfigured in a more comfortable Silver Star seating layout. The new layout provided comparatively luxurious accommodation for fifty-three passengers on the Viscounts, with much more space and comfort, even over the new Boeings. The standard of cabin service and style of refreshments provided were also upgraded considerably. However, this expensive exercise was not a great success. Eventually, following the delivery of more new Tridents for use on its routes from Heathrow, BEA was able to transfer a handful of Comets from London to Tempelhof. Strictly speaking, the four-engine, first-generation jet airliners were highly unsuitable, operationally and economically, for the West German network. For one thing, restrictions imposed in the 'air corridors' to West Berlin called for the aircraft to operate at a fuel-guzzling low altitude of 10,000ft (3,000m). Not until One-Elevens were introduced in 1968 was BEA able to provide an effective jet service from West Berlin.

Changes Afoot in the Med

The BEA contracts to provide capacity for Malta Airlines, Gibraltar Airways and Cyprus Airways continued to involve the Viscount fleet. In 1963 Malta signed a new ten-year operating agreement with BEA, which would conveniently come to an end shortly after Malta was due to achieve independence. After that date it was expected that the new island nation would finally establish its own carrier. In the meantime, jets, in the form of BEA Comets and, later, the new Tridents, would operate most of the longer and more important routes to the UK and mainland Italy, supplemented by Vanguards. However, BEA Viscounts continued to operate some of the local services to Sicily and Libya from Malta for several years.

The first aircraft to carry full Cyprus Airways livery since the days when the carrier had its own DC-3s, the pair of Viscount 806s leased from BEA were used on regional services around the eastern Mediterranean area. Cyprus Airways

In 1963 a DC-3 replaced the Viscount leased from BEA by Gibair. This apparently retrograde step was economically sensible, as only a short sector was regularly flown from Gibraltar to Tangiers. The use of the DC-3, dry-leased from BEA, enabled Gibair to offer more flexibility and economy in its operation. Nonetheless, it was not a popular move among the local population. The DC-3 had actually been purchased by BEA from its associate, Cambrian Airways, ironically operating ex-BEA Viscounts itself by then. The single DC-3 remained with Gibair for a number of years, and even managed to earn itself a place in the local folklore, despite the hostile reaction to its initial arrival.

Cyprus Airways, the joint operator of the first sustained Viscount scheduled service, had continued to lease in capacity from BEA and, by the early 1960s, was using BEA Comets for most of its services from Nicosia to the UK and Europe. Like Malta, on the verge of full independence, the airline wanted to expand its presence in the region, and was concerned that the Comets would be too large to be used in the planned expansion. A temporary solution was found by leasing in a pair of BEA Viscount 806s, G-AOYJ and 'YK. Unlike earlier lease and charter agreements with BEA, the two 'new' aircraft were operated in full Cyprus Airways livery and permanently based at Nicosia. The first aircraft to display Cyprus Airways colours in their own right since the DC-3 days, they were placed into service in November 1965 and were eventually to be seen on routes from Nicosia to Amman, Athens, Beirut, Cairo, Istanbul, Jerusalem, Rhodes and Tel Aviv. The use of the Viscounts under its own name allowed the airline to re-establish and increase its profile throughout the eastern Mediterranean. Cyprus Airways had ordered a fleet of new Trident 1Es from Hawker Siddeley for 1969/70 delivery, and these would, in time, replace not only the BEA Comets but also the pair of leased Viscounts.

Switch from Mainline to Regional

As well as increasing their presence on the Scottish network, as more of BEA's mainline routes from London and other bases were taken over by jets, the Viscounts were seen on more regional English services, especially from Birmingham. As well as the popular routes to the Channel Islands and Scotland, Viscounts were serving Eire, Northern Ireland and European points from the UK regions, where the incumbent traffic was not enough to support newer jet aircraft.

Viscounts reopened BEA services from Southampton in 1966, the first flight to the Channel Islands being operated by G-AOYO on 1 April. The airline had previously served Southampton until 1961, when it withdrew its last DC-3s. At that time Southampton had only a grass runway, and the DC-3s were the only BEA aircraft capable of operating economically from the airport at Eastleigh. Operations were switched to nearby Bournemouth and the routes taken over by the Viscounts, but, nevertheless, the services from Bournemouth failed to attract the commercial loads that Southampton had offered. For one thing, Southampton Airport had the benefit of its own railway station, on the main line from London and the southeast, with the ability to bring in passengers quickly and easily from a much larger catchment area. Once a new concrete runway had been built at Southampton, BEA was quick to switch its flights back from Bournemouth and started operating Viscounts from Eastleigh.

Even the much larger Vanguards began to become more regular visitors to Jersey for BEA during the mid-1960s, after they had made very limited scheduled appearances in 1963 and 1964. By 1966 there were no fewer than nineteen weekly Vanguard flights scheduled between Heathrow and Jersey in the summer season, with nine weekly flights from Manchester and even two from Gatwick. The smaller island of Guernsey remained almost exclusively Viscount territory for BEA, its still restricted runway allowing only very occasional visits by the Vanguards. Some experimental *ad hoc* services were operated by way of 'proving flights', but BEA was reluctant to schedule Vanguards regularly on Guernsey services, owing to the restrictions that would be imposed on traffic loads when operating from the short runway. As a result, it would be some years before the Vanguards became regular visitors to Guernsey.

One Dark Night

Given the high utilization of its Vanguard fleet, BEA had few serious incidents within the day-to-day operation. Naturally, there was the occasional incident. Among the more significant, G-APEF flew into a large flock of birds on take-off from Edinburgh on 11 April 1962. Two engines failed immediately, and the aircraft managed to limp back to the airport for a safe landing, a third engine failing shortly after the aircraft was down. On 29 March 1963 G-APEJ suffered a nosewheel collapse on landing at Dublin, and G-APEE had a similar failure on landing at Glasgow on 6 October 1964. Fortunately, there were no serious injuries to any of the aircrafts' occupants in these episodes.

Just over a year after its Glasgow nosewheel incident, G-APEE was involved in a much more serious occurrence. On 26 October 1965 it was operating a BEA night-rate service from Edinburgh to Heathrow, having taken off at 23.17hr. The aircraft was crewed by Capt N. Shackell and two first officers, I. Cochrane and D. Swanson, and a steward and two stewardesses were working in the cabin, attending to the light load of thirty passengers. It had already been reported that Heathrow was having problems with fog, and Shackell had taken on enough fuel for up to six hours' flight, though the scheduled flying time was only just over an hour. This allowed him plenty of choice in his options for holding overhead or diverting to an alternative airport if the weather was still bad on his arrival. The preselected alternatives had already been filed as Manchester and Gatwick, and the large fuel load permitted a safe return all the way back to Edinburgh, even after a significant holding time over London.

As predicted, Heathrow was still in the grip of fog when 'EE arrived over the capital. However, the visibility was reported as 350m (380yd), the minimum allowed by BEA for an attempted landing. At 00.23hr 'EE was established on the glide path for runway 28R, but Shackell advised the tower that he was overshooting as he had failed to see the runway lights on the first approach. A little under ten minutes later, having received more favourable reports of the visibility on another of Heathrow's runways, another approach was made, this time to runway 28L. Noticing that this approach was slightly out of line, the radar controller advised another overshoot, which was initiated at 00.35hr. The captain reported that they had not 'seen anything that time', and that the fog had seemed 'very patchy'. The crew decided not to make an immediate attempt at another approach, and 'EE began circling over the Garston holding point, awaiting an improvement in the weather.

In the meantime, another BEA Vanguard, G-APED, arrived over Heathrow and made a successful landing on 28R at 00.46hr. Encouraged by this, though weather conditions had not improved at all, G-APEE's crew turned back to Heathrow for another attempt at 00.52hr. During the flight back from the holding point a third Vanguard, G-APEH, attempted to land on 28R but overshot and diverted. Despite this news, Shackell continued his approach and, at 01.22hr was established on the centreline of 28R, three-quarters of a mile (1.2km) from the runway. Nonetheless, twenty-two seconds later Shackell advised that they were overshooting again. The radar controllers saw the aircraft begin to climb as before, but then, inexplicably, it was seen to enter a steep dive. The Vanguard crashed on to the runway 2,600ft (790m) from the threshold and burst into flames. Despite a very quick response by the airport fire and rescue services, which were on the scene within two minutes, all thirty-six occupants died.

Cruel Combination

In the full investigation that followed the loss of G-APEE, several factors were deemed to have contributed to the tragedy. For one thing, although the visibility had been reported as 350m (380yd), exactly on the BEA minimum, it was discovered that this was incorrect, and that the visibility in the fog was actually 50m (55yd) less, and the crew should not have even been considering an approach in the first place. The incorrect reading was a result of the Runway Visual Range lights not having been calibrated properly for some time.

For many years BEA had operated a 'Monitored Approach System'. While one pilot flew the aircraft on instruments, the other looked out of the aircraft, eyes fully adjusted to the outside conditions. If the runway was sighted, the latter pilot would take over and land the aircraft; otherwise he was responsible for calling for the overshoot and retracting the flaps and undercarriage if the attempt was unsuccessful. In the event of a three-pilot crew being present, as was standard on the BEA Vanguards, the third pair of eyes would monitor all the remaining instruments as the other pilot concentrated on the altitude and so on, during the approach.

Although this system seems to have worked well on G-APEE's previous approaches, on the third and last attempt to land it seems to have broken down owing to several factors. According to data extracted from the flight recorders, the overshoot appeared to have been initiated rather violently, probably distracting the other crewmembers from their assigned tasks in the manoeuvre. The distraction would have been enough to break their previously good concentration and lead to a breakdown of the Monitored Approach System. During the resulting climb-out, spatial disorientation and an error on the setting of one of the pressure-controlled instruments led the crew to believe they were climbing when, in fact, the nose had been lowered. Although the crew were operating well within allowed hours, general tiredness and the stress of the previous missed approaches might well have also contributed to crew fatigue as yet another factor.

An incorrect flap setting had also been selected, which contributed to the descent. An inherent design fault in the flap-selector mechanism was thought to have contributed to this error. The instrument inaccuracy would have been only a minor problem had any of the crew looked at the artificial horizon, which would have alerted them to the descent. However, in the apparent confusion this went unnoticed until, according to the flight recorder information, the nose began to lift, presumably as a result of the crew finally recognizing the aircraft's attitude. Unfortunately this was in the very last second of the flight, far too late to affect the outcome.

By coincidence, thirteen days before the loss of G-APEE, another Vanguard, also on an Edinburgh–Heathrow flight, had experienced a similar problem when attempting an overshoot. On approach, also in fog and using the well-tried Monitored Approach System, the overshoot had been initiated at an altitude of 200ft (60m). The captain suddenly heard the third pilot calling for him to climb because he had noticed that the aircraft had inadvertently continued to descend and was only 100ft (30m) above the runway. Swiftly and instinctively pulling back on the control, the captain saw that they were now at a height of only 40ft (12m). A slower reaction, as had apparently been the case with G-APEE, would almost certainly have resulted in an identical tragedy. As a result of the loss of 'EE, not only was the flap-selector redesigned, but the Monitored Approach System was closely examined and a number of revisions made.

African Movements

The heavily utilized Viscount 700 fleet of CAA had continued to provide a popular and reliable service to the citizens of Northern and Southern Rhodesia and Nyasaland, not only within their borders but also to surrounding African nations. The fleet operated throughout central, eastern and southern Africa over a wide variety of routes and environments, connecting both major cities and more regional and local airports, often under difficult conditions.

In 1963 the Federation comprising the three countries broke up and the new British Commonwealth nations of Zambia, Rhodesia and Malawi, respectively, were born in the wake of independence from the UK. A new Central African Airways was constituted to continue to operate in the

Several unfortunate factors came together in the loss of G-APEE at Heathrow, including the apparent breakdown of established and well-proven flight-deck procedures. Nonetheless, following the tragic accident the remaining aircraft managed to regain the Vanguard's hard-won reputation for reliable service. BEA via author

region, though it was now officially operating its services on behalf of Zambia Airways, Air Rhodesia or Air Malawi.

Initially none of the new airlines was operating its own aircraft. A system was devised whereby the Viscounts, still in CAA livery, were fitted with removable stickers for any one of the three carriers. The Viscount operation continued to flourish, an ex-MEA aircraft having already been acquired in 1961. Further Viscounts, in the shape of a pair of ex-Iranian Airlines V.782Ds, arrived in 1966, but by then major political changes were in the air.

The ruling white residents of Rhodesia clung on to power in the country, requiring its native population to continue to live under apartheid and segregation. This brought Rhodesia into ideological conflict not only with Zambia and Malawi but also with the rest of the British Commonwealth of Nations. After Rhodesia was declared a republic, Rhodesia was expelled from the Commonwealth and began to have severe trade and financial sanctions imposed upon it. On 31 December 1966 CAA ceased operations when Zambia imposed a ban on direct air links to Rhodesia. As a result, Air Malawi, Air Rhodesia and Zambia Airways were obliged to become fully operational airlines, instead of being mere 'paper' companies. The CAA fleet was dispersed to the countries of its previous owners, the Viscounts going to the new national carriers of Malawi and Rhodesia, which received two and five aircraft respectively.

Air Malawi maintained close relations with Air Rhodesia, the latter remaining responsible for the maintenance of the Malawi Viscount fleet for many years. One of the Malawi aircraft was actually operated on secondment by Air Rhodesia, in full Air Malawi colours. The remaining Air Malawi Viscount was used for an average of 1,800hr a year on services from Blantyre to Beira in Mozambique, Ndola in Zambia and Salisbury in Rhodesia, and also on a domestic schedule to Lilongwe. Until One-Elevens arrived in the 1970s, the Viscount remained the prestige equipment for Air Malawi.

Following the dissolution of the Central African Federation, the CAA Viscount fleet was fitted with changeable titles, depending on which of the component carriers the aircraft was flying for. Global Air Image

Although South Africa also found itself subject to sanctions, owing to its own political stance and maintenance of an apartheid system, SAA survived intact. In spite of the airline suffering numerous restrictions, such as the banning of its aircraft from over-flying many African nations, SAA continued to flourish. Even though they were replaced on major domestic runs by new Boeing 727s, the Viscount 813s were still heavily used on domestic and regional services, being seen on SAA flights from Johannesburg to Upington and Windhoek, and from Cape Town to Alexander Bay, Keetmanshoop and Windhoek, all the way through to the early 1970s.

Although the Viscount 813s of SAA were displaced on many more important routes by new Boeing jets, they remained heavily used on regional and local services through the 1960s. Jenny Gradidge

Independent Jet Competition

British Eagle International Airlines had successfully built on the merged network of its own original Heathrow-based European services and the acquired Starways system. A steadily growing fleet of Viscounts continued to operate on the scheduled services alongside larger Britannias, with which they also shared a great number of inclusive-tour holiday charter contracts. Extra aircraft continued to be leased-in as required, especially from Channel Airways, and in 1965 four Viscounts were purchased from UAA. British Eagle's chairman, Harold Bamberg, continued to lobby the UK civil aviation authorities frequently for authority to open new schedules and increase frequencies. A major victory was achieved when permission was granted to open scheduled domestic trunk services from Heathrow to Belfast, Edinburgh and Glasgow, in direct competition with BEA. Initially, both Viscounts and Britannias flew against the BEA Vanguards.

Although the British Eagle flights were a commercial success, they were hampered by severely restricted frequencies, in most cases being limited to only one flight a day,

Author's collection

ABOVE: **British Eagle's V.798D G-ATDR *City of Glasgow* was acquired from Egypt to expand the independent airline's scheduled and charter network.** via author

against several daily services operated by BEA. When authority was refused to increase the frequencies of British Eagle's schedules, Bamberg protested by not only suspending the flights, but also by cancelling a multi-million-pound order for new One-Elevens, which had been purchased to operate on the routes. Leased V.701 G-AMOH operated the last schedule on the Belfast route on 19 February 1965, and V.755D G-AOCB flew the last Edinburgh–Heathrow British Eagle schedule the next day.

Eagle Jets

A year later British Eagle began operating jets for the first time since the Cunard Eagle 707 days, when two One-Eleven 200s were leased-in. Bamberg's persistent lobbying had finally borne fruit with the granting of permission to reopen services to Glasgow at an increased frequency. Although still only allowed to operate twice a day over the Heathrow–Glasgow route, the airline was at least now able to offer the important day-return option to business travellers.

On 2 May 1966 one of the new One-Elevens, G-ATTP *Swift*, became the first aircraft to land at the new airport for Glasgow, at Abbotsinch, which was due to replace the original airport at Renfrew. This first landing was on a training flight, and the first scheduled service with the One-Elevens was inaugurated to Abbotsinch on 9 May, replacing Britannias, which had reopened the Glasgow service, operating to Renfrew, in April. More One-Elevens arrived later in the summer, in the form of a batch of three Series 300s. The jets were soon supplementing or replacing the Viscounts on British Eagle's scheduled and charter services to Europe from Heathrow, as well as appearing on the Liverpool–Heathrow route.

In the Starways takeover British Eagle had also inherited a network of seasonal scheduled services to Newquay, Cornwall, from a number of UK cities, including London, Glasgow, Manchester and Liverpool. Although mostly operated by the Viscounts, occasionally supplemented by Britannias, some services to the Cornish resort were also flown by the One-Elevens at busy times. Viscounts also continued to operate on British Eagle's European scheduled routes to popular destinations such as Dinard, Innsbruck, Luxembourg and Stuttgart, as well as on new routes from Liverpool to Cork and Dublin.

While the incumbent BEA Vanguards from Heathrow had been well able to compete against British Eagle's Britannias and Viscounts, the arrival of the One-Elevens finally enabled the independent carrier to give BEA a run for its money. Even with the restricted schedules, British Eagle's One-Elevens were soon attracting respectable loads at BEA's expense.

BUA Challenges BEA

British United Airways was the first airline in the world to introduce the One-Eleven into service, in 1965. Initially supplementing established Viscounts on the schedules and inclusive-tour charters throughout BUA's European services from Gatwick, the One-Eleven also replaced BUA Viscounts on their last long-range Safari route, to West Africa via the Canary Islands. The arrival of the short-haul jet saw BUA start to dispose of its smaller Viscount 700s, and its ex-Air France Viscount 708s actually found their way back across the Channel to join the still expanding Air Inter fleet in Paris, which by then included most of the remaining V.708s.

On its return to BUA after its long lease to Sudan Airways, V.831 G-ASED was leased to Spanish operator Aviaco for the summer of 1965, and placed on the Spanish register as EC-AZK. Aviaco operated the aircraft on inclusive-tour charters from the Spanish resorts and holiday islands. The three ex-Transair V.804s had already

British United's Gatwick-based Viscounts maintained much of the airline's European scheduled and inclusive-tour charter network until the arrival of the first One-Elevens. Jenny Gradidge

LEFT: Spain's Aviaco operated V.831 EC-AZK, leased from BUA, for one summer season on inclusive-tour charters. Airwork and BUA had previously operated the aircraft on behalf of Sudan Airways.
Jenny Gradidge

BELOW LEFT: Three of BUA's Viscounts were sold to Poland's national carrier, LOT, for use on its domestic and European network, based at Warsaw.
Bill Sheridan Collection

been sold by BUA to LOT Polish Airlines in 1962. LOT operated the Viscounts on its European routes alongside a fleet of Russian-built Antonov An-24 and Ilyushin Il-18 turboprops. Most of the remaining BUA V.800s were retained in service on shorter routes, especially to France, the Netherlands and the Channel Islands.

Once the One-Eleven was established in service, BUA started making plans to open new jet routes from Gatwick to Belfast, Edinburgh and Glasgow. Although BUA claimed that the more southerly Gatwick offered service to a whole new catchment area, it was obvious that a percentage of the revenue traffic on the new routes would also be drawn from BEA's existing Heathrow-based traffic. Despite BEA's strong objections, which were overruled by the licensing authorities, BUA began its Interjet flights to Scotland and Ulster on 4 January 1966. Initially, the Glasgow services used the old airport at Renfrew, with restricted traffic loads on the One-Elevens. Operated twice daily, the new Interjet flights were timed to provide connections with BUA's other routes from Gatwick, as well as offering a high-speed link into London for business travellers, via Gatwick's useful direct rail link into Victoria Station.

BEA Replies with Comets

With the opening of Abbotsinch as Glasgow's airport on 1 May 1966, with a longer runway and less obstructed surroundings, BEA was able to consider introducing jets on its busiest domestic trunk route from London, to attempt to combat the new independent competition. From 1 May Comets replaced Vanguards on the peak morning and evening flights, offering competition to the One-Elevens of British Eagle and BUA. Other flights throughout the day continued to be operated by Vanguards.

Less than enthusiastic at finding itself forced, by commercial pressure, to operate Comets on the Glasgow route, BEA issued a statement in late 1965, confirming that:

> Jets will be noisier than the present turboprops and the increase in noise to people living in the vicinity of the airports will not be welcome. We had hoped to avoid this situation, and some months ago publicly offered to ban jets on domestic routes if others would do the same. The Minister of Aviation has, however, authorised jets from Gatwick and Heathrow on domestic trunk routes. Jet services have already started and British Eagle have now confirmed to BEA that they will operate jets from Heathrow. In the face of this situation BEA, if its services are to be competitive, have no alternative but to lead the way with jet aircraft to Glasgow from Heathrow. We do not make money with the present Vanguard flights to Glasgow and we will lose more money with introducing jets. It is a policy decision. We must safeguard our competitive position.

However, it was certainly noted by regular passengers that BEA's standards of service improved considerably once the airline finally faced serious competition on the main domestic services. Initially, the use of jets was confined to the Glasgow route by BEA on its domestic trunk routes, though they were introduced on many of the remaining routes in due time. Manchester was already earmarked to become the main base of the newly delivered fleet of stretched One-Eleven Series 500s, in 1969. Establishment of the new Super One-Eleven Division saw the new twinjets introduced on the Heathrow service from Manchester, replacing the Vanguards, and also displacing the Viscounts at the West Berlin base.

Nonetheless, the Vanguard's basic economy did enable the fleet to score over the jets on some BEA routes, even as more of the glamorous new Tridents came into service. In 1967 a single Vanguard schedule was operated at mid-day over the London–Amsterdam route, supplementing jets, and the following year three Vanguards a day were operating to the Dutch capital. Also in 1967, the Vanguards actually replaced Comets on the London to Budapest route, in competition with the Il-18 turboprops of Hungarian airline Malev. This was one of the few occasions when the Vanguard was directly in opposition with its very similar Russian lookalike. While the BEA Vanguards took three hours to fly to Budapest, Malev's Il-18s were scheduled to take ten minutes less. A seasonal London–Zurich Vanguard service was operated in the winter to cater for the ski-holiday trade, and a summer-season Vanguard flight operated from London to Salzburg, replacing Viscounts.

Aer Lingus Goes Shopping

Although Aer Lingus had already introduced short-haul jets in 1965, in the form of a quartet of One-Elevens, the Irish carrier seemed in no hurry to replace its turboprop fleet *en masse*. In fact, Aer Lingus had soon realized that the original One-Eleven was too small for many of its routes, and was lobbying BAC to produce a larger version, as well as examining other projects around the world. While evaluating its next jetliner orders, in 1966 Aer Lingus took the unusual step of purchasing all nine Viscount 803s from KLM, effectively doubling its Viscount fleet.

The Dutch carrier had been operating its Viscounts very successfully around Europe, without serious incident, since 1957, but had recently started to replace the V.803s, and its remaining Electras, with McDonnell Douglas DC-9 jets. The acquisition of the ex-KLM Viscounts allowed Aer Lingus to dispose of its much smaller Fokker F.27s and standardize on the larger Viscount as its turboprop of choice at a very reasonable cost.

At about the same time, three of Aer Lingus's original V.808s were given a unique 'QC', or 'Quick Change' conversion by Scottish Aviation at Prestwick. This entailed the fitting of a strengthened freight floor, with roller guides and floor locks. Up to nine freight pallets, with a total payload of up to 7 tons (7.1 tonnes), could then be accommodated, moveable bulkheads permitting seating to be fitted for mixed passenger/freight services. To allow the pallets, or any other bulky freight, to be loaded, a large double-opening forward door was installed in place of the forward entry door. These aircraft were put to good use on night-time all-cargo services, as well as operating 'combi' passenger/cargo flights on routes such as Dublin–Cardiff–Bristol and Dublin–Liverpool, on which passenger loads did not always justify the use of an all-passenger aircraft.

New aircraft, such as the DC-9 short-haul jet, finally displaced the popular KLM Viscounts. A search for a new home for the fleet eventually led to their sale, *en masse*, to Aer Lingus. MAP

Originally delivered to KLM as PH-VIF *Leonardo da Vinci*, Viscount 803 EI-AOE *St Damhait/Dympna* found a new lease of life on the Irish airline's network.
Steve Williams Collection

Continental Goes Jet

The 1958 entry into service of Continental Airline's Viscount 812s had soon been followed by the delivery of the US carrier's first Boeing 707s, which were introduced into scheduled service in June 1959. As a result, the Viscount 812s had enjoyed only a brief period as the glamorous new additions to the fleet. Their luxurious first-class interiors were gradually modified with five-abreast all-economy seating as the jets replaced the Viscounts on the longer sectors. The airline's inventive advertising department was even inspired to promote what could easily have been regarded as a backward move in a decidedly positive vein, claiming it allowed 'Even more of Continental customers to enjoy Viscount service!'

As well as the previously mentioned temporary lease of two of the V.812s to Capital, Continental actually sold off two of its Viscount fleet quite early, in August and September 1960. Having become surplus to Continental's requirements owing to the success of the Boeings, the first of the V.812s, N240V, was sold to the Tennessee Gas Corporation for executive use, and N241V was sold to Ansett-ANA, becoming VH-RMK.

Two V.812s were lost in accidents while with Continental, the first being N243V, which crashed at Amarillo, Texas, on 8 July 1962. While taking off with three crew and thirteen passengers on board the aircraft sank back on to the runway and was destroyed in the resulting fire, though all the occupants escaped without serious injury. As no defects could be found in the aircraft, investigators eventually blamed the accident on the captain, who had been distracted during the rotation by some dripping water in the cockpit.

The second accident involving a Continental Viscount was much more serious. On 28 January 1963 N242V was on approach to Kansas Municipal Airport with, unknown to the crew, a 3in (7.5cm) accumulation of ice on its tail. When the flaps were lowered this caused the nose of the aircraft to drop suddenly. Although the landing was still made on the runway, the aircraft was now out of control and overran the runway, crashing into a dyke. All four crew and nine of the passengers died in the resulting fire. The aerodynamic effect of ice on the tail had also been suggested as a possible contributory factor in the crash of Capital V.745 N7437 on approach to Tri-City Airport on 6 April 1958. However, at the time, the investigation gave the most probable cause as the aircraft having stalled during too steep a turn at low altitude with an inoperative stall-warning device.

The remaining aircraft continued to operate on regional services until the introduction of Continental's DC-9-15s in 1966 saw the final demise of the Viscount 812s. The entire surviving fleet of ten was sold to Channel Airways, the aircraft being released and delivered to Southend, in the UK, between April 1966 and June 1967, as the DC-9s gradually took over Continental's remaining Viscount routes.

Continental's Viscount 812s were repainted in a modernized gold-and-black livery to match the airline's 'Golden Jet' Boeings. This one, N242V, was lost in a fatal accident at Kansas in 1963. via Jon Proctor

BEA's Cargo Vanguard

As early as 1966 BEA decided, at least in principal, to make more use of the capacious Vanguard fuselage for all-freight services. The Vanguards had operated a limited cargo contract in the spring of that year, flying a weekly Manchester–Belfast newspaper service. A small fleet of specialized turboprop Armstrong Whitworth Argosies had been in service with BEA since late 1961. With its voluminous cabin and large nose and rear-fuselage doors the Dart-powered Argosy was originally thought to be the ideal all-cargo aircraft for the corporation's freight network. The initial aircraft were found to be slightly underpowered, however, and a new fleet of improved Argosies, larger and with uprated Darts, was introduced in 1965. Even so, operating such a small fleet of specialized aircraft was expensive for BEA, and even the larger version did not offer sufficient capacity on the busier cargo routes. The delivery of new Trident 2s and One-Elevens during 1968 saw capacity released, the new aircraft replacing Vanguards on several of their remaining passenger routes.

Rather than try to dispose of the Vanguards on an already well-oversubscribed secondhand airliner market, BEA considered expanding the use of Vanguards on cargo services, initially supplementing the Argosies. Consequently, in 1968, V.953 Vanguard G-APEL was given an interim conversion to all-cargo configuration, similar to that carried out by Air Canada on its single Cargoliner variation. On 'EL the passenger airstairs and cabin interior were removed, but the passenger windows were not blanked off as on the Canadian aircraft. It was far from being an ideal cargo conversion, and the original forward passenger door was rather small for easy bulk-freight handling. Even so, the other Vanguards also had their forward airstairs removed, allowing a quick adaptation for use on cargo services as required. The converted aircraft was put into scheduled cargo service on the routes from Heathrow to Copenhagen, Milan and Paris.

ABOVE: Many of BEA's Vanguards had their forward airstairs removed in the late 1960s. As well as making any short-term conversion for cargo services much easier, the not-inconsiderable weight saving increased revenue or fuel loads. Steve Richards

LEFT: Author's collection

New Lives to Come

Even as the longest-standing operators of the Vickers turboprops were making plans for their disposal, the first operator, BEA, was still exploring new ventures to occupy its fleet. For other airlines' aircraft that would find their way on to the secondhand market, yet another new generation of airlines and operators was waiting in the wings, ready to put them to work.

CHAPTER NINE

New Admirers and Shifting Roles

Pressures for Change

The arrival of the second-generation short-haul jet airliners in the mid–late 1960s effectively heralded the end of most of the remaining front-line service for the Viscount and Vanguard. However, new operators were attracted by the reasonable prices at which the aircraft could be acquired. In the case of a Viscount 700, the average cost of a good-quality secondhand example was in the region of £100,000, approximately a third of its original price. Interested parties from points as distant as the UK, East Africa, Asia and South America were soon showing a keen interest in the increasingly available fleets.

However, not all of the Viscount fleet withdrawals were voluntary. Following the loss of the MMA V.720 in December 1968, Vickers had been obliged to place a restriction on the life of Viscount inner-wing spars. In Brazil VASP was flying many of the oldest ex-BEA V.701s, mostly on short flights, in particular on the busy Sao Paulo–Rio route, with many short sectors a day. Consequently, most of its Viscount 701s were already well over the permitted number of landings, and several were immediately grounded. The high cost of the engineering work involved in renewing the inner spars was considered prohibitive by VASP, and many aircraft were cocooned at Sao Paulo. Most of them remained so for many years before eventually being scrapped or donated to museums. The airline's three surviving V.827s remained in use, however, until the mid-1970s, when they were ousted from the network by jets. They were then sold on to PLUNA. At Montevideo they replaced the Uruguayan carrier's older Viscount 700s on regional services to Argentina and Brazil, as well as on its domestic network.

BEA's new 'Union Flag' livery, introduced in 1968, was intended to take the airline well into the 1970s. via author

The V.810 prototype, G-AOYV, was converted to a V.827 at the end of its development work with Vickers in 1960. After service with VASP in Brazil the aircraft was sold to PLUNA as CX-BIZ in 1975. via author

Pacific and Far Eastern Moves

New Zealand National Airways had retained its Viscounts even after introducing the first of a fleet of Boeing 737 short-haul jets into service in 1968. In addition to the four V.807s bought new from Vickers, NZNAC had also acquired one of the ex-Transair/BUA V.804s from LOT in 1967. The Viscount operation continued for another six years, three of the V.807s being withdrawn in 1974. Two others, the remaining V.807 and the single V.804, which had been converted to V.807 standard, remained in service, supplementing the smaller F.27s on regional routes for another year, until 1975.

In Japan, ANA had replaced its Viscount 828s with Boeing 727s, finally withdrawing the last of the turboprops from service in 1969. One of ANA's Viscounts had been lost in a training accident near Nagoya in 1962, and the airline scrapped two at the end of their intensive domestic service. Nonetheless, four survived to be sold to an

Indonesian operator, Merpati Nusantara, and two others went to an Ecuadorian airline, Servicios Aereos Nacionales (SAN).

The three original Philippine Air Lines Viscount 748Ds had eventually been joined in 1961 by a V.745D from the undelivered Capital order. However, just over two years later this aircraft was leased out to Hawaiian Airlines of Honolulu. Hawaiian's main rival in the islands was Aloha Airlines, which introduced two Viscount 700s into service, also in 1963, having acquired a pair of V.745Ds returned to Vickers by Capital, that had been operated by Austrian Airlines. Hawaiian disposed of its Viscount within a year, preferring to standardize on its fleet of Dart-powered CV640 turboprop conversions. Aloha, however, went on to acquire two more Viscounts, both ex-Northeast Airlines V.798Ds. The quartet remained the airline's flagships on Aloha's intensive inter-island network, alongside Fairchild F-27s, until the arrival One-Elevens in 1968. Two of the Viscounts remained in service until the early 1970s, long after the One-Elevens themselves had been replaced by Boeing 737s.

Aloha Airlines' Viscounts enjoyed a long career shuttling between the Hawaiian Islands. via author

The remaining Philippine Viscounts continued to operate domestically throughout the country and to neighbouring states until 1967. Following their replacement by One-Elevens, the trio was sold to a Swedish charter airline, Falconair. They then operated over a variety of charter services from their base at Malmö, in the south of Sweden. The Viscounts were later joined by three Lockheed Electras, and continued to fly for Falconair until September 1970, when the company ceased operations owing to financial difficulties.

After ex-BOAC Comets had replaced them, Malayan Airways' two V.760Ds, leased from BOAC Associated Companies, were moved on to another BOAC-controlled airline, Aden Airways, in 1963. They were operated on scheduled services from the southern Arabian territory alongside several DC-3s until one was destroyed by sabotage at Aden in 1967. Aden Airways operations came to an end shortly afterwards, when BOAC withdrew its interest following heavy losses, and the surviving Viscount was returned to the UK.

During 1970 Far Eastern Air Transport (FEAT) of Taiwan bought no fewer than five Viscounts from Ansett-ANA, comprising three V.832s, the ex-Continental V.812 and an ex-Cubana V.818. FEAT had

Aden Airways' two Viscount 760Ds were flown from the protectorate for five years before political upheaval caused the demise of the airline following the destruction of one of the aircraft; VR-AAN eventually returned to the UK. Jenny Gradidge

been operating a small fleet of Dart Heralds on domestic services from Taipei, in competition with China Air Lines, the national carrier. Two more Viscounts arrived from Australia in 1971, this time a pair of V.816s from TAA. In addition, an ex-Austrian Airlines V.837 was added to the fleet in 1972.

The arrival of a single Boeing 727 in 1970 saw Union of Burma Airways' fleet of three Viscount 761Ds displaced from most of the airline's international routes and relegated to the domestic network. One of the three was lost when it was damaged beyond repair after running off the runway at Akyab, Burma, in August 1972. The surviving aircraft remained in service with Burma Airways Corporation, which UBA became in December 1972. Their use was gradually decreased, until they were finally withdrawn and sold in 1976.

Huns Air Viscounts came from surplus Indian Airline's stock. This one, VT-DOE, was eventually scrapped for valuable spares as the struggling airline battled to survive. Global Air Image

Subcontinent Sales

Indian Airlines Corporation's well-utilized fleet of Viscount 700s had been boosted in 1967 by the arrival of the two Indian Air Force examples. This brought the operational fleet up to an impressive level of fourteen, two of the original aircraft having been written-off in service in 1961 and 1963. Another Viscount was lost after overrunning the runway at Jaipur on 9 August 1971. After IAC flew its last Viscount services in late 1973, most of the fleet were up during the next few years.

Two of the IAC fleet did find a new owner in 1974, going to Lane Xang Airlines of Cambodia. They operated in the midst of the war, originally centred on Vietnam, which spread throughout the region at the time. At least one of the aircraft was believed to have been written off during the hostilities. The other was transferred to Royal Air Lao the next year and managed to survive until the 1980s. Three more of the IAC Viscounts were sold to a small independent Indian airline, Huns Air, which operated them on passenger and cargo charters, particularly between Bombay and Sharjah, in the Arabian Gulf. Unfortunately, by 1980 Huns Air was beginning to experience serious financial problems, and one of the Viscounts had to be cannibalized to provide badly needed spares. Following the loss of another aircraft in a landing accident at Vijayawada, the airline ceased all operations and the survivor was broken up.

The PIA fleet of V.815s was replaced by Trident 1Es in 1966. Two of the five Viscounts delivered to PIA had been written-off in accidents in 1959, shortly after delivery, but the three survivors continued in service until they were traded-in to Hawker Siddeley in part payment for the Tridents.

The sole Luxair Viscount 815 was operated alongside Fokker F.27s and Caravelles on European services for three years. Bill Sheridan Collection

It was thought that a new home had been found for all three aircraft with Luxair, the national carrier of Luxembourg, to replace its smaller Fokker F.27s. In the end, though, Luxair took delivery of only one of the trio, the remainder staying with Hawker Siddeley. Nonetheless, the sole Luxair Viscount enjoyed three years of successful solo operations on European scheduled and charter services until it was written off when its nosewheel hit a snow bank during a landing in 1969.

Further west, MEA had gradually reduced its Viscount fleet as initially Comets and Caravelles, and later VC10s and 707s, had taken over the more important routes. The carrier leased two of its Viscount 754Ds to a new operator in neighbouring Jordan from 1961 to 1964. This airline, Jordanian Airways, was later reorganized and replaced by Alia Royal Jordanian Airlines, which, as well as operating Caravelles and DC-6Bs, leased three Viscount 800s from BUA in the winter of 1966/67.

British United eventually withdrew its last Viscounts from service at the end of 1969. One of the first customers for the redundant aircraft was Arkia, Israel's domestic carrier, which operated a small fleet of Dart Heralds. Three ex-HCAT V.833s were sold by BUA to Arkia in 1969, but one was written-off in a night training accident at Tel Aviv only ten days after delivery. The Viscounts were introduced on the major domestic services from Tel Aviv to Eilat and Sta Katarina, as well as operating transport flights for the Israeli military and on the scheduled route to Nicosia from Tel Aviv on behalf of El Al. A steady stream of extra secondhand Viscount 800s and 810s were to follow during the 1970s as Arkia's services were expanded.

The Cyprus Airways V.806s, leased from BEA, remained on the Mediterranean island until 1970, when the carrier introduced its own new Trident 1Es. Once the Tridents were established in service the Viscounts were returned to BEA, which initially placed them back into service, still in basic Cyprus colours but with BEA stickers applied. The following year THY's three surviving V.794Ds were transferred to the Turkish Air Force. These aircraft enjoyed a long operational life with their new owner, as for nearly twenty years they continued to be seen throughout Turkey and the eastern Mediterranean region performing transport and VIP flights. They were not withdrawn from use until 1990.

Last Viscounts at United

In the USA, United remained an enthusiastic operator of the V.745s inherited in the Capital merger. Although the airline's newly delivered Caravelles had taken over many of the longer ex-Capital routes, the still large fleet of over forty Viscounts was still used on much of the East Coast and Great Lakes network. The Viscounts remained popular with United's passengers, many being retained even after later jets, such as the Boeing 727, arrived in 1964.

As well as the Boeing 727 tri-jet, United had also ordered a large fleet of Boeing 737 twinjets. Some of United's Viscount fleet had already been sold off in small numbers, but most of the V.745s remained in regular service until the arrival of the 737. In addition to the Viscounts, United continued to operate many other, piston-engine, propeller-driven types, such as the CV340, DC-6 and DC-7. All of these were expected to be replaced quickly by the 737s and the new, larger, versions of the 727, due for delivery in 1968–69.

As the 737s were delivered and spread their influence throughout the United network, more and more of the Viscounts were removed from service. The last United Viscount schedules were operated on 14 January 1969. For the most part, the Viscounts had continued to be flown, or at least kept available, until they became due for major maintenance checks. They were then stood down from the operational fleet and offered for sale 'as is', the potential buyer being responsible for completing any work required to make them airworthy.

Six of the withdrawn aircraft required only fairly minor work, such as a wing spar check or block overhauls, and were offered as potentially flyable. Most of these were sold to corporate customers for executive use. Twenty-eight others required more extensive work and had their registration plates removed, though they could be returned to the US register if all work was completed on them. These Viscounts were offered at a very reasonable price, though much of the work needed was quite expensive. Companies such as Aero Flite and Cavalier Aircraft acquired several of these aircraft purely for their Dart engines, or stripped them for other spares and scrapped the airframes. Thirteen remaining aircraft were sold to a new organization called the Viscount International Corporation.

These aircraft were all ferried to Georgetown, Sussex County Airport in Maryland and stored. Viscount International also purchased United's remaining stocks of Viscount spares. Various projects to restore at least some of the Viscounts and resell them to travel clubs or executive operators came and went. Eventually a number of their Dart engines were removed and sold, or used for proposed re-engining programmes for piston-powered aircraft. In 1974 a few of them were finally restored to airworthy condition, sold to new owners and went on to varied careers. For the most part, however, the remaining Viscounts lingered in the open air at Sussex County, slowly deteriorating.

The large surviving United Viscount fleet continued to serve the airline long after the aircraft were inherited in the Capital Airlines merger. via Bill Mellberg

Venezuelan Curtain Call

After fifteen years of uninterrupted service, the long-established Viscount 700 operation of Linea Aeropostal Venezolana

LAV-Aeropostal lost Viscount 749, YV-C-AMU, in a crash at Merida in 1971. The aircraft had been delivered new to the airline in 1956. Jenny Gradidge

(LAV) came to a poignant end. The original three V.749s, delivered in 1956, had been joined by an ex-BEA V.701X in 1963. This aircraft was the one damaged while trying to take off on a blocked runway in fog at Heathrow in 1955, and rebuilt. An ex-BWIA V.702 was acquired in 1965, and a V.772, also ex-BWIA, was leased in from 1968 to 1969. The Viscount fleet had proved extremely popular on many of LAVs' routes, operating domestically, to neighbouring countries in South America and around the Caribbean.

On 25 January 1971 one of the V.749s was lost in a crash at Merida, killing thirteen of the forty-seven on board. Later that year, on 1 November, another V.749 was lost at Maracaibo, crashing shortly after take-off. The last of the original three V.749s was lost in a crash on Margarita Island on 14 August 1974, this time with only one survivor of the forty-seven on board. The two remaining aircraft, the V.701X and the V.702, remained in service, albeit at much reduced utilization. They were restricted to a handful of scheduled flights, often only once or twice a week, usually supporting the DC-9s that were by then being operated by LAV. Some charter work was also undertaken with the Viscounts, mostly at weekends. Eventually both aircraft were quietly retired, the V.701X in December 1975 and the V.702 in January 1976.

The first ex-Continental Viscount 812 to be operated by Channel Airways was G-ATUE. Aviation Hobby Shop

Glory Days at Channel

Not surprisingly, the secondhand Viscount market was probably at its most buoyant among the UK's independent operators. The Viscount was most numerous in its home country, and continued to be a common sight at airports throughout the UK. Channel Airways had continued to keep its Viscount 700 fleet busy. The extensive charter contracts and the high-frequency, shorthaul services across the English Channel were soon yielding record utilization figures for its Viscounts. A steadily increasing inclusive-tour charter programme took the Viscounts further afield, and an outstation was established at Manchester specifically to cater for this market from the north of England. An ex-BOAC Associated Companies and BWIA V.703, G-APZA, joined Channel in 1965. It spent most of the winter of 1965–66 back in the Caribbean, on lease to Bahamas Airways, joining its fleet during their winter season peak period to provide extra capacity on routes to Florida

A typical summer Saturday flying programme for just one aircraft of the Channel fleet could involve a night-time inclusive-tour charter from Southend to Barcelona and back, departing the UK late on the Friday evening and returning to Southend at 06.25hr on the Saturday morning. A very quick turn-round would be followed by no fewer than four round trips across the Channel to Ostend, carrying up to seventy passengers each way, and a Southend–Jersey–Southend rotation, all being completed by mid-afternoon. After a Southend–Paris–Southend schedule had been fitted in later in the afternoon, another long night would follow, with the operation of an inclusive-tour charter from Southend to Gerona, in Spain. All of the Viscount fleet would be expected to operate similar busy daily programmes in the summer months. This impressive level of intensive utilization was a feature of Channel Airways' operation, not only with the hard-working Viscounts, but also with its single Douglas DC-4, two remaining DC-3s, its de Havilland Doves and its new Dart-powered HS.748 twin turboprops, which had entered service early in 1966.

Bigger 'Golden Viscounts'

The ex-Continental V.812s, deliveries of which had begun in 1966, were soon reconfigured to match the rather cramped seating of the rest of Channel's fleet, being fitted with eighty-two high-density passenger seats. This was thirty more than were fitted when the aircraft were originally delivered to Continental in their first-class layout. The first of the Channel V.812s, G-ATUE, ex-N244V, entered service on a Southend–Ostend scheduled flight on 12 May 1966. By the end of the summer of 1966 Channel had three V.812s in use, with more on the way, operating a similar mixture of charter and scheduled services to the V.700s.

One of the Viscount 812s was destined never to enter Channel service. Following delivery from the USA, N248V was converted to UK certification standards and, on 3 May 1967, was prepared for a test flight in preparation for the issue of its UK C of A as G-AVJZ. As it left the runway, number four engine was feathered and the aircraft began an uncontrolled turn at low altitude. Its starboard wing struck the ground and it careered into a fenced compound, killing two workmen and seriously injuring a third. Although the crew escaped with only minor injuries, the Viscount was a total write-off.

Channel Airways put One-Elevens into service in 1967, and Tridents were also on order for 1968 delivery. In 1966 the airline had formed its own travel company, Mediterranean Holidays, to sell inclusive-tour holidays, and it also flew for other leading tour companies such as Clarksons and Riviera Holidays. The new jets were expected to take on most of the inclusive-tour charter work, but during 1967 the still more numerous Viscounts undertook a large proportion of the Channel's inclusive-tour programme.

The remaining two Channel Viscount 700s were finally phased out by the end of 1968. The original Channel Golden Viscount, G-APZC, which the airline had inherited from Tradair, and V.702 G-APTA were kept busy even in their last Channel Airways summer season, being seen on new longer-ranging charter routes to Alghero, Malta and Tunis, as well as on more parochial services such as a new weekly Liverpool–Ostend charter.

Invicta and BMA

British Eagle continued to operate its six Viscount 700s, supplementing its much larger fleets of Britannias and One-Elevens. At the end of 1967 a number of the scheduled routes were cut and, as a result, the two ex-Cubana V.755s were sold at the beginning of 1968. These aircraft went to Invicta Airways of Manston, which had been operating DC-4s and Vikings on charters from the Kent airport since 1965. The last of the Vikings were retired shortly before the Viscounts arrived, but the DC-4s continued in service on passenger and cargo charters. Once in service, one of the Viscounts was based at Manston, operating from there and other UK airports on inclusive-tour charters, while the other was based in West Berlin. From there it was contracted by German tour operators for inclusive-tour charters to the Mediterranean, and it also operated charters to popular resorts on the shores of the Baltic.

However, the two Viscounts served with Invicta for just the one summer season. By early 1969 Invicta was owned by Minster Assets, a holding company. Minster already owned British Midland Airways, based at East Midlands Airport, and had plans to combine the operations of its two airlines. BMA had been operating Viscounts since early 1967, having purchased V.736 G-AODG from BUA. The airline had previously operated a fleet of DC-3s and Canadair Argonauts. Initially a small fleet of Dart Heralds had been acquired from 1965 to take the place of the DC-3s, but the airline had decided to replace these, and eventually the Argonauts, with Viscounts. Initially placed into service on the East Midlands–Glasgow route, during the summer 'DG was also operated from several UK airports to the Channel Islands.

The tragic loss of one of the BMA Argonauts in a fatal accident in June 1967 led to the early retirement of the remainder, and the carrier acquired more Viscounts to replace them. Two ex-BUA V.831s and the two remaining ex-PIA V.815s from Hawker Siddeley joined 'DG in 1967, and more aircraft went into service during 1968. The extra Viscounts comprised a V.745 from Alitalia and a V.760D from BOAC Associated Companies. This growing fleet was joined by the two ex-Invicta V.755s that were moved to East Midlands in early 1969 following the merger of the two airlines. However, only one, G-AOCB, entered service with BMA, as G-AOCC was found to be suffering from corrosion and was scrapped soon afterwards. The merger of BMA and Invicta was short-lived, Invicta's original founder, Wg Cdr Hugh Kennard, buying back the Manston-based DC-4 cargo operation from Minster Assets later in the year.

The original BMA Viscount, G-AODG, enjoyed only a brief career with the company, being written off after a heavy landing in appalling weather at East Midlands Airport on 20 February 1969. After a difficult approach at the end of a Glasgow–East Midlands scheduled flight, 'DG struck the ground nosewheel first in a steep attitude, while landing in snow. The nosewheel collapsed and, when the main undercarriage made contact with the runway, the fuselage ruptured in the centre section, breaking

Invicta Airways' pair of Manston-based V.755s saw only one summer season's service, operating charter programmes from West Berlin as well as from several UK points. Aviation Hobby Shop

Early 1969 saw the loss of two of BMA's Viscount fleet. Both of the unfortunate aircraft, G-AVJA and G-AODG, are seen here on the East Midlands airport ramp shortly before their accidents. G.P. Jones via Steve Richards

the Viscount's back. Fortunately none of the passengers or crew was seriously hurt and all were safely evacuated from the crippled aircraft. To replace G-AODG, ex-BWIA and Bahamas Airways V.702 G-APPX was leased in from Field Aircraft Services for the summer of 1969.

Exactly a month after G-AODG's accident, one of BMA's ex-PIA V.815s, G-AVJA, was also destroyed in an accident. On 19 March the aircraft diverted into Manchester owing to bad weather at East Midlands. The next day, it was to be positioned back to East Midlands with only the crew of two pilots and two stewardesses on board. Taking advantage of the otherwise empty aircraft, the captain elected to use the flight to undertake some training for the first officer, en route. One of the stewardesses had asked to sit on the jump seat in the flight deck to observe the training session, and the other took a seat in the rear cabin. Shortly after take-off, at a height of about 200ft (60m), the aircraft was seen to roll and turn to the right. The hapless Viscount continued to roll, and its nose dropped until it struck the ground and burst into flames. All the occupants of the flight deck were killed instantly, but the other stewardess escaped unhurt. The cause of the loss of 'JA was to remain largely undetermined, though it was stated that control appeared to have been lost by the two pilots during the training exercise.

Viscount 739A G-ATDR was one of a quartet of Viscounts still in service with British Eagle in 1968. via author

The End of Eagle

After the disposal of G-AOCB and 'CC, the four remaining British Eagle Viscounts still found plenty of work in 1968, operating daily services from London to Innsbruck; twice-daily, Monday–Friday, Liverpool–Glasgow services; and a Sunday service from London to Luxembourg. In addition, from May to September, the Viscounts operated on the schedules to Newquay from Liverpool, Birmingham and Manchester. One Viscount was leased to Air France, to operate on thinner routes such as Lille–London, replacing a pair of Cambrian Viscounts previously leased. Another of the Viscounts, V.739A G-ATFN *City of Truro*, was tragically lost on 9 August 1968 while on a London–Innsbruck scheduled service. After losing all electrical power while cruising in cloud at 21,000ft (6,400m), the aircraft crashed on to an Autobahn near Pfaffenhofen, north of Munich, killing all forty-four passengers and four crew.

British Eagle chairman Harold Bamberg continued to lobby for permission to expand his airline's scheduled network beyond Europe. A pair of secondhand Boeing 707s were delivered in early 1968 to operate a new programme of inclusive-tour charters to the Caribbean. Bamberg was successful in gaining approval for new scheduled routes from Bermuda to New York, and a brand-new Boeing 707 was ordered in the hope of gaining approval for a London–New York route. Although approval for a transatlantic network was eventually granted, it was later withdrawn. To add to Eagle's troubles, two long-haul charter contracts, to Singapore and Australia, came to an end. The British inclusive-tour market was also in recession in 1968, following the imposition of foreign exchange regulations, and British Eagle suffered losses of over £1 million in cancellations on its inclusive-tour services. In October, British Eagle (Liverpool) was suddenly closed down with the loss of 400 jobs, in an effort to cut the parent company's costs.

All of this made the airline's financiers nervous, and two major banks suddenly withdrew support for underwriting the following year's flying programme. As a result, on 6 November 1968, all British Eagle International Airlines operations ceased at midnight. The three surviving British Eagle

Viscounts never flew commercially again. One of them, V.732 G-ANRS, was sold to Cambrian Airways, which used its fuselage for cabin crew training at Cardiff for many years. The remaining two, G-ATDR and G-ATDU, were stored at Blackbushe and Liverpool respectively, and were eventually scrapped on site.

Treffield's pair of leased Viscount 812s were only to be seen for a few months on charter services before the airline collapsed in disarray, when very dissatisfied travel industry clients cancelled contracts. Aviation Hobby Shop

Channel Summer Leases

As with its Viscount 700s, the excess capacity of Channel's V.812s was soon offered out for lease contracts. The airline signed a potentially lucrative contract for the summer of 1967, for a lease of three of the new fleet to a new operator, Treffield International Airlines of East Midlands. Two of the Viscounts were delivered to Treffield in April 1967, at which time a programme of inclusive-tour charters opened from Bristol, Cardiff, East Midlands, Gatwick and Liverpool, mostly to Spain and Italy. A series of serious operational problems followed, with passengers enduring long delays and a great deal of disruption. As a result, some of the disgruntled travel companies actually cancelled their contracts mid-season. The short-lived airline closed down on 23 June, victim of an inexperienced management and a precarious financial base. The third Viscount was never handed over, having been replaced by a leased Britannia that operated for Treffield for only a few weeks.

Slightly more successful was the lease of two more Viscount 812s in the summer of 1968, this time to Manston-based Air Ferry, which operated charters with a fleet of elderly DC-4s and Vikings. The airline was owned by Air Holdings, which also owned British United, which had supplied a pair of DC-6As to Air Ferry. As with its Manston neighbour, Invicta, Air Ferry based only one aircraft at a time at Manston, on rotation. At the beginning of the year one of the Viscounts was based at Manchester, but later this was changed, the aircraft being based at Perpignan in southern France instead. From there the French-based Viscount operated to several points in the UK.

During 1968, however, Air Holdings decided to close down Air Ferry and transfer its valuable inclusive-tour contracts to BUA's Gatwick-based One-Eleven fleet, which was under-used at the time. Subsequently, all Air Ferry operations ceased on 31 October and the Viscounts were returned to Channel when their lease expired.

The Air Ferry Viscounts split their operations between the company's main base at Manston and Perpignan in the south of France. Air Holdings eventually closed the airline down at the end of the 1968 summer season. Aviation Hobby Shop

The Scottish Flyer

One of Channel's V.812s, G-APPU, had been written off after aquaplaning on landing on a wet Southend runway after a flight from Rotterdam on 4 May 1968. It ended up with a fractured fuselage, almost on the main Southend–London railway line. Of the eighty-three passengers and four crew on board, two crew and sixteen passengers were seriously injured, and thirteen others sustained more minor injuries. Another of the Viscount 812s, G-APPC, was removed from service at the end of 1968, leaving eight in use.

Channel Airways' ambitious plans to expand its pure-jet fleet meant that the inclusive-tour charters would become almost the sole province of the jet fleet by

Viscount 812 G-AVHK wore special 'Scottish Flyer' titles to promote the short-lived multi-stop service from Southend to Scotland. Bill Sheridan Collection

the end of 1969. Noise problems and range restrictions resulting from using Southend's short runway led to the jets being moved to nearby Stansted Airport, and some of the Channel Islands schedules were also moved north to the larger airport, still being operated by the Viscounts.

The eight remaining Viscounts were mostly used on Channel's short cross-Channel scheduled services for 1969, only a handful of charters featuring in their operating programme. The aircraft were, nonetheless, used to pioneer a bold new venture for the airline, with the opening of a new scheduled route. This was a multi-stop Scottish Flyer 'bus-stop' service from Southend to Aberdeen, designed with business and commuter travellers in mind. Stops were scheduled at Luton (later changed to Stansted), East Midlands, Leeds/Bradford, Teeside, Newcastle and Edinburgh. At the time there was very little airline service, north to south, on the eastern side of the UK, and Channel hoped to establish a new niche market in the area. Viscount 812 G-AVHK operated the first service, on 20 January 1969. The route was also shared with the HS 748s, with de Havilland Herons operating feeder flights from Norwich and Liverpool to East Midlands. To promote the service, G-AVHK and one of the 748s wore special Scottish Flyer titles, although other aircraft were also used as required. Despite disappointing loads, Channel persevered with the route, but finally closed the service down on 28 November as a result of mounting losses.

Channel Bows Out

Two of the Channel Viscounts were retired at the end of 1969, followed by two more in early 1970. The last of the 748s were also disposed of by 1970, and the remaining Viscounts and Herons were confined to scheduled services, with only a few *ad hoc* charters operated as required. Consolidation of the turboprop fleet was to have been offset by the expansion of the jet operation, and four One-Elevens and five Trident 1Es had originally been ordered. In the event, as the result of financing and operational problems, only three One-Elevens and two Tridents were delivered. Instead, five secondhand Comet 4Bs were acquired from BEA in 1970. However, both the Tridents and Comets suffered from chronic spare shortages, and the operational chaos that followed led to numerous delays and disruption for the charter passengers, as well as inflicting a great deal of damage on Channel's professional reputation.

By the end of 1971 Channel was forced to retrench and the Tridents were sold. Through all the jet fleet's problems, the Viscounts had continued to hop to and fro over the Channel to Ostend and Rotterdam from Southend, and to the Channel Islands from Southend, Stansted and Bournemouth, supplemented by the Herons. Traffic loads on the scheduled routes were declining, however. The winter of 1971–72 was especially quiet, and V.812 G-ATVR had been retired at the end of 1971. As a result of the increasing financial crisis, an official receiver was appointed on 1 February 1972 to examine the airline's situation. All of the jet fleet was grounded on 15 February, though the remaining Viscounts and Herons continued to operate the scheduled services, albeit with nearly empty passenger cabins.

Defeat was finally admitted on 29 February 1972 and, as no buyer had been found for the ailing airline, all operations were closed down at the end of that day's flying. On the last day, two of the Viscounts, G-ATUE and G-AVJL, were operated. The former flew a Southend–Jersey–Bournemouth–Jersey–Southend schedule, and 'JL operated the morning Southend–Rotterdam–Southend service. The last-ever Channel Airways scheduled flight was operated by a Heron over the Ostend–Southend route later in the day, landing at 19.54hr.

The Arrival of British Air Services

Cambrian Airways acquired more Viscount 701s from Channel from 1965, eventually operating an impressive fleet of twelve. As well as its extensive scheduled and charter passenger services, Cambrian also operated the Viscounts on nightly newspaper and freight runs from Liverpool to Belfast and the Isle of Man. Unfortunately one of the V.701s was lost while operating these contracts when G-AMOL crashed while on approach to Liverpool in

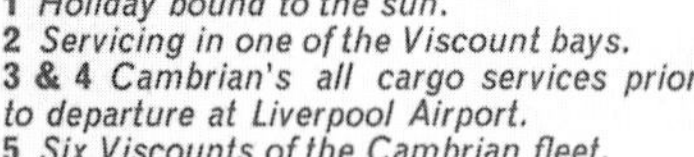
1 *Holiday bound to the sun.*
2 *Servicing in one of the Viscount bays.*
3 & 4 *Cambrian's all cargo services prior to departure at Liverpool Airport.*
5 *Six Viscounts of the Cambrian fleet.*

OPPOSITE PAGE: The success of the Cambrian Viscount 701 fleet was a major factor in the rapid expansion of the Welsh carrier in the mid-1960s. Author's collection

poor weather on 20 July 1965. Both pilots, the only occupants, were killed. The accident was attributed to an asymmetric flap problem, similar to that which had caused the loss of G-ALWE back in 1957. As previously mentioned, two of the Cambrian V.701s were leased to Air France in 1967 in full Air France livery.

Also in 1967, Cambrian Airways became a subsidiary of British Air Services (BAS), a new company formed to administer BEA's holdings in other airlines. In 1964 BEA had also bought a 30 per cent share in BKS Air Transport, which had experienced a welcome turn-round in its fortunes after its near-bankruptcy in 1962. Having survived the traumatic years of the early 1960s, BKS had finally been in a position to reintroduce turboprops into its operation, in the form of ex-BOAC Britannias and new HS 748s. The Britannias were used to supplement the established Ambassadors on schedules and charters from Newcastle and Heathrow. The HS 748s replaced DC-3s at Leeds-Bradford, where their effect on passenger traffic was nothing short of dramatic. The flying time from Leeds-Bradford to Heathrow was reduced from nearly ninety minutes to an hour, in a modern, comfortable turboprop aircraft that offered considerable improvement over the ageing DC-3s. Within months of the HS 748's introduction, passenger traffic had improved by 49 per cent and load factors were averaging 80 per cent. Other BKS routes from Leeds-Bradford saw similar traffic increases with the HS 748s.

This very success was to be the HS 748's downfall with BKS. By 1965 it was becoming clear that the 48-seat HS 748s were having trouble coping with the demand, so BEA Viscount 806s were chartered in for many of the busiest flights to Heathrow from Leeds-Bradford, and Channel's Viscount 701s were chartered on several occasions in 1966 to help increase capacity. Earlier in 1966 BKS began negotiations to lease three Viscounts from Channel Airways, and crew training was even undertaken at Southend. However, instead of the planned trio of Channel aircraft, a single V.745 was acquired from United Airlines and placed in service on the Leeds-Bradford from Heathrow service on 9 June.

The following year BKS acquired a further three Viscounts, one V.786 and one V.798 from TACA of El Salvador and a V.776D from BOAC Associated Companies which had been operating for Kuwait Airways. After ousting the HS 748s, which were disposed of, and also eventually replacing the remaining Ambassadors, the BKS Viscounts also operated to Ulster, Eire, the Channel Islands and Europe on scheduled flights, as well as on the important London service from Leeds-Bradford. A busy inclusive-tour charter programme, in addition to the schedules, kept them well occupied from the Yorkshire airport. The Viscount 700s were also operated on a number of other BKS services from Newcastle and Heathrow.

Later, BEA's financial holding in BKS Air Transport was increased, this shareholding and that in Cambrian being used to help found British Air Services in 1967. As a result, BKS and Cambrian Airways became much closer operationally, though both airlines retained their separate commercial identities. The success of BKS's reintroduction of the Viscount encouraged BEA to provide its associate with even more support, in the shape of six Viscount 806s transferred from BEA between April 1968 and December 1969. Offering much-needed extra capacity on both the scheduled and charter networks, the larger Viscounts initially operated alongside the four smaller V.700s. However, the Viscount 700s were soon relegated to a back-up role, and were finally withdrawn in early 1970. By then BKS was also a pure-jet operator, a pair of Trident 1Es having been introduced.

Cambrian Airways also took delivery of ex-BEA Viscount 806s, transferred from late 1970 to replace its V.701s. By then Cambrian was also a jet operator, having introduced One-Elevens in the winter of 1969–70. The first V.806 joined Cambrian in July 1970, followed by another that October and a third in January 1971. Four more followed in the autumn of 1971, leading to the withdrawal and scrapping of most of the remaining V.701 fleet. Three of the V.701s did, however, earn reprieves. The oldest surviving Viscount, G-ALWF, was initially preserved as an exhibit at Liverpool, though it was later moved to the care of the Duxford Aviation Society in Cambridgeshire, following an unsuccessful attempt to build a museum around it at Speke Airport. In addition, G-AMOG and G-AMON actually managed to remain active, and were operated by Cambrian on charter to BOAC. From 1972 the two Viscounts operated feeder flights from Prestwick to Aberdeen, Belfast and Edinburgh

RIGHT: The BKS fleet of Viscount 700s of various marks were gathered from several sources. The ex-Northeast and Hawaiian Airlines V.798D G-AVED was acquired from TACA International Airlines of El Salvador. Aviation Hobby Shop

TOP: Two of Cambrian's elderly V.701s were given a new lease of life operating in full BOAC colours on feeder flights for transatlantic services from Prestwick. Steve Williams Collection

ABOVE: As well as a new livery, BKS Air Transport was given a whole new image and renamed Northeast Airlines in November 1970. The company was given its own yellow-topped version of the new BAS styling. Bill Sheridan Collection

in full BOAC livery, offering a connecting service to BOAC's transatlantic flights from Prestwick.

New Images

The BAS airlines maintained a rather staid image for their first few years of co-operation. Liveries were standardized, a simplified version of the BKS red, white and blue design being adopted by both carriers, with 'British Air Services' titles displayed prominently. As the 1970s arrived, though, it was decided to update the images of BKS and Cambrian. From 1 November 1970 BKS Air Transport changed its name to Northeast Airlines, the better to reflect its association with the region of England on which its operations were mostly based. A bright new livery was also adopted, with a yellow cabin roof over a white cheat-line and grey underside. Bold black titling in a more-modern font was applied. Cambrian also found itself being brightened up, with an almost identical livery style but with an orange cabin roof and its traditional Welsh Dragon logo modernized.

Winner Airways relied heavily on Vietnam War contracts to keep its Viscount 806 busy. Global Air Image

East-Bound

As well as those joining the BAS component airlines, BEA's other V.806s were sold off, single Viscount 806s being bought by both Lao Air Lines and Winner Airways in 1969. Lao Air Lines operated its single Viscount on daily flights from the capital, Vientiane, to Pakse, Satavane and Savannakhet on a domestic network, and internationally to Phnom Penh and Singapore. The aircraft was lost in an accident on take-off from Phnom Penh in March 1973, and the carrier itself soon ceased operations.

Winner was a small charter airline based at Taipei in Taiwan which held valuable freight contracts, mostly in support of the Vietnam War. When the conflict ended, the war-based transport work for the airline dried up almost overnight. Winner had nursed hopes of gaining licences for scheduled domestic operations within Taiwan, but these were not forthcoming. Instead, all flying ceased and the Viscount was left to languish at Taipei for a considerable time. A dispute between Winner, BEA and the broker that had arranged the sale, delayed any chances of reselling the Viscount, and it was not until 1976 that the aircraft was sold and leased-on by its new owner on to an Indonesian carrier, P.T. Mandala Airlines. Mandala had already bought three V.806s directly from BEA in 1970, and operated them on domestic services within Indonesia, later in association with Seulawah Air Services, on whose routes the aircraft were also operated. Eventually six more Viscounts, V.810s of various marks, also joined Mandala in Indonesia.

More Jets in Europe

The first customer for the Boeing's new 737 short-haul jet had been Lufthansa. The carrier had already been the first European airline to place a fleet of Boeing 727s into service, and had signed up for the first version of the Boeing twinjet, the shorter-bodied 737-100, specifically to replace its remaining Convair and Viscount propliners. When the 737s began arriving in 1968, the Convairs were the first to be disposed of, all but one leaving the operational fleet by mid-1969. However, the Viscounts were retained a little longer.

Three of the V.814s were on lease to Lufthansa's charter associate, Condor, and these were returned to the parent airline by September 1969. Condor had originally leased-in Lufthansa Viscounts for its charter contracts as early as 1961. Even after the arrival of its own jets, Condor continued to fly the Viscounts on inclusive-tour and *ad hoc* charters throughout Europe. Lufthansa itself was in no hurry to dispose of its remaining Viscounts, selling off four in 1969, two in 1970 and the last four in 1971. These last four were removed from scheduled service on 5 February 1971, but were still used for back-up duties until 31 March. For their last few years in Lufthansa service the V.814s were mostly operated on domestic schedules as well as 'thinner' international routes. One of them, D-ANAF, was retained by Lufthansa as a ground instruction training airframe at Frankfurt, where it still remains in use (at the time of writing), over thirty years later.

The smart and well-maintained Viscounts of Lufthansa remained in use on short-haul and regional scheduled services until early 1971. via author

Aeropesca was one of several small Colombian carriers which acquired various marks of Viscount on the second-hand market. Bill Sheridan Collection

Alitalia had maintained its sizeable fleet of Viscount 700s even after Caravelles had taken over many of the denser European and domestic routes. It was only when DC-9-30s arrived from the USA that the airline began to consider disposing of its Viscounts. Two were sold to PLUNA in 1967, and one each to British Midland and a regional Colombian carrier, Aerolineas TAO, in 1968. The latter also bought four more ex-Alitalia Viscounts over the next few years, though two of them were scrapped to provide spares for the other aircraft. Ecuadorian airline SAETA bought two of the Alitalia fleet in 1969 and 1970.

The remaining three aircraft were delivered to Altialia's associate, Somali Airlines in East Africa, in 1968, 1969 and 1970. The Somali aircraft suffered mixed fortunes while flying regional routes in East Africa, one being destroyed in a forced landing after a cabin fire in May 1970. The remaining two continued in service from the Somali capital, Mogadishu, for several years until they were broken up for spares in 1977 and 1979.

Three of Austrian Airlines' V.837s also found their way to Colombia in 1971 and 1972, being sold to Transportes Aereos del Cesar, otherwise known as TAC Colombia. The sale was handled by UK aircraft broker Shackleton Aviation. TAC Colombia leased the aircraft out to another Colombian carrier, Lineas Aereas la Urraca Ltda, in whose service one of the aircraft was destroyed in a mid-air explosion in January 1972. The surviving pair were returned to TAC that September. An ex-ANA V.828 was purchased from SAN in Ecuador in 1975 by TAC, which was renamed Aerovias del Cesar that year. Colombia was also to be the new home for Aloha Airlines' surviving Viscounts, the carrier having sold its last two aircraft to another regional independent airline, Aeropesca, at the end of 1971. Aeropesca operated the Viscounts, still basically in Aloha's late-1960s 'flower power' colour scheme, on domestic services from Bogota.

The difficult operating environment in Colombia led to a great deal of innovation in maintaining the Viscounts in flying condition. One of the TAO aircraft, HK-1061, was badly damaged in a crash-landing at Neiva in October 1971. A little over a fortnight later another TAO Viscount, HK-1057, was damaged in a similar crash at Bucaramanga. The undamaged starboard wing of HK-1057 was used to repair HK-1061. This was the first-ever single-wing change on a Viscount, and was accomplished by TAO with the assistance of BAC and Butler Aviation of the USA. Eventually it was decided to repair HK-1057 as well, and a full set of wings from one of the scrapped 'spares' aircraft, I-LOTT, was used. Yet another accident at Neiva, in May 1972, to HK-1058, led to the use of a wing from the other scrapped aircraft, I-LIRG, in a similar repair.

Irish Disposals

The much-enlarged Aer Lingus Viscount 800 fleet continued to operate alongside the airline's quartet of One-Elevens from 1966, supplementing the new jets on routes to the UK and Europe. However, the advent of the Boeing 737 in the Irish carrier's fleet, early in 1969, brought a swift end to this cosy arrangement.

Aer Lingus had lost three of its Viscount 800s in accidents during 1967–68. The ex-KLM V.803 EI-AOE *St Finghin* was destroyed during a training sortie on 22 June 1967. The V.808 EI-AKK *St Aodhan* crashed on approach to Bristol, from

Dublin, in poor weather on 21 September 1967, and another ex-KLM V.803, EI-AOM *St Feidhlim*, went missing on a flight from Cork to Heathrow on 3 November 1968. The loss of 'AOM was the subject of much speculation. Theories ranged from unexpected structural failure to water spouts and even stray missiles from a military exercise. As none of the unfortunate occupants survived after the aircraft crashed into the sea, and what little wreckage that was recovered offered no definite clues, the true cause remains a mystery.

Swiss charter operator SATA flew HB-ILR, its second Viscount leased from Aer Lingus, for two years. Jenny Gradidge

Lingus Leases

The remaining Aer Lingus Viscounts began to be withdrawn during 1969, six being stood down from operational use during the year. One, V.803 EI-AOE, was leased to Swiss charter operator SATA from March, as HB-ILP. It was operated alongside a single Dart-powered Convair 640 and Caravelles on inclusive-tour and *ad hoc* charters from Swiss cities, most regularly to Barcelona, Palma and Palermo. In November it was returned to Dublin and was replaced by another ex-Aer Lingus Viscount, EI-AJK, which became HB-ALR. This aircraft remained with SATA until December 1971. It was then leased out again a month later, still as HB-ILR, to another Swiss charter airline, Air Tourisme Alpine (ATA), which was based at Basle and operated the convertible V.808C, on newspaper delivery contracts between Geneva, Munich, Paris and Zurich, as well as on temporary charters. In early 1972 'LR was actually leased back to SATA for two months. Shortly after the end of this lease ATA ceased operations, and Aer Lingus repossessed the Viscount.

Another short-lived operator of an Aer Lingus Viscount was Belfast-based Ulster Air Transport, which operated scheduled services as Air Ulster. Its DC-3s were operated from Belfast-Aldergrove to both the Glasgow Airports, Abbotsinch and Prestwick, as well as on short-term charters. A single V.803 was leased from Aer Lingus in July 1969 to upgrade the Glasgow service and offer scope for more charter work, especially on the inclusive-tour market. However, the lease of the Viscount, which retained its Irish registration, EI-APD, only lasted until November. The aircraft saw limited use on the route to Prestwick and the hoped-for inclusive-tour charter contracts failed to materialize, so it was returned to Dublin. In January 1970 Ulster Air Transport/Air Ulster ceased all remaining operations.

The original cross-Channel vehicle ferry operation of BUA, British United Air Ferries, was renamed British Air Ferries in 1967 and became a totally separate airline from BUA, though both airlines were still owned by Air Holdings at the time. Over the years the number of all-passenger services, which operated alongside the vehicle ferry flights, had steadily increased, using the ferry aircraft, Bristol Freighters and Carvairs, with extra passenger seating. To develop the non-vehicle ferry services on its scheduled routes from Southend, BAF leased-in a V.803 from Aer Lingus, EI-AOI flying in full BAF livery from March 1970 to September 1971 and mostly operating from Southend to Ostend, Bruges and Ghent. From November 1970 the Viscount was joined by an HS 748 leased-in from Autair/Court Line, and another 748 from the same source was operated in the summer of 1971.

After the first retirements in 1969, the remaining Aer Lingus Viscounts left the operational fleet in 1970. Many were scrapped after a period spent awaiting possible sale, including most of those that returned to Dublin after lease contracts expired or were cancelled. The lucky exceptions included the ex-SATA/ATA V.808C, which was sold to a UK leasing company, becoming G-BBDK. The other two convertible V.808Cs, EI-AKL and

Air Ulster's single Viscount saw only limited service for a few months. Aviation Hobby Shop

The BAF lease of EI-AOI saw the aircraft operating passenger services that supplemented the established car ferry operation. Aviation Hobby Shop

'AKO, were sold to West German charter operator Air Commerz Flug in 1970. Operating both passenger and cargo charters throughout Europe from their new base at Hamburg, the Viscounts, registered D-ADAM and D-ADAN, were eventually joined by two Boeing 707s. Air Commerz succumbed to bankruptcy on 1 September 1972 and the aircraft were repossessed by Aer Lingus, which was owed a great deal of money for maintenance on the aircraft.

Being highly valuable by virtue of their versatile convertible interiors, the two V.808Cs soon found a new owner. They were purchased by the Sultanate of Oman Air Force (SOAF), which had bought the two RAAF V.816s in 1971. Two Lufthansa V.814s were also acquired in 1972, though one of these was written-off in an accident at Hurn before delivery to Oman. The SOAF Viscounts were used for regional transport work. They could be fitted with canvas seats for troop transport, and also flew in support of the ruler's executive aircraft fleet. Another ex-Aer Lingus aircraft was also bought for spares, being broken up after it was ferried to Hurn in 1973. This aircraft had been earmarked for sale to a Norwich-based UK operator Progressive Airways, and had been painted up in the airline's livery in early 1971. However, Progressive ceased operations before the Viscount could be delivered, and plans for new scheduled services from Norwich to the Channel Islands and Scandinavia, for which it was intended, were scrapped.

The Sultanate of Oman Air Force fleet of Viscounts, some of them equipped with large cargo doors, were operated both on general transport duties and VIP services. Jenny Gradidge

Longevity Sets In

As the 1970s progressed it seemed that both the Viscount and Vanguard had become enduring features, worldwide, despite assumptions that they would have served their original purpose long since and been consigned to history. Many airframes had moved on to enjoy productive lives long after their original purchasers had believed they were no longer viable. A quarter of a century after the Viscount had been created, even more adventures still awaited both of the Vickers turboprop airliners.

CHAPTER TEN

A Busy Middle Age

Air Canada Drops the Turboprops

As at Continental, the arrival of the DC-9 saw the beginning of the end for Air Canada's Vickers fleet. An initially small fleet of DC-9-10s, delivered from 1966 onwards, was later expanded by the purchase of several secondhand aircraft, and also by the addition of a large number of the stretched DC-9-30 series ordered new from McDonnell Douglas.

Air Canada's Vanguards began to be withdrawn from early 1969, as they, too, were replaced by the DC-9s. This process continued over the following two years, the last Vanguard passenger flights being operated on 31 October 1971. The remaining Vanguards spent their last months with Air Canada on routes to the Maritime Provinces, from Montreal to Halifax, via Moncton and also to Gander and St Johns. The sole Cargoliner, CF-TKK, remained in use on all-freight services until May 1972, when it too was withdrawn.

BELOW: **Air Canada's first handful of DC-9s began to arrive in 1966. Later increases in their numbers led to the eventual disposal of the airline's remaining Viscounts and Vanguards.** Air Canada via author

BOTTOM: **The Air Canada Vanguards had operated their last passenger services by the end of 1971.** Air Canada via Bill Mellberg

Viscount Farewells

By the early 1970s most of Air Canada's Viscount 700 fleet had also been withdrawn. One of the aircraft, V.757 CF-THI, had already been presented to the National Museum of Science and Technology as early as 1969, where it is still preserved in its original TCA colours. At the end of 1973, though, five Viscounts remained in full-time service, with another five retained on standby. These were operated in the eastern regions, serving routes linking Halifax, Montreal, North Bay, Ottawa, Toronto and Val D'or. The final scheduled Viscount flights were operated on 27 April 1974, completing over twenty-nine years of turboprop service with TCA and Air Canada.

One of the V.757s, CF-TID, faced a very different future to those of most of its colleagues. In 1972 it was sold to United Aircraft of Canada as a flying test-bed. The company later became Pratt & Whitney Aircraft of Canada. One of the first tasks for the re-registered C-FTID-X was to serve in the development of the Pratt & Whitney PT-6 turboprop engine. After being tried in two different positions on the wing, in place of one of the Darts, a prototype PT-6 was finally fitted in the Viscount's nose and operated as a fifth engine. The nose engine's propeller rotated in the opposite direction to those on the wing, in an effort to retain asymmetry and reduce stress on the airframe. The aircraft continued to serve Pratt & Whitney on similar projects until 1989.

A fifth, nose-mounted, engine was eventually fitted to C-FTID for research and development work. Jenny Gradidge

Canadian Trade-ins

Some of the redundant Vanguards were traded in as part of the purchase of a fleet of new widebody Lockheed L.1011 TriStars. The TriStars were being bought by Air Canada via a third party, Air Holdings (Sales) Ltd of the UK, which had ordered no fewer than thirty of them from Lockheed for resale outside the USA. Initially only five Vanguards were included in the Air Canada deal, but the number was later increased to twelve.

Air Holdings took delivery of eight of the Vanguards during 1969, and three other stored Air Canada aircraft were sold to another aircraft sales company, Aviaco Traders (Lockheed). These were also to be handled by Air Holdings under a separate agreement with Lockheed. The first eight Air Holdings aircraft were all ferried to the UK for storage at Cambridge during 1969, where they were joined by the Aviaco Traders trio the same year. The remainder of the Air Holdings aircraft arrived in 1972, as they were withdrawn from scheduled service in Canada. Four passenger Vanguards and the sole Cargoliner were sold directly by Air Canada to Europe Aero Service (EAS), of Perpignan, France, in 1972–73. These were later joined at EAS by two of the three Aviaco Traders aircraft. The final three unsold Air Canada Vanguards were sold to a Panamanian company, Cie Interamericana Export-Import SA in August 1973. They were all scrapped on site at Montreal, for spares. While CF-TKM was being dismantled, a fire broke out and destroyed it on the ramp at Dorval.

New Lease of Life at BEA

Although Air Canada had decided to dispose of its Vanguards, BEA had other ideas for its aircraft. As early as 1966, speculative tenders had been invited for the conversion of a number of the Vanguards to an all-freight configuration. The experimental cargo services operated by G-APEL had convinced the airline that the aircraft might still have a profitable future in all-freight operations. The small fleet of Argosies was struggling to earn any money at all. Their break-even load factor was approximately 73 per cent, and the average loads carried were barely in the region of 55 per cent. It was calculated that an all-cargo conversion of the Vanguard would offer break-even loads 25 per cent lower than those of the Argosies, placing the freight services on a more viable footing.

The conversion contract was eventually awarded to Aviation Traders Ltd of South-end in Essex. With a well-established reputation for aero-engineering and maintenance programmes, the company had modified a number of Britannias with retrofitted cargo doors and freight floors for several British independent airlines. The Vanguard conversion entailed the fitting of a large, upward-opening freight door, 139in (3.53m) long and 80in (2m) high, in the forward port fuselage. All passenger cabin windows were to be blocked out, and a strengthened roller-floor was to be installed to facilitate the speedy loading of cargo.

The Vanguard's capacious fuselage would be able to accommodate up to 18½ tons (18.7 tonnes) in its 3,850cu ft (109cu m) and could accommodate standard cargo pallets. The airline adopted the name Merchantman for its all-freighter Vanguards. The contract with Aviation Traders covered the Merchantman design and the conversion of two of the five BEA Vanguards initially selected modification. Aviation Traders would supply the components in kit form for BEA to carry out the work itself on the remaining three aircraft, and for any subsequent adaptions.

The newly installed main-deck cargo door gave the Vanguard a new future as a high-capacity dedicated freighter. Jenny Gradidge

Tragedy over Belgium

Although their numbers had been seriously depleted by the Merchantman programme, there were still five V.951s and six V.953 BEA Vanguards in passenger service in 1971. As well as the domestic trunk routes to Belfast, Edinburgh, Glasgow and Manchester, they were also used on international services to Alghero, Gerona, Gibraltar, Madrid, Malta, Palma, Salzburg and Shannon. In the winter of 1971–72 the Vanguards also operated twice a day from Birmingham to Paris, and on a daily Birmingham–Dublin flight.

That summer season's Vanguard flying, which had been as uneventful and dependable as usual, came to a sad end on 2 October 1971. On that day, V.951 G-APEC was scheduled to operate the London–Salzburg flight, and left Heathrow at 09.34hr with eight crew and fifty-five passengers on board. At 10.04hr the aircraft had already crossed the Channel and was over Belgium, en route to its Austrian destination, and routinely reported passing the Wulpen VOR (VHF omnidirectional radio range; a fixed signal-emitting beacon, the most common radio navigation aid) at flight level 190. ('Flight levels' are altitudes in controlled airspace, where altimeters are set to a standard pressure setting of 1013.3mB. FL190 is 19,000ft (5,800m) at this setting, FL150 is 15,000ft (4,500m), and so on.) Five minutes later, however, at 10.09hr, radio messages from the crew reported that they were 'going down', followed by two voices giving the 'Mayday' distress call several times over. Other distorted calls followed to the effect that they were 'going down vertically' and 'out of control', all of which suddenly ceased 54 seconds after the first distress calls. At 10.10.40 the stricken G-APEC smashed into a field close to the village of Aarsele, its impact making a large crater. All on board were killed instantly.

It soon became evident that the outer two-thirds of both tailplanes and left elevator, together with the entire right elevator, were not at the wreckage site, and must have become detached. These were later found, in fragments, scattered downwind from the track of the flight, northwest of the main wreckage. The ensuing investigation showed that the rear pressure bulkhead had apparently ruptured, having suffered corrosion caused by a leaky toilet. The force of the cabin's pressurized air suddenly expelling through the rupture blew off the elevators and tailplane, forcing G-APEC into a dive from which there was no hope of recovery. As a result of the findings, all Vanguards were restricted to a maximum cruising height of 10,000ft (3,000m) until they had been examined and a strengthening modification for the rear bulkhead, recommended as a precaution by BAC, undertaken.

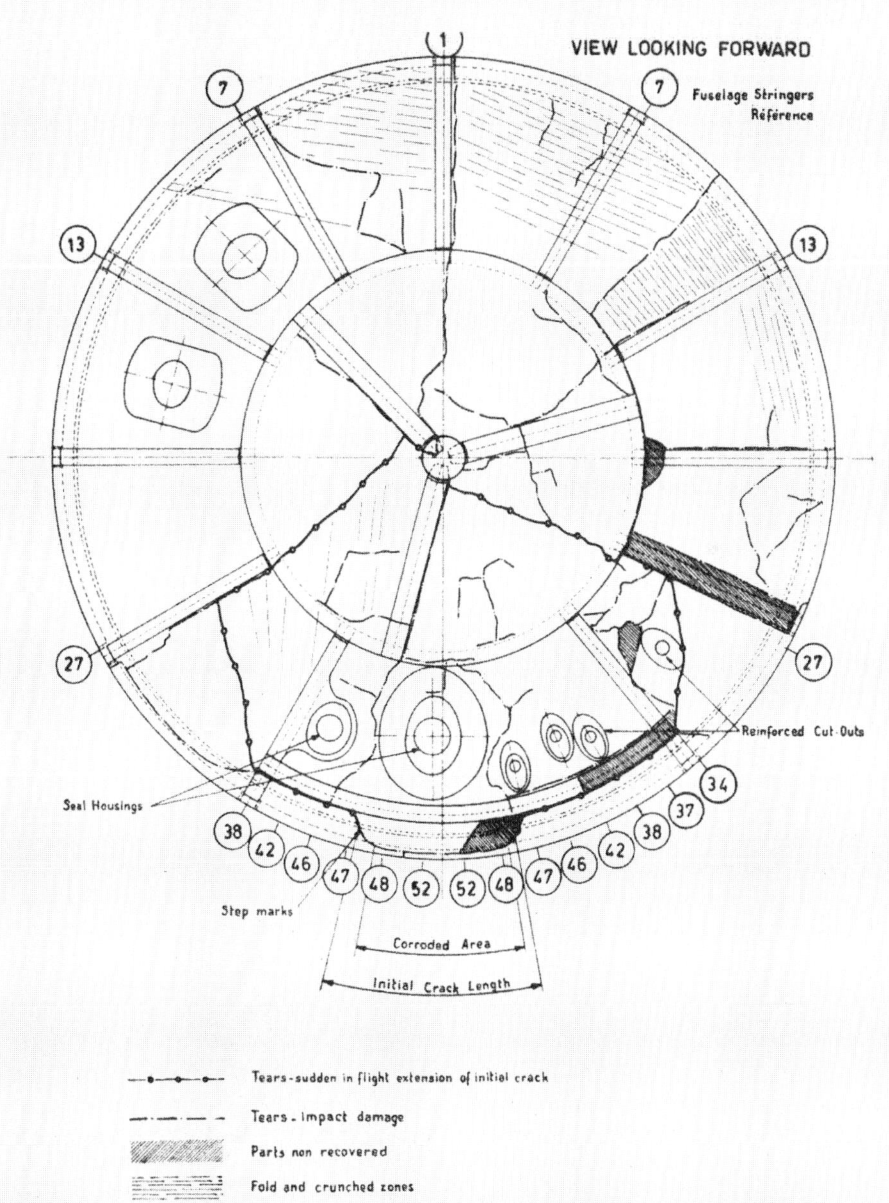

TOP: The unfortunate V.951 G-APEC had served BEA for ten years when it was lost in 1971. via author

BOTTOM: The corrosion and tears in the bulkhead of G-APEC became apparent when the wreckage was recovered and reassembled. via author

First to be earmarked for conversion was G-APEM, which was flown to Southend on 1 October 1968. The second aircraft, G-APEO, was ferried to Southend on 2 January 1969, and BEA began work on G-APEK at Heathrow in May. In November 1969 G-APEG was withdrawn from scheduled service and flown to Cranfield, where it was to take part in trials of the new onboard computer system being designed for the Merchantman.

In the meantime 'EM was rolled out at Southend as a full Merchantman, making its first post-conversion flight on 10 October 1969. Following a number of test flights over the next month, 'EM became the first of the type to receive certification, being delivered back to BEA at Heathrow on 26 November. The first commercial Merchantman service, a Heathrow–Stuttgart–Vienna–Heathrow round trip, was operated by 'EM on 7 February. The second aircraft returned to Heathrow from Southend on 23 February 1970, just under a week after the conversion and certification of 'EK was completed by BEA at Heathrow on 17 February. A fourth Merchantman, G-APES, was awarded its new C of A on 1 April. Two more Vanguards, G-APEL and 'EP, were withdrawn from passenger service in early 1970 to undergo conversion.

With four of the fleet in service, BEA was finally able to dispose of its Argosies, which operated their last BEA services on 30 April. The new Merchantman quartet was operated on the international cargo flights from Heathrow to Amsterdam, Athens, Brussels, Copenhagen, Dublin, Dusseldorf, Frankfurt, Gothenburg, Malta, Milan, Nicosia, Paris, Stuttgart, Turin, Vienna and Zurich. This was in addition to domestic cargo schedules from Heathrow to Belfast, Guernsey, Glasgow, Jersey and Manchester. Encouraged by the success of the first services, BEA had adapted nine of its V.953s by 1973, 'EG and 'EJ following 'EP and 'ES in the programme. The V.951s were deemed unsuitable for Merchantman conversion owing to their lower operating weights, which would restrict their usefulness in all-cargo mode.

BEA's Last Days

The remaining passenger-equipped Vanguards continued in BEA service through 1972 and 1973, gradually reducing in numbers. One V.951, G-APEF, was sold to a leasing broker, Templewood Aviation, in 1972, and two others, G-APEA and G-APED, were retired and scrapped at the end of the summer season. The last of BEA's V.951s, G-APEB, met a similar fate in June 1973. Two more of the V.953s were sold to Templewood by 1974, leaving just three Vanguards in passenger service when BEA was merged with BOAC on 1 April 1974 to create British Airways. The passenger Vanguards' employment for their last few months with the airline was confined to limited use on scheduled routes to Edinburgh, Gibraltar and Jersey from Heathrow. The day of the airline's last Vanguard passenger service inevitably came round, and on 16 June 1974 V.953 G-APEU operated a round trip from Heathrow to Jersey. This last revenue load from the Channel Islands to London brought BEA/British Airway's total number of Vanguard passengers carried in nearly fourteen years of service to an impressive total of 21,874,770.

The Merchantman fleet continued operations after the departure of the last passenger Vanguards. The longest scheduled freight service regularly operated was to Nicosia, usually via Athens, flown once a week. In 1974 and 1975, however, a number of marathon transatlantic trips were made to the USA to collect passenger seats and spares for British Airways' own new L.1011 TriStar fleet from Lockheed's California factory.

Short-Lived Leases

The ex-Air Canada Vanguards, which had been gathered together by Air Holdings, totalled eleven by November 1969. Most were delivered, via Stansted, straight into storage at Cambridge. The first to arrive, CF-TKN, was ferried to Heathrow for overhaul shortly after its delivery flight in March. This work, undertaken by BEA for Air Holdings was completed on 22 December, and the aircraft was given the new UK registration G-AXNT. On its return to Air Holdings at Stansted, the aircraft began a series of crew training flights in preparation for the first lease contract the company had been able to arrange for its new Vanguard fleet.

Indonesian Angkasa Civil Air Transport of Djakarta had been operating a pair of Britannia 102s on charter work in the Far East. In particular, the company was involved in the transport of Muslim pilgrims from Indonesia to Saudi Arabia to visit the holy shrines at Mecca during the annual 'Hadj'. A contract for the lease of one aircraft was signed with Air Holdings, and another Vanguard, CF-TKJ, which had become G-AXOO, was delivered as PK-ICC in February 1970. Configured in a 146-seat layout, the Indonesian Vanguard seems to have arrived too late to operate any of the Hadj flights, which were still operated by the Britannias. The Vanguard was found alternative work, operating cargo charters to Saigon four times a week, and twice-weekly to Sydney. Even this work appears to have been short-lived, though, as 'ICC was returned to Stansted on 26 April and Angkasa ceased all operations.

A single-aircraft lease was arranged with Beirut-based Lebanese Air Transport, and G-AXNT was accordingly delivered on 29 May. Intended to be operated on tobacco charters between Beirut and the UK, the Vanguard was crewed by Air Holdings personnel, but very little commercial flying seems to have taken place. On 10 June G-AXNT was returned to Air Holdings, and Lebanese Air Transport soon faded into history. However, 'NT was idle for only a few months. The reconstituted Invicta Air Cargo had continued to operate three DC-4s on cargo flights from Manston after the airline had extracted itself from the abortive merger with British Midland. Invicta was impressed by the V.952 Vanguard's maximum 18-ton capacity compared with the DC-4's mere 8 tons, and signed up to lease G-AXNT. The aircraft was put into Invicta service in October 1970, flying cargo charters from Manston around Europe and to North Africa.

Another of the Vanguards found a temporary home, CF-TKD, now G-AXOY, being despatched north to Air Viking in Iceland on 2 June 1970 as TF-AVA. Based at Keflavik, the aircraft began operating passenger inclusive-tour charters to Europe. The most popular of these was to Palma, which could take up to five hours to reach from Iceland. A refuelling stop was usually made at Stansted on the return flight. The Air Viking Vanguard also operated a round-trip passenger charter on 2 July on behalf of Channel Airways from Stansted to Palma, as well as several *ad hoc* charters from Keflavik to Denmark, Germany and the UK. By December, however, much of the charter work had dried up for the winter, and the Vanguard was returned to Stansted at the end of the lease.

Only two months later, in February 1971, TF-AVA returned to Iceland. This time it

ABOVE: The first Invicta Vanguard, G-AXNT, offered a huge increase in capacity over the DC-4s. via author

LEFT: Two different Icelandic charter companies operated V.952 TF-JEJ over two years. Air Viking flew the Vanguard on passenger charters in 1970, and Thor Cargo operated it as a freighter in 1971. via author

BOTTOM: The V.952F G-AYLD was the only Merchantman not to be converted specifically for BEA. Aviation Hobby Shop

had been stripped of its passenger fittings and wore the titles of Thor Cargo. It had also been reregistered yet again, as TF-JEJ. A month later a second Vanguard joined the Thor fleet, ex-CF-TKB and G-AYFN, re-registered as TF-JES. The two were employed on cargo contracts that took them mostly between Iceland and Germany, though they also ventured as far south as Italy and North Africa. Unfortunately, Thor Cargo was forced to cease operations on 13 June 1971, and both aircraft were returned to Air Holdings at Stansted.

As part of the investigation into the loss of BEA's G-APEC over Belgium in 1971, one of the ex-Air Canada Vanguards in storage with Air Holdings at Cambridge, CF-TKI, was used for a series of bulkhead pressure tests by the UK accident investigation authorities. Following the tests the aircraft was scrapped and reduced to spares by Air Holdings.

A New Merchantman

Air Holdings soon noticed that the enquiries it was receiving regarding the Vanguards increasingly centred on their possible use as freighters. Putting to use the experience gained by its associate, Aviation Traders, in designing and producing the Merchantman conversions for BEA, the company decided to convert one of the ex-Air Canada aircraft as a demonstrator for potential clients. Having selected CF-TKG, ATEL began work on turning the aircraft into a Merchantman in May 1970, at Southend, and the 'new' Merchantman was rolled out as G-AYLD on 8 July 1971. As well as the new registration, the aircraft was given a fresh livery with Air Holdings (Sales) Ltd titles. This was the first of the ex-Canadian fleet to wear anything but the most rudimentary adaptation of the basic Air Canada livery, its new two-tone blue scheme being based on that of British Air Ferries, which was also owned by Air Holdings at the time.

A series of demonstration flights followed the first post-conversion flight on 21 July, including a Southend–Ostend–Southend service operated for BAF on 24 August. Other demonstration flights were operated to Dusseldorf, and Lubeck was also visited in August. This was the home base of German operator Elbeflug, which Air Holdings hoped it could interest in a Merchantman order to replace its fleet of DC-6As and Nord Nortalases. No orders followed this flurry of activity, however, so G-AYLD was stored at Southend to await new opportunities.

Invicta Returns to Passenger Service

The use of G-AXNT on freight services impressed Invicta's founder and managing director, Wg Cdr Hugh Kennard, to the extent that overtures were soon being made to Air Holdings with a view to acquiring more aircraft. Instead of cargo Vanguards, though, Kennard was now interested in restarting his passenger charter operations, previously operated by Viscounts and DC-4s before the BMA merger.

Consequently, G-AXOO, the ex-Angkasa aircraft, was made ready for Invicta and delivered to Manston on 1 March 1971. The new passenger division was to operate as Invicta International Airlines. On 8 May 'OO was followed by G-AXOP, previously CF-TKV, which had been in storage since its arrival from Canada in June 1969. In the meantime, 'OO had entered service in April, with charters to Basle and Dusseldorf. The passenger Vanguard operations were based at Luton in Bedfordshire, with the cargo aircraft still flying from Manston, though occasional passenger charters were operated from the Kent base as well. Gatwick was also a regular departure point for the Vanguards, services being operated to Le Bourget, Rotterdam and Tarbes in the first few months of operation. Stansted was the starting point for one of the Invicta International Vanguard fleet's more spectacular charters of 1971, 'OP operating a direct passenger charter flight to Tel Aviv on 5 October.

Both passenger Vanguards soon settled into a healthily varied charter programme, with a mixture of inclusive-tour contract flights to the Mediterranean, Ministry of Defence charters carrying servicemen and their families to Dusseldorf, student charters to Milan and Rome, and catholic pilgrim services to Tarbes. The pilgrim flights to Tarbes, serving nearby Lourdes, were also operated from other UK points such as Blackpool and Gatwick. So successful was Invicta's first season with the Vanguards that the passenger fleet was doubled. The ex-Air Viking Vanguard, G-AXOY, and another ex-Air Canada aircraft, CF-TKF, which arrived directly from Canada to become G-AZRE, were both ready in service by May to operate a much-expanded charter programme for 1972.

At a time when most of the larger charter airlines had converted to pure jets for passenger work, Invicta's Vanguards still attracted a number of smaller holiday companies and travel organizations who still appreciated the economics of the turboprop and the aircraft's very useful capacity of up to 146 passengers. Typical of these important sources of regular revenue was a contract signed with Tyrolean Travel for frequent inclusive-tour charter flights to Munich from Edinburgh, Luton and Manchester, from 13 May 1972.

Swedish Interlude

The Air Holdings (Sales) Merchantman G-AYLD remained idle at Southend for several months before it was finally found a new home. A new Swedish cargo charter airline, Air Trader, acquired a lease on the aircraft to operate a series of freight flights from Stockholm to Bangladesh on behalf of the Red Cross. Following repainting in a dramatic blue and orange livery, the Merchantman was delivered to Stockholm's Bromma Airport on 22 January 1972. Crew training followed, and the first commercial service to Bangladesh left Bromma on 12 February, bound for Dacca.

In-between runs to Bangladesh the company found short-term cargo work around Europe and to the Middle East. Another of Aviation Traders' fleet was prepared for lease to Air Trader and delivered to Bromma on 13 April. A third Vanguard, one of the ex-Thor Cargo fleet, followed in July. A fourth

Invicta returned to passenger operations with its pair of Vanguard 952s in 1971. Steve Williams Collection

Following Air Trader's financial collapse, its fleet was returned to Air Holdings.
via author

from Aviation Traders' stock, CF-TKO, was delivered from storage in Canada, via Southend, and ferried immediately to Bromma, where it was cannibalized for spares. The colourful trio were kept busy on flights that often ventured to North Africa and the Middle East. On 31 July the Merchantman even reached as far south as Johannesburg.

However, this early success did not continue, Air Trader finding itself in serious financial difficulties by October. A temporary grounding of the fleet was lifted in November, when a new investor was found. The Merchantman and one of the Vanguards were returned to service and were seen on a number of cargo charters from Scandinavia to the UK in late 1972. Unfortunately the revival proved to be short-lived, and Air Trader had returned all three aircraft to Aviation Traders by early 1973.

Vanguards with a French Flavour

Between May and June 1972 the first three Europe Aero Service (EAS) Vanguards entered service. Replacing a small fleet of DC-6Bs, they were mostly operated from EAS's Paris base at Le Bourget, which was later moved to Orly, as well as from the company's head office and maintenance base at Perpignan in the south of France. The first two aircraft were flown on passenger charters, while the third was configured as a freighter.

As with Invicta's Vanguard fleet, the EAS aircraft were often used on pilgrim flights from various European points to Tarbes, and were also very popular on inclusive tours and student exchange charters. The Vanguards were also occasionally operated on EAS's small scheduled route network, which was usually served by a pair of Dart Heralds. These operated from Perpignan to Nimes, Paris and Palma, and the Vanguards replaced the Heralds when loads warranted it. Two more passenger Vanguards and the ex-Cargoliner had all joined the operational fleet by the end of the year, to be followed by a further pair of passenger aircraft, from Aviaco Traders, in mid-1973. These last two Vanguards were given French 'overseas' registrations and put into passenger service on a year-long contract for the French government, based in Tchad and the Sahara regions. At the end of this contract the aircraft were returned to France, where one was scrapped for spares and the other was placed into European charter service.

Return to Indonesia

Even though Air Holding's 1970 lease of the single Vanguard to Indonesian Angkasa could hardly be regarded as a commercial triumph, within two years the type was once again to be found in the skies above the Far Eastern island nation. At the time, government-owned PN Merpati Nusantara Airlines was experiencing a boom in traffic on its domestic routes. Having already operated a fleet of secondhand Viscounts, Merpati was very inclined to regard the Vanguard as a viable alternative to pure jets.

Initially Merpati leased-in three Vanguards from Templewood Aviation, two ex-Air Canada V.952s from the Air Holdings stock and a single ex-BEA V.951. The first two aircraft arrived in March and May 1972, and the third, the ex-BEA aircraft, arrived that November. The Vanguards were introduced on the airline's busier passenger schedules from Djakarta to points such as Medan, Surabaya and Ujung Pandang. They were soon proving themselves useful on routes serving both business and tourist traffic and, when one of the V.952s was returned to the UK and the V.951 was scrapped at Djakarta in July 1973, the remaining aircraft was soon joined by one of the ex-Air Trader V.953s. These two were returned to the UK in April 1974, but were immediately replaced by British Airways' last three passenger Vanguards, G-APEH, G-APEI and G-APEN, which became PK-MVF, 'MVD and 'MVE respectively.

Europe Aero Service's first Vanguards operated a variety of inclusive-tour and short-term charters from Paris and Perpignan. Jenny Gradidge

BEA Viscount Changes

Even when BEA had finally dispersed its V.806s, either passing them on to its BAS subsidiaries or selling them to new owners, a considerable fleet of V.802s was still available. In 1971 the airline was restructured into a number of smaller divisions, each operating as a separate 'profit centre' in its own right within BEA. The remaining Viscount 802s were split between two new divisions, BEA Scottish Airways and BEA Channel Islands Airways, responsible for the scheduled services from their appropriate UK region. The two 'new' operators were given the resurrected names of two of the original independent airlines that had been taken over by BEA on its formation in the late 1940s.

Seven V.802s were allocated to BEA Scottish Airways and based at Glasgow. Taking over the previous Scottish Division, it operated all the internal Scottish services with the Viscounts and two Herons, as well as schedules to Heathrow from Aberdeen and Inverness, and the Glasgow–Belfast route. The Inverness–Heathrow flight, the longest non-stop service within the UK, was operated in 2hr 10min by the Viscounts. Although BEA Channel Islands Airways was, as indicated by its title, responsible for many of the scheduled services to the two main Channel Islands, Jersey and Guernsey, it was actually based at Birmingham. Allocated the remaining twelve V.802s, Channel Islands also flew the scheduled services from Birmingham within the UK to Eire and Europe, as well as the Channel Island Viscount flights from points such as Heathrow, Gatwick and Southampton.

The Birmingham-based division was also responsible for one of its Viscount 802s leased out to Gibair in Gibraltar. This aircraft had finally replaced Gibair's DC-3 on

ABOVE: Vintage Viscount 802 G-AOJE was assigned to the 'new' BEA Scottish Airways Division. Steve Williams Collection

BELOW: Based at Birmingham's Elmdon Airport, BEA's Channel Island Airways Division was responsible for Viscount operations from several UK and Channel Island airports. Steve Richards

the Gibraltar–Tangiers route, reviving a similar arrangement previously used with BEA's V.701s. Gibair also sub-leased the aircraft to Royal Air Maroc for a number of domestic services from Tangiers and Casablanca in 1971/1972. The use of BEA Viscounts by Gibair ended in January 1974, when an ex-NZNAC V.807 was delivered to Gibraltar. Although ostensibly owned by BEA, G-BBVH was leased to Gibair for its exclusive use, being sold to the airline seven years later. The solitary Viscount was operated by Gibair, later renamed GB Airways, until it was damaged beyond repair in a heavy landing as late as 1988.

As the new divisions became established, the Viscounts were painted with additional 'Scottish Airways' or 'Channel Islands' titling over the BEA livery, though exchanges of fleet members between the two divisions were common. It was by no means unusual for the Scottish Airways internal network to be operated by a Viscount bearing 'Channel Islands' markings, nor for an apparently 'Scottish' aircraft to be seen operating the daily Guernsey–Gatwick flight. Tentative plans to rebrand the two divisions in the style of Northeast and Cambrian and hand their operation over to BAS were overtaken by events when BEA and BOAC merged to become British Airways, and were not proceeded with. Had that come about, it was proposed that Channel Island Airways would have adopted a green version of the BAS livery, and Scottish Airways a blue one.

The British Airways Influence

On the transformation of BEA into British Airways European Division, in 1974, the Viscount operating units of BEA began taking on the new red, white and blue colours, but initially kept their own operating identity. While 'British Airways' was now the predominant titling on the aircraft, small titles on the lower forward fuselage identified the division concerned. Cambrian and Northeast lost their colourful liveries in the changeover, but continued to exist in their own right, with their own administration and operational control. Even the ageing pair of Cambrian Viscount 701s operated on the Prestwick services took up the bright new BA livery and were operated in those colours until March 1976.

In late 1971 BEA had bought Channel Airways' pair of Trident 1Es. One was transferred to Northeast Airlines, and BEA Channel Islands Airways had taken delivery of the other by early 1972. The aircraft replaced Viscounts on scheduled services from Birmingham to Dublin and Paris and Dusseldorf, as well as operating some inclusive-tour charters. Secondhand One-Eleven 400s were eventually acquired by BA for use by Scottish Airways and Channel Islands Airways, and the Trident 1E followed its old Channel Airways stablemate to Northeast. New HS 748s were ordered for some of the Scottish regional services previously operated by the Viscounts. When the secondhand One-Elevens and new 748s were delivered, some thirteen of the higher-hour V.802s were withdrawn and scrapped.

The operations of Cambrian Airways, Channel Islands Airways, Northeast Airlines and Scottish Airways were eventually 'rationalized' into a new British Airways Regional Division, with effect from 1 April 1976. From that date the original constituent airlines ceased to exist and the new division operated the fleets of Trident 1Es, One-Eleven 400s and Viscounts. This brought the surviving V.802s and V.806s back together in the same fleet once again, and British Airways Regional now operated both versions. Although it was now over twenty years since the first scheduled BEA Viscount service, the trusty Viscount was still making its presence felt throughout the UK, and continued to make its own significant contribution to the new British Airways operation.

The absorption of the Cambrian and Northeast Viscount 806s by the new British Airways Regional Division saw the reunification of the survivors from the original BEA Viscount 800 fleet. BA via author

Still Under African Skies

The trio of V.838 Viscounts supplied to Ghana Airways had been reduced to a pair in 1965 when one was sold off to the Royal Aircraft Establishment in the UK. The remaining two continued to lead a busy life operating the carrier's regional international and busier domestic routes from Accra for another ten years, until small regional jets, such as the Fokker F.28 Fellowship, arrived in the mid-1970s to replace them. As well as operating Ghana's own services, a number of joint operations were undertaken in association with Nigeria Airways. Nigeria also leased-in a V.815 from British Midland for the winter of 1968–69.

One of the ex-Burma Airways V.761Ds was leased out to Air Botswana briefly in 1979–80, joining an ex-MEA V.754D that had been in service since 1976. Unfortunately, services were short-lived on scheduled services from the capital, Gaborone, to South Africa and Zambia, and the aircraft were eventually returned to their South African broker owner. The aircraft were both eventually operated, although at separate periods, by South African independent United Air for several years on charter work. Botswana's previous national carrier, Botswana National Airways, had also operated a Viscount, in the form of an ex-TAA V.756D, from 1969, before declaring bankruptcy in 1972.

New Regime, New Name

The ex-CAA Viscount 700s continued to operate with their Rhodesian successor despite the difficulties experienced in operating under strict international sanctions. Air Rhodesia showed a great deal of ingenuity in gathering spares for the aircraft, and managed to keep its fleet viable throughout the 1970s, until Boeing 720s were acquired to take over the more prestigious routes and expand services to Europe once more. Even then, the Viscounts still maintained services on many important regional international routes, such as Salisbury to Blantyre, Johannesburg and Lorenco Marques.

The end of the 1970s saw the Air Rhodesia Viscount fleet caught up in appalling events. A vicious civil war was raging in the troubled country, and on two separate occasions, in September 1978 and February 1979, revolutionary forces shot down civilian Air Rhodesia Viscounts, using ground-to-air missiles.

On 3 September 1978 VP-WAS *Hunyani* was brought down in the Whamira Hills, 10 miles (16km) from Lake Kariba, while en route to Salisbury with four crew and fifty-two passengers on board. In a particularly harrowing sequel to the episode, half-an-hour after the crash, the revolutionaries who had shot the aircraft down arrived on the scene and cold-bloodedly shot dead one man, seven women and two children who had survived the initial impact. Eight other survivors were lucky to escape with their lives. Five months later, VP-YND *Umniati* was similarly brought down, close to the same spot, with the loss of all fifty-nine passengers and crew.

Following these incidents, some of the Air Rhodesia Viscounts were given low-visibility all-grey, colour schemes and carried devices to divert heat-seeking missiles. In 1980, after the fall of the old apartheid-based regime, the airline became Air Zimbabwe, after a short period operating as Air Zimbabwe-Rhodesia. The network was expanded, following the lifting of sanctions, with the Boeing 720s replaced by 707s and operating on new routes as far as Australia, as well as expanding the European network. Nonetheless, the Viscounts remained in service on most of the domestic routes while modern replacements were evaluated and sought. Extra secondhand aircraft were even acquired as late as 1981.

Ghana Airways often operated its Viscount 838s on joint services with neighbouring Nigeria Airways.
Jenny Gradidge

Viscount 782D VP-WAS became a victim of the Rhodesian Civil War when it was callously shot down in an act of terrorism. via author

SAA Viscounts Trek North

The SAA fleet of V.813s enjoyed a long and productive career with the airline until they were replaced by Boeing 727s, and later 737s, by the early 1970s. An ex-Cubana V.818 had been acquired in 1962, though this aircraft was lost in a crash into the sea 22 miles (35km) off East London on 13 March 1967. The seven SAA V.813s found a new home *en masse*, in 1972, when the entire fleet was sold, together with a sizeable spares package, to BMA. The first began to arrive at BMA's engineering base at East Midlands in early 1972.

The Viscount had proved to be ideal for BMA's mixed network of seasonal holiday and business travel-based routes. By mid-1970 all the Viscount 700s had all been replaced by an assortment of Viscount 800 and 810 models, and the type was firmly established as the backbone of the airline's fleet. Although BMA's first pure jets had arrived in 1970, in the form of new One-Eleven 500s and secondhand Boeing 707s for use on charters, the turboprop was still viewed as the ideal aircraft for all but a handful of the scheduled services.

As well as the established East Midlands-based routes, in 1969 BMA took over a number of scheduled routes from Teeside, in the northeast of England, including a potentially lucrative trunk route to London-Heathrow, and seasonal services to the Channel Islands and the Isle of Man. The airline had also been awarded the Southend–Channel Island routes after the demise of Channel Airways. The Viscounts opened most of the new services, though the One-Elevens later took over the Teeside–London route. Before the ex-South African Airways fleet arrived, BMA was still operating one V.815 and three V.831s. Previously, a V.833 had been leased in 1969–70 to replace the V.815 lost in the Manchester accident, and an ex-Lufthansa V.814 which had been written-off following a fire on take-off at Heathrow on 22 January 1970.

The variety of Viscount models in service was a major source of operational and engineering problems for BMA. Differently-rated engines and other variations in equipment fitted in the aircraft required large expensive stores of different spares to be on hand to cover all eventualities. There were even differences in the cabin configurations, which could make fleet scheduling and passenger reservations management a nightmare. In an attempt to introduce more standardization, BMA bought the seven-strong SAA fleet. By late 1973 all three V.831s had been sold off, and four more ex-Lufthansa V.814s were acquired.

Lufthansa had originally sold the V.814s to Nora Air Service GMBH (NAS), a new charter company that planned to fly the aircraft on inclusive-tour charters from northern Germany. In addition, NAS had hoped to use the Viscounts to transport foreign workers from West Germany to their homelands, and no fewer than six ex-Lufthansa V.814s were purchased, though not all were delivered. However, despite the Viscounts being painted up in the rather garish yellow-and-pink NAS colour scheme, the company was unable to begin commercial operations and four of the fleet were acquired by BMA.

With the growth of BMA's Viscount fleet, more scheduled services were opened from East Midlands to Paris, Frankfurt, via Birmingham and Brussels, Birmingham to Heathrow, in partnership with British

British Midland Airways was operating several different models of Viscount by the early 1970s, including ex-Airwork and BUA V.831 G-ASED. Steve Richards

The ex-Lufthansa Viscount 814s originally intended for Nora Air Service arrived at East Midlands for BMA still in their bright yellow-and-pink colours. Steve Richards

The arrival of the ex-SAA V.813s, and subsequent disposal of the dissimilar earlier models, meant that BMA was finally able to enjoy the financial and operational benefits of a standardized Viscount fleet. Steve Richards

Airways, from Gatwick to Belfast and from Heathrow to Newquay and Strasbourg. In contrast, the inclusive-tour market had become so cut-throat that by 1974 the entire inclusive-tour charter programme was scrapped by the airline, rather than lose money trying to compete. As a result the One-Eleven fleet was disposed of and the Boeing 707s leased out. One of the One-Elevens was sold to Brazilian airline Sadia, which traded-in three of its Dart Heralds in part exchange for the jet. From then on BMA concentrated most of its efforts into expanding the scheduled network, based around the economic Dart-powered Viscount and Herald turboprops.

Air International and Air Bridge

The V.702 G-APPX was owned by Field Aircraft Services, an aircraft engineering, leasing and brokering company based at East Midlands Airport which had leased the aircraft to BMA for the summer of 1969. After being returned from this lease, G-APPX was eventually leased out again in 1971, this time to an ambitious new charter operator, Air International, based at Stansted. Air International held several inclusive-tour charter contracts with London-based travel agencies for flights from the UK to central Europe and Scandinavia. Unfortunately all of its operations ceased in November 1972, following the impounding of the Viscount at Gatwick for non-payment of landing fees. The aircraft was returned to Field at East Midlands, limping home on three engines. The airline's management also attempted to register a new carrier, Nor-Air, to operate another leased Viscount, but no commercial operations were undertaken.

Field Aircraft Services also became the reluctant owner of a fleet of three Argosy freighters that it had maintained on behalf of their operator, Saggitair, also based at East Midlands. Saggitair had operated the Argosies on cargo charter work since 1971, particularly on charter flights carrying fresh produce from the Channel Islands to the UK mainland. Unfortunately Saggitair ceased operations in the autumn of 1972, and the Argosies passed to Field in lieu of outstanding debts.

A new airline, Air Bridge Carriers (ABC) was set up by Field Aircraft Services to operate the Argosies on the profitable Channel Islands flights, as well as on general *ad hoc* charters throughout Europe. The Argosy services became a success under Field's ownership, and ABC soon established itself as a cargo specialist. One of the Argosies was sold in 1974, but was replaced by ex-Air Tourisme Alpine V.808C G-BBDK. This aircraft had originally been earmarked for lease to Air International's proposed successor, Nor-Air. Entering ABC service in September 1974, the Viscount was operated on short-term leases to other carriers, its flexible passenger/cargo qualities benefiting several airlines, as well as flying on the established ABC cargo-charter network.

Brief Kestrel Summer

With the arrival of the ex-SAA Viscount fleet, BMA proceeded further with its standardization policy by attempting to dispose of the last V.815 in the fleet, G-AVJB. The aircraft was leased out to yet another new neighbour at East Midlands, Kestrel International Airways. Originally based at Lydd Airport, Kent, Kestrel had started operations in late 1970 with a single DC-3. Business was fairly slow initially, and in early 1971 the company's base was moved to East Midlands, from where it was hoped more charter work might be forthcoming. During the following year the DC-3 operated a number of charter services carrying both passengers and cargo around Europe, and was especially busy with popular twenty-minute pleasure flights from East Midlands on summer weekends.

Expansion plans for 1972 included applying for a number of scheduled service licences for routes from East Midlands and Liverpool to Newquay and from Teeside to the Isle of Man. The licence applications specified the use of both DC-3s and Viscounts. Although the scheduled services were not proceeded with, the Viscount was still acquired from BMA, and entered service in March 1972. Tristar Travel had contracted Kestrel for a regular weekly East Midlands–Palma inclusive-tour charter, which operated via Clermont Ferrand, and the Viscount was acquired to serve this charterer. In addition, a number of services were flown on behalf of 'JB's previous operator on BMA's scheduled network.

For the rest of the summer the Viscount was chartered out to Dan-Air Services, and operated that airline's scheduled services to the Isle of Man from Bristol, Cardiff, Carlisle, Newcastle and Prestwick every weekend, while operating *ad hoc* and inclusive-tour charters for Kestrel during the week. The DC-3 was sold in August, leaving the Viscount as Kestrel's sole fleet member. The Dan-Air contract ended with the close of the summer season and, unable to find sufficient work for the winter months, Kestrel International was forced to close down and the Viscount was repossessed by BMA in November.

Alidair Joins the EMA Viscount Club

Another new venture also began charter services from East Midlands with Viscounts in 1972. Alidair was originally formed in 1971 to provide executive flight services for its parent company, a midlands-based packaging organization. Initially based at Hucknall, it flew two Piper Twin Comanches and a Beagle Pup. With a view to expanding the flying operation, Alidair Cargo was registered in January 1972, to carry out freight charter work from Hucknall. As part of the expansion plan, Alidair had already relocated its head office to East Midlands in preparation for the proposed cargo services, as custom facilities were not available at Hucknall.

However, the demise of Channel Airways in early 1972 offered a unique opportunity for Alidair to transform its proposed operation, and the Alidair Cargo plans were modified to include passenger charter operations. In April the last three serviceable

Viscount 815 G-AVJB was Kestrel's sole fleet member following the airline's sale of its original DC-3. As well as flying a handful of inclusive-tour contracts for Kestrel, the aircraft operated a great many scheduled services for BMA and Dan-Air under charter. Bill Sheridan Collection

Alidair's original Viscount 812s were among the last airworthy members of the defunct Channel Airways fleet. Steve Richards

Viscount 812s of the Channel Airways fleet were ferried to East Midlands Airport. One was scrapped for spares, while the two other entered service with Alidair in June, BMA's V.831, G-ASED, also being acquired in that month. The three aircraft spent a busy summer operating passenger charters to the Channel Islands and mainland Europe.

A scheduled service from East Midlands to Malmö, via Birmingham and Copenhagen, was opened in 1973, using one of the Viscounts configured in a forty-seat, first-class, configuration. The thrice-weekly route was opened on 30 April, but the loads were disappointing and the service was eventually dropped in late 1973. The charter operation was much more successful, however, and 1973 saw inclusive-tour flights operated from Southend to Alicante and Palma, and numerous day-trip excursion flights operated from Coventry and Southend, as well as from East Midlands. One of the V.812s was leased out to BAF in the summer of 1973 for cross-Channel passenger schedules from Southend.

The worldwide oil crisis led to one of the Viscounts being sold in early 1974, though the remaining two aircraft managed to keep busy. An important contract was held with the Volvo Car Company, carrying spares to and from Gothenburg. A number of passenger flights were also operated for Volvo, ferrying UK sales agents to the Gothenburg factory on educational and promotional visits. In addition to the usual short-term, inclusive-tour and day-trip contracts, other charter work for 1974 included several newspaper-carrying contracts and the operation of scheduled services for other airlines, such as for Dan-Air over the Newcastle–Gatwick route. Work was soon so buoyant that an ex-Lufthansa and NAS V.814 was acquired from the Oman Air Force. On 29 July 1975 the V.814, G-AZNH, was used for a very significant Viscount charter. On this day it operated from Northolt to Le Bourget, carrying an invited party of VIPs to celebrate the twenty-fifth anniversary of the first revenue flights for BEA over the same route, made by the prototype V.630 Viscount, G-AHRF.

Alidair, Aberdeen and the Oil Boom

The discovery of North Sea oil brought major benefits to a number of UK carriers in the early 1970s, with many contracts becoming available for the transport of oil-industry workers and technicians from the UK mainland to isolated terminals and facilities. Almost overnight, traffic soared at Aberdeen's Dyce Airport, the site of most of the oil-industry-related activity, with numerous aircraft shuttling between the city and the offshore Scottish islands such as the Shetlands, carrying oil-company personnel and supplies. British Midland briefly based a Viscount at Aberdeen to operate on behalf of a new operator, Site Aviation, specifically created to take advantage of the new business. Unfortunately, despite leasing-in the Viscount capacity and acquiring several DC-3s for the work, Site Aviation soon ceased operations.

Alidair based one of its Viscounts at Aberdeen from February 1975, mainly operating for Burmah Oil and Total Oil. As well as flying frequent services between Aberdeen and Sumburgh, on Shetland, the aircraft also visited Amsterdam, Bergen, Norwich and Stavanger on oil-charter work. From May, most of the oil industry work was taken over by a 'new' fleet of four Viscount 708s and a single V.724, which had been bought from Air Inter. By the early 1970s the French domestic airline had finally replaced the last of its Viscount fleet with jets. Demand

Viscount 700s were obtained by Alidair to expand its oil-industry-related operations from Aberdeen, as well as the established East Midlands-based charter work. via author

for its Aberdeen-based services was now so high, and the V.708s were placed into service so speedily, that they were initially operated by Alidair still carrying their French registrations. When they did take up UK markings, three of the V.708s were revealed as old hands of the UK airline scene, including two of the ex-Maitland Drewery/BKS/BUA aircraft, G-ARBY and G-ARGR, and ex-Starways G-ARIR.

The Viscount 700s were able to offer more-economic payload and range options than the larger V.810s when operating from the Scottish airports. They were easily able to operate a Sumburgh–Heathrow charter, a regular *ad hoc* service, with an economic payload despite runway restrictions at Sumburgh. With the increased dependence on the oil-related work, Alidair also applied 'Alidair Scotland' titles to the V.700s.

New Leasing Revenue

All five of the ex-Air Inter fleet had been delivered to Alidair by June 1975, and the two remaining ex-Channel V.812s had been sold to FEAT in Taiwan by May. Nonetheless, another V.812, N501TL, was acquired from Tenneco in the USA, which had operated it as an executive aircraft since buying it from Continental in 1960.

Also operating on the oil industry charters from Aberdeen was Dan-Air Services, headquartered at Gatwick. Dan-Air eventually transferred most of its sizeable fleet of HS 748 turboprops to Aberdeen to exploit the available contracts. This, however, left Dan-Air short of aircraft to operate its scheduled network. More 748s were being acquired from various sources, but pending their entry into service Dan-Air leased-in Viscount capacity to cover the shortfall. The ABC V.808C G-BBDK was leased-in between March and October 1975, mostly operating on the 'Coach-Air' service between Lydd and Beauvais in Northern France. When 'DK was returned to ABC an Alidair V.708, G-ARBY, replaced it for two months, and was then in turn replaced by another of Alidair's V.708s, G-ARIR. This aircraft remained with Dan-Air for eighteen months, and was painted in full Dan-Air livery.

Another lease saw Alidair V.724 G-BDRC and one of the V,708s, G-BDIK, contracted to Intra Airways of Jersey from March 1976. Intra had been operating scheduled services with a large fleet of DC-3s from Jersey to the UK and Northern France since 1969. The Viscount leases enabled an upgrade of equipment on many of the airline's longer and busier routes, and the aircraft were frequently used on the schedules to Cambridge and Ostend from the Channel Islands, as well as on numerous charter services around the UK and Europe. Although 'IK was returned to Alidair at the end of the 1976 summer season, 'RC was retained by Intra through the next year, not returning to Alidair until October 1977. On its return 'RC was leased out again, this time to Dan-Air on a year-long contract from March 1978.

Tenneco's N50ITL, the first production V.812, remained on the VS register throughout its 13 months with Alidair. via author

Dan-Air Services operated Viscount 808C G-BBDK on a number of scheduled services while it was on lease from Air Bridge Carriers. Aviation Hobby Shop

Cyprus Viscount Revival

In 1974 Cyprus Airways had been forced to suspend operations following the Turkish invasion and eventual partition of the island. Its fleet of Tridents had been devastated, the aircraft being destroyed or severely damaged in the fierce fighting, and the main base at Nicosia Airport was split by the ceasefire line. Once the hostilities ended, the airline was finally able to consider restarting operations, and a new base was established at Larnaca Airport on the southern side of Cyprus in 1975. To open the new services, Cyprus Airways turned to BMA, which was building a reputation as a flexible leasing operator. For the most part, BMA used its Boeing 707 fleet for the leasing services, but any of its fleet could be made available if a customer required it.

The 'new' Cyprus Airways took delivery of BMA V.813s G-ALZR and 'ZS in January and February 1975. Limited services were opened to Athens, with other routes in the region being opened as the airline

The reconstituted Cyprus Airways started operations from Larnaca with Viscounts leased from BMA. Steve Richards

struggled to re-establish itself. Two more BMA Viscounts, another V.813 and a V.814, were added by April, though the original pair were returned to the UK by August as Cyprus Airways found jets, in the form of DC-9s, to lease-in for the more important routes. The remaining two BMA Viscounts were returned in November 1975 and March 1976. However, Alidair also leased its V.812, N501TL, to Cyprus Airways in March–July 1976, followed by V.814 G-AZNH from July to August. An Alidair V.708 was operated by Cyprus in December 1975 to March 1976, and 'NH was leased to Cyprus again from December 1976 to February 1977.

False Last Hurrahs

Some of the fortunate passengers on board G-AZNH who were transported from Northolt to Le Bourget on 29 July 1975 must have mused that they might well be experiencing a final fanfare for Viscount travel. The very fact that they were celebrating the twenty-fifth anniversary of the world's first revenue passenger flight by Viscount would have indicated that the type's days on the aviation scene were numbered.

There were few airports in the UK that still did not have a regular visit from a Viscount or a Vanguard some time in the 1970s and 1980s. Africa, South and Central America, and the Far East were also scenes of continuing Viscount activity, a handful of Vanguards in Indonesia adding to the variety. Even in the USA and Canada, the occasional Viscount could still be found. However, it was becoming debatable whether this situation was likely to be a long-term feature. Few could have realized that there were almost as many years again of productive service ahead for many of the remaining Viscounts, and practically as many for the Vanguards.

The Viscount was still to be found in significant numbers around the world in the mid–late 1970s, especially with UK operators such as BMA. Steve Richards

CHAPTER ELEVEN

Hectic Twilight Years

Lingering in Canada

Despite the withdrawal of the Vanguard and Viscount fleets by Air Canada, the latter type continued to be a part of the Canadian aviation scene for a while. Nonetheless, Transair had retired its single V.724 in January 1971, before Air Canada disposed of the last of its fleet. The aircraft was officially returned to Air Canada, from whom it had been leased, though it remained in storage at Transair's Winnipeg base. In 1974 CF-TGI was sold to a private owner in the USA, and was eventually donated to the Pima Air Museum in Arizona.

Especially long-lived was the operation of a pair of Viscount 700s, a V.737 and a V.797D, by the Canadian Department of Transportation. Delivered in 1955 and 1958, both aircraft were operated on VIP services until 1982, when they were replaced by executive jets. Wabush Mines operated an ex-Air Canada V.757 between 1976 and 1988 on a private, twice-weekly supplies and personnel service from Montreal to Wabush via Sept Isles. Air Cardinal, later renamed Air Caravane, operated two Viscounts, one from Air Canada and one acquired from an operator in Zaïre, in Africa from 1979. One was withdrawn from service in 1982, but the other continued in operation on general charters around Canada and to the USA until 1986.

Following twenty years of serving several private owners and small charter operators, after its seventeen-year airline career with TCA and Transair, the first V.724 was eventually presented to a museum for preservation. Jenny Gradidge

The Viscount 797D flew VIP services for the Canadian government for many years. Jenny Gradidge

Zaïre Haven

The surviving Air Caravane Viscount actually returned to Zaïre, where the Africa nation's airlines had seemingly developed a fondness for Viscounts. A vast country with extremely primitive ground-transport services, Zaïre was able to support a number of independent airlines. Zaïre Aero Service (ZAS) had started the trend by buying-in six ex-Air Canada V.757s in 1978. One of these was repossessed in 1980 and began to operate for another Zaïre-based airline, Scibe Airlift, and another was sold to Zaïrean Airlines in 1981. Air Charter Services and Filair also operated Viscounts from Zaïre's capital, Kinshasa, in the 1980s.

Although flown under difficult conditions, with reliable air traffic services almost non-existent, the Zaïre Viscount operations seem to have returned a remarkable record for safety and reliability. Only one of the ZAS Viscounts was involved in an incident, crashing on take-off from Kinshasa on 28 August 1984 without serious injuries to the occupants. The

Zaïre Aero Service operated several Viscounts, including many acquired from surplus Canadian stocks as well as various other sources. Steve Richards

Zaïrean Airlines aircraft was operated without incident for nearly fifteen years! Although ZAS had ceased Viscount operations by 1985, the type continued to be popular with Zaïre's operators for many years afterwards. Even after a devastating civil war, which severely disrupted all of the country's transport services, a handful of surviving Viscounts still made occasional appearances within the Democratic Republic of Congo, as Zaïre became.

Swedish Viscount Revival

Falconair's Viscounts were idle following the end of operations in September 1970, but a new Swedish carrier, Skyline Air Charter of Malmö, acquired the trio of Viscount 700s in mid-1971. One V.784D, SE-CNK, was flown to Bournemouth, where BAC gave the aircraft a major overhaul, including a spar change. On 20 August the Viscount was delivered back to Skyline, and it operated its first service for the company on 16 September, a Malmö–Gothenburg–Hamburg charter. Although the original plans had called for at least one of the two other ex-Falconair Viscounts to enter Skyline service, in the end neither was returned to airworthiness, both eventually being scrapped for spares.

Configured for up to fifty-eight passengers, 'CNK operated both passenger and cargo flights throughout the winter of 1971–72. However, passenger-carrying work became more frequent with the summer months, and regular charters in 1972 saw the aircraft operating to Amsterdam, Gatwick, Jersey, Paris, Salzburg and Southend. In addition, Sweden's domestic carrier, Linjeflyg, increasingly began to charter the Viscount to operate on its scheduled network in place of its own Convair CV-440s.

Viscount SE-CNK remained Skyline's sole fleet member until the autumn of 1975. Following the award of a contract to operate several Linjeflyg schedules on a more permanent basis, in September two BMA V.814s, G-BAPD and G-BAPF, were delivered from the UK and became SE-FOY and SE-FOX. The first schedules under the new contract were inaugurated by one of these two on 15 September 1975. An ex-Ghana Airways V.838 was also acquired from Field Aircraft Services in August 1976, and the arrival of this aircraft, SE-FOZ, saw the retirement of the V.784D.

Five months later the Skyline fleet was reduced to the V.814s when SE-FOZ was lost on approach to Stockholm's Bromma Airport at the end of a Linjeflyg service on 15 January 1976. Carrying three crew and nineteen passengers, the aircraft suffered the Viscount's old enemy, tailplane icing, and entered a vertical dive, crashing into a car park and killing all on board. In October 1976 the Linjeflyg contracts expired. On 17 October SE-FOX was returned to British Midland, and SE-FOY remained to operate charters and the occasional *ad hoc* Linjeflyg schedule throughout 1977. Eventually, however, Skyline was forced to cease operations, and its last Viscount was returned to BMA in May 1978.

Invicta's Problems

Increasing financial difficulties for Invicta International in the winter of 1972–73 had overshadowed the company's busy Vanguard operations. As a result, Air Holdings repossessed the entire fleet of five aircraft, including the single freighter, on 16 January 1973. The aircraft were placed in storage by Air Holdings at Lydd with the exception of G-AXOO, which remained at Manston. In the meantime, Invicta's owner, Wg Cdr Kennard, began talks with potential new investors.

Only one of the former Falconair Viscount 784Ds acquired by Skyline actually entered commercial service with the Swedish charter carrier. Bill Sheridan Collection

ABOVE: Although operationally successful, Invicta International's Vanguard services were forced to grind to a halt while the financially troubled company was reorganized. Jenny Gradidge

RIGHT: Ex-Air Traders Merchantman G-AYLD flew from Stansted for several months with the revived Silver City Airways. Jenny Gradidge

Silver City Revival

Air Holdings found itself with not only the Invicta Vanguards on its hands, but also, at the same time, the returned Air Trader fleet. This was a worrying situation, but, realizing that a number of lucrative passenger and cargo contracts might become available if Invicta was unable to refinance, Air Holdings set up its own airline operation to fly the aircraft commercially.

The company reincarnated the dormant name of Silver City Airways, to which it still held the rights, and Merchantman G-AYLD was flown to Southend and given Silver City titles over its blue ex-Air Traders livery. Commercial operations began from Stansted in March, on European cargo and livestock charters to Germany and Italy. A second ex-Air Traders aircraft was allocated to Silver City, but was not placed into service. Although 'LD enjoyed a busy summer with Silver City, Air Holdings found a buyer for the aircraft in October, delivering it to Europe Aero Service the following month. One of BEA's V.953s, G-APEI, had been painted up with Silver City titles at Heathrow in October, in preparation for a proposed lease, but the aircraft was never delivered. Subsequently, Silver City Airways ceased operations with the departure of 'LD.

Lost Over Basle

A saviour for Invicta was eventually found by Kennard, in the form of the European Ferries Group, which agreed to buy a 76 per cent stake in the company. European Ferries also bought back the five Vanguards from Air Holdings in time to allow operations to begin again in March 1973. However, the C of A for G-AXOO had expired while the fleet was still grounded, and the aircraft became a source of spares. Despite the relief of renewed operations, within weeks the latest Invicta revival was marred by misfortune.

During the quiet winter months of 1972–73 Invicta had introduced a number of low-cost day-trip services from Bristol to Basle and Munich. At a very reasonable cost, local groups were carried to either city for a day's sightseeing, leaving Bristol in the morning and returning the same evening. These trips had proved very popular, and were restarted when the aircraft were returned following the airline's refinancing. On 4 April 1973 G-AXOP was assigned to operate one of the day trips, and 139 passengers boarded the aircraft for the flight to Basle, which departed Bristol's Lulsgate Airport at 07.19hr. Many of the passengers had been drawn from Women's Institutes and similar young wive's and mother's groups in the local area.

On arrival over Basle, ninety minutes later, the weather conditions were decidedly unpleasant, with low visibility and driving snow. An instrument approach was initiated to Runway 16 by 'OP's crew, Capt Anthony Dorman in command and Capt

Invicta International operated the ill-fated G-AXOP for two years before it crashed near Basle with great loss of life. via author

Ian Terry acting as first officer. Overshooting during the first approach, the crew appears to have become disorientated, and a meandering figure-of-eight course was flown by the Vanguard, doubling back over the airport and finally continuing to the south of where it should have been, flying towards Hochwald, to the southwest of Basle. The crew, however, appeared to be under the impression they were back further north, on course to a second approach.

The Vanguard was glimpsed though the overcast by witnesses on the ground, who judged it to be flying at a height of only 150ft (45m) and heading away from the airport. The crew reported that they were 'established on glide-path and localizer', though the radar controller had questioned the crew's estimation of their position. Shortly afterwards, the crew reported that they had 'spurious readings', and that the automatic direction finder readings seemed 'all over the place'. In fact, by this time, the aircraft had left the Basle radar cover and was flying dangerously low in a hilly area.

Soon after its altitude had been reported by the crew as 1,400ft (425m), 'OP brushed the side of a wooded ridge near Herrenmatt. The aircraft somersaulted into the hillside and caught fire, killing 104 of the passengers, both pilots and two of the cabin crew. Most of the thirty-five passengers and two cabin crew who did survive were located in the rear cabin, which remained fairly intact. At the time of the crash the aircraft was on a southerly course, flying along the extended centreline of the runway, but away from it. The 'spurious', or even possibly misinterpreted, instrument readings had led the crew to believe they were on course for the runway when they were actually flying away from it and into extreme danger. Ironically, G-AXOP had originally been TCA's CF-TKV, which had held together and protected its passengers and crew so well in the clear-air turbulence incident over the Rocky Mountains in May 1963, a little short of ten years earlier.

The accident was officially blamed on 'loss of orientation during the two ILS [instrument landing system] approaches carried out under instrument flight conditions'. It was also noted that this would have been made worse by technical defects in a localizer receiver and a glide-slope receiver on board, which would have confused the situation for the crew.

Soldiering On

Shortly after the loss of 'OP, Invicta took delivery of G-AYFN, which was diverted from its planned delivery to Silver City. Invicta International operated a similar programme to previous years, with the same mixture of varied charter flights. A V.952, G-BAFK, which had been leased by Air Holdings to Merpati Nusantara, was delivered in June 1974. The Cargo Division's G-AXNT continued to operate freight and livestock charters from Manston throughout Europe and to North Africa and the Middle East. In 1975 'NT

The Vanguards took on a revised Invicta livery following the introduction into service of a leased Boeing 720B. Shortly afterwards, the company was put up for sale. Malcolm L. Hill

was replaced in the cargo role by G-AZRE, which was transferred from passenger services. A pair of Boeing 720Bs had been delivered in late 1973, though only one entered Invicta service, the other immediately being leased out.

By 1975 the European Ferries Group had decided that the Invicta operation was not yielding enough profit to justify its continued support. The group announced that the airline would be put up for sale, and that if a buyer were not found by the end of that summer's flying programme, Invicta International would be closed down. The dismantling of Invicta soon began, as no interested parties came forward. Europe Aero Service (EAS) took delivery of passenger-configured G-AYFN in August, and its departure was followed by that of the two freighters, G-AXNT and G-AZRE, later in the year. By October only G-AXOY and G-BAFK remained in service, flying a handful of charters from Luton, as the summer season ran down.

On 21 October 'FK departed for France, leaving G-AXOY to operate the last charter contracts. Finally, on 26 October, 'OY flew one more service for Invicta International, a one-hour enthusiast pleasure flight from Luton. This was the last revenue passenger carrying flight by a UK registered Vanguard. In November G-AXOY was also delivered to the EAS maintenance centre at Perpignan. Only two of the Invicta Vanguards, G-AYFN and G-BAFK, would fly again commercially with EAS. After varying periods of storage and cannibalization for spares, the remainder were eventually scrapped on site at Perpignan.

Air Bridge Carriers' first Merchantman entered service on cargo charters from East Midlands Airport in late 1976. Steve Richards

British Airways continued to operate a reduced fleet of Merchantman freighters until 1979. Steve Williams Collection

French Retirement

The acquisition of the Invicta fleet by EAS assured the French carrier of a ready supply of both serviceable aircraft and spares for its active Vanguards. Although the first of a number of secondhand Caravelles were soon to join EAS, the turboprops were still kept busy on its now established varied passenger and freight charter programme.

Two ex-British Airways Merchantmen joined the ex-Silver City Merchantman in 1976. Their arrival saw the retirement of the original Cargoliner, which had lacked the useful large freight door and other all-cargo refinements. The three Merchantmen were contracted to operate on behalf of Air France on nightly newspaper charters from Paris to Marseilles and Toulouse, as well as flying many of the national carrier's all-cargo services throughout Europe. In addition, EAS found a great deal of *ad hoc* work on its own behalf for the freighters to Europe, North Africa and the Middle East.

The inevitable replacement on EAS passenger service by jets was soon under way, though, all but five of the Vanguards being withdrawn by 1975, and two retiring in 1979. However, during 1979 the remaining three Vanguards were overhauled and repainted in a new livery. They remained in regular passenger service until 16 January 1981, when the last survivor, F-BTOV, was retired following a Paris-Orly to Perpignan flight.

ABC's Merchantman Upgrade

British Airways' decision to dispose of some of its Merchantmen was made after the airline found that its dedicated all-cargo fleet was much less in demand. The arrival of more wide-bodied aircraft on European services saw the normal underfloor hold capacity of its fleet increase to the extent that much of the freight traffic could now be accommodated on passenger flights. As well as the pair sold to EAS in the summer of 1976, another Merchantman, G-APES, was sold by BA to ABC.

Since 1974 ABC had operated a single Viscount 808C, G-BBDK, alongside its established fleet of Argosies. Although the Viscount had spent much of its time leased out to Dan-Air, it had also proved very useful on ABC's general cargo charter services. The opportunity to offer the larger capacity of the Merchantman to its customers was soon recognized by ABC, and

G-APES was delivered to East Midlands on 24 November 1976. After overhaul and repainting in ABC colours, 'ES entered service on 15 December on a cargo charter from Belfast to Cagliari.

A wide-ranging programme of *ad hoc* services followed, the aircraft soon appearing at airports as far away as the Middle East and Africa on services from the UK and Europe. The operation of livestock charters became a regular task for the Merchantman, which made numerous flights to Milan and Venice from points in the UK and Eire. In the meantime, the Viscount was withdrawn from use and returned to its owner, Field Aircraft Services.

In 1979 BA decided to dispose of its remaining Merchantman fleet. The last BA scheduled service was a Heathrow–Stockholm–Gothenburg–Heathrow trip, operated on the night of 1–2 December 1979 by G-APEJ. This ended nearly twenty years of operation of the Vanguard by BA and BEA. In nine years of Merchantman all-cargo revenue services, 12,735 tons of mail and 397,310 tons of cargo had been carried by the aircraft for the airline. Five aircraft were still in service at the beginning of 1979, and ABC, seeing an excellent opportunity to expand its already successful Merchantman venture, snapped them all up as soon as they became available.

Two were delivered to East Midlands from BA at Heathrow in November 1979, followed by two in December, and the last one arrived in January 1980. Among the new contracts obtained to keep the much-enlarged fleet profitable was a six-nights-a-week Luton–Glasgow newspaper charter and a twice-weekly Heathrow–Vienna scheduled cargo service flown on behalf of Austrian Airlines. The carrier's Merchantmen also operated scheduled freight services for Swissair for a month, and increasing *ad hoc* work saw the fleet operating to Belgrade, Forli, Gibraltar, Milan, Rennes, Rhodes and Venice during early 1980.

Intra Airways' Viscount 810s all came from BMA, and operated both scheduled and charter services for the Jersey-based carrier. Steve Richards

UK Viscount Revival

December 1976 saw Intra Airways take delivery of BMA's V.815, G-AVJB, to replace the remaining Viscount 724 it still flew on lease from Alidair. After spending the summer of 1977 on Intra's scheduled and charter operations, 'JB was joined in October by the first of two ex-BMA V.814s, G-BAPE, the second, G-BAPG, following in January 1978. Previously, BMA had operated these aircraft on the BA schedules from Prestwick, replacing the ex-Cambrian V.701s, which had finally been retired. The dropping of transatlantic services from Prestwick by BA had eventually rendered the feeder services redundant, and the Viscounts were returned to BMA.

A busy summer followed, all three Intra Viscounts operating charters throughout Europe, as well as the seasonal and year-round scheduled services from the Channel Islands to the UK. On 19 September all three aircraft were used to ferry stranded Cunard passengers between Southampton and Cherbourg when the shipping line's flagship, *QE2*, was forced to abandon a scheduled stop at the French port after suffering delays en route. Other services took the Viscounts as far afield as Dubrovnik and Faro on both passenger and cargo work.

The three Intra Viscounts were operated through 1979 until the end of the summer season, when the airline underwent a major reorganization. The company was merged with Express Air Services, with which Intra had been co-operating for some time. Only one of the Viscounts, the V.815, was retained in service with the new operation, which was renamed Jersey European Airways (JEA). The V.814s were leased out while a new owner was sought for them. Initially G-BAPE and 'PG were leased to Arkia, in Israel, for the winter, and ended up flying for much of 1980 with their old operator, BMA. The V.815, G-AVJB, flew for JEA on the busier schedules in 1980, but was placed in storage at East Midlands in December, being regarded as too large for the available traffic. Jersey European then reverted to operating its smaller fleet members, such as the Embraer Bandierante and de Havilland Canada Twin Otter, on a much-reduced network.

Alidair Changes

In 1978 Alidair had increased its fleet by buying the last two surviving Iraqi Airways Viscount 735s. One of these was painted in the colours of a new Alidair subsidiary, Guernsey Airlines Ltd, and christened *Sarnia*, the local name for the island. The company had been set up to operate both scheduled and charter services from Guernsey, and the aircraft was also operated on Alidair's services as required. On 25 October 1979 the Guernsey Airlines Viscount was operating a Glasgow–Kirkwall oil industry charter for Alidair when it veered off the runway while landing in a strong crosswind. The number 4 propeller had struck the ground, causing the aircraft to leave the runway, and the nosewheel collapsed. The resulting damage was enough to write off the Viscount, though its forty-seven occupants escaped unscathed.

Alidair subsequently provided Viscounts for Guernsey's operations from its own fleet temporarily, until V.724 G-BDRC was repainted as *Sarnia II* and permanently assigned to Guernsey Airlines. In April 1980 a scheduled Guernsey–Manchester route was opened with the 'new' Viscount and seasonal services were also opened to

Newcastle and Prestwick. Regular inclusive-tour charters also brought tourists to Guernsey from Belgium, and to Jersey from Paris.

The Alidair operation suffered a great deal of adverse publicity following the loss of one of its veteran V.708s, G-ARBY, in a forced landing near Exeter on 17 June 1980. The aircraft had been chartered to rescue stranded UK passengers from a broken-down ship in Santander, northern Spain. One Exeter–Santander–Exeter round trip was operated without incident by a different crew earlier in the day. On arrival back at Santander for the next load of fifty-eight passengers, the aircraft was refuelled. Unfortunately, there appeared to be confusion over the amount of fuel loaded, a situation not helped by an unserviceable fuel gauge.

When the aircraft was only 8 miles (13km) from Exeter, at a height of only 2,000ft (600m), both low-pressure fuel warning lights illuminated and all four engines promptly lost power in rapid succession. Immediately advising air traffic control

ABOVE: Guernsey Airlines Viscount *Sarnia* had spent its previous twenty-three years with Iraqi Airways before becoming the new island airline's flagship in 1978. Author's collection

One of the earliest export model Viscounts built, G-ARBY had been delivered to Air France in 1953. Its long and distinguished career ended in a Devon field in 1980. Steve Richards

of the situation, and then warning the cabin crew and passengers over the public address system, the captain began looking for a suitable place for a safe forced landing, as there was no hope of reaching Exeter Airport. Now reduced to the status of a rather large glider, G-ARBY was guided skilfully along a small grassy valley to the south of the village of Ottery St Mary. As the aircraft crossed a field boundary, its underside struck a tree and it then touched down nose-up, the port wing striking another tree that caused the Viscount to veer to one side as it slid along the field. Fortunately all of the occupants were evacuated safely, only one passenger requiring hospital treatment. The aircraft was declared beyond economic repair. The ensuing public enquiry called into question a number of Alidair's maintenance and crew training practices.

On 1 March 1981 the airline was renamed Inter City Airlines, and the Viscounts were used to open an East Midlands–Edinburgh–Aberdeen schedule on 5 May. Eventually, though, the route was taken over by a pair of new thirty-passenger Shorts 330s which Inter City shared with Guernsey Airlines.

Southern International and Dan-Air

In 1978 a small charter company, Southern International, which had operated a DC-3 on cargo charters, acquired two of NZNAC's redundant V.807s. Both had originally been sold by NZNAC to two short-lived Caribbean carriers, Pearl Air and Air Caribbean, neither of which was successful, and the aircraft were passed to a broker which sold them to Southern International. The aircraft were delivered to the new airline at Southampton early in the year, but only one of them, V.807 G-CSZB, initially entered service, in August 1978.

This aircraft was operated on relief flights for the Red Cross in Ethiopia and Eritrea for two months. On its return to the UK in October 'ZB was operated on a variety of general cargo and passenger charters, mostly from Southampton and Gatwick. The other V.807, G-CSZA, entered service the following March, and spent much of its time operating for Dan-Air on its scheduled services at weekends. By June 1979 'ZA had been repainted in full Dan-Air livery, though it also operated charters for Southern International alongside 'ZB.

A third Viscount, V.808C G-BBDK, was delivered to Southern International in early 1980 and took over the operation of a regular newspaper service between Gatwick and Belfast, which was operated several times a week. Two ex-Intra V.814s were also acquired with a view to replacing the V.807s, but all passenger operations ceased shortly afterwards and both the V.807s and the V.814s were put in storage. The operations base was eventually switched to Stansted and, after an uncertain summer, even the operations of the freighter came to an end in September and Southern International ceased trading.

In addition to chartering-in extra Viscount capacity when required, to operate its scheduled network from the UK regions and the Lydd–Beauvais Coach-Air service between London and Paris, Dan-Air had also placed two Viscount 810s into service in 1979. These were required to replace HS 748s, which were still needed for profitable oil industry work at Aberdeen. The two aircraft were ex-Ghana Airways V.838 G-BCZR, leased from Field Aircraft Services, and ex-Iran Air and Oman Air Force V.816 G-BGLC, which was leased from ABC.

Flown on scheduled services from outstation bases at Bristol and Teeside, the Viscounts were crewed by ABC pilots under contract, with Dan-Air's own locally based cabin staff. Previously, 'ZR had been leased by Field Aircraft Services to BMA and 'LC had been operated briefly by Royal Swazi National Airways on local routes to South Africa during 1978. At the end of 1980 'LC was sold to Air Zimbabwe by ABC, being followed to Harare by 'ZR in May 1981, where they replaced the last of the African carrier's vintage V.700s.

The attractively-styled Viscounts of Southern International had previously been operated in New Zealand for many years by NZNAC. Aviation Hobby Shop

Dan-Air's intermittent use of various Viscounts between 1975 and 1981 included an eighteen-month lease of late-model V.816 G-BGLC. Steve Richards

Executive Decay

Even if the Viscount was managing to maintain its fairly healthy position on the secondhand market as an airliner, in the area of executive operations it was finally entering a decline. The increased production of tailor-made executive jets such as the Gulfstream and Citation ranges, and even the use of converted jet airliners such as the One-Eleven and DC-9, had seen the use of larger propeller-engine executive aircraft wane rapidly.

More up-to-date aircraft soon replaced large Viscount fleets operated by corporations such as Standard Oil, Tenneco, US Steel and others. However, US Steel had operated its Viscount fleet for over thirteen years. Some of the aircraft were passed on to other executive operations, often eventually being broken up for spares. Other executive Viscounts were lucky enough to remain with more-loyal operators, such as the Ray Charles Organization, which had found the aircraft popular with its touring groups of musicians, who appreciated comfortable, reliable Viscount transport throughout the USA. The Viscount also proved popular with evangelical groups such as Cathedral of Tomorrow and John Wesley College, which used their aircraft to fly their followers and staff to rallies on nationwide tours.

A handful of executive Viscounts passed on to airline operators, such as a pair of V.764Ds originally delivered to the US Steel Corporation, which eventually found their way to Servicios Aereos Nacionales (SAN) of Ecuador to operate alongside its ex-ANA V.828s and a V.786D. Unfortunately, both had been written-off in fatal accidents by the end of 1977. Previously, from 1959 to 1967, SAN's ex-LANICA V.786D had been operated as a private aircraft by a Mrs M. Margorie Post and named *Merriweather*. While with Mrs Post, *Merriweather* was used to transport the family between estates near

The exclusive Merriweather served as a personal transport for the wealthy Post family.
MAP

Go Viscounts!

An operator that was to become a noted haven for ex-executive Viscounts in the USA was Go Transportation. Ron Clark Enterprises of Burbank, California, originally founded the operation in 1971, to offer high-quality and discreet VIP flight services for show business personalities and other high-profile individuals.

A single 21-seat V.789D was acquired in 1974, and early customers included Dean Martin, the Beach Boys, Elton John and even Elvis Presley. A second aircraft, an ex-Royal Bank of Canada V.745D, followed in the same year to increase the available capacity, and another six from various sources soon swelled the fleet further. The Go Viscounts featured sumptuously comfortable interiors equipped with high-technology entertainment systems and other executive features.

In 1980 three of the Viscounts were sold to Royal American Airlines, which operated a Fayetteville–Little Rock scheduled service. Unfortunately this was a commercial failure, and The Go Group, Go Transportation's parent company, bought out the ailing airline. The Viscount operation was relocated and new twice-daily scheduled flights from Las Vegas and Tucson to Long Beach and San Diego were inaugurated, as well as charter services. The Royal American Viscounts were competing against several major US airlines in the area, as well as low-fare-operator Pacific Southwest Airlines. Perhaps not surprisingly the Viscounts were unable to tempt enough of the incumbent airlines' passengers from their rival jets, and all scheduled operations were eventually halted as uneconomic. The Royal American fleet included one of the ex-Intra pair of V.814s that had been delivered to Southern International. The ailing UK airline had originally tried to sell its stored V.807s to Go for use by Royal American, but these aircraft failed to gain US certification and the deal fell through.

A further attempt at operating scheduled Viscount services in the USA was made in 1983, when an ex-Royal American V.765 was leased to Atlantic Gulf Airlines, based at St Petersburg, Florida. Intra-state services were operated within Florida, but once again the Viscount was unable to attract sufficient traffic from the established carriers in the region, and Atlantic Gulf was forced to cease operation of these services after only a short time.

Eventually more than thirty Viscounts of different variants were acquired by Go Transportation. Arkia's and PLUNA's remaining Viscounts were among many ferried to Go's maintenance base at Tucson, Arizona. While several aircraft were used by Go, albeit often only sporadically as short-term contracts came and went, several others were refurbished and leased-out or sold to operators such as Aerolineas Republica in Mexico. The Mexican airline operated the ex-executive and SAN of Ecuador V.786D on lease for two years before returning it to The Go Group in 1984. By the mid-1980s the Go operation had become fairly static and, despite several attempts to revive the business right up into the 1990s, the few remaining airworthy aircraft were sold off. The remnants of the fleet languished in various states of disrepair and dereliction at Tucson, in some cases for several years, finally being scrapped.

Ex-executive Viscount 765D N140RA was used by Go Transportation's short-lived scheduled subsidiary, Royal American Airways, on routes from Tucson and Las Vegas to the US west coast.
Global Air Image

Pittsburgh and Washington. The Viscount was also used to transport privileged guests to the Post's mountain retreat at Topridge, near Saranac Lake.

Another handful of Viscounts also found their way into semi-private hands, being operated by that particularly US institution, the travel club. Licensing regulations in the USA made it very difficult for the establishment of inclusive-tour charter operators in the European style. As a result, several travel clubs were established, with the membership operating aircraft on holiday and tour services for the group. With the availability of large numbers of surplus piston-engine aircraft at the beginning of the jet era, a number of these organizations flourished, at least for a short while, though most eventually succumbed to financial difficulties. The concept survived, albeit precariously, into the 1960s and 1970s, and at least two of these clubs, Air World Travel Club and Holiday Air of America, operated Viscounts.

Viscount 806 G-AOYJ operated the last London–Guernsey service for BA in 1980 and, after a further year based in Scotland, was sold the following year. via author

BA Viscount Retirement

At the end of the 1970s BA was still no nearer finding a practical replacement for its own remaining Viscounts. Several options were studied, but none of them was able to offer a financially viable solution. The airline was already in the midst of a financial crisis, and desperately needed to shed any routes that were incapable of making a reasonable profit. Therefore, BA decided that, with the exception of several of the V.806s, which would be retained for Scottish routes in the interim, all of its remaining Viscounts would be retired on 31 March 1980. Any routes exclusively flown by the Viscounts would also be closed down. As a result, all BA operations ceased at Bristol, Cardiff, Guernsey, Leeds-Bradford, Southampton and Isle of Man. In addition, Newcastle operations were greatly reduced, only the Heathrow route, already operated by jets, remaining. Liverpool-based services had already been handed over to BMA in a previous cost-cutting exercise.

Consequently, the last six operational BA V.802s and four V.806s were withdrawn and flown to Cardiff for storage either before, or shortly after, most of the Viscount routes were closed on 31 March. In fact, bad weather conspired to delay the closure, as the last Heathrow–Guernsey service, operated by V.806 G-AOYJ with thirty-five passengers, was delayed by fog until 1 April. The last ten V.806s remained in service on the Scottish routes, their numbers reducing over the following months until May 1982, when even these survivors were retired. The last Viscounts were replaced in Scotland by leased HS 748s. This brought to an end twenty-eight years of continuous Viscount operations by the airline and it predecessor, BEA. In that time a total of seventy-eight Viscounts of various versions had been used.

Route Redistribution

Other UK carriers, some using their own Viscounts, soon snapped up the Viscount routes dropped by BA. The Guernsey–London

British Midland took over several of BA's ex-Viscount routes. The airline expanded its services from a number of local UK points, such as Birmingham. Steve Richards

route was eventually awarded to Guernsey Airlines, and BMA's Viscounts took over the direct routes from the Isle of Man and Leeds/Bradford to Heathrow. Having operated the Birmingham–Heathrow service in co-operation with BA, BMA flew that route on its own at an increased frequency after BA withdrew its daily Viscount flight. By now, BMA had disposed of its Dart Heralds, and the turboprop operations were firmly in the hands of the Viscount 810s, with a growing fleet of DC-9s operating on more important routes. Originally, BMA had opened the Liverpool–London service, after taking it over from BA, with its DC-9s, but it later substituted Viscounts when the revenue loads failed to come up to expectations.

In November 1982 BMA was involved in setting up Manx Airlines, to take over its own and Air UK's services to the Isle of Man. For the first time since the absorption of the original Manx Airlines by Silver City in the late 1950s, the Isle of Man was able to boast its own home-based, scheduled airline operation. For the important twice-daily connection from the island to London Heathrow, BMA transferred V.813 G-AZNA to the new carrier. Manx also operated a mixed fleet of Fokker F.27s, Shorts 330s and some smaller twins on its regional network. In addition, the Viscount was later used on some services to Liverpool or Dublin, as required, in between the morning and evening runs to Heathrow. Although only one Viscount was usually in service at any one time, further aircraft replaced the original aircraft for various periods, until new BAe 146s replaced the type as the airline's flagship in 1987.

The introduction of the first of BAF's 'new' Viscounts was an occasion that called for formal presentation of the aircraft and crews to the travel-trade press. BAF via author

A New Home

Although the Viscounts withdrawn by BA in 1975 had mostly been quickly scrapped or donated to airport fire services, the fleet members that followed them in 1980–82 were more fortunate. A proposed deal for the sale of at least six to Merpati Nusantara was not completed, but a new buyer soon stepped forward with a view to offering the vintage Viscounts a profitable future.

Market changes had seen BAF, no longer a part of Air Holdings and now owned by the Keegan Group, finally end its cross-Channel vehicle ferry operation and replace it with more passenger-orientated services. Dart Heralds had initially been acquired to operate most of the BAF services, a few Carvairs being retained for cargo work. In 1979 BAF reached an agreement with British Island Airways (BIA) to hand over its scheduled services from Southend to the latter company, allowing BAF to concentrate on potentially more lucrative charter and leasing contracts. In the first weeks of 1981 BAF purchased six of the BA Viscounts, two V.802s and four V.806s. The first, V.802 G-AOHV, was flown to BAF's Southend base on 16 January. In addition, another V.802, G-AOHL, was purchased and immediately dismantled on its arrival at Southend in February, its fuselage being adapted as a cabin services trainer.

In short order, G-AOHV was overhauled, refurbished and presented to press and travel trade representatives on 4 February, wearing bright yellow and blue BAF livery details over its basic BA paintwork. The 71–77-seat Viscounts were offered as a more economic vehicle for inclusive-tour charters, as well as offering greater range and capacity for general charter work than the 48/50-passenger Heralds. Soon after the press presentation, 'HV departed Southend on 8 February for a series of demonstration flights with Air Algerie. Following this it was positioned to Tripoli, where it began its first revenue flying for BAF, operating supply and ferry flights for the Oasis Oil Company.

The airline had already been operating its Heralds on North African oil-industry work. Several of the Viscounts were quickly despatched to Libya to be operated on contract to companies such as Occidental Oil and Esso, as well as Oasis, alongside the Heralds. The Algerian demonstration had also proved successful, and Air Algerie leased two Viscounts to operate domestic services from Ghardaia, from March. Back in the UK, in addition to undertaking a number of *ad hoc* contracts, the Viscounts were soon busy operating alongside the Heralds on summer charters to the Channel Islands from several UK regional airports. In addition, holiday services were operated to Jersey from Billund and Copenhagen, in Denmark, and to Beauvais from Southend.

The V.815 G-AVJB joined the BAF Viscount fleet in September 1981, offering greater range and payload and permitting the operation of direct charters to the Mediterranean from the UK. In September 1982 the much-travelled V.808C G-BBDK also arrived, offering the flexibility of its double-size cargo door for freight work. In contrast, Viscount 806 G-AOYH was fitted with a VIP interior, with only thirty-six seats in two cabins, with single and double seats either side of the aisle instead of the more usual, high-density, five-abreast arrangement. After being operated by BAF

Viscount 806 G-AOYH was fitted-out with a unique 36-VIP passenger, all-first-class interior. BAF via author

on several short-term VIP services around the UK and Europe, 'YH was sold to Canadian operator North Cariboo Air of St Johns, Newfoundland, in July 1983.

New Zealand Lease

From the delivery of its first aircraft, the BAF Viscount fleet attracted the attention of other carriers interested in leasing-in the aircraft either short- or long-term. One of the first was a new and ambitious New Zealand carrier, Aqua-Avia Skybus, which planned to operate Viscounts on low-fare domestic routes as a rival to Air New Zealand. Early in September 1981 V.802 G-AOHT was painted in the Skybus livery, and on the 14th it set off on the long delivery flight, routeing via Graz, Athens, Luxor, Bahrein, Muscat, Bombay, Calcutta, Bangkok, Singapore, Denpasar, Darwin, Noumea and Aukland.

This would have been an epic journey for any aircraft, let alone a 25-year-old vintage airliner. Nevertheless, 'HT arrived safely in Aukland on 23 September. There followed a series of political wranglings with the New Zealand licensing authorities, as well as arguments and even internal disputes among the Skybus management, that would probably justify a book of their own. A handful of demonstration flights did take place in October, and the aircraft was eventually re-registered as ZK-SKY. However, it was becoming increasingly clear that the dreams of Aqua-Avia Skybus would never come to fruition and, after reviewing the situation in November, BAF's management felt obliged to cancel the initial five-year lease, as well as preparations to provide at least one more Viscount. Subsequently, ZK-SKY left Aukland on 1 December.

On its eventual return to the UK, restored to the UK register once again as G-AOHT, the Viscount eventually found a new lease customer in the shape of Teeside-based Polar Airways. It was ferried to Teeside in August 1982, and operated a series of charters to Dusseldorf, as well as making several appearances on BMA's scheduled cargo service between East Midlands and Maastricht. A second BAF Viscount, V.806 G-AOYI, entered service in September, and both aircraft were soon visiting Norway, Spain and the Netherlands on both passenger and cargo work, even venturing as far as North Africa. Although 'YI was returned to BAF in March 1983, it was replaced by V.802 G-AOHV, which continued operating the varied charter programme.

A busy summer season was planned, with several inclusive-tour contracts obtained. However, all Polar operations ceased on 21 April when 'HV was impounded by creditors. Both aircraft were taken back by BAF, which also took over the operation of G-AOHT on the Maastricht cargo flight from East Midlands, with its Polar Airways titles removed and replaced by 'Aerolink', the marketing name of the service that was flown for the cargo agent, Pandair.

Euroair's Arrival

In July 1983, following Polar's collapse, G-AOHV was ferried by BAF from Teeside to Southend, where it was prepared for sale to a new client, executive charter operator Euroair, which was associated with another executive carrier, Business Air Centre. Intended for charter by individuals and companies, as opposed to travel agents and holiday companies, the aircraft was to be based at Gatwick. It would be very

Initially, the Euroair Viscounts wore a very discrete livery, with no company titles visible. MAP

discreetly operated, with no airline titling and only the Euroair logo on its tail.

Commercial operations started in September 1983, the 76-passenger Viscount visiting Denmark, France, Sweden, Switzerland and the Netherlands on private and corporate charters in the first month. Euroair was soon attracting new customers, and by 1985 was operating three more Viscounts, also acquired from BAF. Leasing also featured in Euroair's programme, with 'HV operating for small Coventry-based carrier Air Commuter on short-lived scheduled services to Paris. Re-registered G-BLNB, 'HV was joined by V.802 G-AOHT and V.806 G-BNAA (the former G-AOYH, which had returned from Canada in February), and also by ex-Southern International V.807 G-CSZB. The last-named had been neglected since the demise of Southern International in 1980, languishing in storage at various UK airports and eventually ending up at Southend. Jadepoint Engineering, BAF's maintenance organization, gave the aircraft a major overhaul between August 1984 and its delivery to Euroair at Gatwick in December.

As well as the temporary work originally undertaken, Euroair had expanded into limited tour and holiday work, operating regular inclusive-tour charters from and to Beauvais and Rotterdam from several UK airports. Viscount G-BLNB was leased to Tunisavia for use on services from Sfax and Tunis to Malta. British Airways also regularly chartered Euroair's Viscounts when the national carrier was short of capacity. On several occasions Euroair replaced BA's HS 748s on Scottish services, and its aircraft were also seen on London–Jersey schedules replacing One-Elevens. In April 1985 G-AOHT was given the Virgin Atlantic Airlines logo and titling and was used to operate the London–Maastricht route for Virgin.

The BAF fleet was increasingly used for new scheduled services to Europe and the Channel Islands. Steve Williams Collection

Viscount G-AOYR flew in BCal colours for jointly operated BAF/BCal services based at London, Gatwick. Aviation Hobby Shop

BAF Channel Island Expansion

British Air Ferries strengthened its link with the Channel Islands, which had become a major source of charter business for the airline, in April 1983, when it established a Jersey-based subsidiary, Jersey Air Ferries and repainted V.806 G-AOYP in the new airline's colours. However, after only one summer season Jersey Air Ferries was reabsorbed into BAF, all subsequent operations being undertaken in the parent company's name. Shortly afterwards the Keegan Group sold BAF to new owner Jadepoint, a holding company.

Jadepoint also acquired the assets of Guernsey Airlines from the Official Receiver of Inter City Airlines, which was suffering increased financial difficulties. All the Inter City operations eventually ceased in July, a BAF Herald immediately replacing the Guernsey Airlines Viscount 724, which was still owned by Inter City. A V.806 was later transferred to the Guernsey Airlines operation, which retained its separate identity within BAF. The airline also immediately took over the Aberdeen-based oil industry shuttle contracts to Sumburgh, positioning two of its Viscounts to Scotland to take over from the grounded Inter City aircraft.

Business was so brisk that BAF had taken more of the ex-BA fleet as they became available, and by the beginning of 1984 no fewer than eighteen ex-BA Viscounts had been acquired. A new scheduled network was inaugurated from Gatwick in 1985, with a Viscount operating the Gatwick–Rotterdam route in association with British Caledonian (BCal), which also connected with the Guernsey Airlines Gatwick–Guernsey service. Another BAF Viscount, G-AOYR, was repainted in full BCal Commuter livery and took over the route from Gatwick to Brussels and also supplemented One-Elevens on the BCal Gatwick–Jersey service. In August 1985 the owner of Euroair decided to reorganize its airline operations and sold its four Viscounts and their outstanding contracts to BAF for £2.5 million.

Janus's Viscount Summer

After the demise of Inter City Airlines, Lydd-based Janus Airways eventually acquired its surviving three airworthy Viscount 700s. Janus had been formed in 1983 as a subsidiary of Hards Travel, to take up the Lydd–Beauvais route that had been dropped by Dan-Air. The Beauvais services, and a new route from Lydd to Ostend, were to be operated primarily for the benefit of the parent company's coach-air holiday passengers. A single Dart Herald was operated on the short cross-Channel network in 1983. The Viscounts were added to provide extra capacity required for expansion plans for 1984, which included opening new services from Coventry to Beauvais and Ostend.

Of the three aircraft acquired, the two remaining V.708s and the ex-Guernsey V.724, only the V.708s went into service, as the V.724 was suffering from corrosion and was sent on to its destruction at the Manston Fire School. The V.708s enjoyed a busy summer, operating the routes to France and Belgium from Lydd and Coventry, up to four flights a day to Beauvais being flown at the busiest times. On 30 October, however, G-ARGR completed the last scheduled flight from Beauvais to Lydd, and the operation was closed down following increasing financial losses. This was the last time a UK-registered Viscount 700 carried fare-paying passengers.

The two Viscounts were promptly sold to Zaïre, though only one, G-ARGR, made the trip to Africa. The other, G-ARIR, was re-registered as 9Q-CAH for its new owner, MMM Aero Services, but had only got as far as Ostend by November. After a long period of storage it, too, was found to be suffering from corrosion, and was broken up in 1988. Re-registered 9Q-CAN, 'GR was operated in Zaïre until 1987, when it finally succumbed to the scrapman.

Janus Airways obtained one more busy summer season's operations out of the surviving vintage ex-Inter City Viscount 708s. Bill Sheridan Collection

BAF's leasing activities with the Viscounts continued through the 1980s, a single aircraft going briefly to Luton-based London European Airways in 1985. The V.806, G-AOYI, was re-registered G-LOND before delivery and was used for a scheduled Luton–Amsterdam service from 25 February, with charters to the Channel Islands keeping it busy at weekends. All Viscount services ceased at the end of the summer, though, and the aircraft returned to BAF.

Also in 1985, two of the V.806s were sold to Spanish carrier Lineas Aereas Canarias (LAC) of Tenerife. The first Viscounts to be registered in Spain since the lease of a single example to Aviaco in the early 1960s, they were operated on scheduled inter-island services between the Canaries, fitted out in a very-high-density 81-passenger configuration. Operations continued until 1989, when LAC opted to concentrate on inclusive-tour charters with its jet fleet and the Viscounts were withdrawn from use and left to decay in open storage at Tenerife. Although BAF did eventually consider buying back the aircraft for spares, they were found upon inspection to have deteriorated too much in the salty island atmosphere.

BMA Re-equips

In February 1988 the last of BMA's once omnipresent Viscount fleet was retired from service. As the airline began to concentrate more on services from the UK to Europe, the Viscounts were displaced by DC-9s and Boeing 737s. In addition, Fokker F.27s had replaced them on some of the regional and domestic routes, new BAe ATP turboprops also being introduced later. Although some were sold on, a number of the Viscounts were consigned to scrap following their withdrawal by BMA. The V.813 G-AZNA was the only one to survive in use long enough to be repainted in BMA's new 'Diamond' livery, and spent its last few months with the company operating on schedules from Birmingham to Brussels, Guernsey and Jersey. The very last BMA Viscount schedule was a Brussels–Birmingham sector operated on 19 February, ending almost twenty years of Viscount operations by the carrier.

Baltic and Hot Air

BAF's solitary V.815, G-AVJB, was sold in late 1986, to a new Swedish airline, Baltic Aviation. Primarily established as a freight operator, Baltic also eventually opened a Malmö–Southend low-fare scheduled passenger service with the Viscount. This was not a commercially successful venture and was eventually dropped. After a year in Swedish service as SE-IVY, the V.815 was withdrawn and eventually found itself perched atop a pole in the High Chapperal Theme Park at Hillerstop. It remained there until 2003, when a bus, parked underneath it caught fire and the flames soon spread to the hapless aircraft.

The Baltic name was revived in 1988, when the same Swedish owner established a new UK-based operator, Baltic Airlines, to be based at Southend. Five V.810s, comprising two V.813s, two V.814s and a V.816, were acquired from BMA. Following some delays in the issuing of licences and the airline's Air Operator's Certificate, the first commercial flight was a Southend–Twente–Hanover charter on 9 June, operated by V.813 G-AZNA. Baltic intended to operate its charters under the marketing name of Hot Air, the more sedate 'Baltic' being used for any future scheduled services. The colourful Hot Air livery was displayed by V.814 G-BAPF when it operated another charter from East Midlands to Clermont Ferrand, also on 9 June. Much of the airline's early work involved operations for other carriers, and Air UK, BMA and Manx Airlines all chartered the Viscounts. In July G-BAPF was delivered to The Gambia, where it undertook scheduled operations for Gambia Air Shuttle, from Banjul to Bamako, Bissau, Dakar and Sal.

British Midland's last Viscount, V.813 G-AZNA, was disposed of in February 1988.
Steve Williams Collection

Baltic also operated as Hot Air. One aircraft, the ex-G-BMAT, was suitably reregistered G-OHOT.
Bill Sheridan Collection

The fourth Viscount to be delivered to Baltic/Hot Air was G-BMAT, which had previously been G-AZLT with BMA. The aircraft had been re-registered by BMA during repairs following a well-publicized overrun at Leeds-Bradford after a scheduled service from Heathrow in October 1980. With Baltic/Hot Air it became G-OHOT. A contract for a Manchester–Belfast freight service occupied one of the Viscounts, while another was based in West Africa, leaving one available in the UK for *ad hoc* charters, which were operated throughout the UK and Europe. The last Viscount to be delivered to Baltic/Hot Air was ex-Manx and BMA V.816 G-BFZL, which arrived in November.

Operated by BAF as a 'Freightmaster' dedicated cargo aircraft, V.808C G-BBDK was successful enough to inspire the company to convert another passenger aircraft to full cargo configuration. Jenny Gradidge

BAF Reorganizes

Under the ownership of Jadepoint, BAF had greatly expanded the scheduled-service side of its operation. The Southend–Channel Islands market had been abandoned by BMA, and BAF moved in to replace the BMA Viscounts with its own. A fleet of Shorts 330s and 360s had also been acquired, and these opened several new routes such as Southampton–Manchester, which fed into new BAF Channel Islands flights from Southampton.

Unfortunately the move back to scheduled services was not a success and, linked with financial problems within the parent company, this led to BAF being placed under Administration from 8 January 1988. The Guernsey Airlines operation was sold, and most of the remaining schedules were closed down shortly afterwards. The main financial problems had concerned other Jadepoint companies and the loss-making expansion of the schedules. By returning to its core charter and leasing activities BAF hoped to return to profitability, and V.806 G-BLOA, originally G-AOYJ, was converted to all-freight configuration in 1988 to join the V.808C as a dedicated Freightmaster on all-cargo work. Both aircraft soon found themselves in demand on both short-term and temporary contract work, with oil industry services to and from Scotland and Scandinavia proving to be moneymakers for the airline.

A potential buyer for BAF came forward in late 1988, in the form of a new holding company, Mostjet. Among Mostjet's directors was Lennart Hesselburg, the founder and a director of Baltic/Hot Air. Once the legal, financial and licensing negotiations were completed, BAF and Baltic were merged in the spring of 1989, the airline being released from Administration at the same time. The resulting fleet consisted of twenty Viscounts and three Dart Heralds.

Originally Transair's V.804 G-AOXU in 1957, V.807 G-CSZB was still in daily revenue service with BAF over thirty years later. Aviation Hobby Shop

Last Gallop

With the rapid approach of the 1990s, the endurance of the remaining operational Viscounts and Vanguards was becoming increasingly remarkable. Although their numbers were certainly dwindling, the survivors were still earning their keep. Whether on busy domestic passenger schedules around Africa and Indonesia, carrying excited holidaymakers to their leisure destination, or ferrying oil workers to the Shetlands, the remaining Viscounts still provided reliable service to their owners. The handful of Vanguards were nearly all freight-carriers, but the load-hauling capability of the trusty old 'Guardsvan' was proving difficult to replace.

The last decades were finally on the horizon for both types, but they would go doing what they did best; working.

CHAPTER TWELVE

Final Furlongs

The Ultimate Years

Even as the numbers of operational Vickers-Armstrongs-built turboprops were declining from the hundreds of a mere decade before to dozens, or even less in the Vanguard's case, a handful of carriers were still happy to give the aircraft a productive home. As long as the Viscounts and Vanguards were capable of returning a profit there would be operators willing to exploit them, despite their rapidly advancing years.

African Interlude and a Last French Flourish

The use of widebodied aircraft on passenger services also had an adverse effect on the EAS Merchantman fleet. One of its main activities had been the operation of all-cargo flights on behalf of Air France. As the national airline now found itself capable of carrying much of its own freight traffic, the contracts with EAS ended.

In January 1980 one of the ex-BA aircraft was sold to Libreville-based Air Gabon, for which it was to operate on all-freight routes within Africa. Previously Air Gabon had flown a vintage DC-6 on these services, until it was written off in an accident. Initial operations went so well that the ex-Silver City V.952F was sent out to Africa to double the airline's Merchantman fleet. The pair of aircraft operated successfully until 1986, when specialized Lockheed Hercules freighters took over and the Merchantmen were returned to EAS at Perpignan.

The following year the two ex-Gabon aircraft were prepared for cargo operations with a new carrier, Inter Cargo Service (ICS), which had been jointly formed by EAS, Air Inter and another French airline, Touraine Air Transport (TAT). Initial operations centred on a scheduled all-cargo service between Paris-Orly and Montpellier, previously flown by TAT. Flights began on 17 February 1987, the second aircraft arriving in April. Once both aircraft were established in service, nightly sorties were operated linking Orly with Montpellier and Toulouse.

Sadly, the operation was struck by tragedy. The second aircraft delivered, Merchantman F-GEJF, originally BEA V.953 G-APEL, was lost at Toulouse on the night of 29 January 1988. The crash followed an

Both of Intercargo Service's Merchantmen had been lost in crashes by the end of the company's two-year existence. Avimage via author

Far East Movements

On its way back to BAF from New Zealand, the Aqua-Avia Viscount 802 paused for a few weeks in the Far East in the hope of attracting a new leasing contract. The most likely prospect was yet another Indonesian carrier interested in Viscounts, Bouraq Indonesia Airlines. Although Bouraq did not contract the BAF aircraft, the first V.812 built, once Tenneco and Alidair's N501TL, had been leased from FEAT in 1980, but had been lost in a crash near Djakarta in 1980.

Nonetheless, Bouraq had still maintained an interest in joining the local ranks of Mandala and MNA as a Viscount operator, to supplement its large fleet of smaller HS 748s on wide-ranging scheduled and charter services throughout Indonesia and neighbouring regions. In 1983 Bouraq bought the four remaining V.843s from China's CAAC, which had finally been replaced in mainland China by jets and smaller, more modern turboprops. Two of the CAAC Viscounts had been transferred to the Chinese Air Force, but the other four aircraft were all delivered to Indonesia, where Bouraq's engineers noted the excellent condition of the low-hour, well-maintained aircraft. Bouraq had acquired the Viscounts via Hong Kong's HAECO organization, which had been involved with the aircraft continually since their initial delivery from Vickers.

Ironically, both Mandala and MNA had also acquired extra Viscounts from China, but from nationalist Taiwan. Both carriers took delivery of a number of FEAT's Viscount fleet, among other sources. All three airlines were to continue to operate their Viscounts well into the 1980s, and some even into the 1990s. Despite the inevitable accident write-offs, withdrawals and cannibalization for spares, by the mid-1980s MNA was still operating two Viscounts, Mandala was flying four and Bouraq continued to operate its hard-working quartet. The busy Indonesian Viscounts supplemented numerous fleets of not only HS 748s but also the similarly sized F.27, both also Dart-powered, and were a useful link between the smaller turboprop twins and growing numbers of higher-capacity jet fleet members.

Viscount 832 PK-MVN spent its entire working life in Australia and the Far East, flying for Ansett-ANA, FEAT and Mandala Airlines. Visits back to Europe were rare, exceptions including this one to East Midlands Airport for major maintenance and refurbishment. Steve Richards

engine failure on take-off, though all the crew survived unscathed. Decidedly less fortunate were the crew of the original ICS aircraft, F-GEJE, once the Air Holdings and Silver City Merchantman. This aircraft also fell victim to an engine failure, this time on take-off from Marseilles on an Air France service to Casablanca on 6 February 1989. The stricken aircraft plunged into a lagoon and the three crew members were killed. All ICS operations came to an end shortly after the second crash.

Air Bridge Fleet Changes

Although obviously keen to acquire more aircraft, as evidenced by its purchase of the five survivors of BA's Merchantman fleet, ABC resisted the temptation to swamp the market with its capacity. Instead, with the available aircraft now standing at six, the company made a conscious operational decision to rotate the aircraft, keeping about half in day-to-day operation, with the remainder either stored or on major checks, if required. By scheduling the fleet in this way, ABC was better able to control the build-up of hours on the airframes.

Initially, in early 1980, G-APEG, 'EJ and 'EK were operated once the new fleet members had been delivered, allowing ABC's original Merchantman, G-APES, to undergo a major overhaul and repaint. When 'ES returned to service 'EJ was temporarily stored. After this period of inactivity, G-APEJ was prepared for a ferry flight to Gabon the end of June. Once in West Africa it was used for a large contract transporting 1,400 cattle to Gabon from Banjul and Dakar.

In August 1981 G-APEG was also despatched on an overseas contract, being leased out to Singapore-based cargo operator Air Tenggara. The Merchantman was soon seen all over the Far East on charter work, ranging as far afield as Bangladesh and Australia and covering most points in between. In a particularly epic journey, 'EG transported 15 tons of tents from Singapore to Tonga, as disaster relief following a severe hurricane in the area. The 6,250-mile (10,000km) trek was accomplished in under two days, routeing via Australia, New Guinea and Fiji. From March 1982 the Merchantman adopted the titles of Airfast Services and began flying a regular Singapore–Djakarta cargo service. This continued until January 1983, when the much-travelled aircraft returned to East Midlands. On its arrival back in the UK, 'EG was in need of a major maintenance check and was placed into storage. As it transpired, the aircraft remained grounded and was eventually scrapped after donating valuable spares to keep the remaining aircraft flying.

In the autumn of 1982 two of the stored aircraft, G-APEP and G-APEK, were returned to flying status. For 'EP this was the first time it had flown since delivery in 1979, and 'EK had been stored since 1980. The latter aircraft was promptly despatched to West Africa for another Gabon-based cattle-hauling contract. A new Swissair contract, for the operation of services from Glasgow and Manchester to Zurich, awarded in 1984, saw the first entry into ABC service of G-APET, which had been stored since its arrival from British Airways at Heathrow in 1980.

ABOVE: A wide variety of freight contracts awarded to Air Bridge ensured plenty of revenue work for the active fleet members. Steve Williams Collection

More Mundane Tasks

The remaining operational Merchantman fleet was also kept busy flying from the UK, albeit on less exotic labours. As well as the early cargo-carrying work for scheduled airlines such as Swissair and Austrian Airlines, ABC was later contracted by KLM for regular Amsterdam–Manchester and Amsterdam–Gothenburg freight schedules and an East Midlands–Amsterdam feeder cargo service on behalf of Nippon Cargo Airlines. Newspaper contracts saw the Merchantmen flying to Belfast from Liverpool, Luton and Manchester, and from Luton to Glasgow. A weekly military cargo charter was operated from RAF Brize Norton to either Laarbruch or Wildenrath, to supply UK forces in Germany. Varied *ad hoc* work saw the aircraft operating all over Europe, the Mediterranean region and North Africa.

Livestock and bloodstock charters also continued to be a feature of the UK operations, though livestock services later declined as the result of new legislation regarding live animal exports. Bloodstock charters, carrying racehorses, expanded to the extent that G-APES and G-APET were both modified to allow easy conversion for this work in-between their normal freight activities. When used on

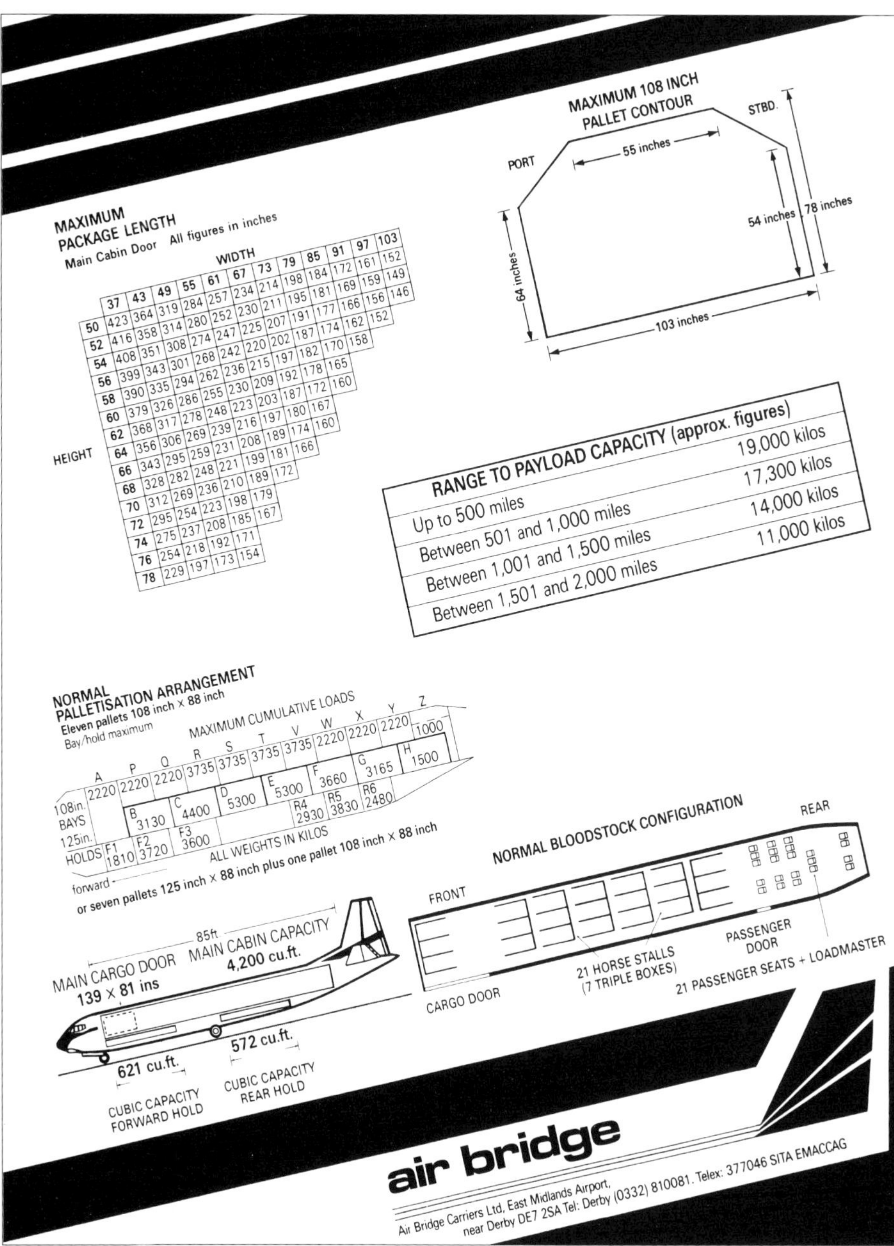

MAXIMUM PACKAGE LENGTH
Main Cabin Door All figures in inches

HEIGHT \ WIDTH	37	43	49	55	61	67	73	79	85	91	97	103
50	423	364	319	284	257	234	214	198	184	172	161	152
52	416	358	314	280	252	230	211	195	181	169	159	149
54	408	351	308	274	247	225	207	191	177	166	156	146
56	399	343	301	268	242	220	202	187	174	162	152	
58	390	335	294	262	236	215	197	182	170	158		
60	379	326	286	255	230	209	192	178	165			
62	368	317	278	248	223	203	187	172	160			
64	356	306	269	239	216	197	180	167				
66	343	295	259	231	208	189	174	160				
68	328	282	248	221	199	181	166					
70	312	269	236	210	189	172						
72	295	254	223	198	179							
74	275	237	208	185	167							
76	254	218	192	171								
78	229	197	173	154								

RANGE TO PAYLOAD CAPACITY (approx. figures)	
Up to 500 miles	19,000 kilos
Between 501 and 1,000 miles	17,300 kilos
Between 1,001 and 1,500 miles	14,000 kilos
Between 1,501 and 2,000 miles	11,000 kilos

RIGHT: The adaptability of the large-capacity Merchantman, including frequent use as a livestock or bloodstock transport, was well promoted by the company to attract custom. Author's collection

bloodstock service up to twenty-one horses could be carried, along with their grooms.

A new and rapidly expanding market was the small parcels business, being developed by a number of freight forwarding companies. Air Bridge Carriers had already become involved in this work, its Argosies operating on behalf of Elan Air from East Midlands to Cologne and Shannon, alongside Elan's own Dart Herald. When the traffic on the route had begun to outgrow the Argosies, an ex-BA Merchantman was purchased from the excess EAS stocks and restored to the UK register as G-APEM in July 1987. It was operated in full Elan colours, taking over many of the services from East Midlands, which were later expanded to include Brussels, London-Heathrow and Luton. Elan was later taken over by DHL, and 'EM's livery was modified accordingly. The ABC Merchantman fleet regularly operated similar small-parcel charters for TNT and UPS, including a Birmingham–Brussels–Copenhagen–Stockholm route.

Beginning of the End

The Merchantman's nemesis with ABC began on the all-cargo airline's services in 1989. Many of the ABC Merchantman fleet were becoming due for expensive major maintenance checks, and, with no suitable Vanguard or Merchantman airframes available, an appropriate replacement was urgently sought. Ironically, ABC decided to acquire examples of the Vanguard's once arch rival, the Electra. Three were initially leased-in from early 1989, and all had entered service by June. The leased aircraft were replaced by second-hand Electra freighters bought from Northwest Territorial Airways of Canada by 1992, by which time the operational Merchantman fleet was reduced to four, comprising G-APEJ, 'EM, 'EP and 'ES.

August 1992 saw the name Air Bridge Carriers changed to Hunting Cargo Airlines. The revival of the Hunting name was possible as Field, the original owner of Hunting Air Transport and Hunting Clan, still held rights to the name's use. However, just one of the ex-ABC Merchantman aircraft, G-APES, was to be repainted in full Hunting Cargo colours. While the 'new' Electras quickly took on the new identity, the remaining operational Vickers fleet merely had 'Hunting Cargo' titles applied over the Air bridge Carriers basic livery.

In December G-APEJ was withdrawn from use and stored at East Midlands. This left the remaining three operating on DHL contract services from Brussels to Belfast, Coventry, East Midlands, London/Heathrow and Luton, as well as performing occasional bloodstock and *ad hoc* work. In January 1994 'EM was also retired, and the last two, G-APEP and G-APES, were mostly operated on DHL flights over the Luton–London/Heathrow–Brussels and Dublin–East Midlands–Brussels routes. More Electra freighters had taken over most of Hunting's remaining operations as the valuable airframe hours on the Merchantmen finally began to be used up. Jets were also on the horizon for Hunting, with second-hand Boeing 727 freighters about to be acquired.

Passenger Vanguard's Last Bastion

In addition to its Viscount operation, MNA still remained faithful to its long-established Vanguard service and, with the cessation of the EAS Vanguard services in 1981, was flying the world's last passenger services with the type. Right up until the early 1980s the MNA Vanguard scheduled services included a daily flight from Djakarta to Medan. Also, a twice-weekly Djakarta–Surabaya–Ujung–Pandang–Biak flight was scheduled to leave Djakarta at 05.00hr on Wednesdays and Saturdays, arriving at Biak at 14.55hr. This service involved a night stop at Biak for the Vanguard before it returned to Djakarta, via the same route in reverse, the next day.

The three ex-BEA V.953s were operated by MNA until 1981, when two were retired. However, two passenger-configured V.952s were acquired from EAS in the same year. These became the sole constituents of the MNA Vanguard fleet in 1982, when the last of the V.953s was withdrawn. Although the Vanguards now faced competition from modern jets varying in size from DC-9s to Airbus A300 widebodies operated by Garuda, they were still popular enough to be retained on the Jakarta–Medan service for several more years. One of the V.952s was retired in 1985, leaving the sole survivor, PK-MVH, to serve until October 1987, when it was finally retired. Ironically, this had also been the last production Vanguard built, CF-TKW, originally flown in 1962. This historic aircraft was eventually returned to EAS at Perpignan in December 1987, but was broken up shortly after its arrival in France.

The last Vanguard in passenger service, Merpati Nusantara's V.952 PK-MVH *Jamdena*, had previously had the distinctions of being both the last TCA Vanguard built and the last Vanguard operated in passenger service in Europe while with EAS. Bill Sheridan Collection

Only one of the Merchantmen took on the full colours of Hunting Cargo Airlines following the company's name change. Aviation Hobby Shop

Research Retirement

In 1992 two Viscount 810s operated from Thurleigh, Bedfordshire, by the UK's Defence Research Agency (DRA) were formally retired. Previously known as the Royal Aircraft Establishment – Bedford, the DRA had operated the two Viscounts, an ex-Austrian V.837 and an ex-Ghana V.838 on radar equipment trials.

Neither aircraft had flown for over a year when it was announced that all DRA operations would be concentrated at Boscombe Down in Wiltshire. The Viscounts had originally been supplied, via the Ministry of Technology and Shackleton Aviation, to the Royal Radar and Signals Establishment at Pershore, Wiltshire, in 1964 and 1965, following their civil airline careers. They had been based at Thurleigh since the closure of Pershore in 1977. Considerable modification had been carried out on them to accommodate test equipment, including large ventral fairings and, in the case of the V.838, a long tube fairing under the lower rear fuselage.

Tasks undertaken by the aircraft included work on the infamous BAC TSR.2 programme in the 1960s, trials of the Thorn/EMI Searchwater radar for the Nimrod maritime reconnaissance aircraft, and development of the infra-red reconnaissance system for the Panavia Tornado GR.1A in the 1990s. The last involved high-speed passes along the runway at a very low 50ft (15m) altitude, in order to emulate the Tornado's performance. Although the Viscounts took such punishment in their stride, the effect of other airframe-straining work of this nature over the years, plus the structural adaptations, took their toll.

The V.837, XT575, was hangared at Thurleigh in 1991, and the V.838, XT661, was stored in the open. By the time their official retirement and offer for sale was announced, it was obvious that neither was suitable to be used commercially again. The repair work required to return them to certifiable airworthiness was too prohibitively expensive to be considered, and both were eventually scrapped in 1993. Nonetheless, the forward fuselage of XT575 was saved and eventually placed on display in the Brooklands Museum at Weybridge in Surrey, established on the old Vickers/BAC factory site.

A number of interesting bulges and fairings appeared on the RAE Viscounts over the years, as they took part in various research programmes. Steve Williams Collection

BAF Recovery

The reorganization of BAF in 1989, after its close brush with bankruptcy and emergence from Administration under new ownership, saw the company's management announcing its confidence in the established charter activities. At the time these were very much based on the combined BAF/Baltic Viscount fleet, with the declining numbers of Dart Heralds playing a much more minor role. As well as the home base at Southend, BAF was operating its Viscounts from outstations at Aberdeen and Manchester. Manchester was generally assigned one aircraft, while Aberdeen frequently had up to three. The remainder were usually stationed at Southend.

The lease of a Viscount to Virgin Atlantic for the Maastricht route continued, and the contract was even expanded with the supply of an additional aircraft to operate Virgin's new Luton–Dublin schedule. The UK terminal for the Maastricht service was also eventually moved from Gatwick to Luton. The Luton–Dublin schedule was so successful that Virgin

After inheriting the initial contracts during the takeover of Euroair's Viscount operations, BAF regularly continued to lease Viscount capacity to Virgin Atlantic Airways. via author

replaced the BAF Viscount with Boeing 727s, this time leased in from Dublin-based Club Air. Unfortunately Club Air ceased all operations a few months later, and a BAF Viscount was again leased-in to operate the service.

However, Virgin eventually decided to drop the Maastricht and Dublin services from its network, and Leeds-based operator Capital Airlines took over the Luton–Dublin route. At the time Capital operated a fleet of Shorts 360s, which would have been far too small for the expected traffic. The airline had BAe 146 jets on order to serve the Luton–Dublin route, and until they arrived a BAF Viscount was once again brought in to fly the service, this time on Capital's behalf, V.806 G-AOYN being delivered to Luton in March 1989. While Virgin had operated a twice-daily service, the Capital schedule called for the Viscount to operate between Luton and Dublin up to four times a day. As each sector took 1hr 20min by Viscount, this gave a very respectable utilization for the aircraft. Capital's BAe 146s duly took over the Dublin flight, but for a few months a Viscount could be seen once again wearing 'Capital' titles, over twenty-five years after the demise of the original US carrier.

More leasing and *ad hoc* charter work for other airlines saw the BAF passenger Viscounts often flying schedules for Aer Lingus, Air Europe Express, Air UK, Birmingham European Airways, BA, Jersey European Airways and Loganair. In 1990 V.836 G-BFZL, which had been acquired from Manx Airlines via BMA by Baltic/Hot Air, found itself returning to its old Isle of Man home for several weeks when BAF leased the aircraft to its previous owner for operation on several Irish Sea routes and to the Channel Islands. Other BAF Viscounts appeared on Manx services on and off through the next few years, usually replacing unserviceable BAe ATPs.

The Viscounts were still capable of undertaking the occasional adventure off the well-beaten tracks of European airspace. In January 1990 V.802 G-AOHM, by then the oldest operational Viscount in the BAF fleet, was despatched at short notice to Africa to replace a Libyan Arab Fokker F.28 jet originally chartered as a support aircraft for the Paris–Dakar car rally. The operation began in Agades, in Niger, on 8 January, and saw the elderly aircraft operating to exotically named West African points such as Tahoua, Niamey, Gao, Tombouctou, Mopti, Nema, Tidjidka, Kiffa, Kayes, St Louis and Dakar, finally arriving in Senegal on 16 January.

Other passenger work for the Viscounts included the well-established Aberdeen–Shetland oil industry shuttles, as well as numerous *ad hoc* services and travel industry contracts. The Viscounts continued to prove especially popular with coach-air inclusive-tour companies and other travel agencies offering coach-air connections. Their passengers were transported by coach from several points in Europe to airports such as Maastricht, Ostend or Rotterdam, from where BAF would ferry them over to Southend. The Channel Islands also remained popular destinations for travel industry charters in the summer months, though on much-reduced frequencies compared with earlier years.

The V.806 G-APIM had been damaged beyond repair when it was struck by another aircraft at Southend on 11 January 1988, but, instead of scrapping it, BAF presented the repaired but non-airworthy aircraft to the Brooklands Museum, for display at the Viscount's birthplace. On 29 July 1990 BAF V.806 G-AOYN made a commemorative passenger flight from Northolt to Le Bourget, this time celebrating no less than forty years of Viscount commercial service. The passengers participating in the historic event enjoyed a low-level fly-past of Brooklands en route.

Vintage Viscount 802 G-AOHM showed that it was still capable of marathon treks in its thirty-third operational year. MAP

Many of the passenger contracts were taken over by a fleet of rather elderly secondhand One-Eleven Series 200s acquired by BAF in 1990. The jets were operated from a new base at Stansted, to overcome operational restrictions in flying them from Southend. This duplicated an almost identical move by another Viscount operator converting to jets, Channel Airways, over fifteen years earlier. Eventually, though Southend would remain BAF's main engineering base, most operations were gradually moved to Stansted. More jets, in the form of new BAe 146s, were also acquired, taking over more of the passenger work from the Viscounts.

As market forces waxed and waned, a handful of BAF Viscounts were withdrawn and scrapped, usually as they came due for an expensive major service. Others were eventually placed in short-term storage, awaiting new contracts. Several times over the next few years individual aircraft were seemingly withdrawn, and even started to lose parts to keep their more active brethren flying, only to be restored to full operating status when required for new contracts. For example, V.813 G-OHOT was placed in storage soon after the BAF/Hot Air merger, at one point being left engineless for some months. However, in late 1991 work started on restoring the aircraft, and 'OT was returned to full-time service as a freighter in February 1992.

Shift to Cargo

As jets displaced the remaining Viscounts as the airline's front-line passenger equipment, members of the fleet increasingly joined the two Freightmaster conversions on all-cargo flights.

Fokker F.27s were supplied by Federal Express for a new cargo contract, and operated on its behalf by BAF on small package contracts. In due course, however, BAF's own turboprops took over the FedEx services and the F.27s were returned to their owner. The Viscounts and Heralds flew over a nightly Heathrow–Brussels–Stansted–Brussels–Heathrow routeing, and also to Brussels from Manchester and Prestwick. In addition, BAF Viscounts operated for Securicor Air on all-cargo routes from East Midlands to Brussels and Dublin.

The growing list of regular cargo contracts for the BAF Viscounts also included newspaper flights, carrying day-old-chicks around Europe, car component charters for Ford and General Motors, and the transporting of fresh eels from Belfast to the Netherlands. The Royal Philharmonic Orchestra's instruments were carried by G-BBDK from Stansted to Seville on 6 July 1991, though a BAF One-Eleven transported the musicians themselves. The large cargo and small package forwarding company TNT also frequently chartered BAF Viscount capacity to carry its consignments around the UK and Europe. Of particular importance to the BAF Viscount fleet was the award of a contract in November 1992 from Parcelforce, the small-package division of the UK Post Office.

On 8 October G-BBDK made a demonstration flight from Coventry to Edinburgh, ably illustrating its ability to carry the very respectable load of 17,640lb (8,020kg) of Parcelforce consignments provided for the occasion. The route was part of a nationwide 'hub and spoke' operation flown on behalf of Parcelforce and the Royal Mail, the hub being at Coventry. Aircraft would fly in from all over the UK, exchange the re-sorted loads at Coventry, and return to their original points with the parcel or first-class letter post destined for the cities they served. Hitherto, Parcelforce had chartered an HS 748 of another airline for the Edinburgh route, but the bulky nature of the cargo meant that the smaller turboprop was sometimes forced to leave some of the load because the cabin was full, though the aircraft was still well below its weight limits. The use of the Viscount eliminated this problem.

The first revenue flight of the contract was operated by V.806 G-AOYP from Glasgow to Coventry on the night of 9 November. Later in the winter the Scottish terminal was switched to Edinburgh. In June 1993 an additional Parcelforce contract saw the Viscounts flying five times a week from Belfast to Coventry. By this time G-BBDK had been repainted in a bright red Parcelforce colour scheme to promote the service.

Stripped of passenger furnishings, and with cargo-handling equipment installed, the Viscount became a very capacious freight carrier. BAF via author

New Name

In April 1993, shortly before the award of the second Parcelforce contract, BAF had officially changed its operating name to British World Airlines (BWA). In fact the name had already been in use commercially since 1 January. Although the company had not operated its original cross-Channel car ferry services since the mid-1970s, there was still a steady stream of enquires from the public every year about the availability of the service. It was obvious that the BAF name was still very much associated with

The only Viscount to carry full British World colours was V.839 G-BFZL.
Aviation Hobby Shop

the previous operation, and it was decided that a new, updated image was badly needed. A number of larger One-Eleven Series 500s had been acquired to replace the older Series 200s, and more BAe 146s had also joined the fleet. Having worked hard to establish a hard-won reputation as an efficient, high-quality, charter and leasing operator, the company wanted to shake off the old identity. A new burgundy-and-white colour scheme, replacing the previous red, white and blue livery, was quickly applied to the high-profile jet fleet.

Unfortunately, BWA's Dart-powered aircraft were less fortunate, only one of the Viscounts, V.836 G-BFZL, being repainted to reflect the new image. The remaining Viscounts were mostly just given 'British World' titles over the old BAF livery, and the last of the Dart Heralds were removed from service altogether shortly after the name change.

Drama Over the Midlands

On the night of 25 February 1994, V.813 G-OHOT was working on the Edinburgh–Coventry Parcelforce contract. Extremely bad weather en route was forecast and, in an effort to avoid it, the crew were instructed to leave earlier than the 19.30hr scheduled departure time. The crew paid particular attention to the Viscount's control surfaces during pre-flight checks, as it was already sleeting, but no significant residual ice or slush was found on the aircraft. Loaded with its cargo of packages, 'OT departed Edinburgh at 18.43hr, initially climbing to Flight Level 190 (19,000ft/5,800m).

As the Viscount passed Manchester on its way to Coventry, it began its descent. At 19.32hr, while still in cloud at Flight Level 150, the number 2 engine failed owing to ingestion of ice. In less than a minute, as the crew completed their shut-down drills on number 2, number 3 engine also started to run down and failed. A diversion and emergency descent was approved by air traffic control and, while still attempting to restart number 2, the crew of 'OT set course for Birmingham. By now at only 7,000ft (2,100m), further attempts to restart both dead engines finally met some success, number 2 being restarted. However, in an especially cruel twist of fate, engine number 4 then failed owing to ice ingestion, and all attempts to restart the two starboard engines failed. The diversion point was changed from Birmingham to East Midlands, which was closer, though the stricken airliner was having trouble maintaining even the 2,500ft (760m) altitude for which it had now been given clearance.

A great deal of ice was now building up on the airframe and, finally, with the crew unable to maintain control, G-OHOT struck a descending forested, slope near Uttoxeter, Staffordshire. The impact occurred at 19.47hr, just fifteen minutes after the first engine failure. The captain was killed in the impact, but two passers-by who witnessed the crash were able to rescue the severely injured first officer from the wreckage. An intense fire broke out and consumed the main fuselage between the flight deck and empennage.

Following an enquiry, the main cause of the accident was attributed to the multiple engine failures, caused by ice ingestion in the extreme flying conditions. However, there was also some criticism of the crew's performance of the emergency drills, which, it was alleged, might have contributed to the failure to restart the failed engines.

Viscount 813 G-OHOT came to a fiery end in Staffordshire in 1994. via author

Signs of the Times

By the end of 1994 three more of the surviving Viscounts were resplendent in the distinctive red Parcelforce livery. From October the contract had been expanded, frequencies on the flights from Coventry to Belfast and Edinburgh being doubled. As a further move to promote the contract, the V.808C freighter G-BBDK was reregistered G-OPFE, V.802 G-BNLB became G-OPFI and V.806 G-AOYP was converted to a freighter and became G-PFBT. Another of the V.806s, G-AOYN, was re-registered G-OPAS on donning Parcelforce colours in October. Although converted for full-time freight services, with the Parcelforce contract particularly in mind, these aircraft still did not boast the double-sized door of the sole V.808C, G-OPFE. The other originally dedicated Freightmaster, V.806 G-BLOA, had been retired from service in May 1993.

For the 1994 season eight airworthy Viscounts were still available for BWA's charter programmes. The active fleet consisted of two V.802s, three V.806s, V.807 G-CSZB, the V.808C and a single Viscount 810 series, V.836 G-BFZL. As well as the continuing Aberdeen-based contracts to Shetland, a handful of European *ad hoc* passenger charters were still undertaken by the Viscounts, though the majority of this work was now undertaken by the One-Elevens and BAe 146s which had deposed the Viscounts as BWA's flagships.

With their available airframe hours before major maintenance becoming very limited, the Viscounts' use was soon being chiefly restricted to their Parcelforce and Oil Industry contracts. By the end of 1995 V.806 G-APAS was so quickly running out of hours that it was relegated to back-up duties to preserve it for use for as long as possible. It was also announced that, although the Aberdeen contracts had recently been renewed by Shell Oil and Production Ltd, for whom they were operated, the Viscounts currently flying the service would be replaced by more-modern turboprops. With the contract being worth £55 million to the company, sentimentality had to give way to business sense and BWA lost no time in confirming an order for two new ATR-72s, due for delivery in April and June 1996.

The usually reliable Viscounts did not seem to take kindly to the impending arrival of their European-consortium-built replacement, and a few weeks of mildly cantankerous behaviour by the elderly airliners ensued shortly after the arrival of the first ATR-72. On 22 March 1996 V.936 G-BFZL damaged its number 3 and 4 engines and propellers after running off the taxiway at Edinburgh and sinking into soft ground. It had just arrived at Edinburgh on a Parcelforce service from Coventry. The usually dormant G-OPAS was rushed back into service to replace 'ZL while repairs were undertaken, G-BFZL finally being returned to service on 17 April.

Two days later, in-between Parcelforce flights, V.808C G-OPFE was assigned a brief training sortie before operating that evening's flight to Coventry from Belfast. This normally routine task was marred when the crew neglected to lower the undercarriage before landing, and 'FE sank on to the runway on its belly, its propellers being irreparably mangled against the ground. After blocking the runway for several hours, the unfortunate Viscount was finally hoisted up by a crane and its undercarriage was lowered so that it could be moved. Although the damage to the fuselage and wings was minimal, G-OPFE was deemed beyond economic repair and scrapped for spares. Its total flying time was 37,591hr, with 32,696 landings for eight different operators in its thirty-eight-year career.

Retirement Celebrations

It was obvious that the withdrawal of the Viscounts from Aberdeen would almost certainly mark the end of passenger Viscount operations, at least in Europe. To mark the occasion, as well as the fiftieth anniversary of the founding of BWA's predecessor, Silver City Airways, a special VIP flight was planned to operate from Heathrow on 18 April. That date also corresponded to the day in 1953 when BEA had opened the first passenger Viscount 700 schedules from London to Cyprus. The vintage V.802 G-AOHM was appropriately chosen for the flight and was positioned from Aberdeen to Stansted the day before, where it was decorated with stickers of sponsors of the event. Unfortunately, while being towed at Stansted on the morning of the 18th, 'HM's wing struck a fence post and was badly damaged. Although it was repairable, the damage was sufficiently serious to cause the Viscount's withdrawal from the event. Instead, V.806 G-APEY was rushed down from Aberdeen, direct to Heathrow, to make the flight.

Among the VIPs gathered at Heathrow were Sir George Edwards, 'father' of the Viscount design and by then 88 years old, Sir Peter Masefield and ex-Vickers test pilot Jock Bryce, all major players in the type's history. After a press presentation and appropriate speeches, the distinguished guests were taken on a 45min champagne flight over London, which also included a fly-past at Brooklands. A buffet lunch and reception, hosted by BA, followed, before a party of press representatives were carried to Stansted by G-APEY. The aircraft then positioned back to Aberdeen to return to its more mundane task of ferrying oil workers to Shetland.

Another BWA Viscount made a celebratory appearance at Heathrow two months later. On 2 June, the fiftieth anniversary of the opening of Heathrow, a massive flypast of types associated with the airport over the years was planned. The V.836 G-BFZL

The arrival of BWA's ATR-72s heralded the end of the airline's use of the faithful Viscounts. Aviation Hobby Shop

Merchantman Retirement

In addition to the much-publicized cessation of passenger services by BWA's Viscounts, the Vanguard/Merchantman was also approaching its final withdrawal from commercial use by HCA. The airline had built up a fleet of Electra freighters that were to displace the last of the big Vickers turboprops. The company's original Merchantman, G-APES, was retired on 4 February 1995, after a Belfast–Coventry charter. Along with the redundant 'EJ and 'EM, 'ES eventually suffered the ignominy of being broken up at East Midlands towards the end of 1995. The nose section of 'EJ was saved and presented to the Brooklands Museum.

The sole surviving HCA Merchantman, and world's last surviving intact Vanguard variant, G-APEP, continued in service for more than a year. It was not until 30 September 1996 that the aircraft, under the command of Capt Gary West, operated the world's very last revenue Vanguard/Merchantman flight, a Belfast–Coventry DHL service. With its reputation for reliability still intact, the type had managed to serve ABC and HCA for over twenty of the Vickers Vanguard's grand total of thirty-five years of service.

Retirement in Style

Unlike its predecessors, however, G-APEP did not succumb to the scrappers. Instead, it followed the remains of 'EJ, being donated to the Brooklands Museum. Unlike 'EJ, though, 'EP was to be flown into the museum, and for the next few weeks Hunting's Capts Peter Moore and Gary West practised short landings at East Midlands to ensure the Merchantman's safe arrival on the rarely used and rather restricted Brooklands runway. Only 2,500ft (760m) of the old runway remained available at the factory airfield, and a row of trees had to be removed before even this could be used. After some frustrating postponements, waiting for the required perfect weather conditions, G-APEP finally roared down the East Midlands runway for the last time at 10.10hr on the morning of 17 October 1996. After performing a spirited fly-past by way of a farewell, the Vanguard headed southwards for its new home.

En route, the aircraft received an unprecedented invitation by air traffic control at Heathrow to perform one last fly-past at its original commercial home base. Slipped in between the regular Heathrow traffic, 'EP crossed the threshold and flew along Runway 27R before climbing away. On arrival at Brooklands yet another fly-past was performed before 'EP finally landed at 10.52hr and taxied to its new position on the museum ramp. Among those present to welcome the aircraft home were the ex-BEA chairman Sir Peter Masefield and Jock Bryce. The meeting of Bryce, the very first Vanguard pilot, with the very last Vanguard crew at the end of the big Vickers turboprop's active, airborne life, must have been especially poignant.

ABOVE: In 1995 G-APES was finally withdrawn from use. Steve Williams Collection

LEFT: Hunting Cargo's last Merchantman, G-APEP, remained at East Midlands while preparations were made for its final flight, to Brooklands. Steve Williams Collection

took part in the airborne jamboree over London, which included types ranging from vintage DC-3s, a DC-4 and de Havilland Rapides to modern-day Boeing 747s and Concorde.

The approaching retirement of the last UK-operated passenger Viscounts saw G-APEY making further farewell appearances, often giving both those who had worked with the aircraft and devotees the chance for one last experience of the aircraft. After making its last flight on the Aberdeen contract on 30 May, G-APEY positioned to Southend on 1 June and operated a special day-trip pleasure flight to Jersey.

Another commemorative day trip, from Southend to Reims in France, was operated four days later, on 12 June. A brief couple of busy weeks for the aircraft then followed, with 'EY operating on the Parcelforce network. In the meantime, V.807 G-CSZB remained at Aberdeen as a back-up for the new ATR-72s. It completed its last rotation on the Aberdeen–Sumburgh–Aberdeen route on 29 June, and operated a return flight charter for Shell on the 30th, carrying passengers both ways between Aberdeen and Newcastle. Also on 30 June, 'EY made an appearance at the Lydd Classic Airliner Fly In, and made three brief pleasure flights from the Kent airport. It had brought in a full load of enthusiasts from Southend to visit the show, and during the busy event the Viscount, commanded by Capt Colin Towle, eventually carried a further 214 people on pleasure flights before returning to Southend.

On June 2 1996 G-BFZL took part in a spectacular fly-past of dozens of airliners to commemorate Heathrow Airport's fiftieth anniversary. Steve Williams Collection

After more Parcelforce work, G-APEY had its passenger interior restored and was prepared for another commemorative flight, celebrating the forty-eighth anniversary of the Viscount 630's first flight, on 16 July. Once again Jock Bryce was among the VIPs assembled for the celebrations. In addition, a further five pleasure flights were made from Southend on 28 July, carrying 368 passengers in total. Finally, on 29 July, the forty-sixth anniversary of G-AHRF's historic inauguration of the world's first turbine-powered passenger services for BEA on the Northolt–Le Bourget route, G-APEY made one last pleasure flight from Southend. Commanded by Capt MacNiece, it carried a full load of seventy-four VIP passengers for BWA on an hour-long pleasure flight that included flypasts at Northolt and Brooklands, as well as a final passenger-carrying fly-past at Southend before landing.

The Last Contract

The unexpected stock of extra Viscount spares supplied by the unfortunate G-OPFE was immediately exploited, providing a

British World's last Viscounts were mostly employed on the lucrative Parcel Force contract. Aviation Hobby Shop

wing-tip to fix the unserviceable G-AOHM. The inauguration of full ATR-72 operations from Aberdeen meant that the V.802 was no longer required for the oil industry contracts by the time it had been repaired. Instead, 'HM's passenger interior was removed and the aircraft repainted in Parcelforce colours. Once the final BWA passenger services were completed, G-APEY and G-CSZB were also transferred to the Parcelforce operation, allowing the high-houred G-OPAS finally to be retired.

The V.807 G-CSZB was retired on 15 October, having completed 46,200hr in its long and varied career. The five remaining Viscounts continued to service the Parcelforce venture, with two nightly rotations each between Coventry and Belfast or Edinburgh. However, the operation was effectively halved from the end of December, when the contract for the Edinburgh–Coventry service was awarded to another operator and V.836 was also withdrawn. Only three aircraft were required for the Coventry–Belfast contract, even with one only on standby, and V.806 G-PFBT was also withdrawn and parked up at Southend in March 1997.

Once delivered to South Africa, the ex-BWA Viscounts were prepared for their planned charter and leasing work. Afavia

New African Haven

A new owner for the Viscount fleet had already been found by BWA. Based at Lanseria Airport, northwest of Johannesburg, South African charter operator Heli-Jet Aviation had already acquired the withdrawn V.836 G-BFZL and V.806 G-PFBT during 1997. Before departure, 'ZL was refitted with a passenger layout and, after a marathon delivery flight via Bari, Cairo, Addis Ababa, Nairobi and Harare, finally arrived at Lanseria on 30 April 1997. A month later 'BT followed, still in all-cargo configuration, and both aircraft became available for both passenger and freight charter work throughout Africa.

Heli-Jet also acquired V.806 G-APEY, and during November 1997 it was flown on a number of enthusiast flights from various UK airports in co-operation with BWA. Several day trips to Jersey were also operated, the last of these being on 15 November from East Midlands. The Channel Island's lucrative tourist industry had benefited a great deal from the loads of holidaymakers carried to Jersey by Viscounts operated by the UK's airlines for over forty-five years, and it was appropriate that it should be included in the itinerary. The last enthusiast flight, a 35min sector from Bournemouth to Southend on 30 November, carried fifty-one passengers, the last of 1,402 carried in the course of the tour. After undergoing maintenance at Southend, G-APEY finally departed the UK for South Africa on 9 January 1998.

The Parcelforce contract between Belfast and Coventry finally ended in January 1998. It fell to the lot of the two most elderly of BWA's Viscounts, V.802s G-AOHM and G-OPFI, to fly the last UK commercial services, on the night of 7/8 January. Both aircraft had been among the first batch of Viscounts acquired from BA by BAF nearly seventeen years earlier, in 1981. The last load of 11,175lb (5,080kg) of Parcelforce cargo was safely delivered to Belfast by G-OPFI at 03.12hr, a little over half an hour after G-AOHM had operated its last Coventry–Belfast sector with its own load of 15,640lb (7,110kg). Characteristically, both aircraft had operated their last BWA revenue flights with no problems and with minimal fuss.

Originally, both of the remaining V.802s had been meant to follow the previous three ex-BWA fleet members to Heli-Jet, but their departure was repeatedly delayed by administrative and financial hold-ups. The Viscounts that had been delivered to Heli-Jet were spending most of their time either in maintenance or storage. Eventually G-PFBT became a spares source, and was soon in no condition for use. It was not until January 1999 that the last two BWA Viscounts left the UK for Africa, and then it was for another customer, an agency called Airwing 2000, on behalf of a Gert de Klerc. Once

Fitted with a 'combi' passenger/cargo interior, 9Q-CGL flew briefly in the Democratic Republic of Congo before being lost in an accident. Afavia

delivered to Lanseria, the V.802s also spent long periods in storage. Eventually G-AOHM departed to Chad and became 5V-TTJ. Sadly it was written off in an accident in July 2001. Viscount G-OPFI also found its way to Chad, and was last heard of flying from Nd'jamena for a local operator, Transtel, as TU-VAB.

The surviving Heli-Jet aircraft eventually found new operators as well. Although they never took up South African registration, they were acquired by a local South African leasing and charter specialist, Planes 'R Us. Having been given a 'combi' passenger/cargo interior, V836 G-BFZL was finally despatched to the Democratic Republic of Congo, previously Zaïre, for use by local airline Trans IntAir as 9Q-CGL. Unfortunately the much-travelled V.836 was written off in an accident in May 2003. The V.806 G-APEY was operated in Angola and also by Air Zimbabwe in late 1999, as 3C-PBH. The use by Air Zimbabwe echoed the long utilization of the Viscount by CAA/Air Rhodesia and Air Zimbabwe from 1956 until their last V.810s had been retired and stored in 1990. The vintage V.806 was last reported at Lanseria with Air Ogooue in 2004.

Epilogue

Just how long the sporadic operations by obscure carriers will keep these last few Viscounts in the air is a question that cannot be answered until long after the appearance of this publication. Already there are rumours of at least one of the originally 'written-off' ex-BWA aircraft being returned to service in Africa!

With only one, irreplaceable, complete airframe left in existence, at Brooklands, the possibility of a Vanguard ever gracing the skies again is almost nil. However, as well as the handful of Viscounts apparently still in daily use, more potentially flyable aircraft lie in various states of 'storage' in Indonesia, Taiwan, the Democratic Republic of Congo and other more obscure parts if the word. Happily there are also several airframes, or at least major parts of airframes, preserved by museums, not only in the UK, but also in Australia, Brazil, Canada, China, Colombia, Eire, France, Germany, Italy, New Zealand, Sweden, Turkey, USA, Uruguay and Zimbabwe. The fact that these countries are concerned enough to preserve examples of the Viscount serves to emphasize the important part played of the Vickers turboprops in developing their airline networks over the decades.

The Viscount was presented to a travelling public used to having its ears assaulted by the pounding vibration of piston engines. In the 1950s it was still quite common for the world's airliners to be unpressurized and subject to the vagaries the weather and the usually rough air found at lower altitudes. Compared with more modern airliners, the noise and vibration in the cabin of a Viscount might still be considered intrusive, but it was positively silent and totally smooth compared with a piston-engine airliner. Although it was overshadowed by the almost simultaneous arrival of the first pure jets, the Viscount's reliability and economy managed to impress commercial operators, as well as its passengers and crews. That the original Viscount model could be developed into even faster and larger versions was a definite sign of its success.

The Vanguard was a victim of the same bad timing that beset other large turboprops, such as the Britannia and Electra. On paper, these bigger turboprops were both logical and financial sensible choices

ABOVE: Viscount 701 G-AMOG, displayed at Cosford, is one of two of BEA's original Discovery Class restored to the airline's 1950s livery and preserved by UK aviation museums. The other, G-ALWF, resides at Duxford. Malcolm L. Hill

LEFT: Although the Vanguard's use as a prestige front-line passenger airliner was limited, the aircraft found a useful new niche as a freighter. Jenny Gradidge

for busier intercity routes. In practice, however, the greater passenger appeal of jets saw the turboprops soon being consigned to less-prestigious routes, charters and even freight work many years before their time. Although only enjoying a brief time in the limelight before being ousted by jets, the Vanguard also earned itself a place in history by simply doing what it was designed to do. It provided a level of economy that ensured that new markets could be encouraged by introducing lower fares.

The Viscount and Vanguard left their marks on aviation history in so many ways. One of the few successes from the 'Brabazon' proposals, the Viscount brought modern, comfortable and reliable air transport to a public that would still have regarded an airline journey as a reckless adventure, only to be endured if absolutely unavoidable. The Viscount was a vital part of the generation of aircraft that brought normality, and even boring routine, to commercial air transport. The success of the aircraft's worldwide sales gave the UK aircraft industry one of its most productive eras, and provided valuable data and new technology that was incorporated in succeeding airliners.

The story started with a single, slightly tubby aircraft, with engines that sounded strangely different, making its first flight in 1948 under clouds of doubt over its future. Several parliamentary, boardroom, design office and even factory floor battles later, this eventually led to new models, worldwide sales, incalculable national and international prestige for the company and even another new, much larger, type. Nearly sixty years later only a brave person would dare to hint that the story might finally be over. Anyone with any experience of aviation knows better than to say 'never again' when it comes to a popular aircraft supposedly reaching the end of its operational life.

Just as these words are being read, somewhere, probably under a tropical or equatorial sky, a quartet of whistling Rolls-Royce Darts might very well be starting up outside large oval windows; presaging yet another profitable, probably uneventful and totally routine flight.

Viscount and Vanguard Variants

The Viscount and Vanguard variants were given model numbers based on the basic type, variant and customer. Whether a customer bought just one or two aircraft, or a whole fleet, that model for that customer would be allocated a separate model number. Unless the aircraft was subject to a major reworking while still on the production line or during a rebuild following an accident, or received a very significant modification, such as being equipped with a totally different model of engine, the original type number would remain with the aircraft throughout its existence.

VISCOUNT

Type Number	Original Owner/Operator	Engines	Notes
V.453		4×turbines	Design study
V.609		4×turbines	Viceroy design study
V.630	Vickers/Ministry of Supply	4×R.Da. Mk502 Dart	Prototype
V.640		4×Napier Naiad	Not completed
V.652		2×Bristol Hercules	Project only
V.653		4×Rolls Royce Dart	Project only (stretched)
V.655		4×R.Da.3 Mk505 Dart	Project, later developed into V.700
V.633	Ministry of Supply	2×R.Ta.1 Tay turbojet	
V.700	Ministry of Supply	4×R.Da.3 Mk505 Dart	V.700 Prototype
V.701	British European Airways	4×R.Da.3 Mk506 Dart	
V.701C	British European Airways	4×R.Da.3 Mk506 Dart	Extra order
V.701X	British European Airways	4×R.Da.3 Mk506 Dart	Rebuild by Marshall's of Cambridge after an accident
V.702	British West Indian Airways	4×R.Da.3 Mk506 Dart	
V.703	British European Airways	4×R.Da.3 Mk506 Dart	Higher-capacity, 53-passenger, project
V.707	Aer Lingus	4×R.Da.3 Mk506 Dart	
V.708	Air France	4×R.Da.3 Mk506 Dart	
V.720	Trans Australia Airlines	4×R.Da.3 Mk506 Dart	
V.721	Australian National Airways	4×R.Da.3 Mk506 Dart	Project only
V.723	Indian Air Force	4×R.Da.3 Mk506 Dart	
V.724	Trans-Canada Air Lines	4×R.Da.3 Mk506 Dart	
V.728	Cyprus Airways/Aden Airways	4×R.Da.3 Mk506 Dart	
V.730	Indian Air Force	4×R.Da.3 Mk506 Dart	
V.731	KLM Royal Dutch Airlines	4×R.Da.3 Mk506 Dart	Project only
V.732	Hunting-Clan Air Transport	4×R.Da.3 Mk506 Dart	
V.734	Pakistan Air Force	4×R.Da.3 Mk506 Dart	
V.735	Iraqi Airways	4×R.Da.3 Mk506 Dart	
V.736	Fred Olsen Air Transport	4×R.Da.3 Mk506 Dart	
V.737	Canadian Dept of Transport	4×R.Da.3 Mk506 Dart	
V.739	Misrair	4×R.Da.3 Mk506 Dart	
V.739A	Misrair	4×R.Da.3 Mk506 Dart	First reorder
V.739B	Misrair	4×R.Da.3 Mk506 Dart	Second reorder

The V.744 N7404 was originally one of the first three Viscounts to be delivered to Capital Airlines. The aircraft was later substantially rebuilt as a V.757 for TCA, following a serious accident at Chicago in 1956. A.R. Krieger via Jenny Gradidge

Type Number	Original Owner/Operator	Engines	Notes
V.740	Queen's Flight	4×R.Da.3 Mk506 Dart	Project only – staff aircraft
V.741	Queen's Flight	4×R.Da.3 Mk506 Dart	Project only – VIP aircraft
V.742D	Forca Aerea Brasileira	4×R.Da.6 Mk510 Dart	
V.744	Capital Airlines	4×R.Da.3 Mk506 Dart	
V.745	Capital Airlines	4×R.Da.3 Mk506 Dart	
V.745D	Capital Airlines	4×R.Da.6 Mk510 Dart	Fully 'Americanized' aircraft
V.746	East African Airways	4×R.Da.6 Mk510 Dart	Project only
V.747	Butler Air Transport	4×R.Da.6 Mk510 Dart	
V.748D	Central African Airways	4×R.Da.6 Mk510 Dart	
V.749	Lineas Aeropostal Venezolana	4×R.Da.3 Mk506 Dart	
V.754D	Middle East Airlines	4×R.Da.6 Mk510 Dart	
V.755D	Airwork Ltd	4×R.Da.6 Mk510 Dart	Sold to Cubana before delivery
V.756D	Trans Australia Airlines	4×R.Da.6 Mk510 Dart	
V.757	Trans-Canada Air Lines	4×R.Da.3 Mk506 Dart	
V.759D	Hunting-Clan Air Transport	4×R.Da.6 Mk510 Dart	
V.760D	Hong Kong Airways	4×R.Da.6 Mk510 Dart	
V.761D	Union of Burma Airways	4×R.Da.6 Mk510 Dart	
V.763D	Hughes Tool Corporation	4×R.Da.6 Mk510 Dart	Sold to TACA before delivery
V.764D	US Steel Corporation	4×R.Da.6 Mk510 Dart	
V.765D	Standard Oil Corporation	4×R.Da.6 Mk510 Dart	
V.766	Fred Olsen Air Transport		Project only
V.767	BOAC Associated Companies		Project only
V.768D	Indian Airlines Corporation	4×R.Da.6 Mk510 Dart	
V.769D	PLUNA	4×R.Da.6 Mk510 Dart	
V.770D			'Americanized' Viscount project
V.771D			Executive 'Americanized' Viscount project

Type Number	Original Owner/Operator	Engines	Notes
V.772	British West Indian Airways	4×R.Da.3 Mk506 Dart	
V.773	Iraqi Airways	4×R.Da.3 Mk506 Dart	
V.776D	Kuwait Oil Company	4×R.Da.6 Mk510 Dart	Converted V.745D
V.779D	Fred Olsen Air Transport	4×R.Da.6 Mk510 Dart	
V.780D		4×R.Da.6 Mk510 Dart	Basic V.700D VIP project
V.781D	South African Air Force	4×R.Da.6 Mk510 Dart	
V.782D	Iranian Airlines	4×R.Da.6 Mk510 Dart	
V.784D	Philippine Airlines	4×R.Da.6 Mk510 Dart	
V.785D	Linee Aeree Italiane	4×R.Da.6 Mk510 Dart	Later aircraft delivered to Alitalia
V.786D	Lloyd Aereo Colombiano	4×R.Da.6 Mk510 Dart	
V.789D	Forca Aerea Brasileira	4×R.Da.6 Mk510 Dart	
V.790		4×R.Da.3 Mk506 Dart	'Local Service Viscount' project
V.793D	Royal Bank of Canada	4×R.Da.6 Mk510 Dart	Converted V.745D
V.794D	Turk Hava Yollari	4×R.Da.6 Mk510 Dart	
V.795	Trans World Airlines	4×R.Da.3 Mk506 Dart	Project only
V.797D	Canadian Dept of Transport	4×R.Da.6 Mk510 Dart	
V.798D	Northeast Airlines Inc	4×R.Da.6 Mk510 Dart	
V.800		4×R.Da.6 Mk510 Dart	Original stretched Viscount project
V.801		4×R.Da.6 Mk510 Dart	Revised stretched Viscount project

The Viscount's heyday in the 1950s and 1960s may be long gone, but despite half a century having passed since their design debut, a handful of survivors still occasionally take to the skies, continuing to represent the world's first successful turboprop airliners. Global Air Image

Before being sold to Poland, SP-LVC of LOT Polish Airlines had been supplied to Transair and was later operated by BUA. After being bought by NZNA the V.804 was converted to V.807 standard to match the other Viscounts already operated by the New Zealand carrier. Global Air Image

Type Number	Original Owner/Operator	Engines	Notes
V.802	British European Airways	4×R.Da.6 Mk510 Dart	
V.803	KLM Royal Dutch Airlines	4×R.Da.6 Mk510 Dart	
V.804	Transair Ltd	4×R.Da.6 Mk510 Dart	
V.805	Eagle Aviation Ltd	4×R.Da.6 Mk510 Dart	
V.806	British European Airways	4×R.Da.7 Mk520 Dart	
V.806A	British European Airways	4×R.Da.7 Mk520 Dart	Development 800/810 aircraft
V.807	NZNAC	4×R.Da.7 Mk520 Dart	
V.808	Aer Lingus	4×R.Da.7 Mk520 Dart	
V.808C	Aer Lingus	4×R.Da.7 Mk520 Dart	'Combi' passenger/cargo conversion
V.810	Vickers-Armstrongs Ltd	4×R.Da.7/1 Mk525 Dart	Prototype 810 Viscount
V.812	Continental Airlines Inc	4×R.Da.7/1 Mk525 Dart	
V.813	South African Airways	4×R.Da.7/1 Mk525 Dart	
V.814	Deutsche Lufthansa AG	4×R.Da.7/1 Mk525 Dart	
V.815	Pakistan International Airlines	4×R.Da.7/1 Mk525 Dart	
V.816	Trans Australia Airlines	4×R.Da.7/1 Mk525 Dart	
V.818	Cubana	4×R.Da.7/1 Mk525 Dart	
V.819	Niarchos Group	4×R.Da.7/1 Mk525 Dart	Order cancelled
V.821	Eagle Aviation Ltd	4×R.Da.7/1 Mk525 Dart	Order cancelled
V.823	California Eastern Airlines	4×R.Da.7/1 Mk525 Dart	Order cancelled
V.825	Black Lion Aviation Ltd	4×R.Da.7/1 Mk525 Dart	Order cancelled
V.827	VASP	4×R.Da.7/1 Mk525 Dart	
V.828	All Nippon Airways	4×R.Da.7/1 Mk525 Dart	
V.829	Transportes Aereos Portugueses	4×R.Da.7/1 Mk525 Dart	Project only
V.831	Airwork Ltd	4×R.Da.7/1 Mk525 Dart	
V.832	Ansett/ANA	4×R.Da.7/1 Mk525 Dart	
V.833	Hunting-Clan Air Transport	4×R.Da.7/1 Mk530 Dart	
V.834	Polskie Linie Lotnicze	4×R.Da.7/1 Mk525 Dart	Project only
V.835	Tennessee Gas Transmission	4×R.Da.7/1 Mk525 Dart	
V.836	Union Carbide Corporation	4×R.Da.7/1 Mk525 Dart	
V.837	Austrian Airlines	4×R.Da.7/1 Mk525 Dart	
V.838	Ghana Airways	4×R.Da.7/1 Mk525 Dart	
V.839	Iranian Government	4×R.Da.7/1 Mk525 Dart	
V.840		4×R.Da.11 Mk541 Dart	Project only
V.842	Iraqi Airways	4×R.Da.11 Mk541 Dart	Project only
V.843	CAAC	4×R.Da.7/1 Mk525 Dart	

TOP: Once the Vanguard's unfortunate early engine problems were solved, the aircraft was able to settle down to a long career, both as an economic passenger aircraft and, in its 'Merchantman' guise, as a high-capacity freighter. Steve Richards

ABOVE: Invicta International referred to its Vanguards as 'Rolls-Royce VC9s' in an effort to boost the aircraft's profile during its last years as a passenger airliner in Europe. via author

V.844	Government of Liberia	4×R.Da.8 Dart	Project only
V.850		4×R.Da.8 Dart	Viscount Major project
V.860		4×R.Da.7/1 Mk525 Dart	Project only

VANGUARD

Type Number	Original Owner/Operator	Engines	Notes
V.870		4×R.B.109 Tyne	Initial Vanguard design study
V.950	Vickers-Armstrongs Ltd	4×R.Ty.1/506 Tyne	Prototype
V.951	British European Airways	4×R.Ty.1/506 Tyne	
V.952	Trans-Canada Air Lines	4×R.Ty.11/512 Tyne	
V.953	British European Airways	4×R.Ty.1/506 Tyne	

Index